Methodology of Educational Measurement and Assessment

Series editors

Bernard Veldkamp, Enschede, The Netherlands
Matthias von Davier, Princeton, USA

10/4/2016

Dear Ida,

thanks for your support of my work on this book series. This is the first of many volumes to come!

Best wishes

This new book series collates key contributions to a fast-developing field of education research. It is an international forum for theoretical and empirical studies exploring new and existing methods of collecting, analyzing, and reporting data from educational measurements and assessments. Covering a high-profile topic from multiple viewpoints, it aims to foster a broader understanding of fresh developments as innovative software tools and new concepts such as competency models and skills diagnosis continue to gain traction in educational institutions around the world. Methodology of Educational Measurement and Assessment offers readers reliable critical evaluations, reviews and comparisons of existing methodologies alongside authoritative analysis and commentary on new and emerging approaches. It will showcase empirical research on applications, examine issues such as reliability, validity, and comparability, and help keep readers up to speed on developments in statistical modeling approaches. The fully peer-reviewed publications in the series cover measurement and assessment at all levels of education and feature work by academics and education professionals from around the world. Providing an authoritative central clearing-house for research in a core sector in education, the series forms a major contribution to the international literature.

More information about this series at http://www.springer.com/series/13206

Monica Rosén · Kajsa Yang Hansen
Ulrika Wolff
Editors

Cognitive Abilities and Educational Outcomes

A Festschrift in Honour of
Jan-Eric Gustafsson

 Springer

Editors

Monica Rosén
Department of Education and
  Special Education
University of Gothenburg
Gothenburg
Sweden

Ulrika Wolff
Department of Education and
  Special Education
University of Gothenburg
Gothenburg
Sweden

Kajsa Yang Hansen
Department of Education and
  Special Education
University of Gothenburg
Gothenburg
Sweden

ISSN 2367-170X   ISSN 2367-1718   (electronic)
Methodology of Educational Measurement and Assessment
ISBN 978-3-319-43472-8   ISBN 978-3-319-43473-5   (eBook)
DOI 10.1007/978-3-319-43473-5

Library of Congress Control Number: 2016946946

Printed on acid-free paper

This Springer imprint is published by Springer Nature
The registered company is Springer International Publishing AG
The registered company address is: Gewerbestrasse 11, 6330 Cham, Switzerland

Preface

We present this Festschrift to our colleague, mentor and friend, Jan-Eric Gustafsson, on his retirement, to express our heartfelt appreciation for his contribution and dedication in education and educational research. Jan-Eric Gustafsson is a prominent figure in the field of education. Throughout his extensive career, Jan-Eric has been interested in many substantive issues in education as well as in methodological problems, far exceeding what this volume covers. However, the chapters reflect at least some very prominent parts of his diversity. The number of collaborators who expressed their interest to contribute to this book is very large, indicating Jan-Eric's broad network of researchers, practitioners, and policy advisers. However, due to the theme of the book series, we have limited ourselves to topics regarding educational measurement and related subjects.

In this volume, we collected 15 comprehensive chapters, authors of which have collaborated with Jan-Eric over different periods of his career. These chapters, being theory driven, empirical, or methodological in character, touch upon three broad topics, namely, *Cognitive abilities*, *Causes and effects of education*, and *Modeling the measurement properties*. All the topics reflect the contribution and involvement of Jan-Eric in his wide-ranging research and teaching.

Many colleagues have been involved in the production of this volume. Specially, we would like to thank all the authors to this book. Without your contributions and collaboration the book would never have come about. Dr. Matthias von Davier took the initiative and suggested publishing this Festschrift within Springer's Methodology of Educational Measurement and Assessment series. We also received first-hand support from Annemarie Keur at Springer during the whole process of publication. Professor Rolf Lander at the Department of Education and Special Education, University of Gothenburg, acted as the external reviewer of all the chapters; his comments helped the authors to improve the quality of the book. Dr. Johan Braeken at the Centre for Educational Measurement (CEMO) and Dr. Trude Nilsen at the Department of Teacher Education and School Research,

University of Oslo, also were involved in the review process of chapters. Thank you! To Berit Askling and Allan Svensson, your experience, advice, and writing in relation to the publication process of this Festschrift have been invaluable assets to our editorial team!

Finally, we want to thank you Jan-Eric for your enormous contributions to the field of education and educational measurement. We dedicate this volume to honour you on your retirement and with this, we hope to inspire and enlighten many young researchers in education to carry on the mission: to acknowledge the educational prerequisites, to improve quality, equity, and efficiency in education, and to enhance educational outcomes.

Gothenburg, Sweden   Monica Rosén
June 2016   Kajsa Yang Hansen
                                                                    Ulrika Wolff

Professor Jan-Eric Gustafsson

Curriculum Vitae

Jan-Eric Gustafsson

Born in 1949, in Falköping, Sweden

University Degree

1970   BA, Education, Psychology, Statistics, University of Gothenburg

Doctoral Degree

1976   Ph.D., Education, University of Gothenburg, "Verbal and figural aptitudes in relation to instructional methods" (Gustafsson 1976), supervisor Professor Kjell Härnqvist

Post-doctoral Exchange Assignments

1979/80   Visiting Scholar, School of Education, Stanford University, mentor Professor Lee J. Cronbach
1988   Visiting Scholar, Social Research Methodology Division, University of California Los Social Research Methodology Division Angeles, hosted by Prof. Bengt Muthén

Qualification as Associate Professor

1977   Associate Professor of Education (Docent in Swedish), University of Gothenburg

Present Position

1986–2016	Professorial chair in Education at the University of Gothenburg
2016	Professor Emeritus, University of Gothenburg

Previous Positions and Periods of Appointment

1971–1976	Research Assistant, Department of Education, University of Gothenburg
1976–1982	Post-doctoral Research Associate, Department of Education, University of Gothenburg, funding from the Swedish Council for Research in the Humanities and Social Sciences
1982–1985	Acting Associate Professor, Department of Education, University of Gothenburg
1986	Associate Professor, Department of Education, University of Gothenburg
1986	Professor, Department of Education, University of Gothenburg

Supervision of Ph.D. Students

Torgny Ottosson, 1987; Eva Björck-Åkesson, 1990; Valentin González, 1992; Monica Rosén, 1998; Berit Carlstedt, 2000; Joanna Giota, 2001; Christina Cliffordson, 2001; Per-Olof Bentley, 2003; Yang Yang, 2003; Ulrika Wolff, 2005; Eva Myrberg, 2006; Mary-Anne Holfve-Sabel, 2006; Caroline Berggren, 2006; Ann Valentin Kvist, 2013

Commissions of Trust

1983–1984	Head of Department, Department of Education, Göteborg University
1986–1989	Member of the Education section of the Swedish Council for Research in the Humanities and Social Sciences
1989–1992	Chair, Council for Research on Admission Procedures, National Swedish Board of Universities and Colleges
1991–1993	Dean, Section of Behavioral, Social and Administrative Educations, Faculty of Social Sciences
1993–1998	Chair, Section of Educational and Psychological Research of the Swedish Council for Research in the Humanities and Social Sciences
1993–1998	Member, Joint Committee of the Nordic Social Science Research Councils; Elected member of the Royal Swedish Academy of Sciences
1993–cont.	Elected member of the Royal Swedish Academy of Sciences
1996–2001	Member, committee on Longitudinal Research, Swedish Council for Interdisciplinary Research
1997–2001	Chair, committee on Longitudinal Research, Swedish Council for Interdisciplinary Research

1997–2002	Member of the Visiting Panel on Research, Educational Testing Service, Princeton, USA
2002–2004	Member of the Board of the Bank of Sweden Tercentenary Foundation
2004–cont.	Member of the Technical Executive Group of the International Association of Evaluation of Educational Achievement (IEA)
2010–cont.	National editor, Scandinavian Journal of Educational Research
2011–2013	Member of the Board of the University of Gothenburg, representing the academic personnel
2013–2014	Acting Director of CEMO, Center for Educational Measurement Oslo at University of Oslo
2006–cont.	Professor II at the Faculty of Education, University of Oslo, Norway

Jan-Eric Gustafsson—A (too) Short Bio Sketch (by Monica Rosén)

I have known and worked next to Jan-Eric since 1987, when I started as a research assistant. He was then at the beginning of his professor's career, while I had just finished my graduate studies. He supervised my Ph.D. and has remained my mentor. Despite a close collaboration that stretches over almost 30 years, the short story I present here will not nearly do him or his academic career full justice. The narrative will by necessity be selective, unbalanced, and imprecise. The purpose is nevertheless to give the reader some background to, and an idea of, some of the things that have rendered Jan-Eric his reputation as an outstanding researcher. For this purpose I have also collected information from other people that are close to him in other contexts or circumstances.

I will begin by telling you about Jan-Eric today, his research interest and the research environments he has built up and appears in. Then, the story will jump back in time to give some of the history. It will be shown that much of Jan-Eric's research interest today can be traced back to the 1970s, to the work of his supervisor Kjell Härnqvist, to the computer development at the time, and to the development of quantitative research methods.

Research Interests

Jan-Eric Gustafsson is a professor of Education at the University of Gothenburg, at the Faculty of Education, Department of Education, and Special Education. He started his academic career at this university and although nurtured and inspired also by many other research environments, he has remained at the University of Gothenburg throughout his career.

At one level, one may say that anything that involves measurement issues engages Jan-Eric, as is clear from his many co-authorships with scholars from other disciplines and also from his many external assignments and commissions. Some of which will be mentioned later.

One of Jan-Eric's research interests relates to individual preconditions for education, where he has worked with different models of the structure of cognitive abilities, and with other ability tests, such as the Swedish Scholastic Aptitude test and other instruments that are used for selection to higher education. Another of his interests is directed towards the effects of education on knowledge and skills, which he often has studied with data from the international comparative studies organized by the International Association for the Evaluation of Educational Achievement (IEA) or by the Organisation for Economic Co-operation and Development (OECD). Moreover, questions concerning the organization of education and the importance of different kinds of resources, such as teacher competence, has attracted his attention more and more during the last few years. Another prominent research activity, which always runs parallel with Jan-Eric's more substantively oriented research concerns the development of quantitative methods with a focus on measurement and statistical analysis.

Jan-Eric's teaching interests coincide primarily with his interest in methodological questions and statistical techniques, and his method classes are very popular as Jan-Eric is an excellent teacher. One of his mottos *one learns as long as one has students* illustrates his humble attitude to the teaching task, and signals the good spirit in which he teaches. He also much enjoys supervising doctoral students.

Research Environments

In the same vein, Jan-Eric's motto could be rephrased to *you learn as long as you have colleagues to share with.* Knowing this has guided Jan-Eric's strivings to ensure and promote capacity building and improve research. Good- and high-quality research requires a good research environment, where ideas, work, and knowledge can be shared and learned in friendly collaboration. Creating such environments has been an essential part of Jan-Eric's agenda ever since his scientific leadership started. At the Faculty of Education, Jan-Eric has founded a research environment where those who share his interests meet on a regular basis to share, collaborate, and learn from each other. The research group goes by the Swedish acronym FUR (Förutsättningar, Utbildning och Resultat) which is short for Prerequisites, Education and Results and within which research is being conducted based on three categories of educational issues: individual prerequisites for education; resources for and organization of education; and educational results at individual and system levels. The FUR environment grew out of two previous activities that Jan-Eric initiated during the 1990s, the quantitative working seminar, and the college for individual differences and education (IDUN, Individuella differenser och utbildning).

FUR is not the sole research environment that Jan-Eric belongs to or has created at the University of Gothenburg; he is also one of the initiators of a multidisciplinary and multifaculty initiative; the Göteborg AMBLE network (Arena for Mind, Brain, Learning, and Environment), which joins researchers from different disciplines for whom the goal is to create a new platform for research, teaching, and communication on early childhood education in west Sweden.

In Norway, at the University of Oslo, where Jan-Eric has been employed as professor II at the Faculty of Education during the last decade, the Norwegian Ministry of Education commissioned Jan-Eric to establish a Centre for Educational Measurement (CEMO), where experts within the field of large-scale assessment today share the task to move the field of educational measurement forward. CEMO now has a very active and highly qualified group of internationally recruited researchers, who continue to enjoy Jan-Eric's expertise, and vice versa.

Aggregated to the group level, Jan-Eric's teaching motto translates; *your environment learns as long as it meets other research environments.* The growing access to international comparative educational data calls for more international collaboration and Jan-Eric has therefore initiated the ICE network (the Network for research on international comparisons of educational achievement), where presently research units from Sweden, Norway, Germany, Belgium, Cyprus, and England are members. ICE has the following objectives: (1) initiation of research projects through the development of proposals for funding directed at both national and international research funding institutions; (2) building of capacity through training of researchers in newly developed methodology; and (3) collaboration and interchange on theoretical, methodological, and empirical issues. ICE-meetings are primarily kept in close connection to the annual ECER conference (European Conference on Educational Research).

The Pre-doctoral Period

Jan-Eric was born and raised in Falköping, a small town located in an agricultural area in the county of Västra Götaland. His university studies started in 1968 at the age of 19, when he signed up at the department of Psychology at the University of Gothenburg to study psychology in parallel with an introductory course in statistics. He had just graduated from the advanced track at the upper secondary school, with good results in both mathematics and humanities. With his affinity for mathematics and strong interest in literature and his early goal was to become a school psychologist. However very soon his career plans changed.

The domain within psychology that Jan-Eric enjoyed the most was psychometrics, and it was through this interest he came to join Professor Kjell Härnquist's[1] special seminar on individual differences.

Härnqvist was deeply inspired by the work of Stanford professors Lee Cronbach and Richard Snow (1969, *Individual differences and learning ability, as a function of instructional variables*) and had at the beginning of 1970 received a major grant for research on individualization from an individual differences perspective. Jan-Eric was immediately hired to learn all about this research and to assist in Härnqvist's newly achieved research project, *Models for the adaption of Individual differences* (MID). The aim was to investigate the interaction between individual differences and teaching methods. One main hypothesis was that pupils with high spatial ability would benefit more from teaching materials based on more content than textual, and vice versa for students who had high verbal ability and low spatial ability. This became the theme of Jan-Eric's dissertation.

In the spring of 1976 and at the young age of 26 Jan-Eric earned his Ph.D. on a thesis entitled *Verbal and figural aptitudes in relation to instructional methods. Studies in aptitude–treatment interaction*. The main contribution from this work was of methodological nature, as the whole thesis demonstrates not only the complexity of the problem, i.e. the number and the complexities of the interactions, but also the many methodological difficulties that follow this line of research.

---

[1]Kjell Härnqvist, Professor at the University of Gothenburg 1958–1986, is the Swedish researcher who has devoted most attention to issues concerning individual prerequisites for education. He earned world recognition for his pioneering studies on individual differences and school differentiation for the Committee on the Final Organization of the Swedish Comprehensive School in the 1950s and 1960s. He is also famous for establishing the longitudinal database, which regularly collects information from samples of 13-year olds and that allows for follow-up and evaluation of the Swedish school reforms.

The Post-doctoral Period

Jan-Eric became associate professor in 1977. Shortly after his Ph.D., Jan-Eric obtained a very favorable research scholarship that allowed him unconditional time for research over 6 years. During the next couple of years, he devoted his time to measurement issues, advancements in quantitative methods and application techniques, and to a research project that would provide valid data for further studies on intelligence and the structure of intellectual abilities.

INSU, the Swedish acronym for learning strategies and teaching methods was from the start designed to continue the studies of aptitude treatment interaction (ATI), but with better instruments and with structural equation modeling techniques, which at this time had become more accessible through the LISREL software and the development of computers. Recruited to this longitudinal project were 50 Grade 6 classes in two communities close to Gothenburg. The test battery was assembled to capture enough primary factors to make possible identification of the broad second-order factors general visualization (Gv—spatial ability), general fluid ability (Gf—non-verbal inductive ability), and crystallised intelligence (Gc—verbal inductive ability). It contained 13 ability tests, 3 standardized achievement tests, and questionnaires. These pupils were followed up in Grade 8 with questionnaires, and in Grade 9 with a test battery including seven of the ability tests given in Grade 6. School marks were later added to the database. With these data and structural equation techniques Jan-Eric has over the years been able to synthesize the research from the past on the structure of cognitive abilities and at the same time developed methodological approaches that have become very useful for assessing measurement instruments and establishing measurement models more widely. The project was launched in 1978, and the data collection in 1980. It started as a 4-year project but ended as a program on ability structures and learning processes, which was stretched over more than a decade.

Early on, Jan-Eric also came in contact with growing methodological advancements, especially confirmatory factor analysis techniques and a computer software LISREL, both developed by the Swedish statistician Karl Jöreskog. Computers with larger computational capacities together with LISREL that could handle larger sets of variables, opened possibilities for making advancements, as this technique better enabled testing of a priori formulated theories. It was here and now that Jan-Eric developed his idea of a hierarchical structure of the intellect with three levels that united the traditions of Spearman (G-factor model) and Thurstone (Primary Factor Analyses) and Cattell and Horn (a handful of broad abilities) where he managed to show that the G-factor at the apex of the structure perfectly coincided with measures of inductive abilities, more specifically the broad factor fluid intelligence (Gf). When he first presented this idea with the support of data at AERA (the annual meeting of the American Educational Research Association) in 1980, it attracted much attention. This also triggered the successful international career that followed after this event, with quite a few international publications in journal and handbooks.

Visiting Stanford

During his post-doctoral period Jan-Eric spent a year as a visiting scholar at
Stanford University in the USA. This year became very influential and stimulating
in many respects. Here, he met a large group of researchers, many of them involved
in research regarding intelligence, cognitive abilities, and their structure, knowledge
of which at the time was quite unsettled. Professor Lee Cronbach became his
mentor, and it was here Jan-Eric made acquaintances with young scholars like
himself that would continue to inspire him over the many years to come, for
example Richard Snow, Henry Levin, Patrick Kyllonen, Richard Shavelson, David
Lohman, and Bengt Muthén (who was also visiting).

30 Years of Full Professorship

Jan-Eric's post-doctoral achievements soon became recognized within Sweden too.
In 1986 the Swedish government awarded Jan-Eric a so-called Professorial chair in
Education at the University of Gothenburg, one of the last of its kind, i.e. directly
funded by the Swedish Government.

From the list of publications it should be clear that Jan-Eric's research widened
during this period to encompass many questions regarding the efficiency of the
school system. The list also bears witness to his capacity; he has authored or
co-authored an impressive number of books, chapters in handbooks, anthologies,
and textbooks, and published innumerable articles. He has also prepared and presented an uncounted number of conference papers and invited speeches.

Jan-Eric's interest for educational system issues can be traced back to the end
of the 1980s, when his interest and expertise in measurement issues got him
involved in the first national evaluation studies in Sweden, initiated by the National
School Authorities. The school system was about to change into a more decen-
tralized system, which is why a first national evaluation to keep track of outcome
and ensure equity was initiated. His engagement in this kind of policy related
research has developed ever since. His expertise has been sought by the governmental authorities not only on matters regarding the design, content, and analyses of
an emerging national evaluation system; he has also been involved in studies that
have evaluated the different grading systems in Sweden, and also the system for
admission to higher education. Furthermore, differentiation has been addressed in a
number of studies regarding the Swedish Scholastic Aptitude Test. During the
1990s his interest for international comparative research grew, as well as for the
data produced by the IEA. Being such an authority on methodological issues, he
was soon invited to be a member of the IEA technical advisory group. His research
based on data from studies like PIRLS (Progress in International Reading Literacy
Study), TIMSS (Trends in International Mathematics and Science Study),
PISA (Programme for International Student Assessment), and PIACC (Programme
for the International Assessment of Adult Competencies) are widely recognized, not
least for his skilful ways to make good use of these data to address important
educational issues. In particular, the studies aimed at causal explanations are
regarded extra impressive and inspiring. His efforts to validly describe and contribute to understanding of the last 15 years of decreasing achievement levels in

reading, mathematics, and natural science in Sweden have been well received but have also caused many animated debates.

During the last 25 years Jan-Eric has been involved in a large number of national research projects. Most of them have been utilizing large-scale data sources in which survey data have been combined with test data and other register information. Among the research projects for which Jan-Eric has been, or still is, the scientific leader, some stand out as more powerful than others in providing internationally significant scientific contribution, creating a rewarding research climate with an impressive production of doctoral theses causing impact on educational policy and practice.

The most important project Jan-Eric manages is the UGU project which he inherited from Kjell Härnqvist. This project was designed for investigations not only of individual differences in cognitive abilities but also of the effects of social background and educational factors on recruitment to education and on outcomes of education. The Evaluation Through Follow-up (UGU, Utvärdering Genom Uppföljning) project was established in 1961 and has since created a large cohort-sequential database which now includes 10 cohorts born between 1948 and 2004. One aim is to provide a basis for evaluation of the Swedish educational system. A second aim is to support longitudinal research in different disciplinary areas in which information about background, aptitudes, and achievements of individuals form interesting control and explanatory variables, for example in research aiming at causal inference. The second aim is becoming increasingly prominent, and the UGU database serves a large number of studies within different disciplinary fields, such as education, economics, medicine, psychology, and sociology. Each cohort comprises about 9,000 pupils. Besides questionnaire and test data from students, information is available from parents, teachers, and principals for some cohorts. Statistics Sweden collects administrative information from the schools. Information from a large number of registers concerning, among other things, education, occupation, income, and health are also added throughout the lifespan of pupils.

A lot of Jan-Eric's research on these data has addressed issues regarding school marks, admission tests, and selection to upper secondary and higher education.

Other Interests—To Develop Useful Research Tools

Jan-Eric early realized the many possibilities that computer development could bring to the social sciences, and he quickly became a skilled programmer. Of the tools that he has developed over the years, there are two that deserve to be mentioned here as they have helped many researchers in their struggles with data and statistical techniques. The first is the software he developed to estimate Rasch models for dichotomous coded items, and the other is the modeling environment he developed for structural equation modeling.

PML Software—Tools for Rasch Modeling

During his Ph.D. studies, Jan-Eric's interest for statistical methods was well nurtured. With the development of computers and computer power followed several methodological advancements, which in many ways coincided with Jan-Eric's research interest. A colleague of his introduced him to the theory and mathematical models of Georg Rasch, an item response theory (IRT) and a mathematical model that allowed test items to have fixed features, that enabled better possibilities to evaluate and compare test takers' performance. To Jan-Eric this appeared as a very promising theory and technique to pursue issues of educational measurement. During the last years of the 1970s, Jan-Eric devoted quite some time to research on, and development of, Rasch modeling techniques. Among his contributions was an estimation procedure that solved the numerical problem for computing the conditional maximum likelihood estimates (CML) for tests with many items, a suggestion of a test for model fit, and a user friendly computer software which was called PML to aid the CML-estimation and the tests of model fit. Together with his friend Peter Allerup, a young statistician at the Georg Rasch department in Denmark, a Nordic post-graduate course was organized, which in turn led to a wider network of scholars with strong interests in measurement issues.

STREAMS—Tools for Structural Equation Modeling

During the mid-1990s, when Jan-Eric and colleagues in one of his projects tried to use structural equation modeling techniques in the secondary analyses of the IEA reading literacy data from 1991, they experienced that the techniques for estimating such models were not only complex and computationally cumbersome, and the model specification tedious and error prone, but also that these problems were aggravated when aiming for more advanced models, such as multilevel models and growth curve models. These problems encouraged Jan-Eric to start a software developing process that would go on for a very long time. It started in 1994 with a pre-processing program for LISREL, that could combine a simple school-level model and a simple student-level model into a two-level model, and it also produced LISREL code complete with start values. However, the need for a more complete modeling environment remained, which was why Jan-Eric, assisted by Per Arne Stahl, a system programmer took on to develop such an user-friendly modeling environment. A full-fledged, non-technical model-building language for describing one- and two-level models in one or more populations was included along with support for other types of complex data, i.e. structurally missing data. Included were also facilities for data handling and a post-processor for easier access and evaluation of the output. The software was labeled STREAMS, Structural Equation Modeling Made Simple, and the first full version was released in 1995. Two years later STREAMS did not only support analyses with LISREL, but also EQS, Amos, and in 1998 Mplus was also included in the STREAMS modeling environment. It is no understatement to say that STREAMS has aided many frustrated researcher over the years, and despite the fact that many of these programs also have become more user friendly over the years, STREAMS continues to do so.

The Third Task of Academia
At universities the so called third task (in addition to research and teaching) belongs to the obligations for faculty members. In this respect Jan-Eric has been an excellent representative in his active engagement for national authorities and associations in undertaking commissioned tasks and also in the dissemination of research results to a wider public. Here I will mention just a few of his many engagements.

The Royal Swedish Academy of Sciences
Since 1993 Jan-Eric has been a member of the *Royal Swedish Academy of Sciences* (Kungliga Vetenskapsakademin). In this Academy Jan-Eric has an active role in a division commissioned to form the Academy's standpoint in school issues, for example in the shaping of a school grade system that meets the expectations of prognostic validity and fairness without having negative effects on teaching and learning in pedagogical everyday life. He was also the Academy chairman for a large, systematic literature review on schools, learning, and mental health, which later also resulted in debate articles in the press.

The Swedish National Agency of Education
Over the years Jan-Eric's expertise on cognitive abilities and their measurement has been called upon whenever the Agency of Education has felt the need to evaluate the grading system and/or the system for national testing in different subject domains. These kinds of tasks have often resulted in considerable work, whilst the results and reports primarily have served as internal working material.

Centre for Business and Policy Studies (SNS)
Jan-Eric is an active and highly regarded member of the Swedish Educational Commission, at the *Center for Business and Policy Studies (SNS)*. The Commission is a collection of interdisciplinary research programs focused on the overarching question of how Sweden can be strengthened as a knowledge-based economy. The program is intended to result in recommendations for the Swedish education policy. Jan-Eric and co-authors (in many cases former students, now researchers in his research group) have prepared a series of popular science reports and taken part in public conferences on themes such as "Equality in Assessment in and by Swedish Schools: Problems and Opportunities", "The Knowledge and Skills of Adults", and "Child and Adolescent Mental Health". The most recently published report, "Policy Ideas for Swedish Schools", discusses the Swedish school crisis in some detail, and contributes a number of suggestions of actions needed to turn the negative trends of decreasing achievement levels and increasing differences between schools. These themes have also been the topic of several debate articles published in influential newspapers.

The Swedish National Agency of Higher Education (Högskoleverket)
Jan-Eric's expertise in educational measurements, in particular in aptitude tests, and his experiences from the Educational Testing Service in the USA were requested when the Government in 1991 decided to offer to all students the chance to take the Swedish Scholastic Aptitude Test (SweSAT) as a second chance for admission to

higher education studies. Until then, the test was used as compensation for grades and only those elder students who lacked comparable grades were allowed to use the test as a basis for their application. The wider usage of the test required a careful examination of its prognostic power compared to grades and, besides, gave researchers access to a rich base of testing data from regular students. An advisory scientific council was established for the purpose of ensuring the quality of the SweSAT, with Jan-Eric serving as its chair for many years.

Assignments from the Government

In 2015, Jan-Eric was appointed member of the Government's School Commission, whose task is to propose different actions aimed to improve quality and enhance achievement and equity in the Swedish school system. Recently, he was also contracted as one of the experts to conduct a politically initiated inquiry on the national assessment system, which has resulted in a comprehensive governmental report.

A Last Comment

It is in a way surreal that Jan-Eric is now about to retire, as everything he does seems to be more successful than ever. His research production and publication rate have never been higher; his sincere involvement in Swedish educational policy development has never been more acknowledged and widely appreciated. When teaching advanced quantitative research methods, he receives the highest marks from the participants, also from those who prefer qualitative approaches. The requests for his unique expertise with respect to both content and methods as a discussant, as a reviewer, as a research advisor, as a collaborator are more frequent than ever. This work capacity, in combination with the research competence that Jan-Eric possesses, is literally unique. So far, no one in the field of education in Sweden has contributed as much as Jan-Eric. It may be that he soon retires from his formal duties as a professor, but his scholarly work and research will hopefully continue for many years to come. I will end this too-short bio sketch by adding to the list of learning mottos what everyone who has worked with Jan-Eric has experienced, namely that *one learns as long as one has Jan-Eric*. We look forward to learning much more.

Contributors' Relation to Jan-Eric— in their own words

Prof. Peter Allerup

I met Jan-Eric in the middle of the 1970s. This happened after a common meeting in Gothenburg with Leif Lybeck, who was at that time conducting teaching experiments, partially based on a set of new principles, where students were taught to identify certain "invariances" in their practical experiments. Like Georg Rasch's basic ideas about creating rigorous grounds for "measurements" or "comparisons" Jan-Eric and I agreed on the need to introduce such basic ideas in a research seminar for Ph.D. students. This seminar took place in 1981 and in the years that followed I have had the pleasure to work with Jan-Eric under activities initiated by the Swedish Skolverket (RUSEK) and whilst reviewing various scientific articles together.

Prof. Sigrid Blömeke

I have known Jan-Eric from literature a long time before I met him in person. His work on cognitive abilities and international large-scale assessments has always been important for my field of research. Our personal collaboration started about 10–15 years ago in the context of the IEA's Teacher Education and Development Study in Mathematics (TEDS-M) where Jan-Eric was supporting the Norwegian team while I was the German National Research Coordinator. Already at that time, I noted a special ability of Jan-Eric that has become more and more important to me, namely his ability to bridge different worlds of research. This ability has been important, first, in the context of competence assessments where fierce dichotomies have been shaping the controversies whereas Jan-Eric was able to bridge and connect these in a productive way so that the best of both worlds could be brought together. The result was a nice paper we wrote together with Rich Shavelson that has changed the discourse about competence assessment. Second, Jan-Eric was crucial in shaping CEMO as a centre that includes both applied and basic research. Again, bridging these two worlds of measurement is a unique feature that has turned out to be very productive. To honor Jan-Eric's contribution in this context, we have created the "Gustafsson & Skrondal Visiting Scholarship" that will be filled for the first time this year.

Prof. Bert Creemers

When Jan-Eric Gustafsson and I met we were both working on educational research, he more from a psychological perspective and I gradually more in the field of educational effectiveness concentrating on the quality of teachers and schools. We had in common our interest in research and the ways to communicate ideas in books and papers. Jan-Eric published in a book about the methods in effectiveness research and he joined and contributed to journals which we established. It was always a pleasure to work with him since he was very focussed, productive, and nice.

Prof. Jan Van Damme

Although I knew some work of Jan-Eric's earlier work, I was specifically impressed by his contribution in 2006 at the IRC meeting in Washington. Therefore, I have stimulated a.o. Hongqiang, Bo Ning and now Kim to do some work in line with this contribution. Jan-Eric was sometimes involved as a member of an advisory commission or a defense commission of a PhD-project at the KU Leuven. It was always great to experience his well-balanced feedback. In addition, I recall the cooperation between us and others in Dortmund to get a European project, which was a nice experience.

Dr. Matthias von Davier

I was influenced by Jan-Eric's seminal work on Rasch models and estimation early on. When starting the project on deriving conditional estimation equations for polytomous mixture Rasch models, I used his work a lot. Later I met Jan-Eric frequently in joint work contexts, such as in the context of methodology conferences, as well as during technical advisory meetings for international studies. I always gained insights when discussing issues with him, and I was very lucky to be able to visit Gothenburg and Jan Eric's group several times.

Prof. Andreas Demetriou

Jan-Eric was very instrumental in the development of my research in the direction of integrating differential with developmental theory. Thus, the development of my theory in the interdisciplinary direction it still follows was influenced by Jan-Eric to a large extent. Moreover, literally, he was my mentor in learning to apply structural equation modeling when only LISREL existed and it was very cumbersome to run. I credit my skill in running SEM to Jan-Eric. We spent many weeks in Gothenburg and Thessaloniki running models on his and my data. We started cooperating 30 years ago, when very young, and our friendship still grows today.

Dr. Patrick C. Kyllonen

I met Jan-Eric in the early 1980s when he came to Stanford as a visiting scholar to study with Dick Snow and Lee Cronbach when I was a graduate student working on Dick Snow's "Stanford Aptitude Research Project" (described in the book *Remaking the concept of aptitude Extending the legacy of Richard E. Snow* by Corno et al., 2001). Jan-Eric was very enthusiastic about the possibilities of significant advances in abilities theory afforded by Karl Jöreskog's then new LISREL software, and he was especially thrilled that he had a year to explore and an extravagant $5,000 budget from his home institution to cover data analysis costs for that year. Back then you had to pay for computer time. After a mere one week, he had spent the entire $5,000 on LISREL runs. Nevertheless he was able to work around the limitations and he had a rewarding, productive year, not only making new lifelong friends, but setting the foundation for his breakthrough HILI model work that he published a few years later.

Prof. Leonidas Kyriakides

I had the chance to collaborate with Jan-Eric to co-organize a workshop for doctoral students in Europe that took place in Gothenburg regarding issues of Educational Effectiveness Research (EER). Through our collaboration, I realized his great interest not only regarding the development and use of quantitative research methods but also in the application of research methods in educational effectiveness research. Jan-Eric has also contributed in our book published in 2010, regarding the methodological developments in the field of educational effectiveness, where he wrote a chapter concerning the use of longitudinal data, thus assisting the further development of the methodology in EER. Jan-Eric and I have also collaborated in many organizations such as the EARLI SIG on educational effectiveness, and every year, together we also successfully organize the EERA spring-school with colleagues from other universities.

Prof. Henry M. Levin

In 1975–1976 I was a Fellow at the Center for Advanced Study of Behavioral Sciences and got to know, well, another fellow, Kjell Härnqvist who was Professor of Educational Psychology at Gothenberg University at that time and later became the Provost. Kjell repeatedly told me about this very interesting and productive colleague of his, Jan-Eric Gustafsson. Later I found out that Jan-Eric was coming to Stanford, as a Visiting Scholar with my close colleague, Dick Snow. I had also heard about Jan-Eric from Torsten Husén, whom I had known for a number of years. Between Kjell and Torsten and Dick Snow, Jan-Eric arrived at Stanford with much fanfare. During the year he was there, I was able to interact with him both at a personal level and at seminars, and I became fascinated with his many interests and insights and his ability to communicate beyond the confines of his professional field. Over these many years, we have maintained these productive ties.

Prof. Ina V.S. Mullis, Research Prof. Michael O. Martin, and Martin Hooper

Ina and Mick first met Jan-Eric more than 25 years ago working on PIRLS 2001, where Jan-Eric and Monica were very influential in the original PIRLS design. Then, Jan-Eric became a member of IEA's TEG and so we have worked with him in that capacity for many years, with considerable appreciation for his insight and expertise. We very much enjoy our discussions and exchanges with Jan-Eric about a number of TIMSS and PIRLS technical issues and greatly admire his expertise and wisdom. After the joint TIMSS and PIRLS assessment in 2011, we collaborated on the "Relationships" report, with Jan-Eric contributing an excellent structural equation analysis of the effects of home background on achievement in reading, mathematics, and science. Jan-Eric's research using aggregated trend data to explain changes in PIRLS achievement over time, as well as differences in achievement among countries, has been an important impetus improving the validity and reliability of the TIMSS and PIRLS context questionnaires, including the doctoral dissertation research being conducted by Martin Hooper our Assistant Research Director for Questionnaire Development and Policy Studies.

Prof. Bengt Muthén

Although Jan-Eric and I had met in Sweden earlier, the times we spent together in the United States were the more memorable. In March 1980, we met at Stanford University where Jan-Eric was visiting. We drove south from Stanford down the Pacific Coast Highway to UCLA where I gave a guest lecture. Along the way we had extensive discussions of whether I should choose a career in the USA or stay in Sweden. Jan-Eric was in favor of the former choice. About 10 years later, he and his family came to visit me at UCLA where I had gotten a professorship. Jan-Eric and I had long discussions about modeling and I remember his enthusiasm about using factor analysis where the influence of a general factor could be extracted from a set of cognitive ability measures in order to pinpoint the specific factors—he was an early proponent of the now very popular bi-factor model.

Prof. Monica Rosén

I have been fortunate to learn from and collaborate with Jan-Eric more or less continuously since I finished my bachelor degree in 1988. I started my research career in his research project and he was one of my supervisors during my doctoral studies. We have thereafter continued to work together in many research projects, in particular on analyses of large-scale assessment data, where we strive to contribute causal descriptions and explanations to differences and change in various educational outcome variables. I have also shared many teaching tasks with him over the year, especially doctoral courses on quantitative research methods and on measurement theory. For me Jan-Eric is an excellent role model in both research and teaching. Like many others in his research group (FUR), I continue to benefit from his rich knowledge and experiences. To work with Jan-Eric is very inspiring; he offers great support as a mentor and, of course, is a very dear friend.

Prof. Richard J. Shavelson

I became acquainted with Jan-Eric's work and ultimately met him through Dick Snow. Years ago Dick had been on assignment from Stanford to the Office of Naval Research in London tasked with traveling through Europe ferreting out the best behavioral scientists emerging out of the period following WWII. Jan-Eric was one such talent, someone who shared deep interests in the nature of human abilities with Dick. Indeed, when Dick was ill with cancer (1996), and knew his career was coming to a close, he gave me a stack of Jan-Eric's papers (a good foot high) to read admonishing me to watch out for Jan-Eric. Jan-Eric and I have had a friendship and collaboration over many years which included my teaching a summer course at the University of Gothenburg and coming to Gothenburg to talk with him and Kjell Härnqvist about (at that time) my research on computer cognitive training for expanding working memory. And most recently, Jan-Eric was behind an invitation to me to give a seminar on generalizability theory for the European Educational Research Association. The seminar turned out to be a joy to teach largely because Jan-Eric was a "student" (actually on the board sponsoring the seminar). To show his great friendship he sat through the entire 3 days! Our collaboration continues and together with Sigrid Blömeke we recently published a paper, Beyond Dichotomies: Competence Viewed as a Continuum, in *Zeitschrift für Psychologie*. I'm looking forward to our next adventure together.

Dr. Norman Verhelst

My first (virtual) contact with Jan-Eric was in the early 1980s when his Rasch program PML (with a Dutch manual, written by Ivo Molenaar from Groningen University) became widely used and admired by Dutch psychometricians. The first real contact dates back from 2010 when I started as a member of the technical expert group of the IEA, an organization where Jan-Eric has been active since … the dawn of time, well probably a bit after that. The real contact, however, started in 2011 or 2012, at a seminar organized by Jan-Eric's colleague at Gothenburg, Gudrun Erickson. Later on I was honored to be one of the first lecturers at the newly founded department of Psychometrics at the University of Oslo (CEMO) where Jan-Eric was the first director. After his retirement, which starts now or very soon, I hope that we both will find the time to continue our collaboration.

Prof. Ludger Woessmann

I think I first met Jan-Eric in person whilst teaching a course at the European Educational Research Association (EERA) Spring School on Advanced Methods in Educational Research in Gothenburg in 2012 on "Methods for Causal Inference from Observational Data". I remember that he sat through my whole course, which I found very impressive. I also fondly remember his stern interest in what econometricians do to get closer to causal inference and our inspiring discussions about the opportunities and limitations of this. It was great to see how open he was to what another field was doing and how he would also express his scepticism about specific approaches.

Prof. Ulrika Wolff

I am happy to say that Jan-Eric was my supervisor. He brought me into the world of more advanced statistical analyses. Today we are colleagues in the same research group. It is a blessing to be one in the big crowd of people he shares his wide experience with. I am also very glad to be able to call him my friend.

Prof. Lisbeth Åberg-Bengtsson

I first got to know Jan-Eric in the mid-1990s when I was a Ph.D. student and took courses in research methodology. With his genuine interest and never-ending patience, he guided us in quantitative research. At that point, Jan-Eric awoke my fascination for factor analyses and structural equation modeling and the possibilities these methods offer. After my dissertation, he became my mentor and colleague at the University of Gothenburg, where we gave courses together and collaborated in several research projects for more than 10 years. In recent years, I have held positions at other universities, but Jan-Eric has never ceased to generously offer expert support and invaluable advice.

Contents

Editors and Contributors

About the Editors

Dr. Monica Rosén is a Professor of Education at the University of Gothenburg. Her main areas of research concern educational results at individual, group, and system levels, and factors associated with differences and change in educational outcome. She also shares a strong interest for the methodological issues that follow these research interests: educational measurement, educational evaluation and assessment, comparative educational research, and statistical modeling techniques.

Dr. Kajsa Yang Hansen is an Associate Professor at the Department of Education and Special Education, University of Gothenburg. Her research lies mainly in the sociology of education, with the main focus on educational quality and equity from a comparative perspective. Studying and explaining the variation in academic achievement between individuals, schools, across countries, and over time has always been her primary research interest. Her methodological interest lies in analytical techniques for large-scale survey data, such as the multilevel analysis, Structural Equation Modeling (SEM), and second-generation SEM. Currently, she is involved in projects investigating trends in Swedish pupils' educational outcomes with respect to changes in opportunities to learn, educational reforms in Sweden, and organizational differentiation across countries.

Dr. Ulrika Wolff is a Professor of Education at the University of Gothenburg. Her primary research interest is on dyslexia, early reading acquisition, and verbal and non-verbal cognitive abilities related to reading. She also has a special interest in analyses of quantitative data and measurement methods.

Contributors

Dr. Peter Allerup is a Professor at Aarhus University. He gained his Master's degree in Mathematical Statistics from the University of Copenhagen in 1970, and has worked as a Senior Research Scientist at The Royal Danish Institute for Educational Research. He has been working as a mathematical statistician in the general field of quantitative data analysis, particularly in the educational research area. He has constructed educational tests and conducted statistical analyses of empirical observations, e.g. in the field of IRT models (Item Response Theory) and Rasch models. He is also the national coordinator of IEA's TIMSS studies of 2007, 2011, and 2015.

Kim Bellens is Research Associate at the Centre for Educational Effectiveness and Evaluation at KU Leuven—University of Leuven (Belgium). Her major research interests are international comparative educational studies, quality and equity amongst educational systems, and multilevel analysis.

Dr. Sigrid Blömeke is the Director of the Centre for Educational Measurement at the University of Oslo (CEMO). Her area of specialization is the assessment of teacher competencies from a comparative perspective across countries and subjects. Blömeke has recently received the 2016 Distinguished Research Award from the German Educational Research Association (GERA). Before she moved to Oslo, Blömeke was Professor of Instructional Research and the Director of the Interdisciplinary Center of Educational Research at Humboldt University of Berlin, Germany, Visiting Professor of Educational Measurement at Michigan State University, USA, and Professor of Teaching and Learning with ICT at the University of Hamburg, Germany. Blömeke was the lead investigator of several large research projects, including the "Teacher Education and Development Study in Mathematics", the funding initiative "Modeling and measuring competencies in higher education", and the longitudinal study "Structure, level and development of preschool teachers' competencies".

Dr. Bert Creemers is Professor emeritus in educational sciences at the University of Groningen, the Netherlands. His main interest is educational quality in terms of student learning and outcomes at classroom, school, and system level. Together with Leonidas Kyriakides he works on the development and testing of the dynamic model on educational effectiveness and the approach, based on this model, for the improvement of education.

Dr. Matthias von Davier is Senior Research Director in the Center for Global Assessment at Educational Testing Service. He is editor-in-chief of the British Journal of Mathematical and Statistical Psychology and co-editor of the Springer book series Methodology of Educational Measurement and Assessment. His research interests focus on the international educational skill surveys, item response theory, Rasch models, latent class models, diagnostic classification models, model-data-fit, estimation methods, and computational statistics.

Dr. Andreas Demetriou is Professor of Psychology and President of the University of Nicosia Research Foundation. He was a Professor of psychology at the Aristotle University of Thessaloniki, Greece (1975–1996) and at the University of Cyprus (1996–2008). He has served as Vice-Rector of the University of Cyprus, foundational President of the Cyprus University of Technology, and also Minister of Education and Culture of Cyprus. He is a fellow of Academia Europaea and the International Academy of Education, an Honorary Professor of Durham University, UK, an Honorary Visiting Professor of the Northeastern Normal University, China, and an Honorary Doctor of Middlesex University, London. He developed an intellectual development theory, integrating the developmental, psychometric, and cognitive traditions. His work is published in more than 200 books and articles.

Eric A. Hanushek Ph.D. is the Paul and Jean Hanna Senior Fellow at the Hoover Institution of Stanford University. He is a leader in the development of economic analysis of educational issues. His research areas include the effects of class size reduction, high-stakes accountability, the assessment of teacher quality, and other education related topics.

Martin Hooper is Assistant Research Director of Questionnaire Development and Policy Studies at IEA's TIMSS & PIRLS International Study Center at Boston College. He coordinates context questionnaire development, technical reporting, and policy studies across the TIMSS and PIRLS assessment programs. He is experienced in higher education administration and is completing his Ph.D. in the Educational Research, Measurement, and Evaluation program at Boston College's Lynch School of Education.

Lars Jenßen is currently researcher at the Freie Universität Berlin, Germany. In 2015 he was invited to take a guest researcher position at the Centre for Educational Measurement at the University of Oslo (CEMO). At CEMO, he worked on the application of established psychological methods, e.g. latent state-trait models or nested-factor models, to educational research questions. His area of specialization is the assessment of preschool teachers' professional competence. Other fields of interests are the relation between student personality and achievement in higher education or the interplay of intelligence and competence in general. During his research career, Jenßen worked as a researcher at Humboldt University of Berlin, Germany, and as a freelance researcher at different psychiatric institutions in Berlin, e.g. Charité Berlin. Currently, he is member of the German project Pro-KomMa which examines the development of preschool teachers' competence in a longitudinal study from training to career entry.

Harrison J. Kell is an associate research scientist in the Center Academic & Workforce Readiness & Success (CAWRS) at Educational Testing Service (ETS). He is interested in how individual differences (e.g. cognitive abilities, personality traits) predict human performance and how basic knowledge about human psychological diversity can benefit the developmental sciences, enhance practice in applied settings, and inform policy development.

Dr. Patrick C. Kyllonen is the Senior Research Director for the Center of Academic & Workforce Readiness & Success (CAWRS) at Educational Testing Service (ETS). The center conducts research on identifying key 21st century skills and methods for measuring these skills in primary and secondary school, higher education, and the workforce. The center also does work on large-scale domestic and international assessments, such as NAEP and PISA.

Dr. Leonidas Kyriakides is Professor in Educational Research and Evaluation and the chair of the Department of Education at the University of Cyprus. His field of research and scholarship is the evaluation of the educational effectiveness of teachers, schools, or educational systems. Currently, his research agenda is concerned with the development of a dynamic model of educational effectiveness, and the application of effectiveness research to the improvement of educational practice. He has acted as the chair of the EARLI SIG on Educational Effectiveness and the chair of the AERA SIG on School Effectiveness and Improvement. He was also a member of the PISA 2015 QEG expert group that was responsible for developing the theoretical framework and the questionnaires of the PISA 2015 study. Finally, he is member of the editorial board of various international journals with referee system and the author of more than 100 papers, 8 books, and 80 book chapters.

Dr. Henry M. Levin is the William Heard Kilpatrick Professor of Economics and Education at Teachers College, Columbia University and the David Jacks Professor of Education and Economics, Emeritus at Stanford University. He is a specialist in the economics of education and human resources.

Dr. Michael O. Martin is Executive Director of IEA's TIMSS & PIRLS International Study Center at Boston College and a Research Professor in the Lynch School of Education. From his early work on IEA's Reading Literacy Study, through 20 years of TIMSS trends and founding PIRLS, his special interests have been in large-scale assessment methods and procedures. Dr. Martin has led and contributed to numerous advances in assessment methods.

Dr. Ina V.S. Mullis is Executive Director of IEA's TIMSS & PIRLS International Study Center at Boston College and a Professor in the Lynch School of Education's Department of Educational Research, Measurement, and Evaluation. She has devoted her career to large-scale assessment, first with NAEP in the USA, and then 20 years with TIMSS and founding PIRLS. She has played a key leadership role in building TIMSS and PIRLS into the global assessment programs they are today.

Dr. Bengt Muthén obtained his Ph.D. in Statistics at the University of Uppsala, Sweden and is Professor emeritus at UCLA. He was the 1988–1989 President of the Psychometric Society and the 2011 recipient of the Psychometric Society's Lifetime Achievement Award. He has published extensively on latent variable modeling and many of his procedures are implemented in the Mplus program that he has co-developed.

Prof. Richard J. Shavelson is Chief Scientist at SK Partners, and emeritus Margaret Jacks Professor of Education, and emeritus I. James Quillen Dean of the Graduate School of Education at Stanford University. His research interests span statistics, psychometrics, and research design to measurement of performance in education, work, and the military, through to education policy and practice.

Dr. George Spanoudis is an Associate Professor of psychology at the University of Cyprus. He studied psychology at the Aristotle University of Cyprus and obtained his Ph.D. from the University of Cyprus. His works focuses on cognitive development, theory of intelligence, relations between intelligence and the brain, and special learning difficulties.

Dr. André Torre is Senior Research Scientist and is working as a statistician in the general field of quantitative data analysis included IRT/Rasch models. He got his science Master's degree in Engineering from Technical University of Denmark, 1989, and Bachelor of Science degree in Mathematical Statistics from the University of Copenhagen, 1999. Since 1999 he has been an academically trained member at Aarhus University, DPU.

Dr. Jan Van Damme is Professor emeritus at the Centre for Educational Effectiveness and Evaluation at the KU Leuven in Belgium. He is interested in the effects of teachers, class groups, schools, and educational systems on the development of students.

Dr. Norman Verhelst has worked 15 years as Associate Professor at the Universities of Leuven, Belgium, University of Nijmegen, and University of Utrecht, the Netherlands, after studying psychology. From 1985 to 2010, he was a senior researcher at the National Institute for Educational Measurement (Cito) in Arnhem, the Netherlands. Since 2011 he has been working as an independent consultant in educational statistics and psychometrics. His main area of research is item response theory.

Edward E. Wiley is senior research scientist at SK Partners. His research interests center on Big Data and advanced statistical analytics, systems of school accountability, teacher quality and compensation, and school choice—initiatives central to the current atmosphere of standards based testing.

Dr. Ludger Woessmann is Professor of Economics at the University of Munich and Director of the Ifo Center for the Economics of Education. His main research interests are the importance of education for economic prosperity—individual and societal, historical and modern—and the importance of institutions of the school systems for efficiency and equity. His research on the determinants of student achievement often applies micro-econometric methods to international student achievement tests.

Dr. Lisbeth Åberg-Bengtsson is a Professor of Education at the Department of Educational Research and Development, University of Borås, Sweden. One of her research interests focuses on dimensionality of large-scale tests. Another interest concerns students' comprehension of graphical representations such as graphs, diagrams, and statistical maps, as well as of illustrations in the form of explanatory pictures and models in educational materials.

Chapter 1
Introduction

Monica Rosén, Kajsa Yang Hansen and Ulrika Wolff

1.1 Cognitive Abilities and Educational Outcomes

The relationship between cognitive abilities and academic achievement is well established (see e.g., Mackintosh 1998). Differences in cognitive abilities as captured by different dimensions of intelligence are often used to explain social and individual variability in educational achievement and to predict academic performance and future career success.

As is frequently observed, there is substantial variation in the level of educational achievement reached by different individuals. Some students experience difficulties acquiring the basic knowledge and skills stipulated by a school's curriculum while others master complex material with ease. According to the investment theory (Cattell 1967, 1971), fluid intelligence is one of the major causes of achievement differences, since it represents the individual's capacity to solve novel problems, to make inferences, to identify relations, and to transform information. The greater a pupil's capacity in this regard, the more efficiently and rapidly they will learn. Through investment in learning experiences, such a capacity is transformed into crystallized intelligence, which is defined as the depth and breadth of knowledge and skills that are valued by one's culture. In this process, school and family act as formal and informal learning environments, along with intrapersonal characteristics, such as, motivation, self-concept and persistence, and cultural belongingness, playing essential roles in the development of an individual's knowledge and skill (see, e.g., Kvist and Gustafsson 2008).

In studying the relationship between educational outcomes and cognitive abilities, issues concerning the malleability of cognitive ability and the educational,

M. Rosén (✉) · K. Yang Hansen · U. Wolff
Department of Education and Special Education, University of Gothenburg, Gothenburg, Sweden
e-mail: Monica.Rosen@ped.gu.se

© Springer International Publishing AG 2017
M. Rosén et al. (eds.), *Cognitive Abilities and Educational Outcomes*,
Methodology of Educational Measurement and Assessment,
DOI 10.1007/978-3-319-43473-5_1

1

social, and environmental determinants of educational outcomes need to be addressed. Typically, schools focus on teaching and promoting students' knowledge and skills in different content areas, according to national curriculums. The imperfect correlation between cognitive abilities and academic performance (e.g., Jencks 1979; Mackintosh 1998) suggests that differences in educational outcome may also be influenced by additional factors.

As has been observed in the educational effectiveness and attainment research, school organizational characteristics and academic processes, such as curriculum, resources, and teacher competence, explain a rather substantial part of the outcome differences. Furthermore, research also indicated that, while the composition of the student body in classrooms and schools has significant impact on student educational outcomes (e.g., Thrupp 1995; Ammermueller and Pischke 2009), the differentiated organizational features, for example, tracking and ability grouping, implemented in different school systems also attribute to a great deal of the variation in educational outcomes (e.g., Woessmann 2009). The ability to identify the determinants of educational outcomes is of particular importance for improving our understanding in effective schools and teachers, and for informing and monitoring educational policies. Also, it may guide our educational practices to enhance students' school performance and their basic cognitive skills.

These categories of determinants have traditionally been treated separately. However, they should be investigated under a common theoretical framework of educational measurement through multilevel methodologies to combine both micro and macro approaches to research on educational outcomes and cognitive abilities. Individual differences in cognitive ability can thus be studied simultaneously with the effects of social, educational, and environmental factors at different organizational levels on the structure and development of abilities.

To allow the investigation and communication of the abovementioned issues, and to make credible inferences from the observations, the measurement properties of instruments used to appraise different constructs in educational outcomes, cognitive abilities, and/or contextual backgrounds need to be addressed in terms of their reliability and validity. In that, classic test theory, item response theory, and factor analysis, among others, are worth special attention.

The inspiration for this book is the contributions of Jan-Eric Gustafsson to the field of educational measurement, honouring his vision to link prerequisites, education process, and cognitive and non-cognitive outcomes together in an integrated framework at both individual and organizational levels as well as from a developmental perspective.

The book is an attempt to reflect at least parts of the broad research areas to which Jan-Eric Gustafsson has been dedicated, and made contributions to, over the years. Jan-Eric started his research in the field of cognitive abilities but subsequently widened his scope to embrace the causes and effects of education, while always residing at the forefront of measurement issues. In accordance with Jan-Eric's research, this Festschrift is organized in three parts, focusing on three broad interrelated themes, namely, *cognitive abilities, causes and effects of educational outcome,* and *modeling measurement properties.* In the following sections we will briefly describe each of these themes and the associated chapters of this book.

1.2 Part I. Cognitive Abilities

The first part of the book covers aspects of research on cognitive abilities and provides an overview of the models for the structure of intelligence.

In the beginning of the twentieth century the first intelligence scale was created by Binet, in France. This was an important contribution to the field of research on cognitive abilities, and similar scales are still in use for both clinical and research purposes. Another crucial contribution to the field at the beginning of the twentieth century was the creation of factor analysis, and the first model of the structure of cognitive abilities by Spearman (1904). Spearman's two-factor theory of intelligence proposes a g-factor of general intelligence and an s-factor of specific cognitive abilities which accounts for individual differences in performance. Thurstone (1938) further refined the factor analysis technique to encompass multiple common factors in a multidimensional model of intelligence, in which a g-factor was not possible to identify.

Throughout the twentieth century, there were strong conflicts within the research of cognitive abilities, and a g-factor common to all tasks was a critical issue. Some researchers supported models with a g-factor (e.g. Burt 1949; Vernon 1950) whereas others supported models without a g-factor (e.g. Guildford 1967; Horn and Cattell 1966). Furthermore, there was a disagreement as to whether all factors should be considered as equal or if hierarchical models with lower order factors subsumed under higher order factors should be used.

In 1966, Horn and Cattell presented a hierarchical model with a set of narrow and broad factors, among which two factors, fluid intelligence (Gf) and crystallized intelligence (Gc) are now regarded as the core concepts in the field of intelligence. Cattell (1963, 1987) suggested that these constructs represent two different aspects of general intelligence (g). Whereas Gf represents the ability to solve novel, complex problems using inductive and deductive reasoning, Gc represents individual differences in language, information and concepts of a culture. Cattell (1987) later proposed Gf to be biologically determined, while Gc he considered was mainly acquired through education and experience. Recent research, however, has provided reasons to believe Gf to be plastic and possible to improve (e.g. Cliffordson and Gustafsson 2008).

The Cattell–Horn–Carroll (CHC) is a consensus model based on three strata. Stratum I comprises around 60 narrow factors, from which around 10 broader factors are identified to Stratum II, among those Gf and Gc. Stratum III includes the g-factor. Cattell (1987) hypothesized Gf to be highly correlated to g. According to Cattell's above-mentioned investment theory, Gf is also an important early determinant of Gc, particularly in areas that require an understanding of complex relations. The capacity to understand complex relations is required in subjects such as reading and arithmetic, even though motivation, instruction and opportunities to learn are important too (Cattell 1987).

Jan-Eric Gustafsson empirically supported the hypothesis of a strong, even perfect, relationship between Gf and a higher order g-factor (Gustafsson 1984; Gustafsson and Undheim 1996), which may be due to the fact that each task that requires learning of new knowledge and skills will be influenced by Gf. In further support of the investment theory (Cattel 1971), Valentin Kvist and Gustafsson (2008) have shown the relation between Gf and g to be close to identical within homogenous groups, who had equally good or poor opportunities to develop knowledge and skills, but not in heterogeneous groups.

Gf can thus be conceived as a domain-general ability, and separate content factors can be identified along with a Gf-factor (Beauducel et al. 2001). This implies that when only one type of content is used, Gf becomes flavored by construct-irrelevant factors. Typically, among young children Gf is measured by visuospatial problem-solving tests only, such as Raven's matrices, leading to bias towards this kind of task. A more valid measure of Gf in young children has been proposed through combining visuospatial tests with working memory and memory span tests (Gustafsson and Wolff 2015). The verbal and visual aspects of the tests were found to be modality specific, and not to represent general processing capacity (Gustafsson and Wolff 2015; Wolff and Gustafsson 2015).

Four chapters are included in Part I:

Patrick Kyllonen and Harrison Kell take a retrospective viewpoint to the developmental structure of intelligence. They relate Jan-Eric's key contributions in the property of Gf (Gustafsson 1984) to the important implications in understanding the nature of general cognitive skills. The authors also summarize the important extension of Jan-Eric's contribution to recent research and the introduction of a new area of research on how understanding the nature of fluid intelligence can help to improve and optimize human performance.

Andreas Demetriou and Georg Spanoudis demonstrate how individual differences in intellectual growth are related to both the state of the core of cognitive processes and its interaction with different cognitively primary domains (e.g. categorical, quantitative, spatial cognition, etc.). They also demonstrate that different levels of intelligence expressed through IQ measures correspond to different types of representational and problem-solving possibilities as expressed through the core of cognitive processes. With their empirical evidence from various learning deductive reasoning studies, the authors show that the abstraction, representational alignment, and cognizance (AAcog) mechanism functions as a general core of mental processes, integrating classic psychometrics, developmental structures as well as different general and specific mental processes into a system of mind, which has strong implications in, for example, enhancing leaning.

Monica Rosén investigates gender differences in cognitive abilities and its relationship with performance on a standardized achievement test in grade six (12-year olds), using data from Jan-Eric Gustafsson's research project on learning strategies and teaching (the INSU-project, Swedish acronym) in the 1980s. Group differences are examined by the nested latent variable approach suggested by Gustafsson (1992), in combination with the missing data modeling approach suggested by Muthén et al. (1987). Her analysis demonstrates that a more complex understanding is needed of both the measures and performances of the compared groups. The results are also discussed in relation to the investment theory of cause and effect in the hierarchical structure of broad and narrow cognitive abilities.

Following Jan-Eric Gustafsson's research on the hierarchical structure of cognitive abilities and investment theory, Sigrid Blömeke and Lars Jenßen describe the relationship between intelligence and content specific skills of preschool teacher students in Germany. They show that general cognitive ability influences the preschool teacher students' domain-specific knowledge. Given this, they propose that the general cognitive ability factor needs to be controlled when learning outcomes are researched.

1.3 Part II. Causes and Effects of Educational Outcome

The second part of the book covers theoretical and methodological aspects within the field of Educational Effectiveness Research (EER). If one is aiming to improve schools in the educational system, many factors, both within school and within the school system, that affect the educational outcomes and cognitive abilities of students in their academic and social development, must be considered. Such factors include teaching methods, school organization, curriculum and learning environments. This makes EER a complex field to study. In order to identify the effects of school related factors, one needs to eliminate effects related to students' family and other social environments intertwined with the effects of school related factors. Therefore: *"The methodological issues of how we analyze complex data from multiple levels of the educational system have had, and continue to have, a salience in EER more than in many other educational specialties"* (Reynolds et al. 2014, p. 198).

Various models have been proposed in the past, but none has achieved to fully account for variations in student educational outcomes. One of the latest models of educational effectiveness is the Creemers and Kyriakides (2007) Dynamic Model of Educational Effectiveness. In designing the model, Creemers and Kyriakides took into consideration a critique on previous models in EER, in order to create a theoretical model of the components affecting student learning outcomes. They argued that, since we live in a constantly changing environment, teaching and learning practices need to be adaptable and dynamic in form, adjusting to the requirements of society.

Based on the assumption that teacher behavior in the classroom is strongly associated with student achievement (Creemers and Kyriakides 2013; Scheerens 2013), the Dynamic Model of Educational Effectiveness can be used to analyze the different actors of educational effectiveness. Scheerens et al. (2013) concluded in their review of 109 studies using the Dynamic Model that there is still a need for research in the domain of effective instruction. Therefore, assessing classroom factors to obtain a better understanding of how they interact with each other and affect learning outcomes remains yet a further valuable endeavor.

In this section, the purpose of five prominent chapters is to shed light on different aspects of the theme of educational effectiveness research. In some of the contributions, data from international large-scale surveys, such as TIMSS (Trends in International Mathematics and Science Study) and PIRLS (Progress in International Reading Literacy Study), provide the empirical materials for testing assumptions and hypotheses concerning causality in the EER framework, but also for reflecting on research methodology and design. In a frequently cited paper, Jan-Eric suggested that longitudinal trend data from TIMSS and PIRLS could be used to provide causal explanations about educational influence on educational outcomes (Gustafsson 2007). Some of the contributions elaborate both theoretically and methodologically on this suggestion.

Leonidas Kyriakides and Bert Creemers address the causality issues in different research methods used to establish causal relations within EER and attempt to identify strengths and methodological limitations in both cross-sectional and experimental studies. Special emphasis is also attributed to the use of international educational evaluation studies such as PISA (Programme for International Student Assessment) and TIMSS in developing and testing the theoretical framework of EER.

Using data from TIMSS 2003 and 2011, the chapter by Jan van Damme and Kim Bellens investigates trends in achievement level and the relationships between achievement and socio-economic status and ethnicity, respectively, as indicators of quality and equality. In their hierarchical multilevel model analysis, they show no consistent relationship between trends in quality and trends in equality.

Eric Hanushek and Ludger Woessmann examine research evidence on the effect of school resources on student achievement. They focus on studies applying quasi-experimental research methods and data from international, large-scale research such as TIMSS and PIRLS. They note that school resources, like expenditure and class size, are not driving forces in student achievement differences. Instead, teacher quality as an important school input plays an essential role.

Lisbeth Åberg-Bengtsson compares Swedish Scholastic Aptitude Test (SweSAT) results between students from different upper secondary tracks, whilst controlling for grade-point average from compulsory schools. Her findings support the assumption that different school tracks may affect performance on cognitive tests differently, in addition to a student's background and earlier school performance.

Tackling the challenge of identifying the characteristics of effective teachers, Henry Levin examines the empirical evidences for causal links between different teacher-related factors and student achievement. Studies have indicated that individual teachers generate substantial differences in student results. However, the teacher characteristics proposed to generate the result differences are not identified in the reviewed, large-scale studies.

1.4 Part III. Modeling Measurement Properties

Over the history of educational research, a parallel theme of any research question has always been the validity and reliability of measures. Creating valid and reliable measures of socially relevant constructs that allow comparisons between individuals and groups across time and cultural settings is an important goal for educational research and a challenge in itself. The limitations of classical test theory (CTT) have long been recognized. However, it was not until later, with the arrival of computers and the progress of computer power, that new models were developed to produce more reliable information about both test and test takers, and the development of test theory and its applications could evolve at a more rapid pace. From the mid-1970s onwards, two major strands of development in the field of educational measurement have grown in parallel, and successively become more accessible to applied researchers. One is item response theory (IRT) and the other is structural equation modeling, taking a multivariate approach to the measurement problem.

The true score model, proposed in 1904 by Spearman, states that any manifest score is due to at least two sources of variance: true variance due to the intended construct and to measurement errors. This model has to become the foundation for CTT (for detailed presentations of CTT see, e.g. Gulliksen 1950; Lord et al. 1968). Although Spearman and others have offered techniques to estimate the true score variance, the difficulty of obtaining a reliable person score has remained, due to the fact that the estimate of person score varies depending on different item characteristics, such as item difficulty level, and the competence level of the sample.

The main weakness of classical test theory is thus that the item parameters change as the group of test takers change. In the mid-1970s, the one-parameter Rasch Model, named after its originator George Rasch, became available and this problem in CTT was statistically solved (Rasch 1960). According to Rasch, performance on test items can only be attributed to one of two sources, item difficulty and a person's ability level. The one-parameter logistic model enabled item difficulty to be separated from respondent's ability and vice versa. As item difficulty is a fixed characteristic of the item, person scores on different sets of items can be compared, a feature which is used for example in all international large-scale assessments. Another advantage of the Rasch Model is that the person parameter is estimated on the same latent scale as item difficulty parameter. This feature has provided researchers with better possibilities to compose well-balanced tests from test items.

However, two problems plagued the Rasch model. One problem was the computational difficulty to estimate the model, especially when there were many items.

The other problem was the difficulty to determine good model fit. Jan-Eric Gustafsson was one of the early enthusiasts and contributed an elegant solution to the computation of the conditional maximum likelihood estimate (Gustafsson 1980a) which in turn gave room for better statistical tests of goodness of fit (Gustafsson 1980b). He also argued that the model fit question during these early days was ill posed, proposing that the question should not be if one item did or did not fit, but rather whether the items fit together. With this solution, he suggested that one way to address poor model fit was to sort items together more carefully rather than excluding items from the scale.

The problem of obtaining good model fit in the Rasch model also resulted in model development. The one-parameter Rasch model was soon developed to include more item parameters. The two-parameter logistic model (also called the Birnbaum model) added item discrimination as another item parameter which allowed for differently discriminating item slopes. The fact that multiple choice items are, to a varying degree, sensitive to guessing was captured by a third parameter in the so-called three-parameter logistic model.

Another line of model development were models allowing for different types of scoring, such as partial credit-models and graded response models. The original Rasch model was based on dichotomous scoring where all items were scored to be either right or wrong. A common trait for all item response models is, however, that they rely on the rather strict assumptions of unidimensionality and local independence. The unidimensionality assumption presupposes that all items in the test share the same latent trait or set of latent traits. Accordingly, the local statistical independence assumption means that the items do so to the same degree and that this holds true for all persons or groups that are to be compared on this scale. Furthermore, local statistical independence does not hold true if some items include clues on how to solve other items in the test, since clues will be advantageous to some test-takers more than others. Establishing measurement invariance across groups is thus an essential prerequisite before comparisons of ability levels are made on any test.

Item response theory remains a valuable tool for developing instruments, constructing scales, linking scales and adaptive testing (Lord 1980). Whilst multidimensional IRT models currently are under development, Rasch models are still the ones most commonly relied on. Achievement tests are not the only aspects scaled with IRT models. The same type of model is now applied for other theoretical constructs that are assumed to influence or explain educational outcome, for example feelings, attitudes, opinions and perceptions.

However, since IRT modeling is not yet optimal for detecting or accounting for multidimensionality or for measuring behavior on complex tasks, other methods and models have been developed in parallel with IRT techniques. The Swedish statistician Karl Jöreskog and his colleague Dag Sörbom in the 1970s developed LISREL, a software incorporating confirmatory factor analysis, simultaneous equation models, and path analysis into a general covariance structure model (e.g., Jöreskog & Sörbom 2001). This technique was then advanced further through the work of Bengt Muthén. Since the end of the 1970s, these techniques are also accessible for dichotomous and categorical data, as well as for complex sampling designs (e.g. Muthén and Muthén 1998–2015).

In contrast to IRT models, confirmatory factor analysis has the advantage of not relying on any strong assumption about item variance distributions. Multidimensionality, as an inevitable part of any educational measure, can with this technique be modeled so that both measurement error and more systematic sources of variance are captured or defined in different latent variables. The hierarchical approach with nested variables (the bi-factor model) suggested by Jan-Eric Gustafsson in his research on the structure of cognitive abilities (e.g. Gustafsson 1988, 1994) has been widely used as a strategy to fit latent factor models to achievement tests as well as measures of other constructs to investigate issues about dimensionality. Gustafsson has also shown the usefulness of the bi-factor model to detect the needs of improvement in SAT (Gustafsson et al. 1992).

For a long time, item response theory was regarded as being completely different from classical test theory due to its strong assumptions about unidimensionality and the absence of measurement error. Today IRT and CTT are used in tandem and, together with the recent advances of structural equation modeling and the increasing availability of more user-friendly software, these methods continue to improve educational research with respect to both the quality of measures and to research questions that now, due to these methodological advances, can be addressed.

Six chapters are included in Part III:

The chapter by Ina Mullis, Michael Martin and Martin Hooper describes how the items in the PIRLS and TIMSS contextual questionnaires are selected and scaled according to IRT principles illustrating the development toward a broader application of IRT models.

In the context of the multivariate latent variable modeling, Bengt Muthén discusses the problem of missing data or selective response patterns, a condition that is common in most large-scale observational studies, whether planned by design or not, which risk distortion of the regression coefficients in any modeling approach. Muthén offers a solution to this problem through an application of the Pearson–Lawey selection formula which in combination with a factor score approach can produce valid means, variances and covariances for the full population. Examples are provided.

Richard Shavelson and Edward Wiley's chapter is an application of bi-factor models (Gustafsson 1984) to examine the structure of the Scholastic Aptitude Test (SAT). Gustafsson has shown the usefulness of the bi-factor model to detect the needs of improvement in SATs. Reflecting upon the interpretation of factor-analytic findings, Shavelson and Wiley also propose the use of both cognitive interviews and predictive studies to validate suggested factor-analytic interpretations.

Matthias von Davier discusses test construction using CTT or IRT, respectively. He shows that, in contradiction to common belief, the Rasch model (or any unidimensional IRT model) and CTT are both conceptually and mathematically connected through their use of conditional odds-ratios to determine the items relation to the overall sum of scores.

Norman Verhelst addresses the difficulty of obtaining measurement invariance, i.e., the same item parameter estimates across groups, as being required by the IRT model to ensure the validity of any group comparisons. Instead of rejecting the model as invalid, a methodology that makes constructive use of the group's deviation from the expected item parameter estimates is offered to identify particular patterns or profiles that can be interpreted in substantive terms.

Glimpses from the early days when scholars learned how to understand, compute and use Rasch models is presented in the final chapter where Peter Allerup and André Torre describe the enthusiasm given to the Rasch model's mathematical beauty and over the potential of finally finding a way to develop truly objective measures that are not only easy to interpret, but also have many application areas.

References

Ammermueller, A., & Pischke, J. S. (2009). Peer effects in European primary schools: Evidence from the progress in international reading literacy study. *Journal of Labor Economics, 27*(3), 315–348.

Beauducel, A., Brocke, B., & Liepmann, D. (2001). Perspectives on fluid and crystallized intelligence: Facets for verbal, numerical, and figural intelligence. *Personality and Individual Differences, 30*, 977–994.

Burt, C. (1949). *The factors of the mind: An introduction to factor analysis in psychology.* New York: MacMillan.

Cattell, R. B. (1963). Theory of fluid and crystallized intelligence: A critical experiment. *Journal of Educational Psychology, 54*(1), 1–22.

Cattell, R. B. (1967). The theory of fluid intelligence and crystalized intelligence in relation to 'culture fair' tests and its verification in children 9–12 years old. *Revue de Psychologie Applique, 17*(3):135–154.

Cattell, R. B. (1971). *Abilities: Their structure, growth and action.* Boston: Houghton Mifflin.

Cattell, R. B. (1987). *Intelligence: Its structure, growth, and action.* New York: Elsevier Science.

Cliffordson, C., & Gustafsson J.-E. (2008). Effects of age and schooling on intellectual performance: Estimates obtained from analysis of continuous variation in age and length of schooling. *Intelligence, 36*, 143–152.

Creemers, B., & Kyriakides, L. (2007). *The dynamics of educational effectiveness: A contribution to policy, practice and theory in contemporary schools.* Routledge.

Creemers, B. P., & Kyriakides, L. (2013). *Improving quality in education: Dynamic approaches to school improvement.* Routledge.

Guildford, J. P. (1967). *The nature of human intelligence.* New York: McGraw-Hill.

Gulliksen, H. (1950). *Theory of mental tests.* New York: Wiley.

Gustafsson, J.-E. (1980a). A solution of the conditional estimation problem for long tests in the Rasch model for dichotomous items. *Educational and Psychological Measurements, 40*(2), 377–385.

Gustafsson, J.-E. (1980b). Testing and obtaining fit of data to the Rasch model. *British Journal of Mathematical and Statistical Psychology, 33*(2), 205–233.

Gustafsson, J.-E. (1984). A unifying model of the structure of intellectual abilities. *Intelligence, 8*, 179–203.

Gustafsson, J.-E. (1988). Hierarchical models of individual differences in cognitive abilities. In R. J. Sternberg (Ed.), *Advances in the psychology of human intelligence* (Vol. 4, pp. 35–71). Hillsdale, New Jersey: Lawrence Erlbaum Associates.

Gustafsson, J.-E. (1992). The relevance of factor analysis for the study of group differences. *Multivariate Behavioral Research, 27*(2), 239–247.

Gustafsson, J.-E. (1994). Hierarchical models of intelligence and educational achievement. In A. Demetriou & A. Efklides (Eds.), *Intelligence, mind and reasoning—Structure and development. Advances in Psychology* (Vol. 106, pp. 45–74). Amsterdam: Elsevier.

Gustafsson, J.-E. (2007). Understanding causal influence on educational achievement through differences over time within countries. In T. Loveless (Ed.), *Lessons learned: What international assessment tells us about math achievement* (pp. 37–63). Washington, DC: Brookings Institution Press.

Gustafsson, J.-E., & Undheim, J. O. (1996). Individual differences in cognitive functions. In D. Berliner & R. Calfee (Eds.), *Handbook of educational psychology* (pp. 186–242). New York: Macmillan.

Gustafsson, J.-E., Wedman, I., & Westerlund, A. (1992). The dimensionality of the Swedish scholastic aptitude test. *Scandinavian Journal of Educational Research, 36*(1), 21–39.

Gustafsson, J.-E., & Wolff, U. (2015). Measuring fluid intelligence at age four. *Intelligence, 50,* 175–185. doi.org/10.1016/j.intell.2015.04.008

Horn, J. L., & Cattell, R. B. (1966). Refinement and test of the theory of fluid and crystallized general intelligences. *Journal of Educational Psychology, 57,* 253–270.

Jencks, C. (1979). Who gets ahead? In *The determinants of economic success in America.* New York, NY: Basic Books.

Jöreskog, K. G., & Sörbom, D. (2001). *LISREL 8 user's reference guide.* Chicago: Scientific Software International.

Kvist, A. V., & Gustafsson, J.-E. (2008). The relation between fluid intelligence and the general factor as a function of cultural background: A test of Cattell's investment theory. *Intelligence, 36*(5), 422–436.

Lord, F. M. (1980). *Applications of item response theory to practical testing problems.* Mahwah, NJ: Lawrence Erlbaum Associates, Inc.

Lord, F. M., Novick, M. R., & Birnbaum, A. (1968). *Statistical theories of mental test scores.* Reading, MA: Addison-Wesley.

Mackintosh, N. J. (1998). *IQ and human intelligence.* Oxford: Oxford University Press.

Muthén, B., Kaplan, D., & Hollis, M. (1987). On structural equation modeling with data that are not missing completely at random. *Psychometrika, 52,* 431–462.

Muthén, B. O., & Muthén, L. K. (1998–2015). *Mplus user's guide.* Seventh Edition Los Angeles, CA: Muthén and Muthén.

Rasch, G. (1960). *Probabilistic models for some intelligence and attainment tests.* Copenhagen: Danish institute of Educational Research. (Expanded ed. 1980) Chicago, Ill.: Chicago University Press.

Reynolds, D., Sammons, P., De Fraine, B., Van Damme, J., Townsend, T., Teddlie, C., et al. (2014). Educational effectiveness research (EER): A state-of-the-art review. *School Effectiveness and School Improvement, 25*(2), 197–230. doi:10.1080/09243453.2014.885450

Scheerens, J. (Ed.). (2013). *Effectiveness of time investments in education: Insights from a review and meta-analysis.* Berlin: Springer.

Scheerens, J., Witziers, B., & Steen, R. (2013). A meta-analysis of school effectiveness studies. *Revista de educacion, 361,* 619–645.

Spearman, C. (1904). "General intelligence," objectively determined and measured. *The American Journal of Psychology, 15*(2), 201–292.

Thrupp, M. (1995). The school mix effect: The history of an enduring problem in educational research, policy and practice. *British Journal of Sociology of Education, 16*(2), 183–203.

Thurstone, L. L. (1938). Primary mental abilities. *Psychometric monographs, 1.*

Vernon, P. E. (1950). *The structure of human abilities.* London: Methuen.

Woessmann, L. (2009). International evidence on school tracking: A review. *Growth, 6.* Paper retrieved at https://core.ac.uk/download/files/153/6630968.pd

Wolff, U., & Gustafsson, J.-E. (2015). Structure of phonological ability at age four. *Intelligence, 53,* 108–117. doi.org/10.1016/j.intell.2015.09.003

Part I
Cognitive Abilities

Chapter 2
What Is Fluid Intelligence? Can It Be Improved?

Patrick Kyllonen and Harrison Kell

Abstract General fluid intelligence (*Gf*) is the ability used in inductive and deductive reasoning, particularly with novel material. It can be contrasted with general crystallized ability *(Gc)* which reflects schooling and acculturated learning, and the two abilities have different developmental trajectories, with *Gf* peaking earlier in the lifespan. Gustafsson has made key contributions to our understanding of *Gf*. He (Gustafsson 1984) introduced hierarchical confirmatory factor analytic models to reconcile Thurstonian (non-hierarchical) and Spearman and Cattell-Horn (hierarchical) models of intelligence and in so doing identified *Gf* as a second-order factor which perfectly correlated with the third-order factor, general ability (*g*). This has important implications for understanding the nature of general cognitive skill. Subsequent research showed that *Gf* can be identified separately from g through variation in culture-related opportunities to learn (Valentin Kvist and Gustafsson 2008). *Gf* has served both as a predictor (Gustafsson and Balke 1993) and outcome (Cliffordson and Gustafsson 2008) in the developmental, cognitive training, cognitive aging, international comparative assessment, genetics, neuropsychopharmacological, human capital theory, and behavioral economics literatures. Understanding the nature of fluid intelligence and how to improve it has become a topic of renewed and general interest for optimizing human performance in school and in the workplace.

2.1 Introduction

General fluid ability (*Gf*) is commonly defined as the ability to solve problems in unfamiliar domains using general reasoning methods (Carroll 1993; Cattell 1963). It is typically contrasted with general crystallized ability (*Gc*), which is the ability to answer questions or solve problems in familiar domains using knowledge and strategies acquired through education, training, or acculturation. These two broad abilities are highly correlated, suggesting a common or general factor (*g*). One

P. Kyllonen (✉) · H. Kell
Educational Testing Service, Princeton, NJ, USA
e-mail: pkyllonen@ETS.ORG

© Springer International Publishing AG 2017
M. Rosén et al. (eds.), *Cognitive Abilities and Educational Outcomes*,
Methodology of Educational Measurement and Assessment,
DOI 10.1007/978-3-319-43473-5_2

explanation for the *Gf-Gc* correlation is given by investment theory (Cattell 1987) which suggests that *Gf* is *invested* in learning so that the rate of learning different tasks depends on *Gf* (along with motivation and opportunities to learn). Therefore school achievement (*Gc*), reflecting the rate of learning, is related to *Gf*. Thorsen et al. (2014) found support for this idea, and further showed that *Gf* is invested in *Gc* not just initially, but continually throughout the school years. They showed that *Gf* measured in 3rd grade predicted *Gc* measured in 9th grade after controlling for *Gc* measured in 6th grade.

Stated this way it might be presumed that *Gf* is an important ability, as solving novel problems is a hallmark of intelligence. It is also essential to learning in school, performance on the job, and in life generally. Empirical studies confirm this intuition. *Gf*, as measured by various tests, has been shown in meta-analyses to predict school grades, and job training and job performance, particularly for high compared to medium complexity (Postlethwaite 2011). Studies based on representative samples show moderate to high correlations between *Gf* (measured by Raven's Progressive Matrices) and national achievement examinations (Pind et al. 2003). *Gf* predicts school achievement, and growth in school achievement, but is not by itself notably affected by the quality of schools (Finn et al. 2014). *Gf* also predicts life outcomes such as earnings, criminality, civic participation, and educational attainment (Borghans et al. 2008; Lindqvist and Vestman 2011). It also is an ability characterizing so called *super-forecasters* (Mellers et al. 2015), people who consistently make accurate predictions about future geopolitical events across a wide range of topics.

In this chapter we address several issues pertaining to general fluid ability. These are (a) what is it? How is it identified? (b) is it distinguishable from g? from *Gc*?, (c) does it improve, and can we improve it?

2.2   What Is an Ability?

The concept or construct of general fluid ability arises from the *abilities model*, or *psychometric model of intelligence* (e.g., Hunt 2011). It is based on the empirical observation that if a group of people are administered a variety of cognitive tests, such as samples of school tasks, intellectual puzzles, problems to solve, or in general, anything that requires learning, memory, or thought, then the most successful people on one test will tend to be the most successful on another, that is, there is a common factor. The factor model formalizes this relationship by positing a common, unobserved (latent) factor to account for correlations among test scores. If there are four tests, there are six (n * [n − 1]/2, n = 4) correlations among them. But a factor model posits a single latent factor (x, serving as an independent variable) with a regression coefficient (factor loading) for each of the four tests (y1–y4, serving as separate dependent variables), thereby accounting for the six observed data points with only four parameters, a savings of two parameters, and therefore a more parsimonious representation of their relationships. Fractal-like, this relationship can be repeated for clusters of tests; and empirically it turns out that there are clusters of tests (e.g., spatial tests, verbal tests) whose interrelationships cannot be completely accounted for by the general factor. This necessitates additional group factors, one for each cluster.

This model of accounting for test inter-correlations parsimoniously through the positing of latent factors is the fundamental basis by which we say that people have *abilities*. Abilities are the unobserved latent variables. There is a general ability (g) and there are group abilities. Carroll (1993, p. 23) refers to a cognitive ability as "an intervening variable, i.e., a calculation convenience, as it were, in linking together a particular series of observations." The abilities concept is not completely dependent on a factor model—other methods of representing the empirical fact of clustering of test-score variables, such as hierarchical clustering or multidimensional scaling also invoke an abilities explanation (Corno et al. 2002, p. 66; Snow et al. 1984). However, the factor model may more easily represent hierarchies of abilities. It was once thought that the general factor (Spearman 1927) and group abilities theories (Thurstone 1938) represented different abilities models, but Gustafsson (1984) showed that both views could be accommodated in the same hierarchical model which provided a better summary of their empirical relationships.

2.3   What Is General Fluid Ability?

Given that there is empirical clustering, what is the nature of those clusters? This can be explored by studying the common features of the tests that are the best representatives of those clusters, that is, the ones that have high factor loadings. A limitation is that factors from factor analysis simply represent what is common to a group of variables studied, and so if a kind of test is never studied then a factor underlying performance on such a test would never be identified; conversely, if a particular kind of test appears in many studies, a factor will be identified to account for that fact. However, reviews of studies that have been conducted on tests and their interrelationships reflect what many researchers have thought important enough to conduct a study on, and therefore the findings that emerge in such reviews will be important in the sense of warranting attention.

One such review was Carroll's (1993) meta-analysis of 460 datasets. He found 241 instances where a reasoning factor (these subsequently were labeled fluid ability tests by Carroll) was identified. Carroll then classified these factors into three categories based on his analysis of their common and unique features. The 236 factors, i.e., the ones that occurred more than once and had relatively high loadings, fell into the categories of

(a) sequential or deductive reasoning factors (e.g., categorical syllogisms ["Some dogs don't bark, Fido is not a dog, can he bark?"], linear syllogisms [Fred is taller than Sam, but shorter than Joe, who's tallest?]), general verbal reasoning [e.g., deductive reasoning, as in identifying a logical conclusion based on verbally stated problem situation],

(b) inductive reasoning factors (e.g., rule discovery, number or letter series tasks, multiple exemplars tasks, matrix tasks, odd element or "odd man out" tasks, and analogies tasks); and

(c) quantitative reasoning factors (these are typically inductive or deductive reasoning tasks but involve quantitative elements, such as number series).

Carroll found that these three main categories of fluid reasoning tests were difficult to distinguish empirically, although there was some tendency for Induction and Sequential Reasoning to be more correlated with *Gf* factors, and Quantitative reasoning to be relatively more related to *Gc* factors. Commercial tests reflect this inconsistency. The Number Series test (Test 24) in the Woodcock-Johnson® III (WJ III®) (Woodcock et al. 2001) test battery is classified both as measuring *Fluid Reasoning* (*Gf*) and as measuring narrower *Mathematics Knowledge* and *Quantitative Reasoning* factors (Schrank 2006). The Woodcock Johnson classification is based on what has come to be known as the Cattell-Horn-Carroll (CHC) theory (McGrew 2005).

Carroll (1993) classified number series tests (Series Tasks more generally) as Inductive Tasks (p. 211), but also pointed out that they can be made more difficult and "thus classifiable as a quantitative task" (p. 213). Wilhelm (2006) reviewed Carroll's classification (and the separation of deductive and inductive reasoning) and pointed out that Carroll viewed series tests as tentative markers of induction due to the fact that analyses are often based on studies that have weak designs and show a single-factor solution. Wilhelm also pointed out that there is often a "content confound," with deductive tasks being primarily verbal, and inductive tasks often being spatial in content. This breakdown suggests that Carroll's Inductive-Deductive (Sequential)-Quantitative split is confounded with a Verbal-Spatial-Quantitative split. A study by Wilhelm (2000) (in German, but reviewed in Wilhelm 2006) suggested that a better representation of relationships is that there is a general fluid ability (*Gf*) factor with Verbal, Figural, and Quantitative sub-factors, and that Number Series was more closely aligned with two deductive measures, *Solving Equations* and *Arithmetic Reasoning,* than with other inductive measures with other contents, such as *Figural Classifications* and *Figural Matrices*.

2.4   Explorations of Measures of General Fluid Ability

In addition to identifying common features of tests that cluster in factor analyses, another approach taken to understand fluid ability has been to explore more systematically features of tasks that are good measures of (have a high correlation with) fluid ability. This approach must be taken with caution as particular measures have considerable task-specific variance (Gustafsson 2002). Nevertheless it can be informative to study several tests in such a way and examine potential underlying commonalities.

2.4.1   Complexity

An example is the complexity hypothesis (e.g., Stankov and Schweizer 2007), which is that because intelligence, particularly *Gf*, is the ability to deal with complexity in some sense, more complex tests must be better measures of intelligence. For example, Stankov and Schweizer (2007) defined complexity as the number of steps needed to reach a solution (their Swaps test), or the level of embedding of a rule used to sort number strings into two categories (their Triplets test), and found that thereby increasing complexity increased task difficulty and led to higher correlations with a *Gf* measure, Raven's progressive matrices. However, Gustafsson (1999) found that an equally plausible measure of complexity—having to switch problem solving sets on every item due to heterogeneous versus homogeneous item type groupings (using figural "odd man out," figure series, and Bongard figure classification tasks)—did not result in higher loadings. In fact, homogeneous groupings tended to lead to higher factor loadings, a result he attributed to the opportunities afforded by homogeneous grouping for within-task learning. He also invoked a working-memory explanation to account for his findings.

Informal approaches to defining complexity might be criticized [akin to Boring's (1923, p. 37) definition of intelligence "as what the tests of intelligence test"]. Halford et al. (1998) proposed a formal specification of the relationship between task features and cognitive complexity called *relational complexity*. Birney and Bowman (2009) applied this framework to both the Swaps and Triplets task as well as to a Latin Square and simple sentence comprehension task. However, they found no advantages to this particular framework over others in predicting *Gf* correlations.

2.4.2   Reasoning Ability and Working-Memory Capacity

The complexity hypothesis, and relational complexity, are essentially working-memory explanations. Working memory is the notion of a limited, short-term system in which temporary storage and information processing of the current focus of thought occurs (Baddeley 2003). The idea that individual differences in working memory capacity might underlie general fluid ability was originally suggested by Kyllonen and Christal (1990), who found correlations above $r = 0.80$ between latent factors of fluid ability and latent factors of working memory. The primary value of the study was to show that tests could be developed to measure working memory capacity using Baddeley and Hitch's (1974) simple definition (tasks that require simultaneous storage and processing of information, such as mental addition) and that capacity measures from those tasks correlated highly with established measures of fluid ability (such as sets, series, and matrices tests).

However, the question of whether the two factors are the same has been an issue addressed. Many factors influence the correlation estimate including measurement error (e.g., correlations between tests vs. latent factors), contents (e.g., verbal, spatial, numerical), item types (e.g., series, matrices, span), speededness, task-specific factors, strategies, and so on. If two large sets of reasoning and working memory measures do not confound these factors, then the latent factor inter-correlation will tend towards unity (e.g., Kyllonen 1995). On the other hand, if random working memory tests are correlated with random reasoning tests without attention to confounding of content, test type, and other factors, then the correlations will be lower. This finding has been evaluated in numerous studies since with a variety of methodologies (Conway et al. 2007; Unsworth et al. 2014). The general view now seems to be that the two factors are highly correlated but not the same (e.g., Kane et al. 2004). One meta-analytic estimate of that correlation is $\rho = 0.85$ (Oberauer et al. 2005), which is based on but higher than Ackerman et al.'s (2005) meta-analytic estimate of $\rho = 0.63$ (between working memory and Gf, controlling for content; p. 38). Much of the source for the distinction between typical reasoning and typical working memory tasks is in content (e.g., Wilhelm 2006) and to a lesser extent, speededness (Ackerman et al. 2005). Chuderski (2015) found that Gf tested under time pressure overlapped considerably with working memory (83 % variance) whereas Gf tested without time limits overlapped considerably less (58 %).

The findings in this literature are at least consistent with the idea that working memory capacity explains or contributes to differences in Gf task performance, but that other task effects (e.g., content, paradigm, speededness) also affect both Gf and working-memory task performance and may differentiate the two categories. It is not clear that factor analysis of tasks that are labeled as Gf or working memory tasks is the best method for addressing the issue. The systematic manipulation approach controlling for other factors such as what was done to explore the complexity hypothesis may be more appropriate. Analyses of Raven's Progressive Matrices have been conducted in this spirit.

2.4.3   Raven's Progressive Matrices

Progressive matrices, in particular, *Raven's progressive matrices*, has long been considered one of, if not the single best measure of general cognitive ability and general fluid ability (Gustafsson 1998). For example, Snow et al. (1984) summarized various studies of cognitive measures that showed Raven at the center of a multidimensional scaling representation, corresponding to having the highest general factor loading. This prompted Carpenter et al. (1990) to conduct a detailed information processing analysis of what the RPM measures, which they found to be the ability to encode and induce relationships between elements and to manage this in working memory. On the applied testing side, the literature findings concerning the matrix test led to the development and inclusion of a new matrix test for the WAIS-III and WAIS-IV IQ tests, the most widely used today. Embretson (2002) developed an adaptive version of a figural matrix test called the adaptive reasoning test (ART), based on the rules identified by Carpenter et al. (1990). Preckel and Thiemann (Preckel 2003; Preckel and Thiemann 2003) also have developed versions.

It is possible in principle to produce a matrix test with materials other than the simple geometric forms used in the Raven's Progressive Matrices (RPM) test. However, in practice the geometric forms work quite well, as Embretson (2002) showed, and as the adoption of a figural matrix test into the WAIS establishes. An advantage of the figural stimuli in the RPM, with regard to it being a good measure of *Gf*, is that their use and the rules that operate on them are novel, which means that cultural and educational effects are reduced relative to what they might be if for example numbers (and numerical relations) or words (and semantic relations) were used instead.

A question is whether inducing rules or keeping relations in mind (active in working memory) is the major source of difficulty on Raven's Progressive Matrices, or on inductive tasks in general. If there were many potential rules linking elements to one another then this might suggest that discovering those rules would be major source of difficulty. But Jacobs and Vandeventer (1972) examined 166 intelligence tests listed in the Buros (1965) Mental Measurement Yearbook and 35 additional tests in the ETS test collection library that fell into Guilford's (1967) category of *cognition of figural relations* (CFR), which overlaps considerably with Carroll's *Gf* category, subject to the stimuli being primarily figural (as opposed to verbal or numerical). Their purpose was to categorize all the rules (relationships between elements in the problem) that were used in such tests. They found that almost all relations between two elements in the 1335 item pool fell into 12 categories such as *shape change* (a change of form, e.g., square to circle, solid to dotted; 53 % of all relations); *elements of a set* (i.e., each element appears three times in a 3 × 3 matrix, 35 % of relations); movement in a plane (e.g., rotating 30°) (28 %).

Carpenter et al.'s (1990) analysis of Raven's Progressive Matrices (RPM) resulted in a set of just five rules, which exhaust those used in the RPM (and which map to Jacobs and Vandeventer's 1972, rules; see also, Diehl 2002; Embretson 2002). These were "constant in a row" (element is the same across columns) (53 %), "distribution of three" (element appears once in each row, once in each column) (35 %), "distribution of two" (same as distribution of three with one being a "null" element) (28 %), "pairwise progression" (an element changes across rows and columns) (26 %), and "figure addition/subtraction" (two entries visually sum to a third entry) (24 %). Carpenter et al. (1990) suggest that most problems can be described by identifying the specific elements within a 3 × 3 matrix cell, then applying one of the five rules to that element.

The Carpenter et al. (1990) study did not establish whether the rules and the processes were sufficient for creating a test that would behave well psychometrically. However, Embretson (2002) did this, and so did Diehl (2002) in her dissertation. Embretson (2002) developed a matrix test called the Adaptive Reasoning Test (ART) based on the five rules and on manipulating the number of elements and rules within an item. Embretson (2002) and Diehl (2002) also provided additional specifications for those rules, and developed a useful notation. In Embretson's (2002) notation, each element (e.g., shape) is represented by a letter, which can be subscripted to define attributes on that element (e.g., pattern, size, shading, thickness, orientation, number, color, etc.). In Embretson's (2002) system, any of 22 objects and 7 attributes appear in any "item structure," and an item structure was assumed to create an item with the same difficulty level, which analysis showed is reasonable.

Increasing the number of rules and the number of elements in a matrix reasoning test item increases processing time, beyond a simple additive function (Mulholland et al. 1980; Primi 2001). It also leads to increased demands on working memory (Primi 2001). Increasing difficulty by increasing the number of rules and elements is one of the main drivers of construct-relevant increased difficulty in matrix reasoning tests. On the other hand, perceptual complexity of the geometrical shapes in the matrix (which affects encoding difficulty) also affects item difficulty (Meo et al. 2007; Primi 2001), but does not affect how good a measure of Gf it is (Arendasy and Sommer 2012), and also tends to have a greater impact on the performance of females. This is also true of the adjacent fusion phenomenon in which adjacent elements become difficult to distinguish perceptually. This may not be a desirable item feature to include. Hornke and Habon (1986) and Arendasy and Sommer (2005) found that figural matrices with fused elements governed by different rules introduce a second dimension, and reduced Gf/g saturation (Arendasy & Sommer 2012).

In summary, several methods have been used to explore the nature of general fluid ability. These include defining common features of tests that cluster in factor analyses, and systematically manipulating features of tests to determine which might serve as *radicals* (construct-relevant difficulty-manipulating factors), or *incidentals* (construct-irrelevant factors) to use Irvine's (2002) terminology. Based on these analyses it appears that working-memory capacity is an important factor contributing to performance on tests of general fluid ability.

2.5 General Fluid Versus General Crystallized Ability

Spearman's (1924) general factor theory was challenged by Cattell (1963) (see also Cattell and Horn 1978) who proposed two general factors, general fluid and general crystallized. The distinction between fluid, crystallized, and general ability is often ignored in the literature (e.g., Herrnstein and Murray 1994; Jensen 1998; Nisbett et al. 2012; Rindermann 2007) as well as in the lay population which does not differentiate between them (Kaufman 2012). The proposal for a fluid-crystallized differentiation was based on the conceptual distinction between tasks reflecting the phenomenon in which "skilled judgment habits have become crystallized" due to schooling or prior learning experiences (Cattell 1963, p. 2) and those requiring adaptation to new situations (cf., Schank 1984). It was also based on the empirical finding that over the life span performance on Gf task peaks sooner and drops more rapidly than does performance on Gc tasks (discussed in more detail below, in "Fluid Ability and Age").

These findings motivated Cattell's (1987) investment theory which posits that in early life, a single general factor, Gf, "primarily associated with genetic factors and neurological functioning" (Valentin Kvist and Gustafsson 2008) is invested in and governs the rate of learning and "as a result of the fluid ability being invested in all kinds of complex learning situations, correlations among these acquired, crystallized abilities will also be large and positive, and tend to yield a general factor" (Cattell 1987, p. 139).

Carroll's (1993) meta-analysis identified a number of crystallized ability factors. These included language development, verbal and reading comprehension, lexical knowledge, foreign language aptitude and proficiency, listening and communication abilities, spelling, grammar, and phonetic coding, and cloze ability (the ability to infer correctly a missing word in a sentence or paragraph). It is clear that these are language-related factors.

Postlethwaite's (2011) meta-analysis showed even higher predictions of educational and workforce outcomes for crystallized than for fluid ability (Table 2.1). His classification scheme was based on McGrew's (1997) cross-battery classification system based on the Carroll-Horn-Cattell $Gf-Gc$ model (however, his classification is subjective, a potential limitation to the study). The analysis found that crystallized ability predicted school grades, job training particularly for high compared to medium complexity jobs, and job performance, particularly higher skill jobs.

Although fluid and crystallized abilities often fail to be distinguished, there is growing recognition in both psychology (Ackerman 1996; Hunt 2011) and

Table 2.1 Correlations of Gf, Gc, and g with outcomes (Adapted from Postlethwaite 2011, Tables 6–14)

	Fluid ability[a]			Crystallized ability[b]			General ability[c]		
	k (N)	r	rho	k (N)	r	rho	k (N)	r	rho
Grades in school	67 (7991)	0.26	0.40	157 (199,642)	0.36	0.65	110 (29,739)	0.47	0.68
High School	26 (4134)	0.30	0.38	18 (2100)	0.43	0.53	32 (13,290)	0.53	0.65
College	41 (3857)	0.22	0.44	139 (197,542)	0.36	0.65	78 (16,449)	0.42	0.72
Job training	20 (3724)	0.25	0.54	114 (38,793)	0.38	0.70	24 (7563)	0.28	0.59
Low skill jobs[e]	11 (2658)[d]	0.23	0.44	29 (8152)	0.41	0.73	2 (156)	0.22	0.53
High skill jobs[f]	5 (569)	0.32	0.67	4 (596)	0.45	0.75	2 (2824)	0.22	0.57
Job performance	23 (3272)	0.14	0.27	199 (18,619)	0.23	0.49	86 (8070)	0.23	0.43
Low skill jobs[e]	2 (251)	0.01	0.01	108 (9307)	0.22	0.45	37 (3420)	0.20	0.37
High skill jobs[f]	2 (132)	0.31	0.64	27 (2214)	0.29	0.59	11 (861)	0.30	0.60

[a]Measured by tests such as Raven's Progressive Matrices and the Cattell Culture Fair test; [b]measured by tests such as the Mill Hill Vocabulary test, ASVAB and AFQT, Differential Aptitude Test; [c]measured by the g factor from the AFTQ and the GATB, Otis-Lennon, Stanford-Binet and others; [d]these are values for middle skill jobs because there were no low skill jobs; [e]O*NET Zone 1 and 2; [f]O*NET Zone 4 and 5
k number of studies; N number of test takers; r observed correlation weighted by N; rho observed correlation weighted by N, corrected for both range restriction and criterion unreliability
Adapted from Postlethwaite (2011), Tables 6–14

economics (e.g., Borghans et al. 2015; Heckman and Kautz 2014) that the two are highly overlapping (correlated) but nevertheless separate and distinguishable, and that crystallized abilities are more strongly predictive of school and workplace outcomes.

2.6 General Fluid Ability Versus General Ability

In a series of studies involving school children and adolescents taking various batteries of cognitive ability tests hierarchical factor analytic models were fit to the data using both exploratory (Schmid and Leiman 1957; Undheim 1981), and confirmatory approaches (Gustafsson 1984; Undheim and Gustafsson 1987). In these analyses general fluid ability (Gf) was found to be indistinguishable from general ability (g). At some level this is not a surprising result because descriptions of general fluid ability and general ability sound similar. Spearman (1904) suggested that general ability involved the "eduction of relations and correlates" which comes close to a description of the processing involved in the progressive matrices test, a prototypical measure of Gf, as discussed in the previous section.

As Valentin Kvist and Gustafsson (2008) pointed out, some studies have not replicated the $g = Gf$ finding (e.g., Carroll 2003), and others have even argued that Gc is closer to g, on the basis of the centrality of Gc tests in particular test batteries. It would seem that this is a difficult issue to resolve given that the makeup of the test variable set will affect the location of factors designed to account for the relationships among those variables.

However, Valentin Kvist and Gustafsson devised a novel and compelling rationale for how the $Gf = g$ hypothesis could be tested. The basic idea is that according to investment theory, Gf develops into a general factor because it drives knowledge and skill acquisition in diverse domains (e.g., vocabulary acquisition, rule induction), causing correlations between performances in those diverse domains. But that relationship assumes roughly equal learning opportunities. If there are differential opportunities to learn, say, between first and second language groups, then the relationship between g and Gf will be reduced. In their words:

> This suggests a way to test both the Investment theory and the hypothesis that g equals Gf, namely through investigating the effect of differential learning opportunities for different subsets of a population on the relation between Gf and g. From the Investment theory follows the prediction that within populations which are homogeneous with respect to learning opportunities there should be a perfect relationship between Gf and g, while for populations which are composed of subgroups who have had different learning opportunities, the relation between Gf and g should be lower (p. 425).

They administered a battery of 15 tests, measuring Gf, Gc, general visualization (Gv), and general speediness (Gs) to 3570 18–60 year olds, mostly men, registered at a Swedish employment office. For the purposes of hypothesis testing the sample was divided into native speakers ($N = 2358$), European immigrants ($N = 620$) and non-European immigrants ($N = 591$). Hierarchical models were fit to the data with first order *Gf*, *Gc*, *Gv*, and *Gs* factors, and a second order *g* factor. When the analyses were conducted within groups, the correlation between *g* and *Gf* was 1.0, as expected, due to roughly equal opportunities to learn. But when the data were pooled, which put together groups with very different learning opportunities, then the correlation between *g* and *Gf* was 0.83. As Valentin Kvist and Gustafsson (2008) point out, the result "provides support for the Investment theory, and for the hypothesis that *Gf* is equivalent to *g*…however…only when the subjects have had approximately equally good, or equally poor, opportunities to develop the knowledge and skills measured" (p. 433).

The Valentin Kvist and Gustafsson (2008) finding is an important one for understanding the relationship between *g* and *Gf*. It also is reminiscent of an argument made almost 40 years ago by Zigler and Trickett (1978) who proposed that IQ tests measure three distinct components, formal cognitive processes, school learning, and motivation. If the school learning or motivation components are unequal, then IQ tests are poor measures of cognitive processing ability (Brent Bridgeman [personal communication, March 30, 2016] pointed this out).

2.7 Does Fluid Ability Change? Can It Be Improved?

This section addresses the issues of the natural change in *Gf* over the lifespan as well as the secular effect or Flynn effect, which is the change in population cohort *Gf* over time. The section also addresses ways to improve *Gf*, either through school, direct training, or pharmaceutically.

2.7.1 Fluid Ability and Age

It is largely accepted that fluid ability decreases, and crystallized ability increases, with age (Hunt 2011). Fluid ability is generally held to peak in the early to mid-20s before declining and crystallized ability to peak in the early 30s and remain fairly stable into the early 60s before declining (e.g., McArdle et al. 2002). Despite the general acceptance of these trends, interpretations of age-related changes in fluid ability are complicated by several factors.

The first factor is differences in research designs. It is mainly cohort-sequential designs that have found that fluid ability peaks in the early 20s (Horn 1989; Tucker-Drob and Salthouse 2011), yet these designs are prey to cohort effects, including different cohorts being differentially affected by the Flynn Effect (the secular growth in *Gf* scores over the past half century); longitudinal research suggests that fluid ability does not decline until at least the early 60s (Schaie 2012). Indeed, a recent longitudinal study actually found an *increase* in fluid ability of about 15 points from age 12 to age 52 (Schalke et al. 2013). Longitudinal studies, however, are susceptible to selective attrition, which can distort findings of construct-level changes over time. Additionally, in order to properly compare the results of cross-sectional and longitudinal studies it is important that these investigations use the same cognitive tests, otherwise differences attributed to changes in fluid ability over time may be confounded with test differences that do not reflect true differences at the construct level. It has been claimed (e.g., Horn and Noll 1997) that longitudinal studies have tended to use tasks that are better characterized as indicators of crystallized than fluid ability and after accounting for this the results of the two research traditions are well-aligned in demonstrating the early-in-the-lifespan decline in fluid ability.

A second methodological factor that must be accounted for is where the studies occurred. Much of the cross-sectional and longitudinal research that is taken to be key to understanding age-related differences in fluid ability is conducted in Western, English-speaking countries, especially the United States. For example, Schaie's (2012) results are based on the Seattle Longitudinal Study and many of the studies conducted by John L. Horn and colleagues drew participants largely from the United States; Deary et al.'s (1998) sample was Scottish. Cultural and environmental influences may moderate the association between differences in age and differences in fluid ability; Schalke et al.'s (2013) study finding an increase in fluid ability scores between 12 and 52 was conducted in Luxembourg. Instructive are investigations finding that socioeconomic status modifies the relationship between fluid and crystallized ability (Schmidt and Crano 1974) and the heritability of IQ scores (Harden et al. 2007). More attention should be paid to within- and between-country differences in changes in fluid ability over time, especially in non-Western countries. In pursuit of discovering some "universal" law (cf. Danziger 2009) governing the association between age and fluid ability it is certainly possible to average over all countries, all cultures, and all socioeconomic strata, but in terms of interpretability and usefulness doing so would be comparable to averaging a person's blood pressure readings over the course of her entire lifetime to derive her "true" blood pressure (cf. Sechrest 2005).

Finally, differences in test-taking motivation over time may further complicate interpreting studies demonstrating age-related declines in fluid ability. Research in the past several years has made clear the importance of accounting for motivation when examining test scores conducted in low-stakes settings (e.g., Duckworth et al. 2011; Liu et al. 2012). Classic accounts of proper procedures for conducting tests of individual differences (Fiske and Butler 1963; Terman 1924) emphasize the need to make the testing situation as similar to an experimental one as possible, the goal being to eliminate all between-subjects variance in all influences on test scores—except variance in the construct that test is intended to measure. It is important to remember that *an individual's* test scores are the result of many variables (e.g., eyesight, psychomotor process), but the goal when measuring individual differences is for *differences* in individuals' scores to solely reflect variance in the construct being assessed (Cronbach 1971).

When cognitive ability tests are given under high-stakes conditions it is assumed that motivation does not play a role in determining differences in test-takers' scores because they are all putting forth maximal effort (Sackett 2012). This is not the case when tests are taken under low-stakes conditions, however, where there is little incentive for individuals to put forth their full effort. It is important to ask why older test-takers in-particular would be fully motivated to perform well on tests whose defining characters include being content- and context-free (Ackerman 1999). After exiting the fairly homogenous compulsory school curriculum, people are able to exert more control over their environments and select themselves into situations that will give them access to content they find (relatively) interesting. Presenting older adults with content of no apparent real-world significance and (that is likely not intrinsically interesting to them), after they have been able to avoid such content for decades, and then asking them to fully engage with that content without offering any major incentives does not appear to be a recipe for eliciting maximal effort. By definition (Carroll 1993), cognitive ability constructs are maximal performance variables that can only be measured when test-takers are fully motivated; to the extent older adults are not fully motivated during fluid ability testing the construct validity of these assessments must be questioned.

This line of reasoning suggests that more consideration should be given to the extent to which test-taking effort plays a role in the observed decline of fluid ability with age. If fluid ability tests are consistently administered under low-stakes conditions, the major incentive for test-takers to do well on them may be reducible to their internal sense of competitiveness, perhaps manifesting in the need to "demonstrate one's full potential" or simply outscore fellow test-takers; giving test-takers an achievement motivation inventory (Freund and Holling 2011) could potentially allow for control of some of this construct-irrelevant variance. Providing test-takers with extrinsic incentives (Liu et al. 2012) is another option for inducing motivation. However, finding which incentives are most effective can be challenging [e.g., calling a test a game can increase motivation (Bridgeman et al. 1974)], and incentive manipulations can have different effects on easy versus difficult tasks (e.g., Harkins 2006).

A related topic is the hypothesis that much of the age-related loss of fluid intelligence is attributable to a declining ability to maintain focused attention. Horn (2008) summarizes several converging lines of evidence supporting this hypothesis from studies on vigilance, selective attention, Stroop (i.e., tasks requiring one to name the color of words, such as the word blue presented in a red font, where the perceptual and semantic information conflict), and distracted visual search tasks. These findings complement more recent research (e.g., Burgess et al. 2011; Melnick et al. 2013) indicating the ability to suppress distracting information and maintain concentration in the face of interference is associated with better performance on fluid ability tasks. If older adults already have more difficulty concentrating, it should come as no surprise that they score more poorly on tasks that demand intense concentration but are of no intrinsic interest to them and scores on which have no impact on their lives once they exit the testing session.

2.7.2 Fluid Ability and the Flynn Effect

The Flynn Effect is a label for the phenomenon of rising cognitive ability test scores over the past century, at an average rate of 0.3 points per year (Hunt 2011). These gains have been demonstrated across industrialized countries and age groups and are primarily observed on components of tests that are categorized as tapping fluid ability (e.g., progressive matrices); scores on crystallized ability tests have either remained constant or declined (Flynn 2007). Many different reasons for the Flynn Effect have been put forth, ranging from increased test sophistication to better nutrition to safer environments, but a definitive explanation has not been identified (Hunt 2011). There is evidence that the Flynn Effect has ceased, at least in some countries—yet there is also evidence that it continues, even among those with cognitive abilities in the top 1 % of the distribution (Wai and Putallaz 2011).

The Flynn Effect has important implications for increasing fluid ability because the rate at which cognitive test score gains have occurred suggest they must be environmental in origin. This implicates learning processes. Flynn (2007), Flynn & Weiss (2007) suggests that the rising scores are partially due to the fact that individuals have learned to think progressively more "scientifically" over the past century. That is, individuals know to consistently map concrete objects (e.g., dawn and dusk) onto higher-order relations (e.g., "separates night from day"), rather than simply thinking of those objects in terms of their immediate properties (e.g., "time of day", "degree of brightness"; Flynn and Weiss 2007). Although this shift in thinking may have occurred largely implicitly due to increased exposure to more formal education and more complex environments, clearly it has occurred through learning processes, suggesting it can be explicitly taught. Intriguingly, this theory calls into question the stark distinction between fluid and crystallized ability, as it posits that increases in fluid ability are rooted in *knowledge* that approaching problems using abstract reasoning tends to be an effective strategy.

2.8 Can Fluid Ability Improvement Be Accelerated?

2.8.1 Through Schooling

There is evidence that fluid intelligence can be improved. Ceci (1991), Ceci and Williams (1997) identified several different types of evidence consistent with the idea that schooling raises IQ. Some of these are simply observational—higher test scores accompany more time in school where differential attendance is due to starting school late, attending intermittently, dropping out before graduation, or conversely, staying in school longer to avoid the draft during the Vietnam war years. Another type of evidence is the summer slump where scores go down during the several months of summer vacation, which suggests that cognitive growth is not solely due to maturation.

Maturation and schooling are confounded, and so one approach to disentangle them is to estimate the effect of maturation by comparing ability or achievement scores of same-grade students who vary in age (because a grade will consist of individuals who range from old for the grade, such as those almost old enough to be eligible for the higher grade, to young for the grade, that is, those almost eligible to be held back to a lower grade). The difference in test scores between the relatively old and relatively young students within a grade (or the slope of the test score on age regression line) provides the age or maturation effect on test scores. Then separately comparing test scores of the oldest in a lower grade with the youngest in the next higher grade, a regression discontinuity, will provide the effect of schooling on test scores. This general approach has been used in several studies (e.g., Cahan and Cohen 1989; Stelzl et al. 1995), with a finding that the effect of schooling on test scores is twice as strong as the effect of age (Cliffordson 2010).

Another approach has been to investigate the effects of compulsory education on IQ by comparing same age students who differ in schooling due to variation in age entry requirements or mandatory attendance. An example of the latter is a study by Brinch and Galloway (2011) who noted that in the 1960s mandatory school attendance was changed from seventh to ninth grade in Norway. Different Norwegian communities enforced the change at different times, and so it was possible to compare the effects of school attendance in communities that were largely similar, in effect a natural experiment. An abilities test given to 19 year olds as part of mandatory military service allowed for an estimate of 3.7 IQ points per year. (Note that this is a convenient shorthand in this literature to express schooling's effect on the convenient, well known IQ scale; it does not imply that growth is linear across grades, as there is not sufficient data to make such a claim.)

Differential effects of type of schooling have also been investigated. Gustafsson (2001) compared performance on a mandatory military enlistment test battery given to 18 year old males who had previously gone through different tracks in secondary school (e.g., technical, natural science, vocational). The battery comprised measures of Gf, Gc, and Gv. He controlled for initial differences in grades (following a common pre-upper-secondary curriculum) and socioeconomic status. He found that students who had completed academic tracks had higher Gf scores, technical and science tracks had higher Gv scores, and both effects were stronger than track effects on Gc. Becker et al. (2012) showed similar effects of academic versus vocational tracking in Germany.

Cliffordson and Gustafsson (2008) treated test scores from measures of Gf, Gc, and Gv as dependent variables similar to Gustafsson (2001), but they included age and amount of schooling at the time of testing as predictors (they also included controls for socioeconomic status, background, and school grades). They found results generally consistent with previous findings, with the effect of schooling double the effects of age, a schooling effect of approximately 2.7 IQ points per year, and differences between tracks in expected directions, such as social science and economics tracks having the highest effect on the Gf measure (4.8 points), the technology track having the highest effect on the Technical Comprehension test (3.4 points), and only Natural Science having an effect on the Gv measure (1.6 points).

2.8.2 Through Working Memory Training

An intriguing experiment published several years ago had individuals practice a working memory task known as the dual n-back task (Jaeggi et al. 2008). Participants were simultaneously shown a square appearing in one of 6 locations on a computer screen, and heard a letter (e.g., "C") at the same time. After 3 s, they were shown another square, and heard another letter. This sequence repeated indefinitely. The task was to indicate independently whether the square location and the letter were the same as they were on the previous trial ("1-back"). If they answered correctly, then the question was made more complex by asking whether the two items were the same as they were 2 trials back. The task continued to adapt (1-back, 2-back, 3-back, etc.) according to whether the respondent was correct or not. Participants engaged in this task for anywhere between 8 and 19 training sessions, and were given *Gf* pretests and posttests (e.g., Raven's Progressive Matrices). The researchers found that treated participants (compared to no-treatment controls) performed significantly better on the *Gf* measures as a result of working memory training.

This study has been replicated a number of times and a recent meta-analysis suggested that there was consistent evidence that several weeks of working memory training, specifically based on the n-back task, transfers to fluid ability tasks (Au et al. 2015). However, another meta-analysis suggested that while working-memory training did produce reliable short-term improvements in working-memory skills, there was no evidence that working-memory training transferred to other skills such as *Gf*, attention, word decoding, or arithmetic (Melby-Lervåg and Hulme 2012). There also seems to be little evidence that "brain training" tasks of a more commercial variety transfer to fluid tests (Owen et al. 2010).

2.8.3 Through Pharmaceutical Agents

Use of pharmaceutical agents to enhance intelligence is a growing area of research (Dance 2016). One wakefulness promoting agent in particular, modafinil, which is FDA approved for treating sleeping disorders, such as narcolepsy, shift-work sleep disorder, and general sleepiness is known as a smart drug for non-sleep-deprived individuals (Geggel 2015). A recent meta-analysis on its effects showed that modafinil enhanced attention, executive functions, learning, and memory, but did not affect creativity or working memory (Battleday and Brem 2015).

2.8.4 Through Attentional Control

A common theme of many efforts to enhance fluid ability is a focus on increasing concentration and attentional control (Nisbett et al. 2012). This accords well with Horn's (2008) hypothesis that declines in these abilities explain much of the age-related decay in performance on fluid tasks and that age is associated with deteriorating performance in jobs with intense attentional demands (Kanfer and Ackerman 2004; Sells et al. 1984). To what extent should these findings inform how we conceptualize the construct of fluid intelligence? Should we consider attentional control and concentration "part of" the fluid ability construct or simply "channels" that assist or undermine its deployment? If the former, this implies that given unlimited time individuals should be able to complete fluid ability tasks of any difficulty level, since by removing time constraints individual differences in concentration and vigilance would be eliminated. This seems absurd, however, as it further implies that individuals' basic problem-solving abilities do not practically differ once differences in their concentration have been accounted for—yet it seems unlikely that all individuals could, for example, derive complex mathematical formulae given even unlimited time.

If the ability to maintain concentrated attention for long periods is not taken as being an aspect of fluid intelligence but simply a facilitator of it this implies that many of the efforts to enhance fluid ability do not actually do so but instead merely allow people to more fully take advantage of their current abstract reasoning skills. Assume that performance on a reasoning test is a function of both current abstract reasoning skills and ability to maintain concentrated attention for long periods, which could be a kind of motivation or personality effect. Perhaps one of the major reasons that fluid ability scores increase with each passing grade but decline with age after leaving school is that schooling implicitly trains people to concentrate their attention for long periods of time on content that they do not necessarily find particularly interesting—and the effects of this training decay after individuals have completed their compulsory schooling and are able to exert more control over their environments and choose content they find more intrinsically interesting to interact with. This line of reasoning suggests that training non-cognitive skills such as self-regulation and self-discipline (Nisbett et al. 2012) could increase scores on fluid ability tasks—but also that such training does not enhance individuals' fluid ability itself, merely the extent to which they are able to take advantage of it.

2.9 Conclusions

General fluid ability is an important and influential concept in psychology, in education, and in policy. The purpose of this chapter was to address the issue of its nature, its measurement, how and whether it is distinguishable from other abilities, such as crystallized ability and general ability, and how it can be improved. Jan-Eric Gustafsson has made key contributions to our understanding of fluid ability with respect to all these topics.

In this chapter we reviewed what we know and what we are learning about fluid intelligence. Fluid ability is the ability to solve problems in novel contexts, using deductive or inductive reasoning such as in letter series problems, or with pro-gressive matrices problems. It is contrasted with crystallized ability, which reflects the ability to apply knowledge acquired in school or through acculturation, as reflected in vocabulary and reading comprehension tests. Fluid ability is sometimes empirically indistinguishable from general cognitive ability, although this depends on test takers having roughly comparable opportunities to learn. Fluid ability peaks earlier than crystallized ability over the lifespan. Test scores on measures of fluid ability have increased in successive cohorts over the past 50 years, a phenomenon known as the Flynn effect, although there is some indication that this is no longer happening, at least in the most developed countries. Fluid ability is highly correlated with working memory capacity, and there is some suggestion that working-memory training, particularly on the n-back task, may transfer to performance on fluid ability tasks. There is evidence from various sources that schooling may improve fluid ability, although much of the evidence is based on observational data. There is also some evidence that particular school tracks, such as academic, and social science, may be particularly associated with improvements in fluid ability. There also is some, albeit mixed evidence that pharmaceutical agents, particularly a wakefulness promoting agent, modafinil, improve fluid ability. There are other influences on test scores besides abilities, such as motivation and attention, and these may be the factors responsible for some of the improvements in fluid ability test scores due to schooling, training, and other variables.

Fluid ability is now a firmly established construct in education, psychology, and the social sciences more generally. It is likely to continue to draw research attention into the foreseeable future just as it has over the past 50 years.

References

Ackerman, P. L. (1996). A theory of adult intellectual development: Process personality, interests, and knowledge. *Intelligence, 22*, 229–259.

Ackerman, P. L. (1999). Traits and knowledge as determinants of learning and individual differences: Putting it all together. In P. L. Ackerman, P. C. Kyllonen, & R. D. Roberts (Eds.), *Learning and individual differences: Process, trait, and content determinants* (pp. 437–460). Washington, DC: American Psychological Association.

Ackerman, P. L., Beier, M. E., & Boyle, M. O. (2005). Working memory and intelligence: The same or different constructs? *Psychological Bulletin, 131*, 30–60.

Arendasy, M., & Sommer, M. (2005). Using psychometric technology in educational assessment: The case of a schema-based isomorphic approach to the automatic generation of quantitative reasoning items. *Learning and Individual Differences, 17*(4), 366–383.

Arendasy, M., & Sommer, M. (2012). Using automatic item generation to meet the increasing item demands of high-stakes assessment. *Learning and Individual Differences, 22*, 112–117.

Au, J., Sheehan, E., Tsai, N., Duncan, G. J., Buschkuehl, M., & Jaeggi, S. M. (2015). Improving fluid intelligence with training on working memory: A meta-analysis. *Psychonomic Bulletin & Review, 22*(2), 366–377.

Baddeley, A. D. (2003). Working memory: Looking back and looking forward. *Nature Reviews Neuroscience, 4*, 829–839. doi:10.1038/nrn1201

Baddeley, A. D., & Hitch, G. (1974). Working memory. In G. H. Bower (Ed.), *The psychology of learning and motivation: Advances in research and theory* (Vol. 8, pp. 47–89). New York: Academic Press.

Battleday, R. M., & Brem, A. K. (2015). Modafinil for cognitive neuroenhancement in healthy non-sleep-deprived subjects: A systematic review. *European Neuropsychopharmacology, 25,* 1865–1881.

Becker, M., Lüdtke, O., Trautwein, U., Köller, O., & Baumert, J. (2012). The differential effects of school tracking on psychometric intelligence: Do academic-track schools make students smarter? *Journal of Educational Psychology, 104,* 682–699. doi:10.1037/a0027608

Birney, D. P., & Bowman, D. B. (2009). An experimental-differential investigation of cognitive complexity. *Psychology Science Quarterly, 51*(4), 449–469.

Borghans, L., Duckworth, A. L., Heckman, J. J., & ter Weel, B. (2008, February). *The economics and psychology of personality traits* (NBER Working Paper No. 13810). Cambridge, MA: National Bureau of Economic Research.

Borghans, L., Golsteyn, B. H. H., Heckman, J. J., & Humphries, J. E. (2015). What do grades and achievement tests measure? Unpublished manuscript, Human Capital and Economic Working Group, University of Chicago, Chicago, IL. Retrieved from https://hceconomics.uchicago.edu/sites/default/files/3_BGHH-Grades-Achievement-Measure-Paper_2015-12-30a_sjs.pdf

Boring, E. G. (1923). Intelligence as the tests test it. *New Republic, 36,* 35–37.

Bridgeman, B., Strang, H. R., & Buttram, J. (1974). "Game" versus "test" instructions for the WISC. *Journal of Educational Measurement, 11,* 285–287.

Brinch, C. N., & Galloway, T. A. (2011). Schooling in adolescence raises IQ scores. *Proceedings of the National Academy of Sciences of the United States of America, 109*(2), 425–430. doi:10.1073/pnas.1106077109

Burgess, G. C., Gray, J. R., Conway, A. R. A., & Braver, T. (2011). Neural mechanisms of interference control underlie the relationship between fluid intelligence and working memory span. *Journal of Experimental Psychology: General, 140*(4), 674–692.

Buros, O. K. (Ed.). (1965). *The sixth mental measurements yearbook.* Lincoln, NE: University of Nebraska Press. ISBN 0-910674-06-X.

Cahan, S., & Cohen, N. (1989). Age versus schooling effects on intelligence development. *Child Development, 60*(5), 1239–1249.

Carpenter, P. A., Just, M. A., & Shell, P. (1990). What one intelligence test measures: A theoretical account of the processing in the Raven Progressive Matrices Test. *Psychological Review, 97,* 404–431.

Carroll, J. B. (1993). *Human cognitive abilities: A survey of factor-analytic studies.* New York, NY: Cambridge University Press.

Carroll, J. B. (2003). The higher-stratum structure of cognitive abilities: Current evidence supports g and about ten broad factors. In H. Nyborg (Ed.), *The scientific study of general intelligence: Tribute to Arthur R. Jensen* (pp. 5–21). Boston, MA: Pergamon.

Cattell, R. B. (1963). Theory of fluid and crystallized intelligence: A critical experiment. *Journal of Educational Psychology, 54*(1), 1–22.

Cattell, R. B. (1987). *Intelligence: Its structure, growth, and action.* New York: North-Holland.

Cattell, R. B., & Horn, J. L. (1978). A check on the theory of fluid and crystallized intelligence with description of new subtest designs. *Journal of Educational Measurement, 15,* 139–164.

Ceci, S. (1991). How much does schooling influence general intelligence and its cognitive components? A reassessment of the evidence. *Developmental Psychology, 27*(5), 703–722.

Ceci, S. J., & Williams, W. M. (1997). Schooling, intelligence, and income. *American Psychologist, 52,* 1051–1058.

Chuderski, A. (2015). The broad factor of working memory is virtually isomorphic to fluid intelligence tested under time pressure. *Personality and Individual Differences, 85,* 98–104.

Cliffordson, C. (2010). Methodological issues in investigations of the relative effects of schooling and age on school performance: The between-grade regression discontinuity design applied to Swedish TIMSS 1995 data. *Educational Research and Evaluation: An International Journal on Theory and Practice, 16*(1), 39–52.

Cliffordson, C., & Gustafsson, J.-E. (2008). Effects of age and schooling on intellectual performance: Estimates obtained from analysis of continuous variation in age and length of schooling. *Intelligence, 36,* 143–152.

Conway, A. R. A., Jarrold, C., Kane, M. J., Miyake, A., & Towse, J. N. (Eds.). (2007). *Variations in working memory.* Oxford, England: Oxford University Press.

Corno, L., Cronbach, L. J., Kupermintz, H., Lohman, D. F., Mandinach, E. B., Porteus, A. W., et al. (2002). *Remaking the concept of aptitude: Extending the legacy of Richard E. Snow.* Mahwah, NJ: Lawrence Erlbaum.

Cronbach, L. J. (1971). Test validation. In R. L. Thorndike (Ed.), *Educational measurement* (2nd ed., pp. 443–507). Washington, DC: American Council on Education.

Dance, A. (2016). A dose of intelligence. *Nature, 536,* S2–S3.

Danziger, K. (2009). The holy grail of universality. In T. Teo, P. Stenner, A. Rutherford, E. Park, & C. Baerveldt (Eds.), *Varieties of philosophical and practical concerns* (pp. 2–11). Concord, Ontario, Canada: Captus University Publications.

Deary, I. J., Starr, J. M., & MacLennan, W. J. (1998). Fluid intelligence, memory and blood pressure in cognitive aging. *Personality and Individual Differences, 25*(4), 605–619.

Diehl, K. A. (2002). Algorithmic item generation and problem solving strategies in matrix completion problems. Unpublished doctoral dissertation, University of Kansas.

Duckworth, A. L., Quinn, P. D., Lynam, D. R., Loeber, R., & Stouthamer-Loeber, M. (2011). Role of test motivation in intelligence testing. *Proceedings of the National Academy of Sciences of the United States of America, 108,* 7716–7720.

Embretson, S. E. (2002). Generating abstract reasoning items with cognitive theory. In S. Irvine & P. Kyllonen (Eds.), *Generating items for cognitive tests: Theory and practice.* Mahwah, NJ: Erlbaum.

Finn, A. S., Kraft, M., West, M. R., Leonard, J. A., Bish, C., Martin, R. E., ... Gabrieli, J. D. E. (2014). Cognitive skills, student student achievement tests and schools. *Psychological Science, 25,* 736–744.

Fiske, D. W., & Butler, J. M. (1963). The experimental conditions for measuring individual differences. *Educational and Psychological Measurement, 26,* 249–266.

Flynn, J. R. (2007). *What is intelligence? Beyond the Flynn effect.* Cambridge, MA: Cambridge University Press.

Flynn, J. R., & Weiss, L. G. (2007). American IQ gains from 1932 to 2002: The WISC subtests and educational progress. *International Journal of Testing, 7,* 209–224.

Freund, P. A., & Holling, H. (2011). How to get really smart: Modeling retest and training effects in ability testing using computer-generated figural matrix items. *Intelligence, 39,* 233–243.

Geggel, L. (2015). 'Smart drug' modafinil actually works, study shows. *Live Science.* Retrieved April 1, 2016 from http://www.livescience.com/51919-modafil-improves-attention-learning.html

Guilford, J. P. (1967). *The nature of human intelligence.* New York, NY: McGraw-Hill.

Gustafsson, J.-E. (1984). A unifying model for the structure of intellectual abilities. *Intelligence, 8,* 179–203.

Gustafsson, J.-E. (1998). Hierarchical models of individual differences in cooperative abilities. In R. J. Sternberg (Ed.), *Advances in the psychology of human intelligence* (Vol. 4, pp. 35–71).

Gustafsson, J.-E. (1999). Measuring and understanding G: Experimental and correlational approaches. In P. L. Ackerman, P. C. Kyllonen, & R. D. Roberts (Eds.), *Learning and individual differences: Process, trait, and content determinants* (pp. 275–289). Washington, D. C.: American Psychological Association.

Gustafsson, J.-E. (2001). Schooling and intelligence: Effects of track of study on level and profile of cognitive abilities. *International Education Journal, 2*(4), 166–186.

Gustafsson, J.-E. (2002). Measurement from a hierarchical point of view. In H. L. Braun, D. G. Jackson, & D. E. Wiley (Eds.), *The role of constructs in psychological and educational measurement* (pp. 73–95). Mahwah, NJ: Erlbaum.

Gustafsson, J.-E., & Balke, G. (1993). General and specific abilities as predictors of school achievement. *Multivariate Behavioral Research, 28*(4), 407–434.

Halford, G. S., Wilson, W. H., & Phillips, S. (1998). Processing capacity defined by relational complexity: Implications for comparative, developmental, and cognitive psychology. *Behavioral and Brain Sciences, 21,* 803–865.

Harden, K. P., Turkheimer, E., & Loehlin, J. C. (2007). Genotype by environment interaction in adolescents' cognitive aptitude. *Behavior Genetics, 37*(2), 273–283.

Harkins, S. G. (2006). Mere effort as the mediator of the evaluation-performance relationship. *Journal of Personality and Social Psychology, 91*(3), 436–455. doi:10.1037/0022-3514.91.3.436

Heckman, J. J., & Kautz, T. (2014). Achievement tests and the role of character in American life. In J. J. Heckman, J. E. Humphries, & T. Kautz (Eds.), *The myth of achievement tests: The GED and the role of character in American life* (pp. 3–56). Chicago, IL: University of Chicago Press.

Herrnstein, R. J., & Murray, C. (1994). *The bell curve: Intelligence and class structure in American life.* New York, NY: The Free Press (Simon & Shuster).

Horn, J. L. (1989). Models for intelligence. In R. Linn (Ed.), *Intelligence: Measurement, theory, and public policy* (pp. 29–73). Urbana, IL: University of Illinois Press.

Horn, J. L. (2008). Spearman, g, expertise, and the nature of human cognitive capability. In P. C. Kyllonen, R. D. Roberts, & L. Stankov (Eds.), *Extending intelligence: Enhancement and new constructs* (pp. 185–230). New York: LEA.

Horn, J. L., & Noll, J. (1997). Human cognitive capabilities: Gf-Gc theory. In D. P. Flanagan, J. L. Genshaft, & P. L. Harrison (Eds.), *Contemporary intellectual assessment: Theories, tests and issues* (pp. 53–91). New York, NY: Guilford.

Hornke, L. F., & Habon, M. W. (1986). Rule-based item bank construction and evaluation within the linear logistic framework. *Applied Psychological Measurement, 10,* 369–380.

Hunt, E. (2011). *Human intelligence.* New York, NY: Cambridge University Press.

Irvine, S. H. (2002). The foundations of item generation for mass testing. In S. H. Irvine & P. C. Kyllonen (Eds.), *Item generation for test development* (pp. 3–34). Mahwah, NJ: Lawrence Erlbaum.

Jacobs, P. I., & Vandeventer, M. (1972). Evaluating the teaching of intelligence. *Educational and Psychological Measurement, 32*(2), 235–238.

Jaeggi, S. M., Buschkuehl, M., Jonides, J., & Perrig, W. J. (2008). Improving fluid intelligence with training on working memory. *Proceedings of the National Academy of Sciences of the United States of America, 105*(19), 6829–6833. doi:10.1073/pnas.0801268105

Jensen, E. (1998). *The g factor: The science of mental ability (Human evolution, behavior, and intelligence).* Westport, CT: Praeger.

Kane, M. J., Hambrick, D. Z., Tuholski, S. W., Wilhelm, O., Payne, T. W., & Engle, R. W. (2004). The generality of working-memory capacity: A latent-variable approach to verbal and visuospatial memory span and reasoning. *Journal of Experimental Psychology: General, 133,* 189–217.

Kanfer, R., & Ackerman, P. L. (2004). Aging, adult development, and work motivation. *The Academy of Management Review, 29*(3), 440–458.

Kaufman, J. C. (2012). Self estimates of general, crystallized, and fluid intelligences in an ethnically diverse population. *Learning and Individual Differences, 22,* 118–122.

Kyllonen, P. C. (1995). CAM: A theoretical framework for cognitive abilities measurement. In D. K. Detterman (Ed.), *Current topics in human intelligence* (Vol. 4, pp. 307–359). New York, NY: Springer.

Kyllonen, P. C., & Christal, R. E. (1990). Reasoning ability is (little more than) working-memory capacity?! *Intelligence, 14*(4), 389–433.

Lindqvist, E., & Vestman, R. (2011). The labor market returns to cognitive and noncognitive ability: Evidence from the Swedish enlistment. *American Economic Journal: Applied Economics, 3,* 101–128.

Liu, O. L., Bridgeman, B., & Adler, R. (2012). Learning outcomes assessment in higher education: Motivation matters. *Educational Researcher, 41,* 352–362.

McArdle, J. J., Ferrer-Caja, E., Hamagami, F., & Woodcock, R. W. (2002). Comparative longitudinal structural analyses of the growth and decline of multiple intellectual abilities over the life span. *Developmental Psychology, 38*(1), 115–142.

McGrew, K. S. (1997). Analysis of the major intelligence batteries according to a proposed comprehensive Gf-Gc framework. In D. P. Flanagan, J. L. Genshaft, & P. L. Harrison (Eds.), *Contemporary intellectual assessment: Theories, tests, and issues* (pp. 151–179). New York, NY: Guilford.

McGrew, K. S. (2005). The Cattell-Horn-Carroll theory of cognitive abilities: Past, present, and future. In D. P. Flanagan & P. L. Harrison (Eds.), *Contemporary intellectual assessment: Theories, tests, and issues* (2nd ed., pp. 136–182). New York, NY: Guilford.

Melby-Lervåg, M., & Hulme, C. (2012). Is working memory training effective? A meta-analytic review. *Developmental Psychology, 49*(2), 270–291.

Mellers, B., Stone, E., Murray, T., Minster, A., Rohrbaugh, N., Bishop, M., … Tetlock, P. (2015). Identifying and cultivating superforecasters as a method of improving probabilistic predictions. *Perspectives on Psychological Science, 10*(3), 267–281.

Melnick, M. D., Harrison, B. R., Park, S., Bennetto, L., & Tadin, D. (2013). A strong interactive link between sensory discriminations and intelligence. *Current Biology, 23*(11), 1013–1017.

Meo, M., Roberts, M. J., & Marucci, F. S. (2007). Element salience as a predictor of item difficulty for Raven's progressive matrices. *Intelligence, 35*(4), 359–368.

Mulholland, T. M., Pellegrino, J. W., & Glaser, R. (1980). Components of geometric analogy solution. *Cognitive Psychology, 12*, 252–284.

Nisbett, R. E., Aronson, J., Blair, C., Dickens, W., Flynn, J., Halpern, D. F., et al. (2012). Intelligence: New findings and theoretical developments. *American Psychologist, 67*(2), 130–159.

Oberauer, K., Schulze, R., Wilhelm, O., & Suess, H.-M. (2005). Working memory and intelligence —Their correlation and relation: Comment on Ackerman, Beier, and Boyle (2005). *Pscyhological Bulletin, 131*, 61–65.

Owen, A. M., Hampshire, A., Grahn, J. A., Stenton, R., Dajani, S., Burns, A. S., et al. (2010). Putting brain training to the test. *Nature, 465*, 775–778.

Pind, J., Gunnarsdóttir, E. K., Jóhannesson, H. S. (2003). Raven's standard progressive matrices: New school age norms and a study of the test's validity. *Personality and Individual Differences, 34*, 375–386.

Postlethwaite, B. E. (2011). *Fluid ability, crystallized ability, and performance across multiple domains: A meta-analysis.* Doctoral dissertation. Retrieved from http://ir.uiowa.edu/etd/1255/

Preckel, F. (2003). *Diagnostik intellektueller Hochbegabung. Testentwicklung zur Erfassung der fluiden Intelligenz [Assessment of intellectual giftedness. Development of a fluid intelligence test].* Göttingen, Germany: Hogrefe.

Preckel, F., & Thiemann, H. (2003). Online- versus paper-pencil-version of a high potential intelligence test. *Swiss Journal of Psychology, 62*, 131–138.

Primi, R. (2001). Complexity of geometric inductive reasoning tasks: Contribution to the understanding of fluid intelligence. *Intelligence, 20*, 41–70.

Rindermann, H. (2007). The g-factor of international cognitive ability comparisons: The homogeneity of results in PISA, TIMSS, PIRLS and IQ-tests across nations. *European Journal of Personality, 21*, 667–706.

Sackett, P. R. (2012). Cognitive tests, constructs, and content validity: A commentary on Schmidt (2012). *International Journal of Selection and Assessment, 20*(1)

Schaie, K. W. (2012). *Developmental influences on adult intelligence: Seattle Longitudinal Study* (2nd ed.). New York, NY: Oxford University Press.

Schalke, D., Brunner, M., Geiser, C., Preckel, F., Keller, U., Spendler, M., et al. (2013). Stability and change in intelligence from age 12 to age 52: Results for the Luxembourg MAGRIP study. *Developmental Psychology, 49*, 1529–1543.

Schank, R. C. (1984). How much intelligence is there in artificial intelligence? *Intelligence, 4*(1), 1–14.

Schmid, J., & Leiman, J. M. (1957). The development of hierarchical factor solutions. *Psychometrika, 22*(1), 53–61.

Schmidt, F. L., & Crano, W. D. (1974). A test of the theory of fluid and crystallized intelligence in middle- and low-socioeconomic-status children: A cross-lagged panel analysis. *Journal of Educational Psychology, 66*(2), 255–261.

Schrank, F. A. (2006). *Specification of the cognitive processes involved in performance on the Woodcock-Johnson III* (Assessment Service Bulletin No. 7). Itasca, IL: Riverside.

Sechrest, L. (2005). Validity of measures is no simple matter. *Health Services Research, 40*(5), 1584–1604.

Sells, S. B., Dailey, J. T., & Pickrel, E. W. (Eds.). (1984). *Selection of air traffic controllers.* Report no. FAA-AM-84-2. Washington, DC: U.S. Department of Transportation, Federal Aviation Administration.

Snow, R. E., Kyllonen, P. C., & Marshalek, B. (1984). The topography of ability and learning correlations. In R. J. Sternberg (Ed.), *Advances in the psychology of human intelligence* (Vol. 2., pp. 47–103). Hillsdale, NJ: Lawrence Erlbaum.

Spearman, C. (1904). "General intelligence," objectively determined and measured. *The American Journal of Psychology, 15*(2), 201–292.

Spearman, C. (1924). The nature of "intelligence" and the principles of cognition. *Journal of Philosophy, 21*(11), 294–301.

Spearman, C. (1927). *The abilities of man.* London, England: Macmillan and Co.

Stankov, L., & Schweizer, K. (2007). Raven's progressive matrices, manipulations of complexity and measures of accuracy, speed and confidence. *Psychology Science, 49*, 326–342.

Stelzl, I., Merz, F., Ehlers, T., & Remer, H. (1995). The effect of schooling on the development of fluid and crystallized intelligence: A quasi-experimental study. *Intelligence, 21*, 279–296. doi:10.1016/0160-2896(95)90018-7

Terman, L. M. (1924). The mental test as a psychological method. *Psychological Review,* 31, 93–117.

Thorsen, C., Gustafsson, J.-E., & Cliffordson, C. (2014). The influence of fluid and crystallized intelligence on the development of knowledge and skills. *British Journal of Educational Psychology, 84*(4), 556–570. doi:10.1111/bjep.12041

Thurstone, L. L. (1938). Primary mental abilities. *Psychometric monographs, 1*, ix–121.

Tucker-Drob, E. M., & Salthouse, T. A. (2011). Individual differences in cognitive aging. In T. Chamorro-Premuzic, S. von Stumm, & A. Furnham (Eds.), *The Wiley-Blackwell handbook of individual differences* (pp. 242–267). Malden, MA: Wiley-Blackwell.

Undheim, J. O. (1981). On Intelligence III: Examining developmental implications of Catail's broad ability theory and of an alternative neo-Spearman model. *Scandinavian Journal of Psychology, 22*(1), 243–249.

Undheim, J. O., & Gustafsson, J.-E. (1987). The hierarchical organization of cognitive abilities: Restoring general intelligence through the use of linear structural relations (LISREL). *Multivariate Behavioral Research 22,* 149–171.

Unsworth, N., Fukuda, K., Awh, E., & Vogel, E. K. (2014). Working memory and fluid intelligence: Capacity, attention control, and secondary memory. *Cognitive Psychology, 71*, 1–26.

Valentin Kvist, A. V., & Gustafsson, J.-E. (2008). The relation between fluid intelligence and the general factor as a function of cultural background: A test of Cattell's investment theory. *Intelligence, 36*, 422–436.

Wai, J., & Putallaz, M. (2011). The Flynn effect puzzle: A 30-year examination from the right tail of the ability distribution provides some missing pieces. *Intelligence, 39*(6), 443–455.

Wilhelm, O. (2000). *Psychologie des schlussfolgernden Denkens: Differentialpsychologische Prfung von Strukturuberlegeungen [Psychology of reasoning: Testing structural theories].* Hamburg, Germany: Dr. Kovac.

Wilhelm, O. (2006). Measuring reasoning ability. In O. Wilhelm & R. W. Engle (Eds.), *Handbook of understanding and measuring intelligence* (pp. 373–392). Los Angeles: Sage. doi:http://dx.doi.org/10.4135/9781452233529.n21

Woodcock, R. W., McGrew, K. S., & Mather, N. (2001). *Woodcock-Johnson III.* Itasca, IL: Riverside.

Zigler, E., & Trickett, P. K. (1978). IQ, social competence, and the evaluation of early childhood intervention programs. *American Psychologist, 33*, 789–798.

Chapter 3
Mind and Intelligence: Integrating Developmental, Psychometric, and Cognitive Theories of Human Mind

Andreas Demetriou and George Spanoudis

Abstract This chapter summarizes a comprehensive theory of intellectual organization and growth. The theory specifies a common core of processes (abstraction, representational alignment, and cognizance, i.e., AACog) underlying inference and meaning making. AACog develops over four reconceptualization cycles (episodic representations, realistic representations, rule-based inference and principle-based inference starting at birth, 2, 6, and 11 years, respectively) with two phases in each (production of new mental units and alignment). This sequence relates to changes in processing efficiency and working memory (WM) in overlapping cycles such that relations with efficiency are high in the production phases and relations with WM are high in the alignment phases over all cycles. Reconceptualization is self-propelled because AACog continuously generates new mental content expressed in representations of increasing inclusiveness and resolution. Each cycle culminates into an insight about the cycle's representations and underlying inferential processes that is expressed into executive programs of increasing flexibility. Learning addressed to this insight accelerates the course of reconceptualization. Individual differences in intellectual growth are related to both the state of this core and its interaction with different cognitively primary domains (e.g. categorical, quantitative, spatial cognition, etc.). We will also demonstrate that different levels of intelligence expressed through IQ measures actually correspond to different types of representational and problem-solving possibilities as expressed through the AACog reconceptualization cycles.

A. Demetriou (✉)
University of Nicosia Research Foundation, University of Nicosia, Nicosia, Cyprus
e-mail: ademetriou@ucy.ac.cy; demetriou.a@unic.ac.cy

G. Spanoudis
University of Cyprus, Nicosia, Cyprus

© Springer International Publishing AG 2017
M. Rosén et al. (eds.), *Cognitive Abilities and Educational Outcomes*,
Methodology of Educational Measurement and Assessment,
DOI 10.1007/978-3-319-43473-5_3

39

3.1   Introduction

The human mind was the focus of several research traditions in psychology, each emphasizing some aspects of it more than others. Although all of them are still active and thriving within their boundaries, they leave important questions open partly because research within single perspectives misses important phenomena lying at their intersections. Differential research uncovered stable dimensions of individual differences, such as general intelligence (i.e., inferential power applied to novelty), and a few strong domains of performance, such as verbal or spatial intelligence (Carroll 1993; Hunt 2011; Jensen 1998), but underestimated their development. Developmental research mapped changes in intellectual possibilities through life span (Case 1985; Flavell et al. 2001; Overton 2012; Piaget 1970) but underestimated individual differences in development. Cognitive psychology mapped cognitive mechanisms, such as working memory (Baddeley 2012) and reasoning (Johnson-Laird 2001), but ignored intra- and inter-individual variation and development. Neuroscience highlights the neuronal bases of cognitive functions and development (Shaw et al. 2006) but we do not yet understand how the brain generates cognition. Understanding the mind as a whole requires a theory that would accommodate (i) its architecture and development, (ii) individual differences between both, and (iii) learning at different phases of development.

This article summarizes one such theory. Here we focus on five aspects of the theory. First, we elaborate on the composition of the central core of intellect. Our aim is to show what processes are involved in understanding and problem solving. Second, we show how this core develops through the years. That is, we will discuss what kinds of executive and inferential possibilities are associated with successive phases of development from birth to adulthood. Third, we will elaborate on the relations between changes in executive and inferential possibilities and two important factors of cognitive efficiency: processing efficiency and working memory (WM). Fourth, we discuss research highlighting how cognitive development may be boosted by systematically organized learning environments. Fifth, we focus on individual differences in intellectual attainment and development.

3.2   Embedding the Mental Core into Mental Architecture

The human mind comprises specialized systems carrying out different tasks for understanding or problem solving. They are as follows:

(i)   Several domain-specific thought systems ground the mind in reality (e.g., quantitative, spatial, causal, and social thought).

(ii) A central workspace allowing representation and processing of current information. Working memory is the classic conception for the nature and role of central workspace (Baddeley 2012).

(iii) Consciousness allowing self-monitoring, self-regulation, and self-evaluation.
(iv) Inferential systems allowing integration of information (e.g. inductive, analogical, and deductive reasoning).

Figure 3.1 illustrates this general architecture.

The interface between all systems is a central triple-process mechanism: abstraction, alignment, and cognizance, the AACog mechanism. Abstraction extracts similarities between representations according to shared statistical regularities or other types of commonalities. Alignment inter-links and relates representations in search of their similarities. Cognizance is the component of consciousness focusing on the mind itself. So defined, cognizance generates reflection and mental models of relations allowing feedback loops where cycles of abstraction, alignment, and inference may become the object of further abstraction and alignment.

AACog lies at the center of interaction between systems underlying various processes studied by research (see Fig. 3.1). Specifically, representation and organization of domain-specific information in working memory allows episodic integration that preserves the particular spatial and time structure of events as required. Imposing an explicitly represented goal on the functioning of working memory underlies executive control of mental and behavioral action. The interaction between consciousness and inference allows metarepresentation which encodes similarities between representations into new representations. Finally, processing, integration and evaluation of domain information and concepts underlies

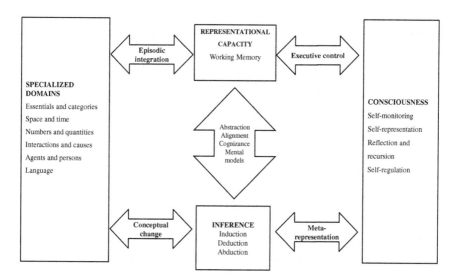

Fig. 3.1 The general architecture of the human mind

conceptual change than enhances one's knowledge base and problem-solving possibilities (Demetriou and Kazi 2006; Demetriou et al. 2008, 2014a, b).

AACog is partly similar to general intelligence as specified by Spearman (1927) or fluid intelligence, as specified by Cattell (1963). In Spearman's (1904) classic theory, general intelligence (or g) is defined as the eduction of relations and correlates. This is relational thought abstracting (i) relations between objects or events based on their similarities and (ii) relations between relations based on the reduction of similarities into rules and higher order principles relating these rules (Carroll 1993; Jensen 1998). In current psychometric theory these processes are associated with fluid intelligence (Gf), which is differentiated from Cf, Gc (i.e. knowledge and skills emerging from the functioning of Gf) (Cattell 1963; Gustafsson and Undheim 1996). In classical developmental theory, this core comprises reversible mental operations allowing understanding of stability and change in the world and grasping the (physical or logical) implications of alternative physical or mental actions (Piaget 1970). This core first organizes mental activity at successive developmental levels. However, cognizance is not even recognized as a factor in psychometric theory (Jensen 1998). Developmental theory did recognize it but considered it a result rather than an effective factor of change (Piaget 2001).

In a similar fashion, cognitive science assumes that there is a language of thought (LOT). According to Fodor (1975), LOT comprises rules underlying the combination of mental elements, such as words or mental images, that preserve stability and truth over the transformation of mental elements: if they are true, their transformation also yields true results. For example, "cat", "dog" and "animal" are all valid symbols standing for some reality. Thus, their combination results in true inferences. For instance, both cats and dogs are animals; thus, they both move around to find food; there are more animals than dogs or cats, etc. That is, once the input is true, the output (conclusions, interpretations, etc.) is also true.

For many, the rules of LOT are the rules of logical reasoning, be they the rules of logic (Rips 1994) or mental models (Johnson-Laird and Khemlani 2014). Carruthers (2002, 2008, 2013) postulated that language is instrumental in the formation of the rules of LOT, especially syntax. He suggested that syntax in language is a major integration mechanism: recursiveness, hierarchical organization, compositionality, and generativity, the fundamental properties of syntax, render language a major influence on reasoning and concept formation. He also maintained that language is related to awareness because language is the vehicle for externally representing mental objects including propositions. Thus, language renders thought available to monitoring and awareness (Carruthers 2008). In a similar fashion, other scholars suggested that language makes executive control possible because it allows individuals to address self-regulatory instructions to themselves (Perner 1998).

In a recent study, we investigated the relation between the psychometric equivalent of AACog, several aspects of executive control and cognizance, and each of several domain-specific processes of language and various domains of reasoning. Specifically, this study involved 9–15 year-old participants who were examined via a large battery of tasks addressed to attention control, flexibility in shifting, working memory, inductive, deductive, mathematical, causal and spatial reasoning, and three aspects of language, namely syntax, semantics and vocabulary. Speaking in terms of structural equation modelling, we created a first-order factor for each of these domains. To capture AACog and specify its relations with language and the various executive control processes we adopted a rather unconventional approach to modeling. Specifically, we created a second-order factor that was related *to all domain-specific language and reasoning factors but one*. This second-order factor was regressed on the domain-specific factor left out of it. Therefore, the domain-specific factor was lifted up to the status of a reference factor or a proxy that may speak about the identity of the common factor. Obviously, a high relation between the reference factor and the common factor would indicate that the common factor carries much of the constituent properties of the reference factor. In turn, the reference factor was regressed on attention control, cognitive flexibility and working memory. For instance, if syntax, as maintained by Carruthers (2002), or inductive reasoning, as maintained by psychometric theory (Spearman 1927), are privileged proxies for the core of intelligence, the relation between these reference factors and the second-order factor would be higher than its relation with any other domain-specific factor. Also, the relations between these reference factors and the executive control factors would be similar to the direct relations between the second-order factors and these executive control factors. The results of these models are summarized in Fig. 3.2.

It can be seen in Fig. 3.2 that the relation between the reference factor and the common factor was always very high (0.8–1.0) regardless of which of the domain-specific factors was lifted to the status of reference factor. These results align with Gustafsson's (1984) finding that gf and g are practically identical. In the same

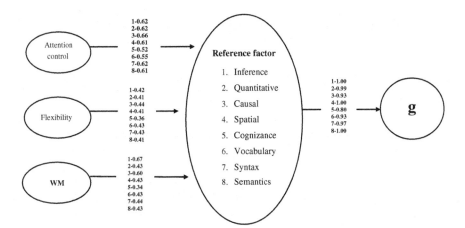

Fig. 3.2 Structural relations between g, reference factors, and attention control, cognitive flexibility, and WM. *Note* The figure summarizes eight models in which first-order factors standing for each of the domains are specified. All but one (the reference factor) was regressed on g, g was regressed on the reference factor, and the reference factor was regressed on all four factors standing for aspects of executive control. The values in the figure come from each run of the model. The fit of all models was always good (all comparative fit index (CFIs) > 0.9)

direction, other research showed that Cf and g relate very highly (Kyllonen and Kell, this volume). Obviously, these results do not support the assumption that syntax or reasoning (in any domain) has a privileged relation with g. Rather, these results suggest that all domains contain the common core to a large extent so that any one of them can reliably stand for it. This interpretation is strongly supported by the fact that all reference factors were significantly, and about evenly, related to all three executive control factors (varying between 0.4 and 0.6), just as in the model where the general factor was directly associated with these executive control factors.

A series of studies focused on the relations between g and cognizance. These studies involved participants from 4 years of age to adulthood, examined by age-appropriate tasks. For example, reasoning in preschool children was examined by various classification, simple arithmetic, and pragmatic reasoning tasks. Cognizance was examined by tasks addressed to awareness of the origin of their mental processing, such as perceptual and environment-based or inferential. We found that cognizance was always an important factor of intellectual functioning and development, if examined by age-appropriate tasks. Specifically, cognizance appears as awareness of the perceptual origins of knowledge at 4–6 years; at 6–8 years the inferential aspects of knowledge took over as a mediator between all reasoning processes and Gf (Spanoudis et al. 2015). Later, in adolescence it was awareness of the logical aspects of reasoning (Christoforides et al. in press). Thus, on the one hand, "self-evaluation and self-awareness concerning the relevant mental operations are very low and inaccurate at the beginning, and they tend to increase and to become more accurate with development until the end of the cycle." (Demetriou et al. 2010, pp. 329). On the other hand, language and cognizance get gradually intertwined with age (Makris et al. in press). However language does not have any privileged role in expressing g. Thus, language may become a tool for the efficient handling of representations in the service of cognizance. However, other types of representation may do this job equally well.

These findings suggest that the common core cannot be equated with psychometric g, Gf, or the mental structures dominating in developmental theories. These classical structures are too dependent on inferential processes, while the core identified here also relates to processes which are minimally inferential, such as vocabulary. As noted in the introduction, AACog is minimally inferential in that it involves abstraction and alignment processes allowing the search for and encoding of similarities or regularities in the environment into representations and concepts. Combinativity and generativity of some sort (including Piagetian reversibility) may be part of this encoding process. However, in itself, AACog is silent about the exact identity of processes as these may vary across domains or developmental levels. In conclusion, one might argue that the seeds for inference, cognizance, and language that contributed to the formation of the core identified here co-evolved for a very long period of time, probably starting since the Neanderthals first appeared, about 500,000 years ago (Dediu and Levinson 2013). Thus, they are so inextricably linked, genetically, brain-wise, ontogenetically, and culturally, that their interactions always go both ways. In combination, these processes allow for the compositionality, recurrence, generativity, and hierarchical integration of mental action sequences engaged by problems requiring understanding and solution. Through the millennia, evolution abstracted this structure from various domains, including language, and projected it to a level higher than any one of them. For instance, these processes might underlie both the interlinking of propositions in deductive reasoning in search of a true inference and the arrangements of words and sentences to convey meaningful messages in language.

3.3 Mapping the Development of the Executive Core and Its Transcription into Reasoning

The AACog mechanism (i.e. abstraction, alignment, and cognizance) is active in its entirety since the beginning of life. However, the operation of each of the three functions and their relative contribution may vary with development and/or experience (Demetriou and Kyriakides 2006; Demetriou et al. 2011, 2014a, b). Specifically, early in development abstraction may induce similarities between objects or patterns of information based on a simple probabilistic inference mechanism sampling over statistical regularities in the environment (Tenenbaum et al. 2011). Later on, in toddlerhood, abstraction may be based on inductive inference, which may grasp relations between representations and bridge conceptual spaces. Later, in primary school, deductive inference is possible, which allows checks for consistency, validity, and truth. Thus, there seems to be an executive core in AACog which comprises the representational capacity to hold a mental or behavioral goal active, the general search and combinativity operations allowing the alignment of this goal with a minimum of one environmental representation and action, and the abstraction–metarepresentation processes that may encode a decision. This may be described as an executive control program that evolves through four major developmental cycles, with two phases in each. New representations emerge early in each cycle and their alignment dominates later. Below we will specify the program for each cycle and highlight how it is transcribed in reasoning. It is noted that the executive programs are transcribed in each of the domains shown in Fig. 3.1, in a fashion similar to reasoning. The interested reader is referred to other sources for an exposition of development in the various domains (e.g. Demetriou et al. 2014a, b).

3.3.1 Executive Control and Reasoning

Episodic executive control. At the age of 15 months, infants recognize themselves in the mirror, indicating awareness of their facial identity (Gallup 1982; Povinelli 2001). By 18 months, infants seem to have an awareness of knowledge as a source of goals and actions; for instance, they infer that someone who saw where a reward was hidden will look for it at that place (Sodian et al. 2012). In fact, infants show signs of explicit reflection on their past experience by the age of 20 months: ND, the first author's grandson, obviously reflecting while traveling in the car, said: "Otherwise ...". What do you mean Nicolas? "Otherwise you will fall down Nicolas". Clearly referring to a conversation with his grandmother who warned him in the morning: be careful, because otherwise you will fall down and harm yourself! (conversations with ND, my grandson, at the age of 20 months). This evidence supports the assumption that infants start to be able to perform executive control by the end of their second year. However, episodic executive control is constrained by the very nature of episodic representations: it is dependent on the availability of stimuli that would sustain an episodic representational sequence (e.g. an interesting object or sound where the infant could turn). Therefore, the scope of control is constrained by the variation of stimuli: by the time a new attractive stimulus appears a new executive concern may initiate which activates a new sequence of actions. However, it is representationally mediated in that the triggering stimulus is represented together with an expected action sequence (pen → write → paper). Thus, in this cycle, the executive program may be described as a "perceive–represent-action" program: It is stimulus-activated (e.g. "this is a pen") but it is mediated by a representation of a past action (e.g. I wrote using it) which is transformed into a present action (writing). Imitation in this cycle may also be analyzed as a focus–represent-program in that an attractive behavioral episode by a model is translated into the infant's own actions (Carey 2009).

Episodic reasoning. Reasoning in this cycle is exclusively inductive, generalizing over episodic representations based on perceptual similarities (Carey 2009), and regularities in the episodic structure of events. Thus, in this cycle, inference emerges as an abstraction of the episodic blocks. When encoded they may resemble schemes of reasoning, such as conjunction or implication. For instance, Nicolas stated, obviously aligning the representations of grandfather and grandmother into a conjunctive complex: "grandma, grandpa; grandma AND grandpa" (conversations with ND, my grandson, at the age of 19 months old). This is evident in language learning. For instance, associating an object with a novel name (i.e. "this is a dax" or "this is a diffle") leads children to infer that other objects of the same shape are "dax" or "diffle" (Becker and Ward 1991; Landau et al. 1988). These inferential sequences may be mapped onto the three components of the "focus–represent–respond" episodic executive program. That is, (i) looking for a relation, (ii) encoding it into a specific representation (e.g. togetherness of grandma and grandpa), and (iii) spelling it out (e.g. AND) would correspond to (i) focus, (ii) represent, and (iii) respond, respectively.

Representational executive control. Early in this cycle, from 1½ to 2 years, episodic representations are projected into representations encompassing properties going beyond their episodic origin. For instance, the "mum and dad" representation is projected from the mother and father pair related to the infant to stand for other "women–men" pairs. As a result, infants start to intentionally scan representations, search for specific elements in them, and align them. Thus, by the age of 3–4 years, executive control is expressed as a *representational control executive program* allowing toddlers to focus on 2–3 interrelated representations and alternate between them while both are in focus. Technically, this program is represented by various inhibition tasks, such as the go/no go and Stroop-like tasks. These tasks require the child to inhibit responding to one perceptually strong stimulus in order to respond to a goal-relevant stimulus that is somehow masked by the strong stimulus. When established at about the age of 4–5 years, it fully accounts for working memory, rule-based sorting, dual representation, theory-of-mind, appearance-reality distinction, and dimensional sorting. All of these seemingly different abilities appear reducible to a simple "focus–scan–choose–respond" program enabling children to stay systematically focused on a goal (Demetriou et al. 2014a, b). This enhances the time perspective of the toddler because earlier experiences underlying representational blocks get into the organization of present action.

Pragmatic reasoning. Inductive reasoning is well functioning in this phase. Preschool children can easily solve Raven-like matrices varying along a single dimension, such as color or size. Deductive reasoning at this phase reflects the sequence of events in an episodic sequence rather than an inference: "It rains, so we need our umbrella." At the second phase of this cycle two-dimensional, Raven-like matrices (animal and color, color and size) may be solved, indicating an ability to search and analyze representations and align their components. Aspects of deductive inference appear at the age of 4–5 years in the form of pragmatic inferences related to deals. For instance: "We agreed that if I eat my food I can play outside; I ate my food; I go to play outside." (Kazi et al. 2012). This sequence, which mimics modus ponens (if p then q; p; thus q), is basically an induction that locks two representations ("A occurs" and "B occurs") together into an inductive rule (i.e. "When A occurs, B also occurs). Children may consider inductive options (i.e. "no eating–no play" and "eating–play") because the "focus–scan–choose–respond" representational executive control program of this cycle allows them to envisage alternative choices.

Rule-based executive control. In the cycle of rule-based concepts the time perspective widens extensively because rules connecting representations bridge the past with the present and future. This gives alternative plans to consider. Thus, in primary school, executive control is upgraded into *a conceptual fluency program* allowing children to shift between conceptual spaces (e.g. various object categories), activate space-specific instances, and interrelate them according to specific conceptual or procedural constraints. This is an "explore–compare–select–shift–reduce" program allowing children to shift between conceptual spaces and inter-link them according to one or more rules. For example, children at 8–9 years of age can perform well on tasks requiring a shift between conceptual spaces by recalling words starting with particular letters (e.g. Brydges et al. 2014), second-order rules in the Dimensional Change Card Sorting (DCCS) task, and second-order theory of mind tasks. We showed that this kind of mental fluency dominates as a predictor of reasoning and problem solving at the end of primary school (Spanoudis et al. 2015; Makris et al. in press). Thus, it seems that mental fluency is added to representational-action inhibition processes.

Rule-based reasoning. Early in this phase, analogical reasoning becomes flexible enough to handle several clearly present dimensions in 3 × 3 Raven-like matrices, suggesting that inference is fluid enough to access individual representations, align them, and bind them together according to underlying relations. This is clearly reflected in deductive reasoning, which emerges explicitly at this phase. It becomes obvious in the integration of modus ponens and modus tolens into a fluent inferential ensemble (i.e. if p then q; $q \rightarrow p$; not $q \rightarrow$ not p). This understanding suggests that the rules underlying relations between objects or events are explicitly metarepresented into a system specifying how different inferential spaces are interrelated. In turn, this metarepresentation transforms inductive imperatives into deductive necessities. The rules are as follows:

(i)   Different representational spaces may have different inferential constraints (e.g. birds fly, mammals walk, fish swim, etc.) yielding different inductive implications about individual elements in each space (e.g. blackbirds fly, elephants walk, sharks swim, etc., respectively).

(ii) Moving across representational spaces is possible; however, shifting across spaces (e.g. imagining that "elephants are birds") implies accepting the constraints of the new space (i.e. "elephants must fly").

(iii) The primary premise defines the constraints of the space; the secondary premise only specifies an application domain of this space.

Therefore, actual properties (e.g. elephants are mammals) are overwritten once they conform to the deductive rule "A & B, $A \rightarrow B$", which cuts across spaces. Obviously, moving across conceptual spaces and integrating into logical rules is possible because the "scan–compare–reduce–select–shift" conceptual fluency program of this cycle allows these possibilities.

Principle-based executive control. Executive control in adolescence integrates the flexibility and planning already established in the previous cycle. Technically speaking, however, changes in executive control in this cycle are not related to changes in selective attention or cognitive flexibility as such because these processes reach a ceiling level by about 13 years. In this cycle, executive control is extended into a suppositional–generative program ("suppose–derive–evaluate") enabling adolescents to co-activate conceptual spaces and evaluate them vis-à-vis each other and truth–validity–value systems that are deemed relevant. Thus, this is *an inferential relevance mastery program* opening the way for fully capturing reasoning and epistemic systems.

Principle-based reasoning. Adolescents in this phase may solve complex Raven matrices requiring grasping a principle underlying several seemingly different transformations. Obviously, these problems require representational alignment that is mastered in the previous phase. In addition, however, they also require explicit encoding of the relations generated by alignment into a representational token of these relations as such. This may be an explicit grasp of the transformation connecting the matrices or the mathematical relation running through a series of mathematical ensembles. Eventually, they may deal with multiple hidden relations or build analogical relations within and across levels of different hierarchies (e.g. students–teachers–education may be related to children–parents–family).

In deductive reasoning, children start to grasp fallacies when expressed in familiar content. Eventually, at the second phase they may process the formal representation of fallacies as in the famous Wason's (1968) task. Grasping the fallacies entails only one further metarepresentational step in concern to the reasoning possibilities mastered at the end of the rule-based cycle. This is the suppositional stance that brings disparate representational spaces back into the deductive rule as a deductive moderator "$A_{(but\ probably\ also\ C,\ D,\ E,\ ...)}$ & B". When A vis-à-vis B is represented as one option among others the modus ponens affirming the consequent and the modus tolens denying the antecedent equivalence necessarily breaks because asserting B (affirming the consequent) or denying A (denying the antecedent) hints to the options beyond A. Obviously, grasping and integrating these rules into a smoothly running metalogical system is a major developmental construction that takes place throughout the last two cycles of development. Thus, the "suppose–derive–evaluate" inferential relevance mastery program of this cycle expresses itself via the deductive moderator that can place truth weights of the various alternative choices that can be deduced from a logical argument (Christoforides et al. in press).

3.4 Changing Patterns in the Speed-Working, Memory-Intelligence Relations

Research in all traditions has sought to decompose the mental core into more fundamental components. Various aspects of attention control (the ability to select and process a stimulus property that is currently relevant, inhibiting more attractive but irrelevant stimuli, shifting between stimuli following relevant directions), executive control (laying down and implementing a plan aiming at a goal by going from step to step), and working memory (storing, accessing, and recalling information according to a goal) were considered as the building blocks of the mental core. A hierarchical cascade was proposed as the model of the relations between these processes. This model postulated that each process is embedded into the next more complex process residing higher in the hierarchy (Fry and Hale 1996; Kail 2007; Kail et al. 2015). Attention control → flexibility in shifting → working memory → reasoning and problem solving.

The cascade model may be promising from the point of view of reductive science because it aims to reduce complex processes to simpler ones. However, it is limited by its assumption that the cascade relation between processes remains stable in development. In a series of studies we explored the development and interrelations between these processes from early childhood to adulthood. Our aim was to pinpoint possible changes in these relations with development. Individuals solved tasks addressed to a succession of reasoning levels according to the cycles described above. These tasks addressed reasoning and problem solving in various domains, such as class, quantitative, spatial, causal, and propositional reasoning. Children also responded to speeded performance tasks addressed to attention control and executive control at various levels of complexity, and they solved working memory tasks addressed to various modes, including verbal, numerical, and visual/spatial information (e.g. Demetriou and Kyriakides 2006; Demetriou et al. 2013). Some of these studies are summarized in Fig. 3.3. Technically speaking, the reasoning curve in Fig. 3.3 stands for a score specifying the developmental phase of individuals. In psychometric terms, this score would be regarded as an index of Gf. The other two curves in Fig. 3.3 stand for performance on processing speed tasks (expressed in seconds) and verbal working memory tasks (varying from 1 to 7 units).

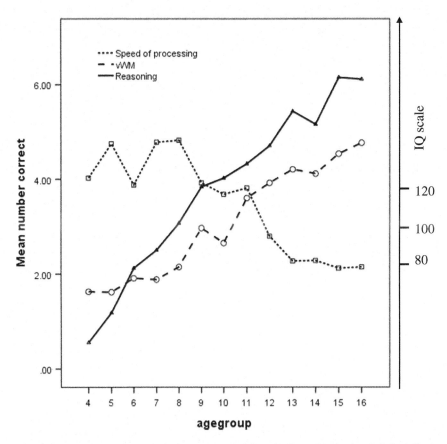

Fig. 3.3 Development of speed of processing, verbal WM (1–7), and reasoning (AACog) (logits +3, 0–1) as a function of age. *Note* Numbers on the left stand for working memory capacity. Numbers on the right stand for IQ points as obtained after the transformation of the reasoning (AACog) logit score into an IQ-like score as explained in the text. Speed varied from 0.73 (at age 15) to 1.66 s (at age 8) and it was adapted in the figure

All processes improved systematically with age. These patterns give the impression of direct and linear causal relations between these processes. However, this is not the case. For instance, we found that reasoning attainment of individuals with high WM was always closer to that of similar aged peers with low working memory rather than to that of older individuals. Results for speed and control were very similar (Demetriou et al. 2013). These results suggest that these factors minimally accounted for age-related changes in reasoning. To further explore these relations, we tested a rather simple structural equations model on each age phase separately (i.e. 4–6, 7–8, 9–10, 11–13, and 14–16 years of age). In this model, reaction time (RT) was regressed on age, working memory was regressed on age and RT, and reasoning was regressed on age, RT, and working memory. This model can show how the relations between these constructs vary with developmental phase, if indeed they do at all. The overall pattern obtained is summarized in Fig. 3.4.

It can be seen that the strength of these relations varied periodically with age. Specifically, in the early phase of each cycle the RT–reasoning relations were high and the working memory–reasoning relations were low. This relation was inverted in the second phase of each cycle, when the RT–reasoning relations dropped and the working memory–reasoning relations rose drastically. Recently, these relations were also tested by modeling the results of a large number of published studies where speed, working memory, and general intelligence were measured in each of the age phases above. It is emphasized that these cycles were fully replicated, indicating that this is a robust developmental phenomenon (Demetriou et al. 2013, 2014a, b).

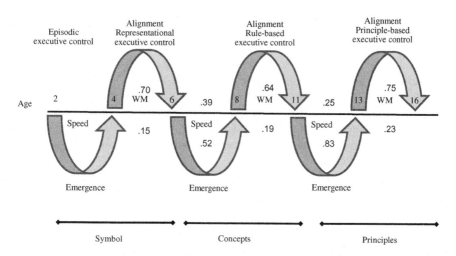

Fig. 3.4 Relations between speed, WM, and reasoning (AACog) according to developmental cycles and phase. *Note* Values show mean structural relations between speed and reasoning (*below the age line*) and working memory and reasoning (*above the age line*) in successive developmental phases

In fact, we recently showed that this recycling model involves executive control as well. That is, the various aspects of executive control are differentially related to AACog, according to developmental phase. Specifically, Demetriou et al. (submitted) showed that control of attentional focus culminates at the age of 5–6 years and then fades out as a predictor of AACog. At 6–8 years inhibition control regarding stimulus–response pairing automates, allowing children to efficiently focus on relevant information. A complementary study involving 9–15 year-old children showed that in the 8–10 year-old phase inhibition control and flexibility in shifting dominate as predictors of AACog. In the 11–13 year-old phase, these two aspects of executive control fade out as predictors of AACog and working memory and cognizance emerge. Eventually, in the 13–15 year-old phase both working memory and cognizance dominate emerge as the best predictors of AACog (Makris et al. in press). These results indicate that, with age, control is passed over from processes interfacing representation with the environment (e.g. stimulus recognition, reading, etc.) to processes primarily applied on the relations between representations and mental processes (e.g., working memory, inference, etc.).

At the beginning of cycles, processing speed on control tasks may increase for several reasons. For instance, individuals master the new executive program, increasingly automating their handling. For instance, in the first phase of realistic representations children become increasingly able to focus on representations, select those which are relevant, and inhibit irrelevant ones. At the beginning of rule-based representations, children become increasingly able to focus on underlying relations and encode them into rules. In short, command of the new control program and related representational unit improves rapidly at the beginning of cycles and thinking in terms of it proliferates to new content. Later in the cycle, when the control program is transcribed in different conceptual domains, and networks of relations between representations are worked out, WM is a better index because alignment and inter-linking of representations both requires and facilitates WM. It is stressed that it is the executive and integrative processes in WM, rather than plain storage, that was found to predict reasoning changes in the second phase of each cycle. However, signifying developmental changes at the beginning of cycles (speed) or individual differences in their implementation at the end (WM) does not imply that these factors are the causes of change or individual differences. Where is then developmental causality if not in speed or WM? We will show in the following section that cognizance is the primary factor of transition across phases and cycles.

3.4.1   Learning to Think and Reason

We conducted several studies to examine if changing intelligence is possible and what is the crucial mechanism that must be targeted to attain change. One of these studies examined whether training inductive reasoning in mathematics would improve performance in several aspects of mathematics and if this would generalize to other aspects of intelligence. This study involved 11-year-old children. We showed that change in the domain of mathematical reasoning was considerable soon after the end of the intervention, although not all of it was sustainable over time. However, the gains did transfer to domain-free analogical reasoning tasks and, to a lesser extent, to other domains, such as deductive and spatial reasoning, differing from the processes trained. Interestingly, gains in deductive reasoning continued to improve from second to third testing, when they dropped in other domains. Also, there was a transfer to domain general processes, reflecting processing and representational efficiency, such as attention control and WM. At the same time, the impact of the program was not significant enough to modify thought processes that belong to a next cycle of development, namely the principle-based cycle.

Another study focused on the critical mechanism for transition. Specifically, this study let 8-year-old and 11-year-old children become aware of the logical characteristics of the four basic logical schemes of conditional reasoning explicated above (i.e. modus ponens, modus tolens, affirming the consequent, and denying the antecedent) and trained them to build and mentally process mental models appropriate for each, and explicitly represent their relations (e.g. that affirming the consequent is not the opposite of modus ponens and denying the antecedent is not the opposite of modus tolens). The aim was to examine if enhancing cognizance about these schemes and processes would result into transition from rule-based to principle-based deductive reasoning. Moreover, we examined how this enhancement influenced transition on the various processing and intelligence processes discussed above, such as processing efficiency, WM, inductive reasoning, and cognitive flexibility. The main findings of this study are summarized in Fig. 3.5. We found that the transition did occur and it was fully mediated by awareness for both age groups. In terms of spontaneous developmental time, this short training program pulled children up by an almost full developmental phase, preserving a distance between ages. That is, trained third graders handled problems at the level of principle-based reasoning if aided by context; sixth graders moved to this level regardless of content and context. Building cognizance was strongly related to attention control and this relation increased systematically with increased training. Thus, awareness training in the cycle of rule-based inference generated insight into the logical implications of the various schemes but this insight was not crystallized into the metalogical rules that would allow handling any problem regardless of familiarity. These rules, which require an explicit representation of the pairwise relations between the schemes, were mastered by the 11-year-old children, who acquired the *suppositional stance*.

This pattern of effects, both positive and negative, bears an important educational implication. Learning programs must cycle along the cycles of development themselves. That is, they must be tailored to successive developmental cycles through the end, each time boosting the processes that relate to the emergence and consolidation of each cycle. Affecting an earlier cycle would not necessarily

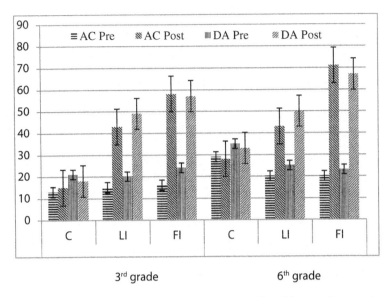

Fig. 3.5 Mean percent success on affirming the consequent (*AC*) and denying the antecedent (*DA*) reasoning tasks as a function of primary school grade and experimental condition (*C*, *LI*, and *FI* stand for control, limited instruction, and full instruction)

transfer to the next cycle, even if it raises its level of readiness. This may render observed gains developmentally specific to a large extent, suggesting that intelligence and related cognitive processes are constrained by powerful developmental cycles that set strong limits to learning. Thus, instruction-based change in various aspects of these processes may be temporary, as shown here. Sustainability and transfer of cognitive change to another cycle may also be constrained by brain-dependent developmental dynamics (Shaw et al. 2006).

This interpretation may explain the distressing fade out effect of learning studies aiming to increase intelligence, such as the Head Start Program. These studies are successful as long as they continue soon after they end. Gains of up to 8 points on the IQ scale were observed by the completion of programs. However, these gains fade out fast and 2–3 years after the end of intervention they are almost completely gone (Protzko 2015). Our studies summarized above suggested that learning gains are developmentally specific. That is, they may change a process at the level targeted, but they do not fully consolidate and automate unless they are embedded in the supportive frame of operating at a next higher level developmental cycle. Therefore, transfer to processes specific to the next cycle, such as scientific thinking, would not be attained unless learning comes repetitively in accordance with the needs of each cycle, until gains are locked into the system as habitual ways of dealing with problems (Papageorgiou et al. 2016).

3.5 Aligning Mental Age with Developmental Cycles

Individuals differ in rate of development and ultimate attainment because of hereditary and environmental reasons. Individual differences in IQ are considered to be generally stable, especially between 5 and 6 years of age to middle age. Correlations between IQ scores obtained at different ages in this span are generally high (between 0.5 and 0.7). However, intelligence within the individual may change, both at the individual and the collective level. At the individual level, it is well established that education increases intelligence by about 1–4 IQ points for each extra year of schooling (Ceci 1991; Gustafsson 2008). At the collective level, according to the so-called Flynn effect, general intelligence increases in the general population over the years. Flynn (1987) discovered that IQ increased by about 10 IQ points every thirty years since the beginning of the 20th century.

What is the developmental implication of these effects? Answering this question requires an integration of psychometrics with the developmental expression of intellectual attainment that would allow one to translate performance on IQ tests into developmental levels. This would enable one to transfer knowledge from developmental research to learning, in order to specify possible developmental constraints to learning aiming to increase intelligence. In sake of this aim, we transformed attainment on our battery of reasoning development into an IQ-like score. This attainment is indicated by the reasoning curve in Fig. 3.3. In a sense, this transformation aligns mental age with the levels associated with the developmental cycles discussed above. The reader is reminded that Binet defined intelligence as the quotient (hence IQ) of (MA/CA) $\times$ 100. Nowadays, IQ is defined as $(z \times 15) + 100$, where z is the z score of the individual on the test and 15 is the standard deviation of the population.

It is noted that this battery involved tasks addressed to all domains of reasoning specified above (i.e. categorical, causal, spatial, analogical, and deductive reasoning). These tasks were systematically scaled in difficulty to tap all three cycles of development spanning from the age of 3–4 to 17–18 years. We also note that the relation between this battery and performance on the WISC test is very high (circa 0.8) (Case et al. 2001). The total score on this battery was transformed into an IQ-like score in the fashion that the raw score on the WISC be transformed into an individual's IQ. That is, the raw score was transformed into a z score and this was then fed into the IQ equation: IQ = $(z \times 15) + 100$. Therefore, this transformation shows how different levels of IQ correspond to the cycles of intellectual development outlined here. It can be seen in Fig. 3.3 that an IQ of 100 points, which is the intelligence of 2/3 of the population corresponds to the attainments of the ruled-based concepts attained at the age of 9–10 years. Intelligence higher than 120 IQ points would require entering the cycle of principle-based thought. It is noted that this transformation was also applied on the performance attained by a Croatian sample of 8–17-year-old participants on Raven's standard progressive matrices (Zebec 2015). We obtained very similar results.

Mapping the effects of education noted above at both the individual and the collective level would suggest that, on average, the sheer effect of 12 years of primary and secondary education would correspond to an increase of about 12–18 degrees on the IQ scale, which is equal to about one standard deviation on the IQ scale. This is important but not dramatic. For most people it would imply improvements within, rather than across, developmental levels, mostly related to the consolidation of rule-based reasoning, provided that principle-based reasoning is rather rare in the general population (Demetriou and Kyriakides 2006). In fact, examination of school effects on the attainment reflected by the curve in Fig. 3.3 showed that each extra year of schooling accelerates development by the equivalent of 1/3 of the developmental level (Kyriakides and Luyten 2009). Our learning studies summarized here indicated that to cause attainment of principle-based thought requires specific learning programs that are not systematically available in our educational systems.

3.6   Conclusions

There are several important messages in this chapter about human intelligence and its development. First, a general core of mental processes does exist. This may have the functions ascribed to it by classical psychometric or developmental theories. Like g, it underlies mental functioning in every domain. Like developmental structures, it systematically changes through the years, causing all other abilities to improve. However, second, this core is defined differently from psychometric g or developmental common structures. It is thought to involve very general processes which are free of content of any kind, be it inferential or representational. These processes simply allow for search, alignment, abstraction (similization and differentiation), and encoding and reduction (metarepresentation) of information into new meaningful mental units. This is the AACog mechanism. In biological terms, this core is for phenotypically distinct mental processes what DNA is for different body cells or structures. It is everywhere, it can be extracted from everywhere, and it can be used to accurately map any specialized process. This was the meaning of the fact that all ability specific factors proved equally good proxies for a second-order factor standing for AACog.

In development, this core is expressed as a minimal executive control program enabling children to manage cycle-specific representations. Specifically, in the episodic cycle, the program allows the infant to represent and handle episodic action sequences joining attractive environmental stimuli with the infant's actions. In the cycle of realistic representations, the executive program allows the toddler to focus on pairs of representations (e.g. day–night) and map them onto respective responses (e.g. day–dark; night–light) in accordance with a rule indicating that the pairing is under mental control rather than automatic association. This ability is made evident in several achievements of this age group where children connect distinct knowledge states with corresponding representations, as in the theory of mind (Wellman 1992) or appearance–reality distinction tasks (Flavell et al. 1995). In the cycle of rule-based representations, the program allows children to mentally search mental spaces, shift between them, (e.g. say first all fruits coming in your mind, then all furniture, then all animals), and operate on them (e.g. say all round fruits, then four-legged furniture, then two-legged animals). The flexibility in searching representational spaces and aligning them to rules is made evident in n-back or backward-digit span tasks requiring a reorganization of information in WM, scan n-dimensional, Raven-like matrices in order to decipher their relation, or properly arrange problem-solving steps in various mathematical problems. This form of attentional control enables the specification of commonalities of representations and their reduction into a representational token that may be mentally handled as such. This seems to be a prerequisite of inferential control that dominates in the next cycle.

Therefore, it seems that there is a developmental snowball effect in the expansion of the AACog core. That is, there is a functional upgrading of this core in each phase such that newfound processes in each next phase sit on the processes acquired in the previous phase and become integrated with them into a smoothly running whole. Changes occur in two dimensions: the nature of representations that are possible with advancing age and the awareness and ensuing control of representations that are available to the individual. In other words, epigenetic interactions transform the mind into a powerful representational machine capable of creating and using complex abstract representations, in the service of different domains of knowledge. Our training study of deductive reasoning showed that self-awareness of logical schemes is crucial in the creation of abstract logical patterns of inference (Christoforides et al. in press). These results suggest that cognizance and second-order reasoning go together (Zelazo 2004). Thus, each of the four cycles is a dynamic state of functioning at both the mental and the brain level. At the mental level, each state may be characterized in terms of representational priorities and AACog (e.g. inferential) possibilities. Changes in cognitive efficiency and WM reflect, rather than cause, representational and control changes.

Domains of reasoning and knowledge emerge from the functioning of the AACog mechanism because alignment of related items (by nature or the environment) is more likely than alignment of non-related items. Cognizance enables revisiting and revising alignments, strengthening domain-specificity. With development, these core processes are elevated into domain-specific operations, such as mental rotation in spatial reasoning, sorting in categorical reasoning, arithmetic operations in quantitative reasoning, hypothesis testing in causal reasoning, and moral reasoning in social interaction. We showed above that working memory as a storage capacity is not a major factor in transitions. Working memory appears to be a major factor to the extent that it carries reflective and metarepresentational processes in the handling of information and inference (Demetriou et al. submitted). This assumption may highlight why relational complexity may be a factor in the transcription of the core in each cycle to domain-specific programs. According to Halford et al. (1998), relational complexity refers to the minimum number of relations that define a concept. For instance, the relational complexity of transitivity is three dimensions because to conceive of it one must hold in mind two relations (e.g. $A > B$; $B > C$) and map them onto a third relation (A ? C). Thus, relational complexity reflects limitations in combinativity and generativity that may be used to implement the executive core of a cycle into the rules underlying various domains. Examples are the rules of inductive or deductive reasoning (Christoforides et al. in press), algebra in mathematics, hypothesis testing and experimentation in scientific thought, etc.

Cognizance may be called upon to contribute to decision making in concern of the kind of criteria or process needed. Our learning studies showed that reasoning develops when cognizance processes are directly trained to be explicitly handled during inference. The study focusing on learning deductive reasoning showed that awareness of logical schemes, the mapping of each with its logical implications, and their metarepresentation were important for mastering reasoning. The study focusing on mathematics showed that learning may affect the AACog core and parameters of its efficiency, such as WM and attention control. However, both studies showed that there is a ceiling to how far learning gains can go which relates to the representational possibilities of the affected. Obviously, this model has several implications for education (Demetriou et al. 2011) and brain science (Demetriou et al. in press) which are discussed elsewhere.

Acknowledgments Special thanks are due to Rolf Lander and Rich Shavelson for their constructive comments on an earlier version of this chapter.

References

Baddeley, A. (2012). Working memory: Theories, models, and controversies. *Annual Review of Psychology, 63,* 1–29.

Becker, A. H., & Ward, T. B. (1991). Children's use of shape in extending novel labels to animate objects: Identity versus postural change. *Cognitive Development, 6,* 3–16.

Brydges, C. R., Fox, A. M., Reid, C. L., & Anderson, M. (2014). The differentiation of executive functions in middle and late childhood: A longitudinal latent-variable analysis. *Intelligence, 47,* 34–43.

Carey, S. (2009). *The origins of concepts.* Oxford: Oxford University Press.

Carroll, J. B. (1993). *Human cognitive abilities: A survey of factor-analytic studies.* New York:

Carruthers, P. (2002). The cognitive functions of language. *Behavioral and Brain Sciences, 25,* 657–726.

Carruthers, P. (2008). Language in cognition. In The *Oxford handbook of philosophy of cognitive science* (pp. 382–401). Oxford: Oxford University Press.

Carruthers, P. (2013). Animal minds are real, (distinctively) human minds are not. *American Philosophical Quarterly, 50,* 233–247.Cambridge University Press.

Cattell, R. B. (1963). Theory of fluid and crystallized intelligence: A critical experiment. *Journal of Educational Psychology, 54,* 1–22.

Case, R. (1985). *Intellectual development: Birth to adulthood.* New York: Academic Press.

Case, R., Demetriou, A., Platsidou, M., Kazi, S. (2001). Integrating concepts and tests of intelligence from the differential and developmental traditions. *Intelligence, 29,* 307–336.

Ceci, S. J. (1991). How much does schooling influence general intelligence and its cognitive components? *Developmental Psychology, 27,* 703–722.

Christoforides, M., Spanoudis, G., & Demetriou, A. (in press). Coping with logical fallacies: A developmental training program for learning to reason. *Child Development*.

Dediu, D., & Levinson, S. C. (2013). On the antiquity of language: The reinterpretation of Neanderthal linguistic capacities and its consequences. *Frontiers in Psychology, 4*, 397, doi. org/10.3389/fpsyg.2013.00397Deary, 2011

Demetriou, A., & Kazi, S. (2006). Self-awareness in g (with processing efficiency and reasoning). *Intelligence, 34*, 297–317.

Demetriou, A., Kazi, S., Spanoudis, G., Zhang, K., & Wang, Y. (submitted). Modeling the mediating role of cognizance in cognitive development from 4–7 years of age.

Demetriou, A., & Kyriakides, L., (2006). The functional and developmental organization of cognitive developmental sequences. *British Journal of Educational Psychology, 76*, 209–242.

Demetriou, A., Mouyi, A., & Spanoudis, G. (2008). Modeling the structure and development of g. *Intelligence, 5*,437–454.

Demetriou, A., Mouyi, A., & Spanoudis, G. (2010). The development of mental processing. In W. F. Overton (Ed.), *Biology, cognition and methods across the life-span. Vol. 1: Handbook of life-span development* (pp. 306-343), Editor-in-chief: R. M. Lerner. Hoboken, NJ: Wiley.

Demetriou, A., Spanoudis, G., & Mouyi, A. (2011). Educating the developing mind: Towards an overarching paradigm. *Educational Psychology Review*. doi:10.1007/s10648-011-9178-3.

Demetriou, A., Spanoudis, G., & Shayer, M., (2014). Inference, reconceptualization, insight, and efficiency along intellectual growth: A general theory. *Enfance, issue 3, 365–396,*. doi:10. 4074/S0013754514003097

Demetriou, A., Spanoudis, G., & Shayer, M. (in press). Mapping Mind-Brain Development. To appear in M. Farisco and K. Evers (Eds.), *Neurotechnology and direct brain communication*. London: Routledge

Demetriou, A., Spanoudis, G., Shayer, M., Mouyi, A., Kazi, S., & Platsidou, M. (2013). Cycles in speed-working memory-G relations: Towards a developmental-differential theory of the mind. *Intelligence, 41*, 34–50, doi:10.1016/j.intell.2012.10.010

Demetriou, A., Spanoudis, G., Shayer, M., van der Ven, S., Brydges, C. R., Kroesbergen, E., et al. (2014). Relations between speed, working memory, and intelligence from preschool to adulthood: Structural equation modeling of 15 studies. *Intelligence, 46*, 107–121.

Flavell, J. H., Green, F. L., & Flavell, E. R. (1995). Young children's knowledge about thinking. *Monographs of the Society for Research in Child Development, 60*, (1, Serial No. 243).

Flavell, J.H., Miller, P. H., & Miller, S. A. (2001). *Cognitive development*. New York: Pearson.

Flynn, J. (1987). Massive IQ gains in 14 nations: What IQ tests really measure. *Psychological Bulletin, 101*, 171–191

Fodor, J. A. (1975). *The language of thought*. Hassocks: Harvester Press.

Fry, A.F., & Hale, S. (1996). Processing speed, working memory, and fluid intelligence: Evidence for a developmental cascade. *Psychological Science, 7*, 237–241.

Gallup, G. G. (1982). Self-awareness and the emergence of mind in primates. *American Journal of Primatology, 2*, 237–248.

Gustafsson, J. -E. (1984). A unifying model for the structure of intellectual abilities. *Intelligence, 8*, 179−203.

Gustafsson, J. -E. (2008). Schooling and intelligence: Effects of track of study on level and profile of cognitiv abilities. In P. C. Kyllonen, R. D. Roberts, & L. Stankov (Eds.), *Extending intelligence: Enhancement and new constructs* (pp. 37–59). New York: Lawrence Erlbaum Associates.

Gustafsson, J. E., & Undheim, J. O. (1996). Individual differences in cognitive functions. In D. C. Berliner, & R. C. Calfee (Eds.), *Handbook of educational psychology* (pp.186–242). New York: Macmillan.

Halford, G. S., Wilson, W. H., & Phillips, S. (1998). Processing capacity defined by relational complexity: Implications for comparative, developmental, and cognitive psychology. *The Behavioral and Brain Sciences, 21*, 803–864.

Hunt, E. B. (2011). *Human intelligence*. New York: Cambridge University Press.

Jensen, A. R. (1998). *The g factor: The science of mental ability*. Westport, CT: Praeger.

Johnson-Laird, P. N. (2001). Mental models and deduction. *Trends in Cognitive Sciences, 5*, 434–442.

Johnson-Laird, P. N., & Khemlani, S. S. (2014). Toward a unified theory of reasoning. In B. H. Ross (Ed.), *The psychology of learning and motivation*. Elsevier Inc.: Academic Press, 1–42.

Kail, R. V. (2007). Longitudinal evidence that increases in processing speed and working memory enhance children's reasoning. *Psychological Science, 18,* 312–313.

Kail, R. V., & Lervag, A., & Hulme, C., (2015). Longitudinal evidence linking processing speed to the development of reasoning. *Developmental Science,* 1–8. doi:10.1111/desc.12352

Kazi, S., Demetriou, A., Spanoudis, G., Zhang, X.K., & Wang, Y. (2012). Mind–culture interactions: How writing molds mental fluidity. *Intelligence, 40,* 622–637.

Kyriakides, L., & Luyten, H. (2009). The contribution of schooling to the cognitive development of secondary education students in Cyprus: an application of regression discontinuity with multiple cut-off points. *School Effectiveness and School Improvement, 20,* 167–186.

Landau, B., Smith, L. B., & Jones, S. S. (1988). The importance of shape in early lexical learning. *Cognitive Development, 3,* 299–321.

Makris, N., Tahmatzidis, D., & Demetriou, A. (in press). Mapping the evolving core of intelligence: Relations between executive control, reasoning, language, and awareness

Overton, W. F. (2012). Evolving scientific paradigms: Retrospective and prospective. In L. L'Abate (Ed.), *The role of paradigms in theory construction.* (pp. 31–65). New York: Springer.

Papageorgiou, E., Christou, C., Spanoudis, G., & Demetriou. A.(2016). Augmenting intelligence: Developmental limits to learning-based cognitive change. *Intelligence.* doi:10.1016/j.intell. 2016.02.005

Perner, J. (1998). The meta-intentional nature of executive functions and theory of mind. In P. Carruthers & J. Boucher (Eds.), *Language and thought: Interdisciplinary themes* (pp. 270–283). Cambridge: Cambridge University Press

Piaget, J. (1970). Piaget's theory. In P. H. Mussen, (Ed.), *Carmichael's handbook of child development* (pp. 703-732). New York: Wiley.

Piaget, J. (2001). *Studies in reflecting abstraction.* London: Psychology Press.

Povinelli, D. J. (2001). The self: Elevated in consciousness and extended in time. In C. Moore & K. Lemmon (Eds.), *The self in time: Developmental perspectives* (pp. 75–95). Mahaw, NJ: Lawrence Erlbaum Associates.

Protzko, J. (2015). The environment in raising early intelligence: A meta-analysis of the fadeout effect. *Intelligence, 53,* 202-210.

Rips, L. J. (1994). *The psychology of proof: Deductive reasoning in human thinking.* MIT Press.

Shaw, P., Greenstein1, D., Lerch, J., Clasen1, L., Lenroot1, R., Gogtay1, N., Evans, A., et al. (2006). Intellectual ability and cortical development in children and adolescents. *Nature, 440,* 676-679. doi:10.1038/nature04513

Sodian, B., Thoermer, C., Kristen, S., & Perst, H. (2012). Metacognition in infants and young children. In M. J. Beran, Brandl, J. Perner, J., & Proust, J. (Eds.), *Foundations of Metacognition* (pp. 110-130). Oxford: Oxford University Press.

Spanoudis, G., Demetriou, A., Kazi, S., Giorgala, K., & Zenonos, V. (2015). Embedding cognizance in intellectual development. *Journal of Experimental Child Psychology, 132,* 32–50.

Spearman, C. (1904). *The abilities of man.* London: MacMillan.

Spearman, C. (1927). *The abilities of man.* London: MacMillan.

Tenenbaum, J. B., Kemp, C., Griffiths, T. L., & Goodman, N. D. (2011). How to grow a mind: Statistics, structure, and abstraction. *Science,* 331, 1279–1285. doi:10.1126/science.1192788

Wason, P. C. (1968). Reasoning about a rule. *Quarterly Journal of Experimental Psychology, 20,* 273–281.

Wellman, H. M. (1992). *The child's theory of mind.* Massachusetts, MA: The MIT Press.

Zebec, M. (2015). Changing expressions of general intelligence in development: A 2-wave longitudinal study from 7 to 18 years of age. Intelligence, 49, 94–109.

Zebec, M., Demetriou, A., & Topic, M. (2015). Changing expressions of general intelligence in development: A 2-wave longitudinal study from 7 to 18 Years of age. *Intelligence, 49,* 94–109.

Zelazo, P. D. (2004). The development of conscious control in childhood. *Trends in Cognitive Sciences, 8,* 12–17.

Chapter 4
Gender Differences in Broad and Narrow Ability Dimensions

A Confirmatory Factor Analytic Approach

Monica Rosén

Abstract This chapter describes investigations of gender differences in cognitive abilities and their relations to performance on standardized achievement tests in grade 6. The data used come from Jan-Eric Gustafsson's projects in the 1980s where cognitive achievement on a battery of 13 different ability tests and 3 different standardised achievement tests were collected from 50 school classes. The nested factor (NF) approach demonstrated by Gustafsson (Multivar Behav Res 27(2): 239–247, 1992) and the missing data modeling approach suggested by Muthén et al. (Psychometrika 52:431–462, 1987) were used to investigate gender differences in latent dimensions of hierarchically ordered cognitive abilities. Based on the results, it is argued that a more complex understanding is needed of the measures, as well as of the observed performances, of the compared groups. Whilst the modeled hierarchical structure of cognitive abilities fitted both groups equally well, the pattern of mean differences in latent dimensions showed both expected and unexpected results. A female advantage was found on general intelligence (g) and on the broad general crystallised intelligence factor (Gc). A male advantage was found on the general visualization factor (Gv), and on several narrow ability dimensions. This was not deducible from the univariate analysis. The chapter ends with a discussion on the degree to which these differences fit the assumptions of the so-called investment theory, that general fluid intelligence (Gf) precedes other broad abilities and narrow ability dimensions.

4.1 Introduction

Cleary (1992) points out that gender differences in aptitudes and achievement were noted long before there were any test scores to compare, referring to both Plato and Aristotle, and always to the male's advantage. Hollingworth's request, in 1914

M. Rosén (✉)
Department of Education and Special Education, University of Gothenburg,
Gothenburg, Sweden
e-mail: Monica.Rosen@ped.gu.se

© Springer International Publishing AG 2017   61
M. Rosén et al. (eds.), *Cognitive Abilities and Educational Outcomes*,
Methodology of Educational Measurement and Assessment,
DOI 10.1007/978-3-319-43473-5_4

(cited in Walsh 1987), bears witness that the introduction of systematic observations would be of great importance for the so-called "woman question". Hollingworth requested that a psychology of women should be written:

> based on truth, not opinion; on precise, not on anecdotal evidence; on accurate data, rather than remnants of magic (Hollingworth 1914, p. 49).

Performances on cognitive tests and beliefs of intellectual abilities are very influential in modern society in general, but particularly so in relation to education and educational opportunities.

In this chapter some results from two previously published studies of gender differences in cognitive abilities will be presented and discussed (Rosén 1995, 1998a). Both were part of my dissertation which had the purpose of investigating gender differences in patterns of knowledge (Rosén 1998b), and both were based on secondary analyses of Jan-Eric Gustafsson's data, the same data that he has used in many of his famous articles on the structure of intelligence (Gustafsson 1984, 1994; Gustafsson and Undheim 1992; Gustafsson and Balke 1993) In this revisit, I will discuss both studies with respect to their findings and with respect to methods used. I will be very brief in reviewing previous research on gender differences in cognitive abilities; such reviews can be found in the original work (Rosén 1998b). The aim here is to demonstrate the power of using confirmatory factor analysis for the investigation and understanding of group differences in cognitive achievement by contrasting the results from differences in manifest performance with the results from a latent variable approach. I will also show the contribution of missing data analysis based on the methodology developed by Muthén et al. (1987) for investigating and reducing the effect of potential selection bias in latent variable models. This methodology is today fully implemented and a default option in the Mplus software (Muthén and Muthén 1998–2007); at the time of my studies in the mid-1990s, however, it required several analytical steps from data preparation to final results. But first, I will introduce a brief description of the theoretical background to the study of cognitive abilities.

4.2   A Theory of the Structure of Human Cognitive Abilities

The question whether human cognitive abilities are unitary or multifaceted has been occupying educational psychologists all over the world ever since Binet and Spearman did their work in the beginning of the twentieth century. Today's scientific view on intelligence has its roots in the beginning of the twentieth century when psychological measurement started. Before that time, the notion of intelligence was founded in personal beliefs and philosophical thoughts among distinguished men (Cattell 1987).

It was Spearman who in those early days developed the first factor analytic method to investigate whether the human intellect should be thought of as "a single power" or "a crowd of faculties" (Spearman 1904). Building on the correlational technique developed by Francis Galton at the end of the nineteenth century, Spearman found that all measures of cognitive performance were positively correlated, and that the correlation was highest among complex and abstract tasks. His interpretation of this pattern was that all tasks share a common dimension, general intelligence (g), and that each task also requires an ability specific to that task (Cattell 1987). Classical test theory is built on this notion. Thurstone (1938) extended Spearman's unidimensional model to encompass multiple factors. With a newly developed factor analytic technique (multiple factor analysis), Thurstone was able to identify about a dozen "primary" factors in large-scale empirical studies. The number of "Primary Mental Abilities—PMAs" was later considerably extended by Thurstone and his followers, and it was soon discovered that many did not seem to have differential predictive power for achievement in different subject matter areas, which questioned the value of primary abilities in practical applications (Gustafsson 1992). Broader abilities were thus needed for both theoretical and practical reasons.

One way to bring order among PMAs is to analyze the correlations between factors, and thereby identify so-called second-order factors. This approach yields a hierarchical organization, which includes both broad and narrow ability dimensions. Horn and Cattell (1966) applied such techniques to construct a hierarchical model with two broad factors, fluid intelligence (Gf) and crystallised intelligence (Gc). They also identified some further broad factors (e.g. general visualization, Gv, and general fluency, Gr).

Carroll (1993) used exploratory factor analysis—in his renowned reanalyses of most studies conducted of the structure of abilities—and he extended the Cattell and Horn model into a model with three levels. Using confirmatory factor analysis instead, Gustafsson (1984) also arrived at a hierarchical model with three levels. This model is depicted in Fig. 4.1 and described in greater detail below.

4.2.1   General Intelligence (g)—Fluid Intelligence (Gf)

At the apex of the model there is g, general intelligence. Current interpretations regard g as a combination of Spearman's general intelligence concept and Gf from Cattell and Horns Gf–Gc theory (Cattell 1943, 1971, 1987; Horn and Cattell 1966). Findings from correlational and experimental research (e.g. Undheim 1981; Undheim and Gustafsson 1987; Gustafsson 1984, 1988, 1994, 1997; Kyllonen and Christal 1990; Carlstedt 1997) provide evidence in support of equating Gf and g. Gustafsson (1997) describes Spearman's (1923, 1927) theory of g, which involved both a quantitative and a qualitative aspect. The qualitative aspect is expressed in terms of three

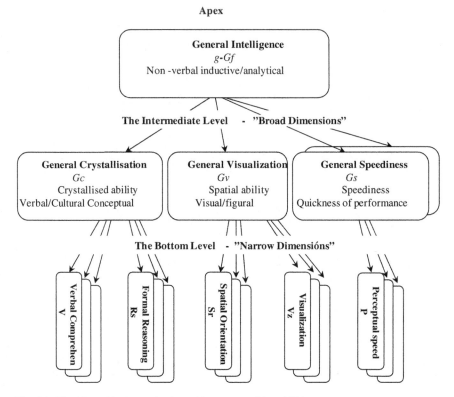

Fig. 4.1 The hierarchical organization of human cognitive abilities

principles: "eduction of relations" (rule inference), "eduction of correlates" (rule application), and "apprehension of experience". The first two principles aim to capture basic aspects of reasoning, while the third corresponds to what is now called metacognition. The quantitative aspect of g was formulated in terms of "mental energy", which should be understood as expressing individual differences in limitations on the ability to keep more than a limited number of items in mental focus at the same time (Gustafsson 1997). Gustafsson concludes that this finding supports putting Gf at the apex of the hierarchy, which thus emphasizes reasoning as the central component of intelligence.

Other research has indicated that the g–Gf dimension may be a reflection of "working memory" (*WM*) (Kyllonen and Christal 1990), which would connect the principles of Spearman's theory and the definition of g as an analytical non-verbal reasoning dimension. However, whether *WM* is part of, or associated with, Gf seems to be an ongoing discussion (cf. Lohman and Lakin 2011).

4.2.2 Broad Cognitive Ability Dimensions

On the intermediate level, a number of broad ability dimensions have been identified, of which the most important one in educational contexts seems to be *Gc*, crystallized intelligence. The term "crystallized" is meant to imply the "*freezing shape of what was once fluid ability*" (Cattell 1989, p. 115). *Gc* like *Gf* is also thought to reflect the capacity for abstraction, concept formation, perception, and eduction of relations. The difference is that *Gc* is associated with the systematic influence of acculturation and is central in tasks of a verbal–conceptual nature (Gustafsson and Undheim 1996).

Gv is another broad dimension spanning over a range of tasks with spatial content, a dimension which according to Cattell (1989) reflects good visualization resources. Another broad dimension, *Gs*, general speediness, is thought to reflect speed and accuracy in cognitive performance, and *Gr* is thought to reflect retrieval from memory storage (Cattell 1989). Later research has proposed a few additional broad dimensions (Carroll 1993; Gustafsson and Undheim 1996).

4.2.3 Narrow Dimensions

At the lowest level of the hierarchical model, a large number of narrow, specialized ability dimensions emerge, similar to those identified in the Thurstonian multiple factor tradition. Examples of primary abilities are verbal comprehension (*V*), numerical ability (*N*), cognition of figural relations (*CFR*), visualization (*Vz*), spatial orientation (*Sr*), and flexibility of closure (*CFR*). Narrow dimensions, over and above the preceding broad abilities, are thought to be determined by practice and experience as well as by interest and motivation.

4.3 Data and Methodology

The data analyzed here come from Jan-Eric Gustafsson's large research project on learning strategies and teaching methods (called INSU, Swedish acronym). A central research question for this project dealt with the structure of human abilities and, above all, the question whether intelligence is unitary or multifaceted. For this purpose, the design included a number of the most promising cognitive tests previously developed in traditional, differential psychological research. The test battery was assembled in such a way that enough primary factors would be represented to make possible identification of the second order factors *Gv*, *Gf*, and *Gc*.

Three standardized achievement tests from regular activities in the sampled schools were also included in the test design. The INSU project and the data collected are described in greater detail elsewhere (Gustafsson et al. 1981; Gustafsson 1984); hence, for the present purpose, only a brief description will be given here.

4.3.1   Sample and Tests

The sample consisted of 1224 students in grade 6 from 1980, which represented more or less all students in two communities on the Swedish west coast. In the first semester of grade 6 (fall of 1980), when most of the students in the sample had reached the age of 12, members of the research project administered a test battery of 13 ability tests to the students. These tests are described in Table 4.1, including also which broad and narrow ability dimensions each was hypothesized to measure.

As part of their regular activities in grade 6, schools were also recommended, by the national educational authorities, to administer three standardized achievement tests (Swedish, English, and mathematics), which also represent measures of *Gc*. No narrow ability dimensions were hypothesized in advance. The three standardized achievement tests, described in Table 4.2, consisted of 4–7 sub-tests, and for the analysis in both the first and the second study, the sub-scores from these three tests were used. The total number of test scores included in the analyses was 29. The number of students with complete data on both test battery and the three standardized achievement test was 981, the number of missing girls and boys being the same (121 girls and 122 boys).

The overarching aim of both studies presented here was to investigate gender differences in hierarchically ordered latent ability dimensions. The method used to formulate the latent variable model was the nested factor (NF) modeling approach suggested by Gustafsson and Balke (1993). Gender differences in the first study were investigated by specifying the NF-model as a two-group structural equation model, which enabled the investigation of gender differences not only in terms of latent mean differences, but also in latent variable variance and, importantly, in the structure. Investigated in the second study was the impact of missing data on the previous results. In this study, gender differences were investigated through means of a dummy variable by which the correlation with each latent variable could be estimated. The tools used for conducting the analyses were SPSS (SPSS Inc. 1988) for the univariate part and LISREL 8 for the confirmatory factor analysis (Jöreskog and Sörbom 1993), with some being conducted within the user friendly environment of STREAMS 1.7 (Structural Equation Modeling Made Simple) developed by Jan-Eric Gustafsson (Gustafsson and Stahl 1997).

Table 4.1 The cognitive test battery

Test	n of items	Time limits in min	Description	Broad ability	Narrow ability
1. Opposites	40	10	In each of the items the task is to select the word which is the antonym of a given word	Gc	Verbal comprehension (V)
2. Number series II	20	10	In each item a series of 5 or 6 numbers are given, and the task is to add two more numbers to the series	Gf	Induction (I)
3. Letter grouping II	20	10	The items consist of groups of letters, and the task is to decide which group of letters does not belong with the other	Gf	Induction (I)
4. Auditory number span	19	12	This is a conventional digit-span test, with digits in series of varying length being read for immediate reproduction	Gf	Memory span (Ms)
5. Auditory letter span	19	12	This test is identical to auditory number span but uses letters instead of digits	Gf	Memory span (Ms)
6. Raven progressive matrices	33	3 × 15	The items present a matrix of figures in which the figures change from left to right according to one principle, and from top to bottom according to another principle. One figure is missing, and the task is to identify this figure	Gf	Cognition of figural relations (Cfr)
7. Metal folding	40	10	The task is to find the three-dimensional object which corresponds to a two-dimensional drawing	Gv	Visualization (Vz)
8. Group embedded figures	9	2 + 5	The task is to find a simple figure within a more complex figure	Gv	Flexibility of closure (Cf)
9. Hidden patterns[a]	400	3 + 3	Each item consists of a geometrical pattern, in some of which simpler configurations are embedded. The task is to identify those patterns which contain the simple configuration	Gv	Flexibility of closure (Cf)

(continued)

Table 4.1 (continued)

Test	n of items	Time limits in min	Description	Broad ability	Narrow ability
10. Copying[a]	64	3 + 3	Each item consists of a given geometrical figure, which is to be copied onto a square matrix of dots	Gv	Flexibility of closure (Cf)
11. Card rotations	28	4 + 4	Each item gives a drawing of a card cut into an irregular shape, the task is to decide whether other drawings of the card are merely rotated, or turned over onto the other side	Gv	Spatial orientation (S)
12. Disguised words	24	2.5 + 2.5	In this test, words are presented with parts of each letter missing; the task is to identify the word	Gv	Speed of closure (Cs)
13. Disguised pictures	24	3 + 3	In this test, drawings are presented which are composed of black blotches representing parts of the objects being portrayed; the task is to identify the object	Gv	Speed of closure (Cs)

Descriptions compiled from Gustafsson et al. (1981)

[a]Speeded

Table 4.2 The grade 6 standardized achievement tests in mathematics, English and Swedish

Standardized achievement tests (SA)	n of items	Time limits in min	Description	Broad ability
SA mathematics			*Standardised test in mathematics composed of 5 sub-tests*	Gc
Numerical calculation	20	35	Items test the understanding of the number line. The ability to carry out addition, subtraction, multiplication, division, and calculations with fractions	Gc
Percent calculation	16	25	Items test the ability to carry out calculations involving the percent concept	Gc
Estimates	21	10	Items test the ability to make rapid estimates of the approximate result of an expression. Multiple choice	Gc
Geometry and diagrams	14	Nd	Involving 8 geometry items, i.e. computing areas of rectangles; 6 items assessing the ability to understand information presented in graphs and tables	Gc
Applied computation	12	Nd	Involving 12 verbally stated problems, most of which require a mixture of arithmetic rules	Gc
SA English			*Standardized test in English composed of 4 sub-tests*	
Vocabulary	40	30	The items present a one or two sentence context. One missing word is required. Multiple choice	Gc
Listening comprehension	35	30	A brief piece of information is presented via tape recorder, in relation to which questions are asked. Multiple choice	Gc
Forms and structures	40	30	Items test the knowledge of grammar, e.g. do-construction and flexion of verbs. Fixed response options	Gc
Reading comprehension	29	30	Involving 9 items requiring the identification of missing words in a sentence. Multiple choice. Five texts of 75–200 words are presented, accompanied by 3–5 multiple choice items	Gc
SA Swedish				
Spelling	25	Nd	The task is to spell dictated words	Gc
Reading comprehension	21	35	Measures pupils' ability to understand texts written in different styles and with different content. Six short texts of 100–200 words with 2–5 multiple choice items	Gc
Words of relation	12	12	Items test the ability to use conjunctions and adverbs. An 8 sentence text is presented in which 12 words are missing; the task is to select the correct word from a list of 28 options	Gc

(continued)

Table 4.2 (continued)

Standardized achievement tests (SA)	n of items	Time limits in min	Description	Broad ability
Vocabulary	25	12	Presents items in which the synonym of a word in a one sentence context is to be selected from a list of 5 choices	Gc
Word list	11	10	Items test the ability to use a word list to find the meaning, spelling, and flexion of a word	Gc
Sentence construction	18	15	Presents a text lacking punctuation; the task is to add 18 missing punctuation marks	Gc

Descriptions compiled from Gustafsson et al. (1981)
Nd = Not documented

4.4 Analytical Considerations

A major advantage of the hierarchical modeling approach is that it allows for simultaneous identification of general and specific abilities. There are at least two ways to formulate a hierarchical model, higher order (HO) modeling and nested factor (NF) modeling. One problem with the HO-approach is that it does not offer procedures for analysis of differences between groups in structure, means, and variances on HO-factors (Gustafsson 1992), another is that it does not easily provide information about the relative importance of the broad and narrow variables as predictors of achievement. Following Gustafsson's NF-approach, the first step was to specify a general factor (*g*) with direct relations to every manifest variable. In the next steps, and based on the residual variance unaccounted for by *g*, narrower latent variables were successively specified, also with direct relations to the manifest variables that they were hypothesized to influence. In this way, the final model

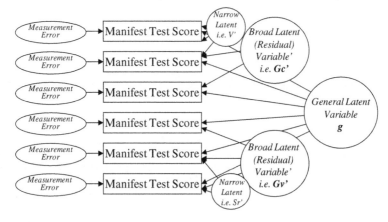

Fig. 4.2 A simplified NF-model

Table 4.3 Means and standard deviations on the ability tests for three groups; the full sample, the sub-sample with complete data, and the sub-sample lacking the standardized achievement test

Test battery	Scale	Full sample n = 1224		Completers n = 981		Attriters n = 243	
		Mean	Sd	Mean	Sd	Mean	Sd
1. Opposites	1–40	21.81	5.75	22.08	5.69	20.72	5.83
2. Number series II	1–20	7.82	3.75	8.04	3.78	6.93	3.51
3. Letter grouping II	1–20	10.96	3.61	11.18	3.56	10.10	3.96
4. Auditory number span	1–19	4.41	2.68	4.49	2.68	4.11	2.64
5. Auditory letter span	1–19	4.52	2.17	4.57	2.20	4.33	2.04
6. Raven progressive matrices	1–45	24.16	5.96	24.44	5.83	23.05	6.36
7. Metal folding	1–30	18.53	6.13	18.70	6.00	17.82	6.58
8. Group embedded figures	1–16	10.60	2.89	10.69	2.79	10.26	3.24
9. Hidden patterns	1–9	70.42	23.99	71.08	23.73	67.74	24.91
10. Copying	1–32	22.42	8.19	22.67	8.12	21.44	8.42
11. Card rotations	1–224	96.39	38.05	97.37	37.32	92.45	40.68
12. Disguised words	1–24	11.72	3.41	11.89	3.36	11.02	3.56
13. Disguised pictures	1–24	12.68	3.25	12.79	3.28	12.23	3.09

resulted in orthogonal latent variables of a broader or narrower nature. Any manifest variable is influenced by a minimum of two latent dimensions, e.g. g and *measurement error*, but often also by some more broad ability and narrow dimensions. With NF-models, it is easy to interpret group differences in means on the latent factors, as the factors are orthogonal in the model. Depicted in Fig. 4.2 is a prototypical model, which illustrates the described features of the NF-model. Squares represent manifest variables. Latent variables are represented by ovals or circles and their labels are written in italics. A prime (′) after the latent variable label denotes that the latent variable is based on residual variance. In a measurement model like this, the manifest variables are dependent, and the latent variables independent, as shown by the arrows.

The NF-model formulated by Gustafsson and Balke (1993) on these data served as a starting point for my two studies. Some extensions of the hierarchical model were made, as I chose to use the sub-tests in the standardized achievement test instead of their total score in order to get a better understanding of observed performance on regular achievement tests. It also enabled better identification of narrow verbal and numerical ability dimensions, which, in relation to previous research, seemed relevant for the investigation of gender differences. Including the three standardized tests in the analyses reduced the initial sample from 1224 to 981 cases having complete data. As shown by the descriptive statistics in Table 4.3, comparing the sub-sample of 981 cases with the results from the full 1224-case sample did not indicate any systematic deviation in the manifest variables; thus, the attrition in the first study was assumed to be random in the same manner as it had been in previous studies of the data. I have labeled the sub-sample with complete data "the completers" and the sub-sample with missing data "the attriters".

Table 4.3 shows that the differences between the full sample and the completers were very small and not statistically significant. Attriters however, show somewhat lower performance on all tests, but the only statistically significant differences are those on two *Gf* tests, 'letter grouping' and 'number series', and on the *Gc* test 'opposites'. One may say that this pattern confirms what has often been observed, that the group lacking standardized achievement tests contains proportionally more low achievers.

Soon after the first study, a technique (Muthén et al. 1987) became available with which one could estimate the latent variable model also for groups with incomplete data making use of the information they do have, and thereby obtaining more reliable estimates. Missing data is often regarded as a purely statistical problem, but the problem may also be addressed from a more substantial point of view. Whether to take part in a high-stakes test situation or not, as was the case for the standardized achievement test, may be a decision which interacts more strongly with gender than gender interacts with the performance. Previous research has shown such differential effects with respect to both socio-economic background and gender in studies of self-selection to the Swedish Scholastic Aptitude Test, which besides school marks is used for admission to academic studies, and in which males have been shown to be more positively selected with respect to their ability than females. The highest performing girls choose to a lesser degree to take the admission test, as they are admitted to higher education based on their high school marks from upper secondary school (cf. Reuterberg 1998). Standardized achievement tests in grade 6 had the purpose of supporting teachers in their duty to assign equal and fair school marks. Taking the standardized achievement tests in mathematics, Swedish, and English was, in the early 1980s, up to the local schools or teachers to decide. In the data used here, the proportion that lacked such achievement test were about the same, 121 girls and 122 boys, and about half of those missing cases came from classrooms which had chosen not to administer the standardised achievement tests. This limited the missing data question only to whether the selection mechanism differed between the sexes with respect to differences in cognitive abilities.

4.5   Analyses and Results

The results from traditional univariate analysis is contrasted below with the results from the multivariate latent approach, serving two purposes: it distinguishes between *manifest performance* on tests and the *latent cognitive dimensions* of the test that cause differences in performance. This means that common interpretations of test performance can be problematized not only theoretically but also empirically. The contrast also demonstrates that both approaches are needed, since the relations between the observed and the latent contribute to a more complex understanding. A second contrast is added by the results from the missing data analysis in the second study. This will illustrate how such analysis can contribute to the understanding of social group differences in addition to yielding more accurate estimates.

4.5.1 Observed Gender Differences in Test Performance

Based on traditional univariate analysis, gender differences in the observed test scores were more absent than present on the 13 ability tests, only 4 showing significant t-values for mean differences. The largest difference was found on letter grouping, a Gf test in which girls performed a higher mean ($r = 0.23$). A higher female mean was also found on the spatial hidden pattern test ($r = 0.16$) and on Raven's progressive matrices ($r = 0.11$), an inductive test. Boys, on the other hand, showed a little higher mean on the number series test ($r = -0.071$). Larger variability was found for boys on Raven's matrices, and on the short-term memory test, that is the auditory number span, as well as on the number series test.

In a traditional analysis, it would have been difficult to draw any strong conclusions on the basis of the results from the 13 ability tests. Three of these are considered to be typical tests of Gf, that is 'number series', 'letter grouping', and 'Raven's progressive matrices'. A minor male advantage on the first, and a somewhat larger female advantage on the two latter, would make any conclusion about an advantage in either direction doubtful. The idea that there could be any "real" gender differences in g or Gf is not socially acceptable, but would there be signs of a female or male advantage in some tests of Gf, the acceptable explanations would most likely refer to them as either accidental, caused by chance or by specifics in the test, or as a sign of maturity level.

Gender differences on spatial tests were shown in two cases in my study, and both were found to benefit girls. Taking into account that none of the other spatial tests in the test battery revealed any gender difference, a reasonable conclusion may have been that the consistent male advantage in this domain finally seems to have vanished, at least in Sweden. The often found male advantage in spatiality has in the research community caused many animated debates (e.g., *American Psychologist*, September, 1986).

4.5.2 Gender Differences on Standardized Achievement Tests

Gender differences on the observed sub-tests of the three standardized achievement tests in Swedish, English, and Mathematics were more frequent, mostly to the advantage of girls, whilst in general small, ranging from $r = 9.12$ to $r = 0.23$. Boys showed a higher mean performance on two of the sub-tests in maths: $r = -0.15$ for estimates and $r = -0.08$ on percentage calculations. Larger variability was found in the boys on four of the six sub-tests in English and on the spelling sub-test in Swedish. There were no differences in variability on the overall scores for the three standardized achievement tests, but somewhat higher averages were found for girls in Swedish ($r = 0.15$) and in English ($r = 0.14$) and for boys in mathematics

($r = -0.076$). Only on the Swedish sentence construction sub-test did gender differences account for as much as 5 % of the variance.

The female advantage on the standardized tests in Swedish and English seem to confirm and validate the fact that females gain higher school grades. This would also confirm the rather consistent pattern of female advantage in verbal abilities reported over the years (e.g. Anastasi 1958; Maccoby and Jacklin 1974; Hyde and Linn 1988; Willingham and Cole 1997). The almost gender-neutral result on the standardized test in mathematics from my first study, seems to support the conclusion that there no longer exists a male advantage in mathematical abilities, at least not among young people in Sweden.

4.5.3 Gender Differences in Variability

In the observed distribution of scores in my study, greater male variability was found from the tests for Gf, that is in one short-term memory test, in most sub-tests in English, and in one sub-test of Swedish. When gender differences are found in the tails of the distribution, they only concern a very limited number of people. Furthermore, these people deviate the most from the average within the group. However, the observed differences in the lower end of the distribution confirm reports of male students as having more difficulties in school subjects (e.g. Wernersson 1989). A common hypothesis is that this has to do with maturity level and/or negative student–teacher interaction (Entwisle et al. 1997).

4.5.4 Gender Differences Among Attriters

With regression analyses, the hypothesis of a differential missing data pattern with respect to achievement on manifest test scores was investigated. Each test score was regressed on the dummy coded variables for completers(0)/attriters(1), boys(0)/girls (1), and on the interaction term (attriters x gender). The only gender-attrition interaction effects found were on the number series test (Beta $= -0.11$ $p = 0.01$) and on the opposites test (Beta $= 0.11$ $p = 0.01$), perhaps indicating some differential ability levels among boys and girls in the attriters' group. However, no such conclusion could be drawn based on these findings, as the interaction effects are so few and so small.

In Table 4.4, the statistically significant mean and variance differences in manifest scores are summarized by their correlations (r) and variance ratios (F) for both completers and attriters.

Table 4.4 Statistically significant gender differences in manifest scores

	Completers		Attriters	
	$n = 981$	$F_{crit} = 1.16$ Df 479/500	$n = 243$	$F_{crit} = 1.36$ Df 121/120
	r	F	r	F
1. Opposites	ns		0.24	
2. Number series II	−0.07	1.33	ns	ns
3. Letter grouping II	0.23		0.35	
4. Auditory number span	ns	1.40	ns	1.57
6. Raven progressive matrices	0.10	1.36	0.18	
9. Hidden patterns	0.16		0.18	
10. Copying		ns		1.59
13. Disguised pictures		ns		1.68
14. SA mathematics (a–e) total	−0.08			
c. Estimates	−0.16			
15. SA English (a–d) total	0.14			
a. Vocabulary	0.13	1.34		
c. Forms and structures	0.16			
d. Reading comprehension	0.16	1.34		
16. SA Swedish (a–f) total	0.16			
a. Spelling	0.21	1.31		
b. Reading comprehension	0.07			
c. Words of relation	0.18			
e. Word List	0.16			
f. Sentence construction	0.23			

Positive r-coefficients indicate female mean advantage. F variance ratios, estimates >1 indicate larger variability in the male group. All estimates are significant at the 0.05 level

4.5.5   Gender Differences in the Latent Structure

Before any latent mean and variance differences could be meaningfully investigated, a well-fitting latent variable model was needed. As mentioned before, in the NF-model by Gustafsson and Balke (1993) these data served as a starting point, but were extended through the inclusion of the sub-tests in the standardized achievement test for better identification of the more narrow verbal and numerical ability dimensions. In Table 4.5, summary information about the relations between latent ability dimensions and observed test scores in the final NF-model is presented.

With the two-group latent variable models, gender differences were investigated with respect to several aspects. The first questions asked regarded the model fit. Would this particular structure fit boys and girls equally well? Were the patterns of relations between manifest variables and latent constructs the same? Was the strength of the relations equal? If the model was found to fit one group much better than the other, then group comparison with respect to means and variances in latent

Table 4.5 Aptitude variables included in the analysis in grade 6 with standardized factor loadings (full quasi-likelihood, FQL)

Test name	Label	Latent factors	Std factor estimates, FQL			
1a. Opposites-odd items	Op-O	g (0.57)	Gc' (0.29)	V' (0.36)	Words' (0.41)	
1b. Opposites-even items	Op-E	g (0.57)	Gc' (0.31)	V' (0.28)	Words' (0.44)	
2. Number series II	NS	g (0.75)				NumAch' (0.24)
3. Letter grouping II	LG	g (0.70)				
4. Auditory number span	ANS	g (0.28)		Ms' (0.56)		
5. Auditory letter span	ALS	g (0.35)	Gc' (0.10)	Ms' (0.70)		
6a. Raven-odd items	Ra-O	g (0.56)	Gv' (0.20)	CFR' (0.71)		
6b. Raven-even items	Ra-E	g (0.60)	Gv' (0.18)	CFR' (0.63)		
7a. Mental folding-odd items	MF-O	g (0.50)	Gv' (0.61)	Vz' (0.40)		
7b. Mental folding-even items	MF-E	g (0.51)	Gv' (0.63)	Vz' (0.38)		
8. Group embedded figures	GEFT	g (0.59)	Gv' (0.32)	Gs' (0.21)		
9. Hidden patterns	HP	g (0.57)	Gv' (0.25)	Gs' (0.43)		
10. Copying	Co	g (0.55)	Gv' (0.27)	Gs' (0.46)		
11a. Card rotations, Part I	CR-I	g (0.45)	Gv' (0.21)	Gs' (0.31)	Sr' (0.57)	
11b. Card rotations, Part II	CR-II	g (0.51)	Gv' (0.26)	Gs' (0.25)	Sr' (0.68)	
12. Disguised words	DW	g (0.37)		Gs' (0.12)	Cs' (0.65)	
13. Disguised pictures	DP	g (0.25)	Gv' (0.25)		Cs' (0.41)	
14. Std ach test mathematics						
14a. Ma percentage calculation	Ma PCC	g (0.55)	Gc' (0.25)	Gv' (0.10)	NumAch' (0.50)	
14b. Ma estimates	Ma Es	g (0.53)	Gc' (0.10)		NumAch' (0.44)	
14c. Ma geometry and diagrams	Ma GD	g (0.66)	Gc' (0.18)	Gv' (0.08)	NumAch' (0.43)	
14d. Ma applied computation	Ma AC	g (0.70)	Gc' (0.14)		NumAch' (0.40)	
14e. Ma numerical calculation	Ma NC	g (0.63)	Gc' (0.22)		NumAch' (0.50)	
15. Std ach test English						
15a. En vocabulary	En Vo	g (0.59)	Gc' (0.51)	V' (0.08)	EngAch' (0.45)	
15b. En listening comprehension	En LC	g (0.54)	Gc' (0.33)	V' (0.23)	EngAch' (0.51)	
15c. En forms and structures	En FS	g (0.61)	Gc' (0.49)		EngAch' (0.34)	
15d. En reading comprehension	En RC	g (0.60)	Gc' (0.48)	V' (0.17)	EngAch' (0.39)	
16. Std ach test Swedish						
16a. Spelling	Sw Sp	g (0.51)	Gc' (0.54)			

(continued)

Table 4.5 (continued)

Test name	Label	Latent factors	Std factor estimates, FQL		
16b. Reading comprehension	Sw RC	g (0.61)	Gc' (0.33)	V' (0.36)	
16c. Words of relations	Sw WR	g (0.62)	Gc' (0.40)	V' (0.19)	
16d. Vocabulary	Sw Vo	g (0.54)	Gc' (0.38)	V' (0.47)	$Words'$ (0.12)
16e. Word list	Sw WL	g (0.66)	Gc' (0.31)		
18f. Sentence construction	Sw Sc	g (0.59)	Gc' (0.37)		

Data compiled from Rosén (1998b)

dimensions would have been both impropiate and meaningless. If there were only minor differences in the model between the groups, then there are modeling procedures with which one can investigate if, and how, these aspects affect the pattern of differences in latent means. In this case, the patterns of relation between latent constructs and observed test performance were the same for boys and girls, although the strength of a few relations differed to some extent (cf. Rosén, 1995, for details). These few, small differences did not affect the means on any of the latent dimensions in any substantial way and the model fit was quite acceptable (Chi-square = 726, df = 406, RMSEA = 0.03, GFI = 0.96, NFI = 0.96, NNFI = 0.98).

By squaring the standardized factor coefficient, the proportion of variance accounted for by different latent dimensions is obtained. The influences from the different latent variables indicate that several different ability dimensions are involved in solving the tasks in these tests, and this is true also for the ability tests that have been designed to measure primarily one ability dimension. Noteworthy is also the substantial part in all manifest variances that is due to measurement error. For example, the observed variance in the spatial mental-folding test g accounted for 24 %, Gv' accounted for another 38 %, and yet another 15 % was accounted for by the narrow visualization (Vz'). Together these latent factors explained about 77 % of the variance in the test, while about 23 % of the variance was due to measurement errors.

The influences of different ability dimensions in the standardized achievement tests were notable. The different variance contribution from each latent factor is illustrated in the graph in Fig. 4.3. Take for example the numerical calculation sub-test; about 40 % of the variance was due to the $g–Gf$ factor, another 5 % was due to Gc', and about 25 % to the narrow $NumAch'$ factor. Furthermore, about 30 % of the variance could not be attributed to any systematic source. In fact, measurement error (measurement error/test specific residual variance is labelled err-spec' in Fig. 4.3) accounted for on average 25–50 % of the variance across all achievement tests. This latent pattern in the manifest variables accentuates two important things: each task can obviously be solved in more than one way, using one or more cognitive abilities, and, it is easy to draw the wrong conclusions about which ability it might be that causes differences between groups.

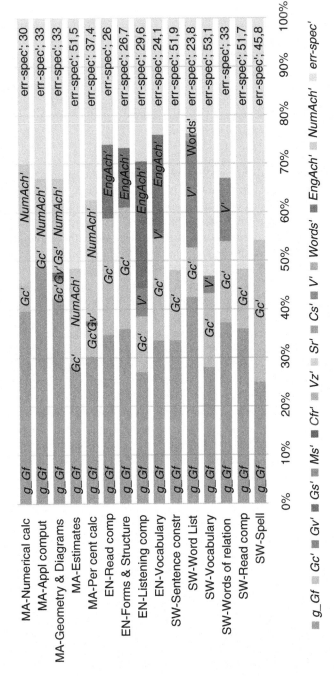

Fig. 4.3 Proportion variance in school achievement tests accounted for by latent ability dimensions

In the next part of the analysis, gender differences in latent means and variances were investigated by successively allowing the means and variances in the latent factor model to vary between the two groups. The mean differences were estimated in a number of models to see to what degree they were affected by different assumptions. The mean differences in the two-group model, with all free parameters allowed to vary between the two groups, did not deviate in any interpretable way from the mean differences found in the two-group model, where all free parameters were restricted to be equal across the two groups. The mean differences in the two-group analysis were also compared with the mean differences obtained in a one-group model, in which gender was included as a dummy variable. The pattern of mean differences remained stable across all these tests. However, the results in the first study relied on the sub-sample with complete data. There was still a possibility that the differences found were biased to an unknown degree, due to some differential selection mechanism. The influence of missing data was investigated in the second study, with unexpected findings.

This technique for investigating the missing data in latent variable models, in the mid-1990s, required another multiple group analysis, where the groups were defined based on their missing data pattern. The results using the original listwise quasi-maximum (LQL) estimation could then be compared with Muthén's full quasi-maximum (FQL) estimation, which offers more accurate estimates, i.e. based on the full sample. Furthermore, to obtain correct degrees of freedom and chi-square, this technique required that two models were fitted to the data; the so called H0-model, which is a model where restrictions are imposed on the data; and the H1-model, which tests if the covariance matrices and the mean vectors for the groups come from the same population. The correct fit statistic was then obtained by subtracting the chi-square and df of the H1-model from the H0-model. In the missing data models, gender was entered as a dummy variable, allowing only for the investigation of mean differences in latent dimensions.

Gender differences in latent means are displayed in Fig. 4.4. For comparative reasons, both the LQL estimates and the FQL estimates are included, and the pattern of results is commented on below.

4.6 Gender Differences on Broad and Narrow Latent Ability Dimensions

Figure 4.4 shows the pattern and size of mean differences in the latent ability dimensions expressed as correlations. Positive estimates indicate female advantage and negative estimates indicate male advantage.

As can be seen, the pattern of mean differences between boys and girls in latent constructs was strikingly different from the pattern in observed scores. Girls showed a substantially higher mean on general intelligence (g) and on the broad crystallized intelligence (Gc') dimension. Boys on the other hand showed a somewhat higher

Gender differences in latent ability dimensions

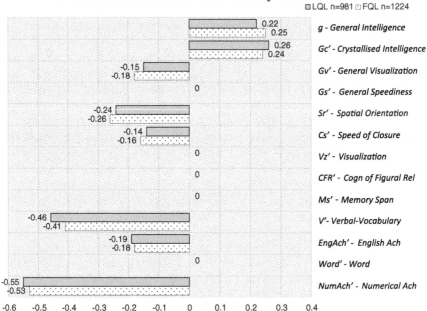

Fig. 4.4 Gender differences in broad and narrow ability dimensions. Contrasting LQL and FQL estimates of maximum likelihood

mean on the broad spatial dimension general visualization (Gv'), on the narrow spatial speed of closure (Cs') and on spatial orientation (Sr'). Boys also had remarkably higher means on the narrow dimensions of numerical achievement ($NumAch'$) and verbal-vocabulary (V'). Gender accounted for some 30 % of the variance in the $NumAch'$ factor and some 20 % in the V' factor.

The rather large difference in g to the female advantage was quite unexpected, given the above-mentioned assumption of equality in this respect. When gender differences in this broad intellectual ability have been reported, it has only been on the basis of performances from IQ scores and similar composite scores (Feingold 1988). Such types of tests have almost always shown a male advantage, whenever gender differences have been found (Willingham and Cole 1997). The male advantage has, however, only been found in purposive samples, which makes comparison between females and males in this respect more complicated to interpret. This is also a circumstance that is easily lost in the public debate.

General intelligence in the modern theoretical sense is not easily captured by any single test, but is instead always involved in all test performances, as demonstrated here. Lack of valid measures is therefore one of the reasons why such findings have not been reported previously. The empirical support for Gf, being inseparable from g described earlier, has helped in defining the construct of g; hence, more studies of gender differences in this respect can be expected in the future. Investigations of group differences in g thus require tests of Gf to differentiate between general intelligence and any general dimension. As Gustafsson (1994) has pointed out, it is impossible to differentiate between g and Gc in IQ tests, unless some of the tasks measure Gf exclusively, with the variance decomposed in a latent variable model, similar to the one in this study.

The fact that history lacks findings of this kind also makes the result somewhat doubtful. There is, however, one parallel study that shows similar results. Härnqvist (1997) too found a female advantage on g. One possible explanation for the female advantage has to do with the age group that is investigated (12–13 year olds). It has been suggested that girls' earlier onset of puberty may be accompanied by an earlier spurt in mental growth (e.g. Ljung 1965).

The female advantage on the broad crystallised intelligence dimension (Gc') was more expected, both from previous research and from the data reported here. Females have consistently been reported to have been awarded higher average school marks (Willingham and Cole 1997; Emanuelsson and Fischbein 1986), which together with the average higher performance on most of the verbal school achievement tests makes this advantage reasonable. In my studies, the observed female advantage on most sub-tests of the standardized achievement tests in Swedish and English is a reflection of this Gc advantage. In the verbal tests, Gc and g together account for the main part of the variance. The female advantage is thus due to their relative advantage on both these broad latent dimensions. However, in the narrower dimensions of the school achievement tests, males were on average substantially stronger ($NumAch'$, $EngAch'$, and V'). The observed pattern did not indicate any difference in mathematics, therefore, the difference in the narrower underlying numerical construct needs some explanation. The hypothesis offered from my studies is that boys and girls use different approaches in solving mathematical tasks. The pattern found may be an indication that male performance to a higher degree is explained by their proficiencies on narrow dimensions, while female performance to a higher degree is explained by their proficiencies on broad dimensions.

If the quantitative domain is established as a "male domain", the verbal domain is an equally established "female domain", so the huge male advantage on the narrow verbal dimension (V') was even more surprising. Verbal comprehension is interpreted as a narrow verbal factor involved in tasks that require some specific vocabulary knowledge. In the present test battery V' was involved in six of the ten language sub-tests and in the opposites ability test. The proportion of variance accounted for by the factor varied between 1 and 22 %. The female advantage in observed performance on these tests is due to their advantage on the broad dimensions of g and Gc rather than to their level on the narrower verbal-vocabulary dimension. One reasonable explanation of the male advantage on V', is that the tests were developed under the awareness of a historically consistent female advantage within this domain, therefore, the choice of words and content in these tests more or less unknowingly has been selected to compensate for this expected difference

(Härnqvist 1997). Such biases were discovered during the mid-1990s on the Swedish Scholastic Aptitude Test (SweSAT) (Reuterberg 1997).

The male advantage on the narrow English achievement dimension (*EngAch'*), although not as large, is equally unexpected. The factor accounted for 12–26 % of the variance in the English tests, while *g* and *Gc'* accounted for the main part. On all the observed scores, girls performed significantly better than boys, which again has to do with their advantage on *g* and *Gc'*. The male advantage on the *EngAch'* factor may perhaps be attributed to the content of the tests, i.e. a similar hypothesis to the advantage on *V'*. Another hypothesis is that some of the male spare time activities, such as TV-games, role play games and computer games which are often in English, may offer extra training opportunities as has been suggested in more recent research (e.g. Sylvén and Sundqvist 2012; Olsson 2016).

The substantial male advantage on several latent spatial dimensions found here was not warranted by their manifest performance, which instead showed a pattern that is more consistent with contemporary understanding. Here, the historical and consistent male advantage in the spatial domain seems to reappear in the latent pattern. Gender similarity may have been reached in solving spatial tasks, but this is obviously not the same as gender similarity in spatial abilities.

4.6.1 The Impact of Missing Data

My own expectations before the missing data analysis were that gender differences would decrease and perhaps disappear altogether in some of the latent dimensions. Again the results were somewhat a surprise; when cases with missing data were accounted for, the pattern of mean differences in observed scores changed differently than the pattern of mean differences on the latent variables. The female average advantage in *g* increased, as did the average male advantage on the spatial dimensions *Gv'*, *Sr'*, and *Cs'*. Gender now accounts for 1 % more of the variance in those dimensions. The male average advantage on the narrow *V'*, *NumAch'*, and *EngAch'* dimensions decreases similarly as the female average advantage on *Gc'*. The amount of variance accounted for by gender hardly drops at all, indicating that the magnitude of gender difference is not dramatically altered in any latent dimension.

In the univariate regression analysis, when attrition and gender-attrition interaction were taken into account, the pattern of gender differences changed in favor of females on almost all observable performance scores. This made sense, since the female attriters performed equally well on all of the ability tests as did the female completers, while the male attriters performed a bit worse than did the male completers. While the missing females seemed to match the missing data at random assumption, the missing males did not.

From the changes in the observed pattern, one may have suspected that the female advantage on *Gc'* would increase, while the male average level on most latent dimensions would remain the same, and that the level on the achievement factors (*V'*, *EngAch'*, and *NumAch'*) would decrease. However, the pattern of differences on the latent dimensions changed differently.

The female advantage on *Gc'* decreased, while their average advantage on *g* increased. Male average advantage on the more achievement oriented factors *V'*, *NumAch'*, and *EngAch'* decreased a little as expected, while their average on the broad *Gv'* factor and the narrow spatial dimensions of *Sr'* and *Cs'*, quite surprisingly, increased. In a way, this pattern supports the idea that spatial abilities are developed outside of the school context, and particularly so in male activities.

The general findings from the missing data study were that the pattern of difference changed, despite the almost invisible deviation of mean differences between boys and girls in the small group with missing data, as compared to the larger group with complete data. This result implies that missing data analysis may be of importance to understand gender differences and to identify and control for differential selection mechanisms, even in cases when attrition seems trivial.

4.6.2 Reflections on Possible Explanations

The overall pattern suggests that females to a larger degree than males have developed broad ability dimensions, which they can use on almost any cognitive task. Males, on the other hand, seem to a larger degree to specialize in narrow ability dimensions, which is profitable in specific tasks. In this way the male group becomes less homogeneous than the female group, since the tendency to specialize may be the uniting trait, but the choice of area for specialization may differ.

The developmental tradition would suggest that the female advantage on general intellectual dimensions at the age of 12–13 is due to females' earlier maturation. However, as Härnqvist shows, the female advantage has not decreased at the age of 16 (Härnqvist 1997). Given that the maturity explanation does not fit with the male advantage found, a socio-cultural explanation may be equally reasonable. That the difference may have a material grounding in the social environment, is another and perhaps not too far-fetched idea. Such thought implies that the difference may be due to other differences such as power, experience, interests, and in normative expectancies from surrounding society. Such an explanatory framework also indicates that this pattern may change as the relations between males and females change in society. The inconsistent pattern of gender differences in the large number of large-scale comparative studies available today (e.g. PIRLS, TIMSS, and PISA) supports the idea that differences also have a socio-cultural basis.

4.6.3 Gender Differences Through the Lenses of the Investment Theory

I will end this chapter by discussing the pattern of male/female differences in hierarchically ordered cognitive abilities that were found in my two studies in relation to Cattell's investment theory from the 1970s (referred in Valentin Kvist and Gustafsson 2008). Based on his findings that g loads higher on Gf than on Gc, Cattell offered the *investment theory* to account for this pattern. According to this theory, Gf should be understood as a single relation-perceiving ability which develops with maturation of the brain, before all other cognitive ability factors, and that a child's rate of learning of different tasks (e.g. conceptual, numerical, and spatial) depends on this ability. However, other factors, such as effort, motivation, and quality of education, may also play a part in the growth of these later developed second-order and first-order abilities.

As Gf has been defined as a non-verbal inductive reasoning factor, it is easy to accept that this general factor needs to be involved more or less in all learning activities, both directly and indirectly through later developed cognitive abilities, such as Gc. Support for this line of reasoning is recognized in Lohman's (2004) example, where he points to the fact that the meaning of most new words are learned by inferring from the context in which the words are embedded. A more general expression of the same phenomenon is offered by Landaure and Dumais (1997) who argue that most knowledge development occurs through inductive inference of partial information encountered in different contexts. The fact that all test performance is due to several ability dimensions of different degree of generality, as was demonstrated by the latent variable model, also explains why the pattern of gender differences deviates from one another when latent differences are contrasted with manifest differences.

In Cattells' investment theory, Gf is assumed to be more biologically determined than other ability dimensions. The other broad and narrow factors were thought to be more determined by environmental factors, such as learning and schooling. Today, several studies have produced evidence that Gf is also malleable by social factors, as is Gc (cf. Rindermann et al. 2010). Most well-known is perhaps the Flynn effect (Dickens and Flynn 2001), which shows a higher secular rise in Gf as compared to Gc in the twentieth century, which is attributed to the increased amount, and quality, of education. There are also other studies: for example Cliffordson and Gustafsson (2008) were able to separate the effect of age from schooling, and their results indicated positive effects of schooling on inductive tests (from the Swedish military enlistments), whereas the effect of age declined and became negative. Yet others have been able to show positive effects from interventions, in which inductive reasoning was trained (Klauert and Phye 2008), with Rindermann et al. (2010) presenting results that indicate a reciprocal relationship between Gf and Gc.

How should this pattern of gender differences in cognitive abilities be understood if the development of narrow ability dimension is dependent first on the level of Gf and second on the level Gc? One possibility is of course that these narrow ability dimensions are nothing but test-specific factors, and that the tasks specificities involved in these are more familiar among young boys than girls. Härnqvist (1997) found similar results in his study, and suggested that this unexpected pattern in narrow dimensions may have something to do with the selection of stimulus words.

If the test bias hypothesis is true or partly true, and gender differences are built into high-stake tests, this is not only unfair but also problematic, as these factors account for around 20 % of the variance in these tests. Otherwise, if these narrow factors actually represent important ability dimensions, and the group differences found are valid, then these need to be better understood as the investment theory does not suffice as the causal mechanism behind this pattern.

Härnqvist (1997) mentioned, a female advantage in general intelligence was also identified in his reanalysis of the data from a study conducted in the early 1960s. Intact classrooms were followed from grade 4 to grade 9 (age 10–16) and enabled analyses over school grades. Härnqvist used the same nested modeling approach in his reanalysis of the data as I used, and he found that girls to the same degree as in my study excelled over boys on g–Gf and, although there were no signs of diminishing differences over the school years, the most plausible explanation suggested was girls' earlier maturation. The maturation hypothesis implies that this condition should be understood as temporary, and boys are expected catch up later. Studies that cover a wider age range are still needed to test this hypothesis.

The relative advantage shown by boys on the general spatial ability (Gv) dimension is even more difficult to explain. From an investment theory standpoint, girls underachieve on this spatial factor, given their higher level of g–Gf. Boys on the other hand overachieve on both Gv and on the narrower verbal and numerical dimensions, regardless of their lower level of g–Gf and Gc and regardless of their less developed maturity level. One may ask why the investments in these ability dimensions are relatively less pronounced in the female group. Valentin Kvist and Gustafsson (2008) argue that if sub-groups within a population have had different opportunities to acquire the knowledge tested, as for example may be the case with immigrants, this relation between Gf and less general factors will break down. However, such differences in opportunity are not easy to identify in this case, as the boys and girls in this study came from the same areas, and were taught together in the same classrooms and schools. It is possible that boys were more exposed than girls to tasks that require spatial abilities outside of the school context, in their leisure time activities. Boys' larger variability in this ability dimension may indicate that such an explanation is applicable for a sub-group only within the male population.

Today, there are researchers who argue that investment in a specific ability boosts similar abilities but retards competing abilities, for example verbal versus mathematical ability, so that those who excel in one of these tend to nurture this profile at the expense of the other (Coyle et al. 2015). In my study, boys excelled over girls in both narrow verbal dimensions and in the narrow numerical dimension, however, such an explanation does not fit at a general level. Perhaps it could be that girls to a higher degree boost their general inductive reasoning and crystallized abilities at the expense of more narrow ability dimensions, while boys to a higher degree boost expertise within more narrow ability domains?

The questions about what causes these differences remain for future research, as does the need to continue investigating group differences. The results here need to be validated in other studies, and stronger longitudinal designs are needed to support any causal hypotheses. The strength and fruitfulness of using Gustafsson's NF-modeling approach in combination (Gustafsson and Balke 1993) with Muthén's estimator (Muthén et al. 1987; Muthén and Muthén 1998–2015), for incomplete data (which today is easily accessible in the Mplus software) has been demonstrated, and should lead the way.

References

Anastasi, A. (1958). *Differential psychology*. New York: MacMillan.

Carlstedt, B. (1997). Test complexity and measurement of the general factor. Manuscript submitted for publication.

Carroll, J. B. (1993). *Human cognitive abilities: A survey of factor-analytic studies*. Cambridge: Cambridge University Press.

Cattell, R. B. (1943). The measurement of adult intelligence. *Psychological Bulletin, 40*, 153–193.

Cattell, R. B. (1971). *Abilities: Their structure, growth and action*. Oxford, England: Houghton Mifflin.

Cattell, R. B. (1987). *Intelligence: Its structure, growth and action*. Amsterdam: Elsevier Science Publishers.

Cleary, A. T. (1992). Gender differences in aptitude and achievement test scores. In J. Pfleiderer (Ed.), *Sex equity in educational opportunity, achievement and testing. Proceedings of the 1991 ETS Invitational Conference* (pp. 51–90). Princeton, NJ: Educational Testing Service.

Cliffordson, C., & Gustafsson, J.-E. (2008). Effects of age and schooling on intellectual performance: Estimates obtained from analysis of continuous variation in age and length of schooling. *Intelligence, 18*(1), 143–152.

Coyle, T. R., Snyder, A. C., & Richmond, M. C. (2015). Sex differences in ability tilt: Support for investment theory. *Intelligence, 50*, 209–220.

Dickens, W. T., & Flynn, J. R. (2001). Heritability estimates versus large environmental effects: The IQ paradox resolved. *Psychological review, 108*(2), 346.

Emanuelsson, I., & Fischbein, S. (1986). Vive la différence? A study of sex and schooling. *Scandinavian Journal of Educational Research, 30,*, 71–84.

Entwisle, D. R., Alexander, K. L., & Olson, L. S. (1997). *Children, schools & inequality*. Oxford: Westview Press.

Feingold, A. (1988). Cognitive gender differences are disappearing. *American Psychologist, 43*(2), 95–103.

Gustafsson, J.-E. (1984). A unifying model for the structure of intellectual abilities. *Intelligence, 8*, 179–203.

Gustafsson, J.-E. (1988). Hierarchical models of individual differences in cognitive abilities. In R. J. Sternberg (Ed.), *Advances in the psychology of human intelligence* (Vol. 4, pp. 35–71). Hillsdale, New Jersey: Lawrence Erlbaum Associates, Inc.

Gustafsson, J.-E. (1992). The relevance of factor analysis for the study of group differences. *Multivariate Behavioral Research, 27*(2), 239–247

Gustafsson, J.-E. (1994). Hierarchical models of intelligence and educational achievement. In A. Demetriou & A. Efklides (Eds.), *Intelligence, mind and reasoning: Structure and development*. Amsterdam: Elsevier.

Gustafsson, J.-E. (1997). *Measuring and understanding G: Experimental and correlational approaches*. Paper presented at the conference "The Future of Learning and Individual Differences research: Processes, Traits and Content", University of Minnesota, October 9–12.

Gustafsson, J.-E., & Balke, G. (1993). General and specific abilities as predictors of school achievement. *Multivariate Behavioral Research, 28*(4), 407–434.

Gustafsson, J.-E., Lindström, B., & Björck-Åkesson, E. (1981). *A general model for the organization of cognitive abilities* (Report 1981:06). Göteborg, Sweden: Göteborg University, Department of Education and Educational Research.

Gustafsson, J.-E., & Stahl, P. A. (1997). *STREAMS User's Guide*, Version 1.7. Mölndal, Sweden: MultivariateWare.

Gustafsson, J.-E., & Undheim, J. O. (1992). Stability and change in broad and narrow factors of intelligence from ages 12 to 15 years. *Journal of Educational Psychology, 84*(2), 141–149.

Gustafsson, J.-E., & Undheim, J. O. (1996). Individual differences in cognitive functions. In D. Berliner & R. Calfee (Eds.), *Handbook of educational psychology* (pp. 186–242). New York: Macmillan.

Härnqvist, K. (1997). Gender and grade differences in latent ability variables. *Scandinavian Journal of Psychology, 38*(1), 55–62.

Hollingworth, L. S. (1914). Variability as related to sex differences in achievement. A critique. *The American Journal of Sociology, 19*, 510–530.

Horn, J. L., & Cattell, R. B. (1966). Refinement and test of the theory of fluid and crystallized intelligence. *Journal of Educational Psychology, 57*, 253–270.

Hyde, J. S., & Linn, M. C. (1988). Gender differences in verbal ability: A meta-analysis. *Psychological Bulletin, 194*(1), 53–69.

Jöreskog, K. G., & Sörbom, D. (1993). *LISREL 8: User's Reference Guide* (2nd ed.). Chicago: Scientific Software.

Klauer, J. K., & Phye, G. D. (2008). Inductive reasoning: A training approach. *Review of Educational Research, 78*(1), 85–123.

Kyllonen, P. C., & Christal, R. E. (1990). Reasoning ability is (a little more than) working-memory capacity. *Intelligence, 14*(4), 389–433.

Landauer, T. K., & Dumais, S. T. (1997). A solution to Plato's problem: The latent semantic analysis theory of acquisition, induction, and representation of knowledge. *Psychological Review, 104*(2), 211.

Ljung, B.-O. (1965). *The adolescent spurt in mental growth*. Acta Universitatis Stockholmiensis. Stockholm Studies in Educational Psychology 8. Stockholm: Almqvist & Wiksell.

Lohman, D. (2004). Aptitude for college: The importance of reasoning tests for minority admissions. In R. Zwick (Ed.), *Rethinking the SAT. The future of standardized testing in university admissions* (pp. 41–56). New York and London: Routledge Falmer.

Lohman, D. F., & Lakin, J. M. (2011). Intelligence and reasoning. In R. J. Sternberg & S. B. Kaufman (Eds.), *The Cambridge handbook of intelligence* (pp. 419–441). New York, NY: Cambridge University Press.

Maccoby, E. D., & Jacklin, C. (1974). *The psychology of sex differences*. Stanford, California: Stanford University Press.

Muthén, B., Kaplan, D., & Hollis, M. (1987). On structural equation modelling with data that are not missing completely at random. *Psychometrika, 52*, 431–462.

Muthén, B. O., & Muthén, L. (1998–2015). *Mplus User's Guide*. Seventh Edition Los Angeles, CA: Muthén and Muthén.

Olsson, E. (2016). *On the impact of extramural English and CLIL on productive vocabulary*. Diss. Gothenburg : Acta Universitatatis Gothoburgensis.

Reuterberg, S. E. (1997). *Gender differences on the Swedish scholastic aptitude test* (Report no 1997:02). Gothenburg: University of Gothenburg, Department of Education.

Reuterberg, S. E. (1998). On differential selection in the Swedish scholastic aptitude test. *Scandinavian Journal of Educational Research, 42*(1), 81–97.

Rindermann, H., Flores-Mendoza, C., & Mansur-Alves, M. (2010). Reciprocal effects between fluid and crystallized intelligence and their dependence on parents' socioeconomic status and education. *Learning and Individual Differences, 20*(5), 544–548.

Rosén, M. (1995). Gender differences in structure, means and variances of hierarchically ordered ability dimensions. *Learning and Instruction, 5*, 37–62.

Rosén, M. (1998a). Gender differences in hierarchically ordered ability dimensions. The impact of missing data. *Structural Equation Modeling, 5*(1), 37–62.

Rosén, M. (1998b). *Gender differences in patterns of knowledge*. Göteborg studies in educational sciences 124. Göteborg, Sweden: Acta Universitatis Gothoburgensis.

Spearman, C. (1923). *The nature of 'intelligence' and the principles of cognition*. London: MacMillan.

Spearman, C. (1927). *The abilities of man*. London: MacMillan.

Spearman, C. (1904). "General Intelligence," objectively determined and measured. *The American Journal of Psychology, 15*(2), 201–292.

SPSS. (1998). *Base. SPSS 8.0 for Windows User's Guide*. Chicago: SPSS.

Sylvén, L. K., & Sundqvist, P. (2012). Gaming as extramural English L2 learning and L2 proficiency among young learners. *ReCALL, 24*(03), 302–321.

Thurstone, L. L. (1938). Primary mental abilities. *Psychometric Monographs, No 1*.

Undheim, J. O. (1981). On intelligence II: A neo-Spearman model to replace Cattell's theory of fluid and crystallized intelligence. *Scandinavian Journal of Psychology, 22*, 181–187.

Undheim, J. O., & Gustafsson, J.-E. (1987). The hierarchical organization of cognitive abilities: Restoring general intelligence through the use of linear structural relations (LISREL). *Multivariate Behavioural Research, 22*, 149–171.

Valentin Kvist, A., & Gustafsson, J.-E. (2008). The relation between fluid intelligence and the general factor as a function of cultural background: A test of Cattell's investment theory. *Intelligence, 36*(5), 422–436.

Walsh, M. R. (1987). *The psychology of women: Ongoing debates*. New Haven: Yale University Press.

Wernersson, I. (1989). Olika kön samma skola? En kunskapsöversikt om hur elevernas könstillhörighet påverkar deras skolsituation [Different gender same school? A research review of how the students gender affect their school situation]. Skolöverstyrelsen, Vad säger forskningen F 89:1.

Willingham, W. W., & Cole, N. S. (1997). *Gender and fair assessment*. Mahwah, NJ: Lawrence Erlbaum Associates.

Chapter 5
A Question of Validity: Clarifying the Hierarchical Nature of Teacher Cognition

Sigrid Blömeke and Lars Jenßen

Abstract Domain-specific cognitive constructs often show strong empirical correlations with each other if not controlled for g, although they are conceptually different, because individuals invest their general ability in all types of learning processes. Based on the investment theory and Jan-Eric Gustafsson's work, the present paper examines for the first time the relation between prospective preschool teachers' cognitive facets. Data from 354 prospective preschool teachers from 3 different federal states in Germany are used. As hypothesized, g was significantly, and with large effect sizes, correlated with the domain-specific constructs mathematical content knowledge (MCK), mathematics pedagogical content knowledge (MPCK), and ability to perceive mathematics-related preschool situations (PERC). The hierarchical relation of g, PERC and MCK or MPCK respectively was modeled by applying nested factor (NF) and second-order models. As hypothesized, the strength of the predictive effect of MPCK on PERC was substantially lower but still significant in both the direct hierarchical and the indirect hierarchical model if g was controlled for. Again as hypothesized, the effect of MCK on PERC was not significant anymore once g was introduced—and this applied again to both hierarchical models. These results suggest that intelligence was invested in preschool teachers' learning of the domain-specific constructs and needs therefore to be controlled for if domain-specific effects of teacher education on outcomes are to be examined. The data revealed furthermore that a difference in the relevance of MCK and MPCK for PERC exists. The NF and the second-order model did not differ significantly with respect to their fit to the data.

S. Blömeke (✉)
Centre for Educational Measurement, University of Oslo,
Oslo, Norway
e-mail: sigribl@cemo.uio.no

L. Jenßen
Department of Education and Psychology, Freie Universität Berlin,
Berlin, Germany
e-mail: lars.jenssen@hu-berlin.de

© Springer International Publishing AG 2017
M. Rosén et al. (eds.), *Cognitive Abilities and Educational Outcomes*,
Methodology of Educational Measurement and Assessment,
DOI 10.1007/978-3-319-43473-5_5

Individuals with high achievement on general cognitive ability (g) tests often show high achievement in specific cognitive domains as well (Carroll 1993; Gustafsson and Undheim 1996; Jensen 1998). At the same time, domain-specific cognitive constructs often show strong empirical correlations with each other if not controlled for g although they are conceptually different because individuals invest their general ability in all types of learning processes (Cattell 1987).

Such a strong empirical correlation between two conceptually different constructs applies, for example, to the mathematical content knowledge (MCK) and the mathematics pedagogical content knowledge (MPCK) of future mathematics teachers (Blömeke and Delaney 2012). Whereas MCK includes mathematical knowledge in typical areas such as algebra or geometry, MPCK is knowledge around how to teach this mathematics to students. This includes knowledge of teaching strategies or typical student errors. In many countries, which had participated in the "Teacher Education and Development Study in Mathematics" (Blömeke et al. 2013; Tatto et al. 2012), the manifest correlation between MCK and MPCK was up to $r = 0.60$ in the case of primary teachers or even up to $r = 0.70$ in the case of lower secondary teachers if one did not control for g (Blömeke and Delaney 2012).

A similarly strong relation between conceptually different constructs showed up in a study with prospective preschool teachers that examined how strongly MCK and MPCK predicted situation-specific skills such as the skill to perceive mathematics-related preschool situations (PERC). PERC is very different from MCK; and, despite of some overlap, PERC is also conceptually different from MPCK in that MPCK is systematic knowledge whereas PERC involves recognizing mathematics-related opportunities to learn (OTL) for children in unstructured, typically play-based preschool situations although these OTL are not at all obvious (Mason 2011). Despite the conceptual differences, MPCK predicted significantly, and with a substantial effect size, PERC ($\beta = 0.60$; Dunekacke et al. 2015b). Even more stunning was that MCK was also a strong predictor of PERC ($\beta = 0.45$; Dunekacke et al. 2015a; Fig. 5.1 displays this structural model; for similar results with respect to mathematics teachers see Blömeke et al. 2014).

None of these studies had controlled for g although it is a crucial question of validity to disentangle the effects of domain-specific knowledge and g on skills. Gustafsson's (2002) research on the structure of cognition, in particular the nested factor (NF) and the second-order approaches, suggests ways in which we can examine this question of validity in more detail. In line with the Cattell–Horn–Carroll (CTC) theory (McGrew 2005), a hierarchical order of teachers' general and domain-specific cognitive abilities can be hypothesized. The present chapter examines the nature of prospective preschool teacher cognition in this respect by applying such a hierarchical perspective to the relation between MCK and PERC or to MPCK and PERC respectively.

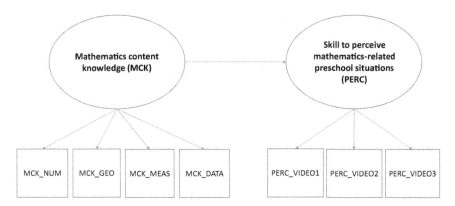

Fig. 5.1 Preschool teachers' cognitive skill to perceive mathematics-related preschool situations (PERC with three item-parcels as indicators) predicted by their MCK (four indicators: number, geometry, measurement and data) without controlling for g (for reasons of clarity residuals are omitted from the figure; a similar model was estimated with MPCK as a predictor)

5.1 Conceptual Framework

5.1.1 Preschool Teacher Cognition

Blömeke et al. (2015) developed a conceptual framework of teacher cognition that includes several systematic knowledge and situation-specific skill facets. Relying on Shulman (1986) and Weinert (2001), teacher knowledge was conceptualized as a multidimensional construct including content knowledge and pedagogical content knowledge as domain-specific facets. Preschool teachers' mathematics-related knowledge includes MCK and MPCK. MCK consists of knowledge about numbers and operations; geometry; quantity, measurement, and relation; as well as data, combinatorics and chance (Jenßen et al. 2015b). Although developed in the national context of Germany, this framework fits well to discussions elsewhere (Clements et al. 2004; National Research Council 2009). MPCK consists of knowledge about how to diagnose children's developmental state in mathematics and how to design informal learning environments that foster mathematical learning in children (Jenßen et al. 2015b). This framework is under discussion in other countries as well (NAEYC 2009).

As a crucial cognitive skill of preschool teachers, Dunekacke et al. (2014) identified the skill to perceive mathematics-related preschool situations (PERC). The informal situations in which preschool teachers are working are complex and characterized by a multitude of features (Perrez et al. 2001). For the teachers, it is important to perceive these features precisely, so that they can use them to foster mathematics learning in children (van Es and Sherin 2008). The perception process involves identifying what is important in the preschool situation, becoming aware of the mathematics-related opportunities in it, and of the ways in which children learn mathematics (Mason 2011).

Since Blömeke et al. (2015) had hypothesized that teachers' domain-specific knowledge predicted their domain-specific cognitive skills, Blömeke et al. (2015) and Dunekacke et al. (2014) developed a test-battery consisting of paper-and-pencil and video-based assessments to test this hypothesis.[1] The conceptual framework for this battery was derived from systematic analyses of all preschool teacher education curricula in Germany and of all German preschool standards (Jenßen et al. 2015a). Construct maps (Wilson 2005) summarized the results of these analyses in terms of sub-dimensions and specific descriptors representing the range of mathematics-related opportunities to learn during preschool teacher education and preschool objectives. Based on these, assessments of MCK, MPCK, and PERC were developed.

5.1.2 General and Domain-Specific Cognitive Abilities

Domain-specific cognition can be regarded as an element of crystallized intelligence (Gc) (Carroll 1993). Teachers acquire Gc in domain-specific opportunities to learn, for example during teacher education. We have evidence for this with respect to primary and lower secondary mathematics teachers' MCK, MPCK, and PERC (Blömeke et al. 2012; Perrez et al. 2001; Star and Strickland 2008). Gc is hypothesized to be influenced by a factor g which reflects broader general verbal, numerical, and figural cognitive skills.[2] Whether such an influence of g also applies to preschool teachers' domain-specific cognition has—to our knowledge—not yet been examined. Furthermore, the precise hierarchical relationship between g and the domain-specific facets is an open question too, because it can be modeled in different ways.

Gustafsson and Balke (1993) introduced the idea of conceptualizing g as a broad cognitive factor on which all cognitive indicators load. Additional smaller factors represent domain-specific constructs which account for additional systematic variance by allowing a second loading of the respective domain-specific indicators on the underlying construct. A set of generic indicators loads in this model on g only. Such a measurement approach is known as a NF model. Data from early studies by Gustafsson (1994) or Härnqvist et al. (1994) as well as recent studies, for example by Gignac (2008), supported such a direct hierarchical model with g directly impacting all cognitive indicators—no matter whether they are domain-specific or generic.

Transferred to the context of preschool teachers, such an NF model would mean that g was invested in the learning of MCK, MPCK, and PERC and that the

---

[1]We are grateful to Simone Dunekacke for providing us with her dataset for the purpose of this chapter.

[2]The many controversies around the relation of g and Gf or around the development of g, whether it is "nature or nurture", are not the topic of this paper and therefore are neglected.

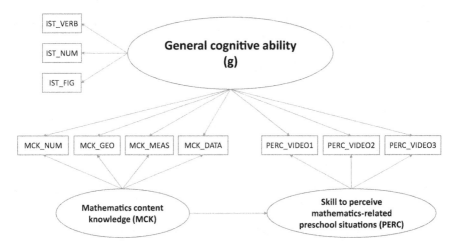

Fig. 5.2 An NF model of preschool teachers' MCK predicting their cognitive skill to perceive mathematics-related preschool situations whilst controlling for g (Verbal, Numerical and Figural subscores from the Intelligence Structure Test; a similar direct hierarchical model was estimated with MPCK as predictor)

teachers' probability to solve each item correctly, no matter whether it assesses MCK, MPCK, PERC, or g, was influenced by g (see as an example Fig. 5.2 displaying the effect of MCK on PERC while controlling for g). All observed variables have, thus, direct functional relationships with g. This approach should, at the same time, provide valid estimations of the predictive effect of MCK or MPCK respectively on PERC because the shared variance with g is "partialed out".

A competing hierarchical model to this NF model—with a shift in the conceptualization of g—is a second-order model in which g is conceptualized more narrowly (Holzinger and Swineford 1937) and where the effects of g, located at the higher level, are fully mediated by domain-specific latent constructs located on the lower level. The empirical results of these two models should be similar because the models are closely related from a mathematical point of view (although they are not completely the same because the second-order model is fully equivalent only to a constrained NF model; Gustafsson and Balke 1993; Yung et al. 1999).

An important difference exists with respect to conceptualization. A second-order model conceptualizes an indirect hierarchical relation between g, domain-specific latent constructs, and manifest indicators. In this case g is conceptualized as a latent construct directly underlying g-specific indicators only but not the indicators of the domain-specific latent constructs. Instead, the domain-specific indicators load on the domain-specific constructs which in turn are hypothesized to be influenced by g which, thus, explains the relation between the latent domain-specific constructs (see Fig. 5.3, again using the relation of MCK and PERC as an example). This traditional and widely used approach to intelligence research (Thurstone 1947) should also provide valid estimations of the predictive effect of MCK or MPCK respectively on PERC because g is controlled for.

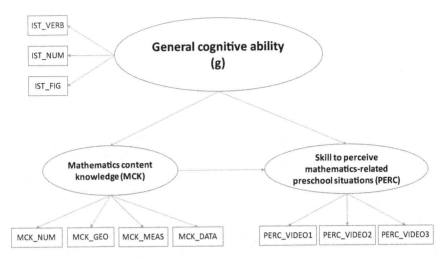

Fig. 5.3 Second-order factor model of preschool teachers' MCK predicting their cognitive skill to perceive mathematics-related preschool situations controlling for g (with three item-parcels from the Intelligence Structure Test (IST) as indicators; a similar indirect hierarchical model was estimated with MPCK as predictor)

5.2   Hypotheses

Based on the investment theory, g plays a role in all cognitive learning processes. First, it is therefore, hypothesized that MCK, MPCK, and PERC are significantly correlated with g (Hypothesis 1).

Second, it is hypothesized that due to the investment theory the strong predictive effect of MPCK on PERC, typically stated in models that do not include g, is weakened once g is included (Hypothesis 2). Given that a conceptual overlap exists between MPCK and PERC, the effect should still be significant though, and this no matter whether an NF model or a second-order model is applied. Hypothesizing a weakened but still significant effect is supported through evidence that MPCK and PERC are partly acquired through the same type of OTL (Blömeke et al., 2016).

The conceptual overlap of MCK and PERC is much smaller, if it exists at all. The level of mathematics needed to foster mathematical literacy of children aged between 3 and 6 is elementary (NCTM 2006). Furthermore, the amount of opportunities to learn MCK during preschool teacher education is low to non-existent (Blömeke et al. 2016) so that chances to develop this knowledge facet are weak. It may therefore be that basic numerical, figural, and verbal intelligence is of higher importance for the skill to perceive mathematics-related preschool situations than MCK so that the relation between MCK and PERC disappears once intelligence is introduced—and this again in both the NF model and the second-order model (Hypothesis 3).

The fourth research question concerns the model fit of the direct versus the indirect hierarchical approach. The question is whether the NF model or the second-order model fits better to the data. One limitation has to be noted here though and that is sample size. Mulaik and Quartetti (1997) pointed out that large samples are needed to identify empirical differences between the two approaches. We will therefore work with an open research question without formulating a specific hypothesis (Research Question 4).

5.3 Significance of the Study

Successfully assessing the impact of preschool teacher education on domain-specific teacher cognition independently of generic dispositions such as g is important given that the development of children's mathematical literacy strongly depends on the quality of the support provided by preschool teachers (Reynolds 1995). Therefore, preschool teachers should be competent at fostering children's mathematical development (Burchinal et al. 2008; Klibanoff et al. 2006).

After a long period of quietness around the structure of teacher cognition, a renaissance of debates about their hierarchical structure is to be noted due to an increase in research on teacher knowledge and skills. Teachers have previously not been covered by intelligence research because of a lack of instruments; this situation has changed substantially during the past five years. Several research groups in the context of the German research program "Modeling and measuring competencies acquired in higher education" (KoKoHs; Blömeke et al. 2013) have built on Gustafsson's work and transferred it to different domains of teacher cognition to assess the effects of education on domain-specific outcomes independently of the impact of intelligence as a generic disposition on these outcomes.

5.4 Methodology

5.4.1 Sample

The present study is part of the research project KomMa[3] which took place in Germany. The sample consisted of $n = 354$ prospective preschool teachers from 16 classes located at 5 vocational schools in the federal states of Berlin, Bremen, and Lower Saxony. The majority of the participants were female (about 83 %), and participants were on average 23 years old. In the study, 42 % of the participants

---

[3]KomMa was a joint research project of the Humboldt University of Berlin and the Alice Salomon University of Applied Sciences Berlin. It was funded by the Federal Ministry of Education and Research (FKZ: 01PK11002A) and part of the funding initiative "Modeling and Measuring Competencies in Higher Education (KoKoHs)."

were in their first year of training, 33 % were tested during their second year, and 26 % were in their final year of training.

Preschool education in Germany is voluntary and can be sub-divided into institutions covering 1–3 year olds and institutions covering 3–6 year olds. Teachers of the latter children represent the target population of this study. At this age, more than 90 % of the children are enrolled at least part-time—mostly during the morning—although parents have to pay a small fee (Statistisches Bundesamt 2014). Preschools are typically run by local municipalities, a church (mostly protestant or catholic), or a charity organization; some are organized privately with a special pedagogical profile, for example based on Montessori's work. Preschools are not part of the school system but of the child and youth welfare system and therefore assigned to ministries of family affairs instead of ministries of education so that care is much more stressed than formal education (Oberhuemer et al. 2010).

All 16 German states have recently implemented standards for preschools which mark ambitious cognitive objectives with respect to early reading, mathematics, and science literacy. Preschool teachers are trained differently in the 16 German states. The majority of preschool teachers (more than 90 %) are trained at vocational schools providing teacher education on the secondary or post-secondary level after 9 or 10 years of general schooling as well as having completed 2–4 years of vocational training in a caring profession (or similar type of education). This applies to the sample used for this paper.

5.4.2 Measures

The MCK test consisted of 24 items distinguishing between 4 mathematical domains, namely number and operations; geometry; quantity, measurement, and relation; as well as data, combinatorics, and chance. Half of the test items were presented in a multiple-choice format and half of the items in an open-response format. For the open-response items, coding directions were developed during the process of item construction (inter-rater reliability Cohen's $K = 0.95$–0.99). Cronbach's α was satisfying ($\alpha = 0.80$). The MPCK test consisted of 12 items covering the domains "diagnosing children's mathematical development" and "designing informal learning environments that foster mathematical learning". Most of the items were presented in a multiple-choice format, one item had an open-response format ($K = 0.88$). Test reliability was $\alpha = 0.65$.

Several studies with different samples confirmed factorial validity of the two knowledge tests (Blömeke et al. 2015). Content validity was also confirmed, and this through systematic expert reviews (Jenßen et al. 2015a).

The video-based assessment developed to measure PERC consisted of three 2–4 min clips which showed typical preschool situations with children between 3 and 6 years old, for example playing with building blocks, rule games, or situations during free play. The situations were recorded in the real context of a preschool and were used as item prompts. Clips were shown to the participants only once. After the presentation of each clip, participants had 6 min to work on 12 open-response items, e.g. "Please describe three aspects relevant from a mathematics education perspective in this situation and provide examples of evidence for each." Reliability was marginally satisfying ($\alpha = 0.53$). Content validity of the clips and of the items was confirmed in expert reviews (Dunekacke et al. in press). The experts' answers to the open-response items as well as data from pilot studies were used to generate coding directions. The inter-rater reliability was good (Yules Y $\geq$ 0.8).

In this study, g was assessed with the screening version of the Intelligence Structure Test (IST-screening; Liepmann et al. 2012) that provides information about numerical, verbal, and figural intelligence based on 20 items for each sub-scale. Reliability was satisfying ($\alpha = 0.87$).

Participants had firstly 80 min to complete the MCK and MPCK assessments. The IST and the video-based assessments were implemented on an additional occasion, one day to one week after the first one. Participants had 30 min to complete the intelligence screening and another 30 min to complete the video-based assessment. All assessments were given either by the authors or trained project assistants so that procedural objectivity was ensured.

5.4.3 Modeling and Data Analysis

The hypotheses were examined in a series of confirmatory factor analysis (CFA). Item-parcels were used as indicators, which meant that in the case of MCK the items of each of the four mathematical sub-domains, in the case of MPCK the items of two randomly generated test-halves that balanced mean and variance, and in the case of PERC the items of each of the three videos, were added up. Item-parceling is recommended when the structure of the latent constructs is the focus of interest of the research (Little et al. 2002) and when the sample is small so that it is desirable that fewer parameters have to be estimated (Bandalos and Finney 2001).

Data analysis was carried out using MPlus 5.2 software. The clustered data structure was taken into account by using a maximum-likelihood estimator with robust sandwich standard errors to protect against being too liberal (Muthén and Muthén 2007). Missing data were handled using the full-information maximum-likelihood procedure implemented in Mplus. The model fit was evaluated with the chi-square deviance and fit indices. A ratio of chi-square deviance and degrees of freedom of <2 indicates a very good model fit, estimates of <3 indicate a good fit. Estimates of the comparative fit index CFI > 0.95 indicate a very good model fit, estimates of >0.90 indicate a good model fit (Hu and Bentler 1999). Estimates of the root mean square error of approximation RMSEA < 0.05 indicate a very good model fit, estimates of <0.08 indicate a good model fit.

The hierarchical relation of intelligence, PERC, and MCK or MPCK respectively was modeled by applying NF models and second-order models (Gustafsson and Balke 1993). In the NF model, the general factor g is orthogonal to the domain-specific factors. Since the two models are nested within each other (see the formal prove provided by Yung et al. 1999), a chi-square difference test for NF models can be used to compare their model fit.

5.5 Results

5.5.1 Hypothesis 1: Latent Correlation Between MCK, MPCK, PERC, and g

As can be seen from Table 5.1, g is not only significantly correlated with MCK, MPCK, and PERC but this coincides also with a large effect size. Thus, the pre-condition is given that g indeed may have been invested in the learning of these domain-specific constructs. The correlation of $\Psi = 0.81$ between g and MCK was even near the threshold of $\Psi = 0.90$ above which constructs are commonly seen as empirically not distinguishable anymore.

The correlation matrix reveals in addition a convincing pattern in the sense that the two knowledge facets MCK and MPCK, as well as the two classroom-related constructs MPCK and PERC, tend to be more strongly correlated with each other ($\Psi = 0.66$ or $\Psi = 0.64$ respectively) than the knowledge facet MCK and the cognitive skill PERC ($\Psi = 0.55$). The same applies to the correlation pattern between g and PERC, MPCK, or MCK respectively.

5.5.2 Hypothesis 2: Strength of the Effect of MPCK on PERC When g Is Controlled for

Replicating the state of research, MPCK strongly predicted PERC in a model that did not include g (see Table 5.2). The effect size was large ($\beta = 0.64$). However, as hypothesized in both models that included g, the second-order model as well as the NF model, the strength of this relation was substantially lower in these cases ($\beta = 0.42$). Thus, the data supported Hypothesis 2.

Although the relation between MPCK and PERC was weakened when g was included in the model, MPCK still predicted significantly PERC as hypothesized,

Table 5.1 Correlation matrix of the latent constructs

	MCK	MPCK	PERC
MPCK	0.66 (0.07)	–	–
PERC	0.55 (0.10)	0.64 (0.10)	–
g	0.81 (0.06)	0.67 (0.07)	0.59 (0.13)

Note: *MCK* mathematics content knowledge, *MPCK* mathematics pedagogical content knowledge; *PERC* skill to perceive mathematics-related preschool situations

Table 5.2 Modeling the hierarchical relation between g, MPCK, and PERC

	MPCK1	MPCK2	PERC1	PERC2	PERC3	gVERB	gNUM	gFIG	PERC on MPCK	p	PERC on g	p	MPCK on g	p
Without g	0.74 (0.10)	0.68 (0.11)	0.49 (0.10)	0.50 (0.07)	0.60 (0.08)	–	–	–	0.64 (0.10)	<0.01	–	–	–	–
Second-order model	0.72 (0.09)	0.70 (0.10)	0.47 (0.09)	0.50 (0.06)	0.62 (0.07)	0.64 (0.06)	0.44 (0.10)	0.70 (0.09)	0.42 (0.21)	<0.05	0.31 (0.23)	0.18	0.65 (0.07)	<.01
Domain-specific nested factors in NF model	0.52 (0.06)	0.56 (0.06)	0.47 (0.08)	0.39 (0.06)	0.42 (0.07)				0.42 (0.18)	<0.05				
General factor in NF model	0.47 (0.09)	0.46 (0.07)	0.26 (0.08)	0.28 (0.09)	0.38 (0.08)	0.64 (0.06)	0.44 (0.10)	0.69 (0.10)			–	–	–	–

Note: *MPCK* mathematics pedagogical content knowledge; *PERC* skill to perceive mathematics-related preschool situations; table displays standardized factor loadings of the item-parcels on the respective latent construct (MPCK1–gFIG) and standardized regression coefficients with standard errors in brackets and this applied both to the NF model and the second-order model. The loading of the item-parcels of MPCK and PERC on the respective nested domain-specific factors were at least equal if not higher than those on the general factor. Thus, we can conclude that a significant domain-specific effect exists.

5.5.3   Hypothesis 3: Effect of MCK on PERC When g Is Controlled for

Again replicating the state of research, MCK significantly predicted PERC in a model that did not include g (see Table 5.3). But as hypothesized, the effect of MCK on PERC was not significant anymore once g was introduced—and this applied again to both the NFmodel and the second-order model. The relation between the two domain-specific constructs was even close to 0. Thus, the data supported Hypothesis 3. This conclusion was further supported by the high factor loading of the MCK item-parcels on g compared to the loadings on the domain-specific nested factor.

5.5.4   Research Question 4: Fit of the Hierarchical Models to the Data

Table 5.4 documents the fit parameters. All MPCK models showed a good fit, and all MCK models showed a very good fit to the data. The difference in fit between the NF model and the second-order model was negligible. In any case, it needs to be stated that the NF model did not show a better fit than the second-order model. In interpreting this result, one has to have in mind that the sample size does not meet the requirement set out by Mulaik and Quartetti (1997).

5.6   Discussion and Conclusions

The data clearly supported the hypotheses developed for this study with respect to prospective preschool teachers based on the investment theory (Cattell 1987) and Gustafsson's (2002) work. In this study, g was significantly, and with large effect sizes, correlated with the domain-specific constructs MCK, MPCK, and PERC. MPCK strongly predicted PERC, and this applied both to models that did *not* and that *did* control for g. However, the predictive effect was substantially lower in the latter case, no matter whether a second-order model or an NF model was applied. In contrast, although MCK significantly predicted PERC in a model that did not

Table 5.3 Modeling the hierarchical relation between g, MCK, and PERC

	MCK1	MCK2	MCK3	MCK4	PERC1	PERC2	PERC3	gVERB	gNUM	gFIG	PERC on MCK	p	PERC on g	p	MCK on g	p
Without g	0.74 (0.05)	0.75 (0.05)	0.66 (0.04)	0.59 (0.06)	0.50 (0.11)	0.51 (0.08)	0.57 (0.07)	–	–	–	0.47 (0.09)	<0.01	–	–	–	–
Second-order model	0.75 (0.04)	0.75 (0.04)	0.66 (0.03)	0.58 (0.06)	0.46 (0.11)	0.51 (0.06)	0.61 (0.07)	0.61 (0.04)	0.50 (0.09)	0.70 (0.08)	-0.08 (0.41)	0.85	0.63 (0.42)	0.14	0.80 (0.06)	<.01
Domain-specific nested factors	0.40 (0.07)	0.37 (0.06)	0.47 (0.08)	0.42 (0.06)	0.47 (0.08)	0.39 (0.06)	0.43 (0.07)	–	–	–	-0.01 (0.28)	0.86	–	–	–	–
General factor in NF model	0.62 (0.06)	0.63 (0.06)	0.50 (0.07)	0.43 (0.08)	0.27 (0.08)	0.27 (0.08)	0.35 (0.08)	0.61 (0.04)	0.49 (0.09)	0.69 (0.08)			–	–	–	–

Note: MCK mathematics content knowledge; PERC skill to perceive mathematics-related preschool situations; table displays standardized factor loadings of the item-parcels on the respective latent construct (MCK1–gFIG) and standardized regression coefficients with standard errors in brackets

Table 5.4 Fit of the different models to the data

	MCK as predictor of PERC						MPCK as predictor of PERC					
	X^2	df	p	X^2/df	CFI	RMSEA	X^2	df	p	X^2/df	CFI	RMSEA
Without g	19.8	13	0.10	1.5	0.98	0.04	14.0	4	0.01	3.5	0.95	0.09
Second-order model	47.7	32	<0.05	1.5	0.97	0.04	35.5	17	0.01	2.1	0.94	0.06
NF model	50.0	32	<0.05	1.6	0.97	0.04	36.0	17	<0.01	2.1	0.94	0.06
Δ second-nested	2.3	0			0	0	0.5	0			0	0

Note: *MCK* mathematics content knowledge; *MPCK* mathematics pedagogical content knowledge; *PERC* skill to perceive mathematics-related preschool situations

include g, this effect was not significant anymore once g was introduced—and this applied again to both the NF model and the second-order model.

First, these results suggest that intelligence was invested in the learning of the domain-specific constructs MPCK, MCK, and PERC and needs therefore to be controlled if the domain-specific effects of teacher education on outcomes are to be examined. Currently, this investment has not been acknowledged sufficiently in educational research. In the model of professional competencies developed by Blömeke et al. (2015), cognitive dispositions represented a fundamental requirement for all other competence facets. Intelligence is a cognitive disposition as well but has not yet been explicitly taken up in this model. Gustafsson's (1994, 2002; Gustafsson and Balke 1993; Gustafsson and Undheim 1996) previous work called for that, and provided suggestions about how to think of the relationship between these constructs. The present paper followed these suggestions and supported Gustafsson's call.

Second, of particular interest for teacher education is the relation between intelligence and the skill to perceive preschool situations appropriately. The conceptual overlap between preschool teachers' MCK and intelligence is rather obvious because in many studies mathematics items of this kind were chosen as indicators for intelligence (c.f. Anastasi 1964; McCallum et al. 2001); in particular numerical and figural abilities were often part of the definition of both constructs (see Liepmann et al. 2012). At the same time, Jenßen et al. (under review) provided for the first time evidence with respect to the assumption of a conceptual overlap between preschool teachers' MPCK and intelligence in that MPCK items comprise longer texts and reflect an interpersonal or communicative part of professional competence and, thus, include verbal intelligence as an inherent part. With the present paper, we could now also provide evidence with respect to such a conceptual overlap of PERC and intelligence. Intelligence can be seen as the ability to identify relations between objects and to interpret these relations (Thorndike 1921; Spearman 1927) which is close to perceptual skills. Correspondingly, neuroscience points out that the processing of visual information involves higher order cortical structures. Together with the need to evaluate and verbalize, processing the information presented in the videos is overlapping with intelligence.

Third, the results of the present study suggest that a substantial difference in the role and relevance of MCK and MPCK for prospective preschool teachers' cognitive skills exists. PERC was only predicted by g but no longer by MCK if g was included. Direct inferences from research on primary or even secondary teachers where MCK is of high relevance for instructional quality and student achievement to research on preschool teachers may therefore be too simplistic. Caution has to be applied given the difference in the level of mathematics involved. However, we need to point out that the sample used in this study was restricted to preschool teachers trained at vocational schools but not at pedagogical colleges. Opportunities to learn preschool mathematics "from a higher point of view" were almost non-existent. Future research should address this lack of heterogeneity with drawing students from colleges where they had appropriate OTL in mathematics.

Fourth, based on our study we cannot decide whether the NF model or the second-order model fit better to the data. Thus, we cannot decide whether it is more appropriate to conceptualize g as a rather broad construct with a direct functional influence of g on all items or as a narrower construct with direct effects on the latent constructs MCK, MPCK, and PERC, which in turn only influence the probability to solve the items correctly. The difference between the two models was not significant. One limitation has to be noted here though and that is the sample size. Mulaik and Quartetti (1997) had pointed out that large samples are needed to identify empirical differences between the two approaches. Thus, another urgent research gap calls for attention.

Acknowledgments In light of the significant contributions to educational measurement by Jan-Eric Gustafsson, the Centre for Educational Measurement at the University of Oslo (CEMO) in Norway honors this outstanding colleague—together with another Nordic scholar, Anders Skrondal—through creating the *Gustafsson and Skrondal Visiting Scholarship*. Each year the visiting scholar program will host up to two young researchers to participate in and enrich the research community at CEMO. All Gustafsson and Skrondal scholars are expected to embody the principles of sound scientific inquiry and intellectual vibrancy of this namesake.

References

Anastasi, A. (1964). Culture-fair testing. *Educational Horizons, 43*, 26–30.

Bandalos, D. L., & Finney, S. J. (2001). Item parceling issues in structural equation modeling. In G. A. Marcoulides & R. E. Schumacker (Eds.), *Advanced structural equation modeling: New developments and techniques*. Mahwah, NJ: Lawrence Erlbaum Associates, Inc.

Blömeke, S., & Delaney, S. (2012). Assessment of teacher knowledge across countries: A review of the state of research. *ZDM—The International Journal on Mathematics Education, 44*, 223–247.

Blömeke, S., Suhl, U., Kaiser, G., & Döhrmann, M. (2012). Family background, entry selectivity and opportunities to learn: What matters in primary teacher education? An international comparison of fifteen countries. *Teaching and Teacher Education, 28*, 44–55.

Blömeke, S., Zlatkin-Troitschanskaia, O., Kuhn, Ch., & Fege, J. (Eds.) (2013). *Modeling and measuring competencies in higher education: Tasks and challenges*. Rotterdam, The Netherlands: Sense Publishers.

Blömeke, S., Busse, A., Suhl, U., Kaiser, G., Benthien, J., Döhrmann, M., & König, J. (2014). Entwicklung von Lehrpersonen in den ersten Berufsjahren: Längsschnittliche Vorhersage von Unterrichtswahrnehmung und Lehrerreaktionen durch Ausbildungsergebnisse. *Zeitschrift für Erziehungswissenschaft, 17*(3), 509–542.

Blömeke, S., Jenßen, L., Dunekacke, S., Suhl, U., Grassmann, M., & Wedekind. H. (2015). Professionelle Kompetenz von Erzieherinnen messen: Entwicklung und Validierung standardisierter Leistungstests für frühpädagogische Fachkräfte. *Zeitschrift für Pädagogische Psychologie, 29* (3–4), 177–191.

Blömeke, S., Dunekacke, S., Jenßen, L., Grassmann, M., & Wedekind, H. (2016). Process mediates structure: The relation between preschool teacher education and preschool teachers' knowledge. *Journal of Educational Psychology*. http://dx.doi.org/10.1037/edu0000147

Blömeke, S., Gustafsson, J.-E., & Shavelson, R. (2015). Beyond dichotomies: Competence viewed as a continuum. *Zeitschrift für Psychologie/Journal of Psychology, 223*, 3–13.

Burchinal, M., Howes, C., Pianta, R., Bryant, D., Early, D., Clifford, R., & Barbarin, O. (2008). Predicting child outcomes at the end of kindergarten from the quality of pre-kindergarten teacher-child interactions and instruction. *Applied Developmental Sciences, 12*(3), 140–153.

Carroll, J. B. (1993). *Human cognitive abilities: A survey of factor-analytic studies.* Cambridge: Cambridge University Press.

Cattell, R. B. (1987). *Intelligence: Its structure, growth and action.* New York: North-Holland.

Clements, D. H., Sarama, J., & DiBiase, A.-M. (Eds.). (2004). *Engaging young children in mathematics: Standards for early childhood mathematics.* Mahwah, NJ: Lawrence Erlbaum.

Dunekacke, S., Jenßen, L., Grassmann, M., & Blömeke, S. (2014). Prognostische Validität mathematikdidaktischen Wissens angehender Erzieher/-innen: Studiendesign und Datengrundlage. In J. Roth & J. Ames (Hrsg.), *Beiträge zum Mathematikunterricht* (= Tagungsband der 48. Tagung für Didaktik der Mathematik in Koblenz). Münster: Verlag für wissenschaftliche Texte und Medien. http://www.mathematik.uni-dortmund.de/ieem/bzmu2013/Einzelvortraege/BzMU13-Dunekacke.pdf

Dunekacke, S., Jenßen, L., & Blömeke, S. (2015a). Effects of mathematics content knowledge on pre-school teachers' performance: A video-based assessment of perception and planning abilities in informal learning situations. *International Journal of Science and Mathematics Education, 13*, 267–286.

Dunekacke, S., Jenßen, L., & Blömeke, S. (2015b). Mathematikdidaktische Kompetenz von Erzieherinnen und Erziehern: Validierung des KomMa-Leistungstests durch die videogestützte Erhebung von Performanz. *Zeitschrift für Pädagogik; 61. Beiheft*, 80–99.

Dunekacke, S., Jenßen, L., Eilerts, K., & Blömeke, S. (in press). Epistemological beliefs of prospective pre-school teachers and their relation to knowledge, perception and planning abilities in the field of mathematics: A process-model. *ZDM—The International Journal on Mathematics Education.*

Gignac, G. E. (2008). Higher-order models versus direct hierarchical models: g as superordinate or breadth factor? *Psychology Science Quarterly, 50*, 21–43

Gustafsson, J.-E. (1994). Hierarchical models of intelligence and educational achievement. In A. Demetriou & A. Efklides (Eds.), *Intelligence, mind, and reasoning: Structure and development.* Amsterdam: Elsevier Science B.V.

Gustafsson, J. -E. (2002). Measurement from a hierarchical point of view. In H. I. Braun, D. N. Jackson & D. E. Wiley (Eds.), *The role of constructs in psychological and educational measurement* (pp. 73–95). London: Lawrence Erlbaum Associates.

Gustafsson, J.E., & Balke, G. (1993). General and specific abilities as predictors of school achievement. *Multivariate Behavioral Research, 28*(4), 407–434.

Gustafsson, J.-E., & Undheim, J. O. (1996). Individual differences in cognitive functions. In D. Berliner & R. Calfee (Eds.), *Handbook of Educational Psychology* (pp. 186–242), New York: Macmillan.

Härnqvist, K., Gustafsson, J.-E., Muthén, B.O., & Nelson, G. (1994). Hierarchical models of ability at individual and class levels. *Intelligence, 18*, 165–187.

Holzinger, K. J., & Swineford, F. (1937). The bi-factor method. *Psychometrika, 2.* 42–54.

Hu, L. T., & Bentler, P. M. (1999). Cutoff criteria for fit indexes in covariance structure analysis: Conventional criteria versus new alternatives. *Structural Equation Modeling, 6*, 1–55.

Jensen, A. R. (1998). *The g factor: The science of mental ability.* Westport, CT.: Praeger.

Jenßen, L., Dunekacke, S., Gustafsson, J.-E., & Blömeke, S. (under review). The relation of intelligence and competence: Clarifying the hierarchy of preschool teachers' cognitive abilities.

Jenßen, L., Dunekacke, S., & Blömeke, S. (2015a). Qualitätssicherung in der Kompetenzforschung: Empfehlungen für den Nachweis von Validität in Testentwicklung und Veröffentlichungspraxis. *Zeitschrift für Pädagogik, 61. Beiheft.*

Jenßen, L., Dunekacke, S., Baack, W., Tengler, M., Koinzer, T., Schmude, C., Wedekind, H., Grassmann, M., & Blömeke, S. (2015b). KomMa: Kompetenzmodellierung und Kompetenzmessung bei frühpädagogischen Fachkräften im Bereich Mathematik (pp. 59–79). In B. Koch-Priewe, A. Köker, J. Seifried & E. Wuttke (Eds.), *Kompetenzerwerb an*

Hochschulen: Modellierung und Messung. Zur Professionalisierung angehender Lehrerinnen und Lehrer sowie frühpädagogischer Fachkräfte. Bad Heilbrunn: Klinkhardt.

Klibanoff, R., Levine, S.C., Huttenlocher, J., Vasilyeva, M., & Hedges, L. (2006). Preschool Children's Mathematical Knowledge: The effect of teacher "math talk". *Developmental Psychology, 42*(1), 59–69.

Liepmann, D., Beauducel, A., Brocke, B., & Nettelnstroth, W. (2012). *Intelligenz-Struktur-Test Screening (IST-Screening).* Göttingen: Hogrefe.

Little, T. D., Cunningham, W. A., Shahar, G., & Widaman, K. F. (2002). To parcel or not to parcel: Exploring the question, weighing the merits. *Structural Equation Modeling, 9,* 151–173.

Mason, Sh. D. (2011). *The relationship between teachers' preparation and perceived level of technology use in mathematics with middle school African American males.* Doctoral dissertation, Texas A&M University.

McCallum, R. S., Bracken, B. A., & Wasserman, J. D. (2001). *Essentials of nonverbal assessment* (Essentials of psychological assessment series). Hoboken, NJ, US: Wiley.

McGrew, K. S. (2005). The Cattell-Horn-Carroll theory of cognitive abilities: Past, present, and future. In D. P. Flanagan, J. L. Genshaft & P. L. Harrison (Eds.), *Contemporary intellectual assessment: Theories, tests, and issues* (pp. 136–182). New York: Guilford.

Mulaik, St. A., & Quartetti, D. A. (1997). First order or higher order general factor? *Structural Equation Modeling: A Multidisciplinary Journal, 3,* 193–211.

Muthén, L. K., & Muthén, B. O. (2007). *Mplus User's Guide* (5th ed.). Los Angeles, CA: Muthén & Muthén.

NAEYC (2009). *Developmentally appropriate practice in early childhood programs serving children from birth through age 8: A position statement of the National Association for the Education of Young Children.* https://www.naeyc.org/files/naeyc/file/positions/PSDAP.pdf

National Research Council (2009). *Mathematics learning in early childhood: Paths toward excellence and equity.* Washington, DC: National Academies Press.

NCTM = National Council of Teachers of Mathematics (2006). *Curriculum focal points for pre-kindergarten through grade 8 mathematics: A quest for coherence.* NCTM.

Oberhuemer, P., Schreyer, I., & Neuman, M. J. (2010). *Professionals in early childhood education and care systems: European profiles and perspectives.* Opladen & Farmington Hills, MI: Barbara Budrich.

Perrez, M., Huber, G.L., & Geissler, K.A. (2001). Psychologie der pädagogischen Interaktion. In A. Krapp & B. Weidenmann (Hrsg.), *Pädagogische Psychologie – Ein Lehrbuch* (pp. 357–413). Weinheim: Urban & Schwarzenberg.

Reynolds, A. (1995). One year of preschool intervention or two: Does it matter? *Early Childhood Research Quarterly, 10,* 1–31.

Shulman, L. (1986). Those who understand: Knowledge growth in teaching. *Educational Researcher, 15,* 4–14.

Spearman, C. (1927). *The abilities of man: Their nature and measurement.* London: Macmillan.

Star, J. R., & Strickland, S. K. (2008). Learning to observe: Using video to improve preservice mathematics teachers' ability to notice. *Journal of Mathematics Teacher Education, 11,* 107–125.

Statistisches Bundesamt (2014). *Statistiken der Kinder- und Jugendhilfe: Kinder und tätige Personen in Tageseinrichtungen und in öffentlich geförderter Kindertagespflege am 01.03.2014.* Wiesbaden: Statistisches Bundesamt.

Tatto, M. T., Schwille, J., Senk, S. L., Ingvarson, L., Rowley, G., Peck, R., et al. (2012). *Policy, practice, and readiness to teach primary and secondary mathematics in 17 countries: Findings from the IEA Teacher Education and development Study in Mathematics (TEDS-M).* Amsterdam: IEA.

Thorndike, E. L. (1921). Intelligence and its measurement: A symposium. *Journal of Educational Psychology, 12,* 123–147, 195–216, 271–275.

Thurstone, L. L. (1947). *Multiple factor analysis.* Chicago: University of Chicago Press.

van Es, E. A., & Sherin, M. G. (2008). Mathematics teachers' "learning to notice" in the context of a video club. *Teaching and Teacher Education, 24,* 244–276.

Weinert, F. E. (2001). Concept of competence: A conceptual classification. In D. S. Rychen & L. H. Salganik (Eds.), *Defining and selecting key competencies.* Göttingen, Germany: Hogrefe.

Wilson, M. (2005). *Constructing measures: An item response modeling approach.* Mahwah, NJ: Lawrence Erlbaum Associates.

Yung, Y.-F., Thissen, D., & McLeod, L. (1999). On the relationship between the higher-order factor model and the hierarchical factor model. *Psychometrika, 64*(2), 113–128.

Part II
Causes and Effects of Educational Achievement

Chapter 6
Searching for Causality to Develop and Test Theoretical Models of Educational Effectiveness Research

Leonidas Kyriakides and Bert P.M. Creemers

Abstract Educational Effectiveness Research (EER) addresses the question of what works in education and why. Because the topic of causality is rarely addressed explicitly in the field of education, in this chapter we discuss its meaning by looking at different orientations within the research methodology and examine the potential importance of searching for causality within EER. This chapter also refers to different research methods that have been used to demonstrate causal relations within EER and seeks to identify the strengths and methodological limitations of demonstrating causality through cross-sectional studies and experimental studies. Emphasis is also given to the use of international educational evaluation studies in developing and testing the theoretical framework of EER.

6.1 Introduction

Educational Effectiveness Research (EER) can be seen as an overarching theme that links together a conglomerate of research in different areas: including research on teacher behavior and its impacts, curriculum, student grouping procedures, school organization, and educational policy. The main research question underlying EER is the identification and investigation of which factors in the teaching, curriculum, and learning environments (operating at different levels such as the classroom, the school, and above-school) can directly or indirectly explain measured differences (variations) in the outcomes of students. Further, such research frequently takes into account the influence of other important background characteristics, such as student

L. Kyriakides (✉)
Department of Education, University of Cyprus, Nicosia, Cyprus
e-mail: kyriakid@ucy.ac.cy

B.P.M. Creemers
Department Educational Science, Faculty of Behavioural and Social Sciences,
Educational Science, University of Groningen, Groningen, The Netherlands

© Springer International Publishing AG 2017
M. Rosén et al. (eds.), *Cognitive Abilities and Educational Outcomes*,
Methodology of Educational Measurement and Assessment,
DOI 10.1007/978-3-319-43473-5_6

ability, socio-economic status (SES), and prior attainment. Thus, EER attempts to establish and test theories which explain why and how some schools and teachers are more effective than others in promoting better learning outcomes for students. The proposed models are multilevel in nature and refer to factors which are expected to have direct and/or indirect effects on student learning (Scheerens 2013). As a consequence, EER deals in one way or another with causal relations. However, most effectiveness studies refer to factors that are associated with student achievement but successful prediction of learning outcomes is something quite different from identifying causal relations between effectiveness factors and student learning outcomes (Creemers et al. 2010). Because the topic of causality is rarely addressed explicitly in the field of education (Angrist 2004), in this chapter we discuss its meaning by looking at different orientations within the research methodology and discuss the importance of searching for causality within EER. Thus, this chapter refers to different research methods that have been used to demonstrate causal relations within EER and seeks to identify their strengths and methodological limitations. Specifically, we discuss the strengths and limitations of searching for causality by conducting experimental and cross-sectional studies. Special emphasis is also given to the use of international educational evaluation studies such as PISA and TIMSS in developing and testing the theoretical framework of EER. It should be acknowledged that qualitative as well as mixed research methods can also be used to search for factors that may affect student learning outcomes under specific conditions (Teddlie and Sammons 2010). Denzin and Lincoln (1998) have argued that besides experiments and quasi-experimental, large-scale studies, life-world stories based on observational data (subjected to analytical induction) can also contribute in identifying factors affecting dependent variables (e.g. student learning outcomes). Although we see the benefits of using this approach in exploring cause and effect relations, the limitations in generalizing the results of these approaches should also be acknowledged.

6.2 Searching for Causality to Understand the Concept of Educational Effectiveness

Locke (1975) argues that a cause is any construct that makes any other variable change its functioning over time. For instance, in the case of EER cause can be attributed to a specific school/teacher factor that is shown to make schools more effective (i.e. helping students improve their achievement in relation to specific learning aims). At the same time an "effect" is seen as a variable which is influenced by another construct. However, Shadish et al. (2002) claim that we very rarely know all of the potential causes of our observed effects or indeed how they may relate to one another. Moreover, Holland (1986) argues that a cause can never be determined unequivocally and it is likely that some effects represent the result of combinations of factors or interactions between them. For EER, this implies a need to try and identify the probability that particular effects will occur.

Estimating *the likelihood* that an effect will occur gives the opportunity for researchers to explore why certain effects seem to occur in some situations but not in others. This also fits well with the kind of statistical approaches used in EER models that typically identify the proportion of variance in outcomes that can be statistically explained or accounted for by different combinations of predictors (Creemers et al. 2010).

Further to the issues of causality and statistical modeling, it is helpful to distinguish between the inference model that is used to specify the relationship between a hypothesized causal factor and its predicted effect and the statistical procedures that are used to determine the strength of this relationship. Researchers should make the focus of their study explicit, deciding whether it is concerned with identifying the effect of a cause or the cause of an effect. For example, if we investigate the extent to which the use of the dynamic approach to teacher professional development (Creemers et al. 2013) promotes quality of teaching as compared to other approaches (e.g. the competency based approach), then an experiment can be designed in which the effect of each approach is compared by using some appropriate measure of teaching skills. If teachers who are exposed to one approach score higher (on average) in the scale measuring quality of teaching than do those exposed to the other, and if the teachers in the two groups are equivalent in all respects other than their assignment to groups adopting each approach (as can often be achieved by randomization), then the researcher can conclude that the higher scores are likely to be the result of the use of one approach rather than the other. This argument implies that when correctly implemented, the randomized controlled experiment is a powerful design for detecting the treatment effects of interventions. A random assignment of participants to treatment conditions assures that treatment group assignment is independent of the pre-treatment characteristics of group members. It is therefore assumed that differences between the groups can be attributed to treatment effects rather than to the pre-treatment characteristics. However, this assumption cannot be easily tested especially since it is not feasible to allocate an individual (in the same time) at the treatment and the control group. Moreover, randomized experiments search for treatment effects and attempt to measure the magnitude of these effects; they do not help us understand the underlying mechanisms (i.e. why treatments differ in their impacts) that are contributing to such effects. In turn, this necessitates a role for theory. When there is a strong reason to believe that one treatment may be more effective than another, an experimental approach is warranted for detecting such likely treatment effects (e.g. as in research on the impact of reductions in class size where it is hypothesized that student attainment should be higher in smaller classes). Although randomized controlled experiments are designed to detect average differences in the effects of different treatments on outcomes of interest, researchers need to recognize that there are a series of important and necessary steps that precede the design of an experiment and these are discussed in the second part of this chapter. It should also be acknowledged that an experimental study is not always the best approach for demonstrating causality. For example, if we already have valid evidence in favor of one treatment, it would be unethical to administer the old treatment to a group of students simply because we want to measure the size of the effect of this treatment. Thus, the use of cross-sectional studies for demonstrating causality is also discussed in this chapter.

6.2.1   Demonstrating Causality Through Cross-Sectional Studies

Researchers within EER made use of studies involving multisample comparisons since several international comparative studies were being (or had been) conducted such as TIMSS and PIRLS. Some of the most important theoretical and method-ological work in educational research has resulted from data analyses using large-scale national datasets such as the Early Childhood Longitudinal Study (ECLS) and the National Education Longitudinal Study of 1988–2000 (NELS). In addition, the number of dissertations, articles in refereed journals, and other pub-lications that have been written from these national datasets is extremely high. This can be attributed to the fact that large-scale datasets that are drawn from multistage probability samples allow for predictive analyses and thereby tentative causal inference (Gustafsson 2013). With such data, researchers can estimate the probable effects of certain conditions for specific populations over time. In instances where there are data elements about school or pedagogical practices, analytic techniques can estimate the likelihood of what would happen if certain organizational, insti-tutional, or instructional reforms were implemented on a larger scale. At this point, we acknowledge the advantages of using longitudinal rather than cross-sectional designs to study causality. When multiple observations of each subject are avail-able, this offers additional possibilities for causal inferences (Gustafsson 2010; Scherer and Gustafsson 2015). Within social sciences, longitudinal designs have frequently been employed to collect information about background variables, possible independent (e.g. effectiveness factors) and dependent variables (e.g. student learning outcomes). In this way, researchers can search for variables that change or remain stable over time. Since it is assumed that the units under study have characteristics which remain constant over time and others which change, the difference-in-difference analysis can be used to search for causal relations. However, longitudinal designs are costly, and fraught with problems caused by attrition. In this respect, a study need not be longitudinal at the individual level, but can be so at other levels of observation. For example, the international studies of educational achievement (e.g. PISA, TIMSS) measure trends in the development of achievement and can have a longitudinal design at the country level (Gustafsson 2013). Thus, secondary analyses of PISA by using the country-level longitudinal dimension of this international study searched for the effect of various educational policies on student learning outcomes (Hanushek et al. 2013)

Datasets of cross-sectional studies can also be used to approximate randomized controlled experiments. For example, matched sampling can be used to assess the causal effects of interventions when randomized experiments cannot be conducted (Rubin 2006). Over the past three decades in particular, statisticians and econo-metricians have developed several methods of analysis for making causal inferences with observational data such as those found in large-scale national datasets. There are several advantages to using large-scale nationally representative datasets to search for factors associated with differences in student achievement (Gustafsson 2013). As one would expect, such studies are based on nationally representative samples of students, their parents, schools, and teachers (readers should bear in mind that international studies may not have representative samples: for instance TIMSS does not have a representative sample of teachers). However, when the matched sampling approach is used some students are removed in order to establish two comparable groups. As a consequence, the two groups upon which the analysis is based are likely not to be representative of the whole population. Obviously, this limitation is rather small compared to what one may achieve (i.e. establishing a kind of "randomized experiment" with large-scale (inter)national studies). Another problem that researchers may have to face is ending up with less statistical power in detecting differences between the two groups especially if the two groups end up to be much smaller in size. On the other hand, randomized controlled experiments are designed to yield valid causal results but often have limited generalizability in establishing the impact of specific interventions. By comparison, large-scale national educational studies are typically designed to be generalizable to specific populations of students and allow changes in the outcomes of interest (e.g. in overall educational standards). This permits large-scale datasets to be seen as rich sources of descriptive information on students, teachers, and schools.

Because they are based on large, nationally representative samples, large-scale (inter)national datasets are also useful in studying the characteristics and achievement of sub-groups such as minority and low-income students, groups that are often tar-geted for educational interventions that aim to improve school effectiveness. In addition, such datasets are often longitudinal which makes it possible to measure achievement gains at both the individual and group levels over time (De Fraine et al. 2007). They can also be used to develop plausible hypotheses regarding the likely causes of differences in student achievement gains and can inform the design of subsequent randomized controlled trials for hypothesis-confirming purposes. For example, these datasets can be used to identify promising interventions and target sub-groups that are thought to be most likely to benefit. They may also suggest potential causal mechanisms that may explain why the functioning of a school factor (e.g. school policy on parental involvement) may have positive effects on student achievement. Moreover, when randomized controlled trials are not feasible (e.g. for measuring the absolute effect of schooling) large-scale nationally representative studies may provide the best source of data on which to base studies that seek to explore the existence of possible causal relations using alternative approaches such as regression discontinuity (Kyriakides and Luyten 2009), propensity score matching (Rubin 2006), or instrumental variables (IV) regression (Winship and Morgan 1999).

Despite the strengths of these studies however, one can also identify some serious methodological weaknesses in attempts by researchers to claim causality by using cross-sectional data and searching for correlations between the functioning of specific factors at different levels (e.g. teacher, school, country) and variation in student achievement outcomes. The main problem of this approach is that large-scale observational datasets do not typically feature a random assignment of individuals or schools to treatment and control groups. Therefore, researchers must be aware of the trade-offs that are involved in choosing experimental versus non-experimental designs when both can be used to address a particular research question and both are logistically and ethically feasible. The most important weaknesses of the cross-sectional approach are outlined below.

First, an issue that needs further attention is the measurement of effectiveness that is based only on a measure of student outcomes without controlling for differences in prior achievement. For example, the inclusion of aptitude variables in IEA studies could lead to more coherent conclusions since the effect of this variable in effectiveness studies, which have collected data on various background characteristics (e.g. aptitude/prior attainment level, gender, SES), has consistently revealed that the effect of aptitude/prior attainment is stronger than the effect of student SES. Moreover, studies that do not take into account aptitude may not be able to explain significant proportions of the variance in later student achievement that is situated at the student level and so such models are very likely to lack appropriate statistical control (or these are under or misspecified). From this perspective, it can be argued that the inclusion of variables such as prior attainment in future comparative and cross-sectional studies should be taken into account. However, even if such measures are taken into account, there are still important problems in arguing that the results of the usually employed multilevel modelling procedure reveals a causal relation between the explanatory variables situated at different levels and student outcome measures which are treated as dependent variables.

A typical effectiveness study following a cross-sectional design usually measures the achievement outcomes of students in a set of schools within a country. Information is collected about specific factors situated at different levels such as student characteristics (e.g. SES, gender), teacher characteristics (e.g. teacher behavior in the classroom, teacher experience/knowledge), and school characteristics (e.g. school policy on teaching, school learning environment). Using different kinds of statistical analyses (such as regression analysis) these background and contextual factors are treated as independent variables and their statistical relation with achievement (ability to predict variation in achievement) is determined. However, it is possible to confuse the direction of causality in cross-sectional data and so caution should be exercised before attempting to make causal statements based on analyses of such data. For this reason, a theory that refers to how and why specific factors affect student learning outcomes should be taken into account when interpreting the findings of an effectiveness study (Creemers and Kyriakides 2015).

The problem of confusion over the direction of causality is well known in virtually every social science. Sociologists and psychologists refer to this difficulty as the problem of "reversed causality". In econometrics, the difficulty in drawing causal relations from cross-sectional data is called an "endogeneity" problem. This term is more general and refers both to the problem of "reversed causality" and omitted variables (see, Hanushek and Woessmann 2011). Yet another term used for the difficulty of drawing causal relations is the "selection bias", which means that the levels of performance of the different groups of our sample may not be comparable before they received a treatment and this has then biased subsequent results. A typical example of this problem is provided by Lazear (2001) who has developed a model to account for the effects of variation in class size. This model shows that there is a selection bias in studies searching for the effect of class size since it is demonstrated that larger sized classes tend to be populated by higher performing students (because in many schools lower ability students may be taught in smaller groups as a form of support). However, irrespective of the term that is used to describe this problem, one should be aware that this difficulty is very likely to occur in cross-sectional studies, especially when a study is conducted at the individual/student level. One way to minimize this problem is to statistically control for the differences between students that existed before a treatment was applied. This approach requires the measurement of pre-existing differences but in cross-sectional studies, such measures are usually not taken into account. Although researchers may address this problem by using the IV approach, in practice it is difficult to find appropriate IV variables (especially within the context of educational research). As a consequence, this technique has not been systematically used so far in the field of EER. In this respect, during the last decade longitudinal designs have become used more frequently and thereby data has become available on prior achievement and/or other aptitude variable(s) as well as on these measures after treatment (i.e. at the end of a school year or a specific period of schooling). This implies that it is now possible for researchers in the area of EER to use such designs and draw stronger arguments about likely cause and effect relationships. These designs could also be used to search not only for causal but also for reciprocal relations (see, Kyriakides et al. 2015).

Before we move to the discussion of other methodological problems that tend to arise from using cross-sectional studies to search for causal relations, it also is acknowledged that national datasets are now available and researchers within EER should make use of the different procedures that have been developed in order to adjust for selection bias. One of the earliest and best known of these techniques was developed by Heckman (1979). In a two-step procedure, a multiple regression model is first estimated for an outcome of interest (e.g. mathematics achievement) before a selection model is then estimated that compares those who participated in a program against those who did not. If differences between participants and non-participants are detected, then adjustments are made to the first model to correct for these. However, there are limitations to the procedures used to correct for selection bias. These mainly arise from the fact that the selection model used to detect and correct for selection differences may be misspecified, such as when important variables are missing. Another method that can be used to try to correct for selection bias is adjusting outcomes for relevant observed variables that are correlated with both the outcome and the independent variables of interest (termed *observable selection bias*; Barnow et al. 1980). Nonetheless, it should still be acknowledged that unobserved characteristics may continue to bias estimates of program effects even when this method is employed.

From the notion of observable selection bias comes the observation that a potential source of erroneous causal inference from cross-sectional data is that concerned with the problem of omitted variables. For example, when an independent variable is related to a dependent variable in a statistical model and the estimated relation is interpreted in causal terms, it is assumed that there are no other independent variables associated with the independent variable being studied (no multicolinearity). However, if such omitted variables do exist they will lead to bias in the estimated causal relations if they are correlated with the regression residual associated with the dependent variable, possibly leading researchers to ascribe causality to variables other than the ones that are really involved. Theoretically, one approach to solve this problem would be to measure and analyze all potential variables. However, it is practically impossible to include all relevant variables even if a strong theory is available to help researchers select all of these. Therefore, the problem of omitting variables may lead researchers to consider some independent variables as causes whereas in practice, the independent variables that are really involved in a cause and effect relationship may have been ignored because they were either not measured, or not included in a statistical model.

Further to the point of omitted variables, social scientists have developed several methods to adjust for observed and/or omitted variables when making comparisons across groups using observational data. The following three methods are mainly used: (a) fixed effects models, (b) propensity score matching, and (c) regression discontinuity designs. Some studies within EER used the regression discontinuity design and indicated the possibility of measuring the effect of schooling (Heck and Moriyama 2010; Kyriakides and Luyten 2009). Concerning propensity score matching, this is a technique aiming at estimating the predicted probability that individuals with certain characteristics would be assigned to a treatment group when assignment is non-random (Rubin 2006). The main advantage of using propensity score matching is that it aggregates a number of characteristics that individually would be very difficult to match amongst those in the treatment and the control groups. For example, if researchers are interested in measuring the impact of remedial teaching on student achievement, one could assume that students from disadvantaged families are much more likely to attend this type of provision in schools. On the other hand, students of upper middle class families might have a relatively smaller probability of attending such provision because of the link between SES and achievement level. To approach a random assignment trial, a comparison should be made between individuals who have a reasonable probability of being chosen to be in either the treatment (e.g. remedial teaching program) or the control group. Students with similar propensities to be in the treatment group (whether they are actually in the treatment group or not) can then be matched on the basis of their propensity scores. As a consequence, the difference in subsequent achievement scores would then be closer to the difference we would expect in a random assignment of these students to the two groups.

Propensity scores address an important issue in empirical research, namely providing estimates of effects for certain groups when randomization is not possible (e.g. remedial teaching), and where sample elements have self-selected themselves into treatment or control conditions (e.g. when teachers decide by themselves which INSET programs they will attend). However, propensity score matching adjusts only for *observed* characteristics. Because a large number of background characteristics are used in calculating propensity scores, the probability that a relevant variable has been omitted from analysis, although reduced, is not eliminated. Nevertheless, it is also possible to test the sensitivity of subsequent results to hypothesized omitted variables (Rosenbaum 2002). Because an aggregate of characteristics is used to compute propensity scores and analytic samples are restricted to individuals (or schools) that can be matched across treatment conditions, propensity scores are more effective at approximating randomized assignment when large, nationally representative datasets are used. In such cases, the samples on which these datasets are based are sufficiently large to allow for the analyses of a sub-sample and contain comprehensive information on the background characteristics of students and schools. If selection into the analysis is unbiased (e.g. exclusions due to missing data do not result in differences between the analysis sample and the larger sample) then subsequent results may also be generalizable back to the population of students or schools.

There are important limits to survey analysis even when adjustments for selection bias and multiple levels of analysis are used. Since populations are heterogeneous, an estimate of the relationship between an effectiveness factor and student outcomes (that have been corrected for selection bias) may not be applicable to groups that have a low probability of falling into either the treatment or control group. However, in the last few years, analyses of large-scale datasets using the methods mentioned above have produced several important findings concerning educational effectiveness, some of which have implications for causal inference and for the design of randomized experiments. Similarly, longitudinal research from the Effective Provision of Pre-School, Primary, and Secondary Education (EPPSE) project in England has demonstrated the impact of both duration and quality of pre-school on young children's cognitive and social behavioral development (Hall et al. 2013).

6.2.2 Demonstrating Causality Through Experimental Studies

The foregoing discussion about the advantages and limitations of cross-sectional studies reveals the need to consider the possibility of carrying out experimental studies in order to demonstrate causal relations between certain factors of interest and changes in student achievement. However, it should be acknowledged that so far, only few experimental studies within EER have been conducted to identify cause and effect relations between school factors and improvements in school effectiveness (e.g. Demetriou and Kyriakides 2012; Tymms et al. 2011). This can be attributed to practical reasons like funding and obtaining consent to allocate students randomly into experimental and control groups but also to the initial interest of EER in *describing* practices which are effective rather than trying to create effective practices based on theory (Scheerens 2013). When conducting experimental studies, attention should be given to the ecological validity of the experiment as well as to associated ethical issues whilst threats to internal validity should be taken into account. However careful use of well-constructed experimental studies may yet provide strong evidence for hypothesized cause and effect relations and contribute both to the testing of theoretical models and to the establishment of stronger links between EER and improvement practices.

Another issue raised in this chapter is the importance of using *group randomization* to study the effects of teacher and school-level factors on student achievement (Antoniou and Kyriakides 2011). Readers are reminded that interventions aiming to change teacher behavior and/or school factors are designed to affect the behavior of groups of interrelated people rather than of disparate unconnected individuals. Therefore, it is generally not feasible to measure the effectiveness of these interventions in an experiment by randomly assigning each student to each of the groups. Instead, by randomizing at the level of groups (i.e. teachers or schools) researchers can still reap most of the methodological benefits afforded by random assignment. Further, the use of group randomization to study the effects of reform policies is now spreading across many fields in the social sciences (Demetriou and Kyriakides 2012).

Problems in implementing experiments can also present substantial threats to their validity. The ideal example of an experimental study assumes that an innovative program is implemented with fidelity, that students do not move between treatment and control groups, and that they remain in their assigned groups for the longevity of the study. This is because the statistical solution to the fundamental problem of causality relies on an assumption of independence between pre-treatment characteristics and treatment group assignment. This independence is very difficult to achieve in non-randomized studies. As a result, statistical models are typically used to adjust for potentially confounding variables (i.e. characteristics of students, classrooms, or schools that predict treatment group assignment and also predict outcomes) when outcomes for different groups are compared. However, as Raudenbush (2005) points out, "No matter how many potential confounders [analysts] identify and control, the burden of proof is always on the [analysts] to argue that no important confounders have been omitted" (p. 28). By contrast, because randomized assignment to treatment groups takes into account observed and unobserved characteristics, such control is not deemed necessary. This is why randomized field trials are often considered as the "gold standard" for making causal inferences (Slavin 2010). Nevertheless, implementing experiments with randomized assignment can also present problems for researchers, such as break-downs in randomization, treatment non-compliance, attrition, and variation in fidelity of program implementation. To counter these, methodologists have developed a number of procedures, which are briefly outlined below. However, the proposed solutions are not always adequate.

6.2.2.1 Breakdowns in Randomization

There is sometimes resistance to randomization, particularly when a promising new treatment is being tested. For example, parents may lobby to have their children included in a promising new treatment program. Such problems can be avoided by monitoring both the randomization process and the actual treatment received by each participant following randomization. Another strategy to minimize break-downs in randomization is to isolate the units under study. For example, when different treatments are given to different schools (high isolation of units), it is less likely that breakdowns in randomization will occur than when different treatments are given to different classrooms within the same school (low isolation of units). However, when schools or other groups are assigned to treatment conditions, randomization occurs at the group rather than at the individual level (i.e. group or cluster randomization). The assumption that individual responses are independent ceases to be valid because individuals within the same group are more likely to provide similar responses than individuals in different groups. At the same time, this problem can be dealt with by the use of multilevel modeling techniques which can simultaneously provide estimates of causal effects at both the individual and group levels.

6.2.2.2 Treatment Non-compliance

Individuals who are randomly assigned to treatment and control conditions may not actually receive treatment as some may simply fail to show up for the particular program to which they have been assigned. For example, randomly assigning teachers to receive different teacher professional development courses does not mean that they will attend these courses. There are several practical ways to encourage participation however, such as providing incentives, removing obstacles (e.g. providing the courses at convenient time), and including only those individual who are willing to participate. However, even when such steps are taken, some of those selected for participation in a study may still fail to participate. Three statistical strategies have been used in cases where there is participant non-compliance.

In the first approach, known as the *intention to treat analysis,* the mean responses of those assigned to the treatment condition (regardless of whether they actually received treatment) are compared with the mean responses of those assigned to the control condition. Assuming that the treatment has positive effects, the mean for the treatment group will typically be found to be lower than it would be if all individuals assigned to the treatment condition had actually received treatment. Therefore, this analysis usually yields conservative estimates of treatment effects. The second approach eliminates individuals assigned to the treatment condition who do not actually receive the treatment. However, unless it can be shown that those who drop out of the treatment condition are a random sample of the participants in that condition, this analysis will yield a biased estimate of the treatment effect. The third strategy focuses on estimating the intention to treat effect (i.e. to take part in the intervention) for the sub-set of participants who are "true compliers." True compliers are those who will take the treatment or the control when assigned it. Non-compliers are those who will not take what they are assigned, whether it is the treatment or the control condition. Non-compliers are of three possible types: (a) never takers (who never take treatment no matter what condition they are assigned to); (b) always takers (who always take treatment no matter what condition they are assigned to); and (c) defiers (who always do the opposite of what they are assigned). Because only the true compliers can be observed both taking and not taking treatment, they are the only sub-group for which we can learn about the effect of taking a treatment versus being in a control group. An additional assumption of this strategy yields the *instrumental variable estimate* for the non-compliers where there is no effect of the assignment on what would be observed. That is, the "exclusion restriction" says that if the assignment to treat versus control cannot affect which condition a participant will take (i.e. the non-compliers will do what they want regardless of the condition to which they are assigned), it cannot affect the participants' outcome.

6.2.2.3   Attrition

In many cases, individuals who are selected for study initially participate but later drop out. It is not always possible to maintain contact with all participants, and those who are contacted may refuse to continue their participation. As such, researchers have developed strategies for estimating the effect of attrition on outcomes of interest. Little and Rubin (2002) reviewed several techniques for dealing with missing data, including data missing due to attrition. In cases of attrition from randomized experiments, researchers typically have information on the pre-treatment characteristics of participants as well as their treatment group assignments and can conduct analyses to determine whether there are significant differences in initial measures between those who dropped out of the study and those who remained. Significant differences between leavers and stayers indicate that the characteristics of those who left differ from the characteristics of those who remained and suggest that the study findings may not be generalizable to the population of interest. Furthermore, when the characteristics of participants who drop out of the treatment group differ from the characteristics of those who drop out of the control group, the estimate of the treatment effect may again be biased. In such cases, researchers are advised to cautiously explore techniques for adjusting for potential bias (e.g. imputing missing values, modeling the effects of attrition on responses, and estimating maximum and minimum values to bracket the treatment effect).

6.3 Concluding Comments

This chapter raises the importance of searching for appropriate research designs in order to identify cause and effect relations within the field of EER. It is argued that while experiments provide the best evidence with respect to treatment effects, they may yield results that are local and may hence jeopardize generalizability. Statistically, the only formal basis for ensuring the generalization of causal effects is to randomly sample from a well-defined population. Although formal probability sampling is viewed as the ideal with respect to generalizing to populations and settings, it is also extremely difficult to implement in practice (and in education especially) when participation in the experiment is voluntarily. Randomly selecting settings (e.g. schools), while possible, may be difficult to implement in practice due to the cost of studying more than a few sites. It is hence important to look closer into strengths and limitations of using cross-sectional data to search for cause and effect relations. These have been discussed in the current chapter along with the importance of conducting secondary analyses of international comparative studies. By aggregating the data at the country level, comparative studies may also enable us to use the difference-in-difference technique to search for causality. Given that each approach has its own strengths and limitations, researchers have often relied on study replication to generalize results from single studies to other outcomes, populations, or settings (Raudenbush and Liu 2000). In this context, the importance of conducting meta-analysis of effectiveness studies in order to search for cause and effect relations is acknowledged (see, Creemers et al. 2010). Moreover, the use of different approaches in analyzing datasets of experimental and cross-sectional studies may also help researchers within EER to develop and test theoretical models. To clarify the importance of this argument, we refer to a secondary analysis of TIMSS data conducted by Gustafsson (2013) who made use of the following three different approaches to systematically investigate the effect of homework on student achievement: (a) two-level regression, which is applied to separate student-level relations from class-level relations, (b) instrumental variable regression, using teacher-reported homework time to instrument student reported homework time, and (c) a difference-in-difference analysis investigating country-level change between 2003 and 2007. All three methods revealed a positive effect of homework time on student achievement. In this way, stronger arguments about the impact of homework on student learning outcomes can be provided. The approach followed in this study can be used by other researchers within EER to systematically examine cause and effect relations when only cross-sectional data are available. In this way, Jan Eric Gustafsson had a significant impact on the methodological development of EER and especially on testing its theoretical framework by using international comparative studies.

References

Angrist, J. D. (2004). American education research changes tack. *Oxford Review of Economic Policy, 20*(2), 198–212.

Antoniou, P., & Kyriakides, L. (2011). The impact of a dynamic approach to professional development on teacher instruction and student learning: Results from an experimental study. *School Effectiveness and School Improvement, 22*(3), 291–311.

Barnow, B., Cain, G., & Goldberger, A. (1980). Issues in the analysis of selectivity bias. In E. Stromsdorfer & G. Farkas (Eds.), *Evaluation studies* (Vol. 5, pp. 43–59). Beverly Hills, CA: Sage.

Creemers, B. P. M., & Kyriakides, L. (2015). Developing, testing and using theoretical models of educational effectiveness for promoting quality in education. *School Effectiveness and School Improvement, 26*(1), 102–119.

Creemers, B. P. M., Kyriakides, L., & Antoniou, P. (2013). *Teacher professional development for improving quality of teaching.* Dordrecht, the Netherlands: Springer.

Creemers, B. P. M., Kyriakides, L., & Sammons, P. (2010). *Methodological advances in educational effectiveness research.* London, UK: Routledge.

De Fraine, B., van Damme, J., & Onghena, P. (2007). A longitudinal analysis of gender differences in academic self-concept and language achievement: A multivariate multilevel latent growth approach. *Contemporary Educational Psychology, 32*(1). 132–150.

Demetriou, D., & Kyriakides, L. (2012). The impact of school self-evaluation upon student achievement: A group randomization study. *Oxford Review of Education, 38*(2), 149–170.

Denzin, N. K., & Lincoln, Y. S. (1998). *Collecting and interpreting qualitative materials.* Thousand Oaks, CA: Sage.

Gustafsson, J.-E. (2010). Longitudinal designs. In B. P. M. Creemers, L. Kyriakides, & P. Sammons (Eds.), *Methodological advances in educational effectiveness research* (pp. 77–101). London, UK: Taylor & Francis.

Gustafsson, J.-E. (2013). Causal inference in educational effectiveness research: A comparison of three methods to investigate effects of homework on student achievement. *School Effectiveness and School Improvement, 24*(3), 275–295.

Hall, J., Sylva, K., Sammons, P., Melhuish, E., Siraj-Blatchford, I., & Taggart, B. (2013). Can preschool protect young children's cognitive and social development? Variation by centre quality and duration of attendance. *School Effectiveness and School Improvement, 24*(2), 55–176.

Hanushek, E. A., Link, S., & Woessmann, L. (2013). Does school autonomy make sense everywhere? Panel estimates from PISA. *Journal of Development Economics, 104*, 212–232.

Hanushek, E. A., & Woessmann, L. (2011). The economics of international differences in educational achievement. In E. A. Hanushek, S. Machin, & L. Woessmann (Eds.), *Handbook of the Economics of Education* (Vol. 3, pp. 89–200). Amsterdam, the Netherlands: North Holland.

Heck, R. H., & Moriyama, K. (2010). Examining relationships among elementary schools' contexts, leadership, instructional practices, and added-year outcomes: a regression discontinuity approach. *School Effectiveness and School Improvement, 21*(4), 377–408.

Heckman, J. J. (1979). Sample selection bias as a specification error. *Econometrica, 47*(1), 153–161.

Holland, P. W. (1986). Statistics and causal inference. *Journal of the America Statistics Association,* 81, 945–970.

Kyriakides, L., Creemers, B. P. M., Antoniou, P., Demetriou, D., & Charalambous, C. (2015). The impact of school policy and stakeholders' actions on student learning: A longitudinal study. *Learning and Instruction, 36*, 113–124.

Kyriakides, L., & Luyten, H. (2009). The contribution of schooling to the cognitive development of secondary education students in Cyprus: An application of regression-discontinuity with multiple cut-off points. *School Effectiveness and School Improvement, 20*(2), 167–186.

Lazear, E. P. (2001). Educational production. *Quarterly Journal of Economics, 116*(3), 777–803.

Little, R. J., & Rubin, D. B. (2002). *Statistical analyses with missing data.* New York, NY: Wiley.

Locke, J. (1975). *An essay concerning human understanding.* Oxford, UK: Clarendon Press.

Raudenbush, S. W. (2005). Learning from attempts to improve schooling: The contribution of methodological diversity. *Educational Researcher, 34*(5), 25–31.

Raudenbush, S. W., & Liu, X. (2000). Statistical power and optimal design for multisite randomized trials. *Psychological Methods, 5*(2), 199–213.

Rosenbaum, P. R. (2002). *Observational studies* (2nd ed.). New York, NY: Springer.

Rubin, D. B. (2006). *Matched sampling for causal effects.* New York, NY: Cambridge University Press.

Scheerens, J. (2013). The use of theory in school effectiveness research revisited. *School Effectiveness and School Improvement, 24*(1), 1–38.

Scherer, R., & Gustafsson, J. E. (2015). Student assessment of teaching as a source of information about aspects of teaching quality in multiple subject domains: An application of multilevel bifactor structural equation modeling. *Frontiers in psychology, 6.* doi:10.3389/fpsyg.2015.01550

Shadish, W. R., Cook, T. D., & Campbell, D. T. (2002). *Experimental and quasi- experimental designs for generalized causal inference.* Boston, USA: Houghton-Mifflin.

Slavin, R. E. (2010). Experimental studies in education. In B. P. M Creemers, L. Kyriakides & P., Sammons (Eds.), *Methodological advances in educational effectiveness research* (pp. 102–114). London, UK: Routledge, Taylor & Francis.

Teddlie, C., & Sammons, P. (2010). Applications of mixed methods to the field of educational effectiveness research. In B.P.M Creemers, L. Kyriakides & P., Sammons (Eds.), *Methodological Advances in Educational Effectiveness Research* (pp. 115-152). London: Routledge Taylor & Francis.

Tymms, P., Merrell, C., Thurston, A., Andor, J., Topping, K., & Miller, D. (2011). Improving attainment across a whole district: School reform through peer tutoring in a randomized controlled trial. *School Effectiveness and School Improvement, 22*(3), 265–289.

Winship, C., & Morgan, S. L. (1999). The estimation of causal effects from observational data. *Annual Review of Sociology, 25*, 659–706.

Chapter 7
Countries Strive Towards More Quality and Equity in Education: Do They Show Success or Failure? Evidence from TIMSS 2003 and 2011, for Grade 4

Jan Van Damme and Kim Bellens

Abstract Over the past decade, countries have been striving to increase the quality and equity of their educational systems. This study aimed to investigate to what extent countries have succeeded in both. Trends over time in educational quality and social and ethnic equity amongst 17 countries were investigated through hierarchical multilevel model analysis using data from TIMSS 2003 and 2011. Results indicated an overall increase of math achievement levels, a stable level of science achievement, an overall decrease in social equity, and an overall increase in ethnic equity. However, differences between countries were noticed, with opposite trends occurring in some countries. This study not only looked at trends in average achievement, but also investigated trends in achievement gaps by looking at trends in achievement of the highest and lowest 10 % performing students, which revealed nuances in the conclusions made. Finally, no systematic relationship was found between trends in quality and trends in equity.

Joint first authors. Kim Bellens was responsible for setting out the objectives of the project, performing the analyses and writing the text. Jan Van Damme supervised the research project, giving feedback during all phases.

J. Van Damme (✉) · K. Bellens
Centre for Educational Effectiveness and Evaluation, University of Leuven, Leuven, Belgium
e-mail: jan.vandamme@ppw.kuleuven.be

K. Bellens
e-mail: kim.bellens@kuleuven.be

© Springer International Publishing AG 2017
M. Rosén et al. (eds.), *Cognitive Abilities and Educational Outcomes*,
Methodology of Educational Measurement and Assessment,
DOI 10.1007/978-3-319-43473-5_7

127

7.1 Background

7.1.1 Introduction

Quality and equity are two largely agreed upon goals of educational systems in all countries, explicitly stating them both in their policy aims. This is e.g. the case in the "No Child Left Behind" Act of 2001 in the USA, the Strategic Framework for Education and Training of the European Union (European Commission 2016), and in the Report on Primary Education Review and Implementation (PERI) in Singapore (Ministry of Education Singapore 2009).

7.1.2 Strive for Quality

A strive for quality can be seen as a self-evident goal for countries, based on research stating the positive effects of education on different domains. Amongst the numerous indicators of quality (e.g. student achievement, years of schooling, low drop-out rates), cognitive achievement is the most important predictor of both individual as well as societal desirable outcomes (Hanushek and Woessmann 2008).

7.1.3 Strive for Equity

A strive for educational equity can be framed within the issue of social justice, asking the question "how can we contribute to the creation of a more equitable, respectful, and just society for everyone?" (Zajda et al. 2007, p. 13). As education is one of the primary ways to obtain status in society (Breen and Jonsson 2005), a striving for educational equity arose. However, visions on social justice and educational equity are diverse (Atkinson 2015; Paquette 1998), with a main distinction between meritocracy and egalitarianism. In a meritocratic view, status in society is the reflection of one's own merits, talents, and effort (Gulson and Webb 2012; McCoy and Major 2007). Hereby, acceptable educational inequity points to differences between students in talents and amount of effort. However, it has been argued that the meritocratic vision is hard to implement due to different hidden mechanisms which make it harder for some to develop their talents than for others, even when given the same (access) opportunities (Lim 2013). Therefore, the egalitarian vision nowadays has evolved as the mainstream vision, in which main responsibility to guarantee equity is given to society as a whole. Positive discrimination of different groups is legitimated within this vision to truly obtain equity in educational results between different groups. Or, as Kyriakides and Creemers (2011, p. 240) argue: "a commitment to equity suggests that differences in outcomes should not be attributable to differences in areas such as wealth, income, power, or possessions." Both visions hold a different view on educational equity and in this sense, the meaning of educational equity is less straightforward and globally accepted than in the case of educational quality. That is one of the reasons why we treat equity as distinct from quality, although equity can also be considered as part of quality.

Based on the egalitarian vision, contemporary research on equity is investigated through (1) the relationship between background variables and student achievement (Kyriakides and Creemers 2011; OECD 2012) or (2) the achievement gap between different sub-groups (e.g. immigrants versus natives) (Bower 2013; Johnson 2002). Two background characteristics frequently investigated are socio-economic status (SES) and ethnicity. SES can be defined as "the relative position of a family or individual in an hierarchical social structure, based on their access to, or control over wealth, prestige, and power" (Mueller and Parcel 1981). As Coleman (1988) states, family social standing is characterized by three forms of capital: economic, cultural, and social. As indicated by Yang (2003), SES consists of, at least, an economic and cultural capital component. Economic capital accounts for family wealth or income, determining physical resources. Cultural capital serves as the cognitive environment for the child, including parental education (Coleman 1988; Bourdieu 1986). Various indicators exist in the literature, including home possessions, parental education, occupation, etc., and come to terms to a more or less extent with both components of SES. Ethnicity refers to "the enduring and systematic communication of cultural differences between groups considering themselves to be distinct" (Eriksen 2002, p. 58). The concept of ethnicity covers a variety of realities, viewed differently in different societies. In European societies ethnicity mainly points to different religion, country of birth, and/or mother tongue, in the USA ethnicity is most closely related to race. As a result, different operationalizations exist depending on the actual experience of ethnicity in societies.

7.1.4 Achievement Gap

Both researchers and policy makers have taken it for granted that the achievement gap (without considering student background characteristics) also indicates equity. The aim is to reduce the gap and keep the standard deviation of the achievement distribution to a minimum (e.g. Konstantopoulos 2008; Nicaise et al. 2005). However, it might be argued that the greater the achievement gap, the more all students (especially the strong ones) develop their talents to a maximum (Luyten 2008). This implies that the achievement gap as such cannot unequivocally be considered as an indicator of equity.

7.1.5 Quality and Equity: A Necessary Choice?

Literature on the question whether quality and equity can be strived for simultaneously is scarce and mainly restricted to secondary education. Results suggest that they might be complementary (e.g. OECD 2012; Woessmann 2004), arguing that when students are not predetermined by their background, they can obtain optimal educational outcomes (OECD 2010). Although the same might hold for primary education, to the best of our knowledge, to date, no study has investigated the complementarity between quality and equity in primary education across countries.

7.1.6 Beyond Boundaries: Research on Quality and Equity

Several boundaries seem to exist when investigating quality and equity. First, there appears a geographical one, as many studies on trends in quality and equity are limited to one country (e.g. Everett et al. 2011; Machin et al. 2013; Mattei 2012). However, various cross-country studies (e.g. OECD 2005, 2012; Hanushek and Woessmann 2008) show how comparisons between countries shed additional light on one's own realizations.

Second, most research uses a cross-sectional design, studying quality and equity at one point in time (e.g. Atweh et al. 2011; Condron 2011, 2013; Kohlhaas et al. 2010; OECD 2005). However, taking into account the starting point different countries gives valuable insight into the extent to which their efforts pay off.

Although some studies have been conducted to look at the trends over time in quality and equity across a multitude of countries (e.g. Schleicher 2009), they exclusively focus on the trend in average achievement level and achievement variation. Looking additionally at the achievement levels at the extremes of the distribution provides further insight into the educational quality of different countries.

International, large-scale databases (e.g. Programme for International Student Assessment, PISA; Trends in Mathematics and Science Study, TIMSS; Progress in International Reading Literacy Study, PIRLS) contain sufficient information to break through these boundaries and allow a research design in which trends over time across countries can be investigated to give further insights into how well countries succeed in raising educational quality and equity. Different studies have shown the possibilities opened up by these databases, each with its specific focus and therefore advantages as well as limitations. Important work was done by Gustafsson (2007), who showed that looking longitudinally at the educational systems of different countries can contribute to our understanding of educational development and improvement. Gustafsson (2007) argued how relating within-country changes in explanatory variables to within-country changes in achievement over time can keep both selection bias and omitted variables to a minimum, making causal inferences possible. As an example, he investigated the effect of age and class size on math achievement, based on TIMSS 1995 and 2003 data. Liu et al. (2014) replicated the effect of age and class size for reading achievement (based on PIRLS 2001, 2006, and 2011), in which they also took into account SES as an explanatory variable. As countries are considered separately in this approach, a direct comparison between countries is not possible. Lenkeit and

Caro (2014) show the possibilities made available by large-scale international data by making use of multilevel models, looking at development over time across countries in educational quality whilst considering the country as the highest level. PISA 2000–2009 data were used to investigate how the educational effectiveness of a country is affected by socio-economic differences. Although no causal inferences can be drawn from this approach, it makes comparison between countries over time possible. Our study is mainly in-line with the research approach of Lenkeit and Caro (2014), as we make use of hierarchical models at the country level to investigate systems' quality and equity. However, we also study trends within countries in separate analyses, as questions can be raised when considering a group of non-randomly chosen countries as a level in an analysis.

7.2 Research Questions

This study has three main objectives:

(1) To investigate the trend in educational quality in primary education (Grade 4) between 2003 and 2011, both between countries as well as for separate countries. We then look at the trend in mean achievement for mathematics and science, and investigate the trend in achievement level for the 10 % of students with the highest and lowest achievement levels. Looking at the extremes of the distribution sheds light on the trend for achievement gap.

(2) To investigate the trend in educational equity between 2003 and 2011. We look at the trends in the relationship between background characteristics and achievement. Again, we investigate the trend across countries as well as for each country. Both social and ethnic equity, as the two major issues in the equity debate, are investigated.

(3) To explore whether a trade-off exists between trends in quality and trends in equity.

7.3 Methodology

7.3.1 Data

We used data from the Trends in Mathematics and Science Study (TIMSS), which is organized by the International Association for the Evaluation of Educational Achievement (IEA) and assesses the achievement in mathematics and science for fourth (and eighth) grade students. This study started in 1995 and was repeated every four years (IEA 2013). As Grade 4 students have only been tested on a regular basis since 2003, we used data from TIMSS 2003 and 2011. This time span of 8 years is assumed to show the effects of possible changes that have taken place during the past decade. Twenty-one countries (or economies) participated in both years. However, due to issues of comparability, some countries were excluded from the analyses,[1] which led to the inclusion of 17 countries (see Appendix).

Two issues need to be taken into account. First, England and New Zealand sampled fifth rather than fourth graders both in TIMSS 2003 and 2011 due to their exceptionally early starting age of schooling. Second, in Armenia, the age of students in Grade 4 decreased in the period from 2003 to 2011 due to educational reforms, which might affect the achievement level.

7.3.2 Variables

Trends in quality. Achievement scores are used as measures of quality in mathematics and science. Both scores are represented by five standardized plausible values with means of 500 and standard deviations of 100 in 1995. To reduce the total variance, we divided the achievement scores by 50, resulting in scores with a mean of 10 and a standard deviation of 2. Trends in quality were indicated by the difference in achievement between 2011 and 2003. The 10th and 90th percentile in achievement scores were considered within each country, showing the *trends in achievement gap*.

Trends in equity. Trends in equity were investigated by means of the non-existence of a relationship between achievement and background characteristics. Both social and ethnic equity were looked at. Based on the available information in TIMSS, the amount of books at home (hereafter referred to as "books") was used as a proxy for student social status. Information was retrieved by means of a student questionnaire. Five categories were distinguished: (1) 0–10 books, (2) 11–25 books, (3) 26–100 books, (4) 101–200 books, and (5) >200 books. Usage of test language at home (hereafter referred to as "home language") was used as a proxy for ethnicity. Three categories were distinguished: (1) never, (2) sometimes, and (3) always (or almost always) speak test language at home.[2] The appendix shows the mean of both variables per country.

---

[1]The Russian Federation sampled third graders from some regions and fourth graders from other regions in 2003 whereas in 2011 only fourth graders where sampled. This was due to structural changes in the age at which children entered schools which were ongoing in 2003. More or less the same was true for Slovenia. Additionally, data of Slovenia of 2011 on language spoken at home (cf. infra) were deleted from international databases due to students' misunderstanding of the question asked. Furthermore, we excluded Morocco and Yemen from the analyses as the achievement scores of Yemen and Morocco could not been estimated reliably in TIMSS 2011, because the percentage of students with achievement scores too low for estimation was above 25 %.

[2]In 2003, four categories were distinguished, i.e. (1) never, (2) sometimes, (3) almost always, and (4) always speak language of test at home. To enable comparison between 2003 and 2011, categories (3) and (4) have been merged.

7.3.3 Analyses

We used MPlus (Muthén and Muthén 2012) to conduct the analyses. To investigate the overall trends in quality and equity across countries, three-level hierarchical linear models (HLM) were estimated, with students nested within schools within countries (see Eq. 7.1). Considering the country as the highest level in the analyses assured that standard errors for the parameter estimates accounted for dependence in the data due to differences between countries. Stegmueller (2013) shows in his Monte Carlo simulation study that a minimum of 15 countries is required to largely reduce the bias in estimates and standard errors. However, standard errors are biased when random slopes are introduced, i.e. Bayesian intervals are overestimated whereas maximum likelihood which are underestimated (Stegmueller 2013). Furthermore, in a three-level model, introducing random slopes for countries will imply that for countries with high (or low) estimates the estimates will shrink to the mean, based on information for all the other countries involved. However, there is uncertainty whether the original estimate is the result of chance or whether it reflects the real situation in that country. Therefore, and since we had sufficient data within countries, we also investigated country specific trends by running a two-level analyses within each country separately (see Eq. 7.2).

In all analyses, we used the five plausible values, generating five estimates of the statistics and combining them in line with the prescriptions of the IEA (von Davier et al. 2009). Furthermore, to ensure every country contributes equally to the analyses, we included *senate weights*—summing up to 500 in each country—at the student level in the three-level models. In the two-level models, the *house weight* was included, summing up to the sample size in each country.

$$\text{Achievement}_{ijk} = \beta_{0jk} + \beta_{1jk}\text{Year}_{jk} + e_{ijk} \tag{7.1}$$

$$\text{Achievement}_{ij} = \beta_{0j} + \beta_{1j}\text{Year}_j + e_{ij} \tag{7.2}$$

where i = student, j = school, k = country, Year = year of assessment as a dummy variable (0 = 2003; 1 = 2011), and β_1 = performance level change between 2003 and 2011.

To investigate the trend in achievement of the top and bottom 10 % and the trend in achievement gap, we looked at the mean score within each sub-group in both assessment years. To determine the cut-off score for both groups, we used the mean of the five plausible values. After groups were determined, five plausible values were used as described above. The model is as follows:

$$\text{Achievement}_{ijk} = \beta_{0jk} + \beta_{1jk}\text{Year}_{jk} + \beta_{2jk}\text{Group}_{ijk} + \beta_{3jk}\text{Year}_{jk} * \text{Group}_{ijk} \tag{7.3}$$

with Group = −0.50 for the 10th percentile and 0.50 for the 90th percentile.

Here, both three-level and two-level models were estimated. In the three-level models, a linear rescaling of the weights was done in such a way that the weights in each assessment year summed up to 50 in each country, making each country contribute equally to the analyses.

To investigate social and ethnic equity, we added books and home language to the HLM analyses. A logarithmic transformation of both variables is appropriate to come to terms with the assumption of a linear relationship between independent and dependent variables. Furthermore, we centered both variables on their overall mean. The trend in equity was modeled as an interaction effect of year and social or ethnic background variables.

The trade-off between quality and equity was investigated by plotting the trends in the country specific models. Finally, we tested whether significant Pearson correlations existed between trends in quality and trends in social or ethnic equity.

As we are interested in countries' total trend in quality and equity, we did not control for institutional or school features. However, predetermined factors that relate to (trends in) quality and equity of educational systems, without the possibility for educational systems to change and/or influence them, should be controlled for in order to make a fair comparison (Lenkeit 2013). One important factor indicated in the literature is the overall developmental state of a country (Lenkeit 2013). Research indicates a strong, reciprocal relation between the developmental status and education level in a country (Condron 2013; Hanushek and Woessmann 2008). The Human Development Index (HDI, Unesco 2013) is a composition of three factors, i.e. life expectancy at birth, educational attainment (mean years of schooling and expected years of schooling), and income (gross national income per capita). Although the HDI of countries changed in the period of 2003–2011, we only took into account the HDI of countries in 2000, so as not to rule out the possible effects education might have on the HDI at a later point in time. A second factor we controlled for is situated at the individual level, i.e. gender, as research indicates that the relation between achievement and family background characteristics might be confounded by gender (Schütz et al. 2008).

Missing data in gender, books, and home language were dealt with by means of multiple imputation, using SPSS. Data were imputed for each country separately.

7.4 Results

Table 7.1 and Fig. 7.1 show the *trend in average achievement* in mathematics and science between 2003 and 2011. Whereas some countries are characterized by an increase in both math and science achievement (e.g. Norway), other countries show a stable achievement level in both subjects. Still others show different trends between domains, with an increase or decrease in math achievement combined with

Table 7.1 Trends in average achievement between 2003 and 2011 per country

	Math achievement			Science achievement		
	2003	2011	Trend	2003	2011	Trend
Armenia	9.11	9.08	−0.03	8.74	8.36	−0.38**
Australia	9.93	10.28	0.34***	10.41	10.30	−0.12
Belgium (Flanders)	11.02	11.01	−0.01	10.38	10.19	−0.19**
Chinese Taipei	11.28	11.85	0.57***	11.03	11.06	0.04
England	10.61	10.79	0.19	10.79	10.53	−0.26*
Hong Kong	11.51	11.99	0.48***	10.86	10.66	−0.20*
Hungary	10.54	10.25	−0.29**	10.56	10.62	0.07
Iran	8.18	8.61	0.43***	8.67	9.04	0.37**
Italy	10.05	10.11	0.06	10.32	10.43	0.11
Japan	11.29	11.71	0.41***	10.87	11.17	0.30***
Lithuania	10.72	10.69	−0.03	10.26	10.32	0.06
Netherlands	10.84	10.77	−0.06	10.52	10.59	0.07
New Zealand	9.82	9.71	−0.11	10.34	9.91	−0.43***
Norway	9.01	9.92	0.91***	9.31	9.90	0.60***
Singapore	11.80	12.06	0.27*	11.20	11.60	0.41***
Tunisia	6.79	7.41	0.62***	6.28	7.14	0.86***
United States	10.25	10.80	0.56***	10.58	10.84	0.27***
Overall	10.16	10.42	0.27***	10.06	10.17	0.10

$*p < 0.05; **p < 0.01; ***p < 0.001$

a stable science achievement level, or even an increase in one subject combined with a decrease in the other (see Hong Kong). Worth noticing is that Armenia is characterized by a stable achievement level in math, which implies that it succeeded in maintaining its average mathematical achievement level, while the age of the students diminished.

The trend in achievement level of the students situated at the *extremes of the distribution* is reported in Table 7.2. It also sheds light on how the achievement gap evolves within a country.

In some countries, the achievement gap widens significantly. How this wider achievement gap is obtained, varies between countries. In Iran, for instance, the achievement level of the bottom 10 % increases less than the level of the top 10 %. The achievement gap in mathematics in Hungary, however, increases because the achievement level of the bottom 10 % significantly decreases, whereas the top 10 % is characterized by a stable achievement level. A third way to widen the gap is by increasing the level of top performing students together with decreasing the level of low performing students (see e.g. Hungary concerning science achievement). A final possibility is shown by Australia and Chinese Taipei for mathematics, showing a stable level of low performing students together with a significant

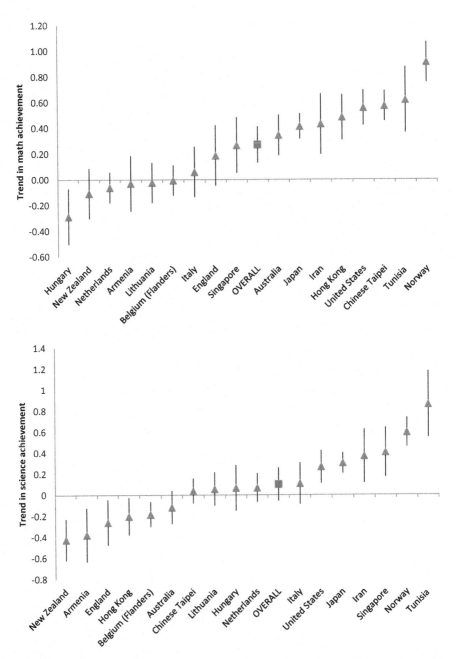

Fig. 7.1 Trends in average math and science achievement between 2003 and 2011, accompanied by confidence intervals (95 %)

Table 7.2 Trends in math and science achievement scores of the 10 % highest and lowest performing students between 2003 and 2011, per country

	Math achievement (Diff.)			Science achievement (Diff.)		
	10 % Lowest	10 % Highest	Gap	10 % Lowest	10 % Highest	Gap
Armenia	0.04	0.02	−0.03	0.08	−0.52***	−0.60***
Australia	0.11	0.54***	0.43**	−0.09	−0.11	−0.02
Belgium (Flanders)	0.02	0.06	0.04	−0.25**	−0.13	0.12
Chinese Taipei	0.10	0.76***	0.66***	−0.21	0.08	0.29**
England	0.11	0.18	0.07	−0.17	−0.33**	−0.16
Hong Kong	0.48*	0.54***	0.06	−0.49***	0.17*	0.66***
Hungary	−0.77***	0.11	0.87***	−0.30*	0.20*	0.50***
Iran	0.37**	0.81***	0.44**	0.44**	0.72***	0.29
Italy	0.48***	−0.20*	−0.67***	0.51***	−0.21*	−0.71***
Japan	0.50***	0.36***	−0.14	0.74***	0.04	−0.70***
Lithuania	0.06	0.04***	−0.01	0.00	0.12	0.13
Netherlands	0.05	−0.13	−0.18	0.09	0.02	−0.07
New Zealand	−0.08	−0.20		−0.32*	−0.40***	−0.09
Norway	1.38***	0.55***	−0.83***	1.31***	−0.11	−1.42***
Singapore	0.47**	0.05	−0.41***	0.37*	0.41***	0.04
Tunisia	0.34**	0.16	−0.18	0.63***	0.27	−0.35*
United States	0.44**	0.40***	−0.03	0.30*	0.10	−0.20**
Overall	0.23**	0.29**	0.06	0.13	0.07	−0.05

$*p < 0.05$; $**p < 0.01$; $***p < 0.001$

increase of the level of the top performers. In other countries, the achievement gap narrows significantly. In the same manner this narrowing is achieved in different ways.

Table 7.3 shows the results of three-level hierarchical models that estimate overall *trends in social and ethnic equity*. Both books and home language show a positive relationship with both math and science achievement (Model 2). Furthermore, the relationship between books and home language with math/sciene achievement is significantly different in 2011 compared to 2003 (Model 3). Figures 7.2 and 7.3 show that the relationship between books and math/science achievement strengthened between 2003 and 2011, whereas the relationship between home language and math/sciene achievement weakened over the years. In total, 13 and 16 % of the variance in math and science achievement respectively is explained by taking into account all mentioned variables.

Table 7.3 Results of the HLM analyses concerning math and science achievement

	Math achievement								Science achievement							
	Model 0		Model 1		Model 2		Model 3		Model 0		Model 1		Model 2		Model 3	
	b	S.E.	b	S.E.	b	S.E.	b	S.E.	b	S.E.	b	S.E.	b	S.E.	b	S.E.
Intercept	10.16***	0.30	6.64*	3.1	7.31*	2.92	7.29*	2.92	10.06***	0.29	5.90*	2.89	6.67*	2.69	6.65*	2.69
Year	0.27***	0.07	0.27***	0.07	0.30***	0.07	0.30***	0.07	0.10	0.08	0.10	0.08	0.15	0.08	0.15	0.08
Gender			0.06**	0.02	0.09***	0.02	0.09	0.02			0.05	0.03	0.08*	0.03	0.08**	0.03
HDI			0.43	0.37	0.35	0.35	0.35	0.35			0.52	0.34	0.41	0.32	0.42	0.32
Books					1.44***	0.13	1.28***	0.11					1.50***	0.12	1.27***	0.11
Home language					1.04***	0.24	1.49***	0.34					1.52***	0.28	1.86***	0.33
Year × books							0.31***	0.09							0.45***	0.10
Year × language							−0.76**	0.22							−0.57**	0.21
Variance																
Student	1.84		1.84		1.76		1.76		1.97		1.97		1.88		1.88	
School	0.71		0.71		0.58		0.57		0.77		0.77		0.60		0.60	
Country	1.48		1.28		1.19		1.19		1.20		0.90		0.81		0.81	
ICC																
School	0.18		0.18		0.16		0.16		0.20		0.20		0.17		0.17	
Country	0.37		0.37		0.35		0.35		0.30		0.30		0.27		0.28	
Proportion explained variance																
Student			0.00		0.04		0.04				0.00		0.05		0.05	
School			0.00		0.18		0.20				0.00		0.22		0.22	
Country			0.14		0.20		0.20				0.25		0.33		0.33	
Total			0.05		0.12		0.13				0.08		0.16		0.16	
Loglikelihood	−297929.43		−297886.39***		−293895.37***		−293804.04***		−303874.79		−303846.00***				−299312.61***	
−299206.87***																

*p < 0.05; **p < 0.01; ***p < 0.001

b regression coefficient

S.E standard error

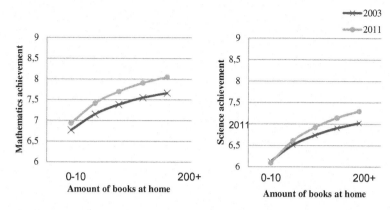

Fig. 7.2 Overall trend in social equity: "year × book" interaction effects on math and science achievement

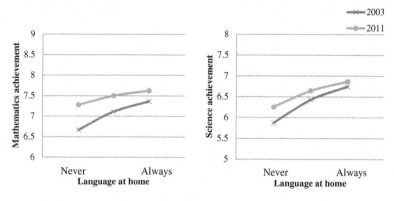

Fig. 7.3 Overall trend in ethnic equity: "year × language" interaction effects on math and science achievement

Table 7.4 shows the estimates of the regression coefficients of the two-level models in each country. In six countries the interaction effect of *books* and year on both math and science achievement is confirmed. The largest effect sizes can be found in Chinese Taipei, Hungary, Hong Kong (especially in science), and Singapore, indicating the largest decrease in social equity during 2003–2011. The interaction effects of *home language* and year on achievement are in many countries in line with the overall trend, with largest effects noticed in Japan and Norway. In Flanders (Belgium) a significant opposite trend is shown in science achievement.

Table 7.4 Estimates of interactions in each country

	Math achievement						Science achievement					
	Intercept	Year	Book	Book × year	Home language	Language × year	Intercept	Year	Book	Book × year	Home language	Language × year
Armenia	9.08***	0.05	0.85***	−0.24	1.96**	−2.00**	8.70***	−0.28*	0.70***	0.04	2.30***	−2.29***
Australia	9.66***	0.36***	1.66***	0.51*	1.18*	−0.55	10.17***	−0.06	1.79***	0.15	1.58*	−0.19
Belgium (Flanders)	10.88***	0.02	1.27***	−0.12	1.38***	−0.17	10.23***	−0.18*	1.23***	0.20	1.18***	1.17***
Chinese Taipei	11.27***	0.59***	1.43***	0.70***	1.79***	−1.06**	10.93***	0.04	1.54***	0.64***	2.05***	−1.61***
England	10.34***	0.29*	2.14***	0.54*	1.69	−1.09	10.55***	−0.14	2.12***	0.44	2.55*	−1.00
Hong Kong	11.46***	0.46***	0.47***	0.36*	2.12***	−1.31***	10.83***	−0.22*	0.35***	0.65***	1.98***	−0.92**
Hungary	10.12***	−0.20	2.18***	0.51*	4.77***	−0.30	10.10***	0.11	1.92***	0.76***	5.21***	0.36
Iran	8.33***	0.46***	0.93***	0.07	0.80***	−0.15	8.86***	0.44***	1.00***	0.17	1.20***	−0.07
Italy	9.89***	0.12	0.74***	0.35*	2.54***	−1.06**	10.21***	0.15	0.91***	0.51***	2.14***	0.12
Japan	10.97***	0.73***	1.91***	0.30	5.90***	−6.39***	10.55***	0.60***	1.64***	0.36	5.65***	−5.98***
Lithuania	10.60***	0.07	1.44***	0.29	2.27**	−0.66	10.17***	0.14	1.27***	0.42*	1.84**	−0.37
Netherlands	10.64***	0.02	1.31***	0.07	1.39**	−0.37	10.29***	0.15*	1.18***	0.32	1.73***	−0.31
New Zealand	9.61***	−0.01	1.81***	0.06	3.19***	−1.99***	10.14***	−0.32**	1.60***	0.49**	4.18***	−1.90***
Norway	8.66***	1.04***	1.78***	0.01	3.67***	−2.49***	8.98***	0.72***	1.68***	0.33	4.54***	−2.47***
Singapore	11.81***	0.21*	1.06***	0.76***	0.59***	−0.08	11.18***	0.36**	1.28***	1.08***	1.51***	0.02
Tunisia	6.94***	0.58***	0.86***	−0.05	−0.27	0.14	6.57***	0.92***	1.10***	0.28	0.01	0.24
United States	10.09***	0.60***	1.31***	0.35**	2.61***	−1.31***	10.42***	0.30**	1.25***	0.52***	3.09***	−0.92***

$*p < 0.05$; $**p < 0.01$; $***p < 0.001$

Table 7.5 Pearson correlations between trend in quality and trend in equity

		Math achievement			Science achievement			
		Trend in social equity	Trend in ethnic equity	Trend in gap	Trend in quality	Trend in social equity	Trend in ethnic equity	Trend in gap
Math	Trend in quality	0.07	−0.21	−0.25	0.61**	−0.04	−0.29	−0.35
	Trend in social equity		0.08	0.30	0.01	0.74**	0.05	0.38
	Trend in ethnic equity			−0.25	−0.03	−0.13	0.96**	−0.51*
	Trend in gap				−0.30	0.01	0.19	0.74**
Science	Trend in quality					0.12	0.00	−0.34
	Trend in social equity						0.12	0.34
	Trend in ethnic equity							−0.49*

$*p < 0.05$; $**p < 0.01$; $***p < 0.001$

Table 7.5 shows the trade-off between trends in quality and equity. We have also added the achievement gap. For clarity reasons, the interaction terms of both books and year, and home language and year, are inversed with positive signs indicating higher ethnic equity in 2011. *Correlations between trends in quality and trends in equity* are insignificant, indicating no general trend in the relation between trends in quality and trends in equity across countries. Figure 7.4 visualizes these results. Whereas in some countries trends towards higher math and science achievement go hand in hand with trends towards a weaker relationship between books or home language and achievement, in other countries, an opposite tendency can be seen. Worth mentioning is that, within domains, the *correlation between the trend in equity (and in quality) and the trend in achievement gap* is rather low and insignificant, except for the correlation between trends in ethnic equity and in the science achievement gap, indicating that countries who develop more ethnic equity also tend to widen the achievement gap ($r = 0.49$).

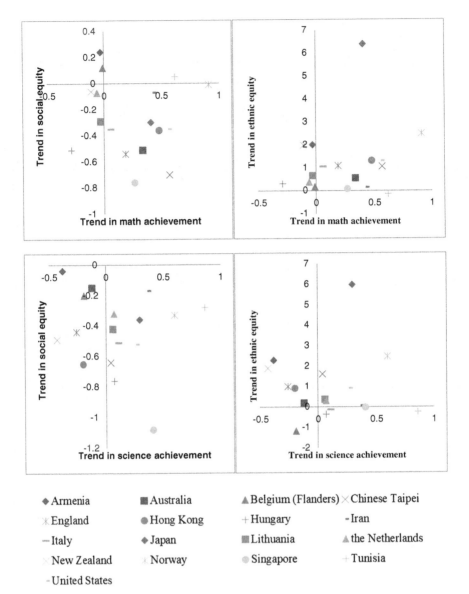

Fig. 7.4 Trade-off between trends in quality and trends in social and ethnic equity

7.5 Discussion and Conclusion

This study investigated the trends in achievement level and equity as well as asking whether a trade-off exists between quality and equity. Seventeen countries were taken into account whilst investigating these objectives. Although the overall level of math achievement increased and the science level remained stable in the period 2003–2011, results show large differences across countries.

First of all, it is worth noting that comparisons over time and between countries are only valuable if made concerning grade, age, and curriculum assessed (Rust 1994). Since some countries are not completely comparable on these characteristics (i.e. England, New Zealand, and Armenia), caution needs to be paid when comparing the achievement scores of these countries. Furthermore, caution needs to be paid in generalizing our results to countries which were not included in our study, as our sample exists of countries which voluntarily participated in TIMSS. Consequently, it cannot be argued that this is a random sample of countries.

Whilst looking at trends in achievement, we also focused on trends of the 10 % highest and lowest achieving students. These insights into the (change in) achievement level are a valuable addition to the currently available research. For example, Armenia and Hungary both kept a stable achievement level for science, but in Armenia the achievement level of the top performing students decreased over the years, whereas in Hungary their achievement level increased.

Along with the trends of both extreme groups, the trend in achievement gap was also reported. Although social justice is often narrowly defined and investigated with a focus on minority groups, in origin it applies to all students, including highly talented students. Looking at the results, the question arises whether it is fair to decrease the gap by means of decreasing the achievement level of the top performing students.

In our study, widening the achievement gap only takes place by means of (1) increasing the achievement level of top performers together with a stable or decreasing level of low performers and (2) by a steeper decrease in the achievement level of low performers. Both these methods can reasonably be argued to indicate more educational inequity. However, this does not mean that closing the achievement gap always indicates more educational equity. A smaller gap can be achieved by means of (1) an increase of the achievement level of low performers together with a stable or decreasing achievement level of top performers or (2) a steeper increase in the achievement level of low performers than that of the top performers. Of course, ceiling effects might take place, which means that it might not (or not to the same extent as for low performers) be possible to increase the achievement level of top performers. Therefore, a stable achievement level for the top performing students or a less steep increase in the achievement level of these students might be acceptable. Other countries might serve as a benchmark to evaluate whether or not stabilization of achievement scores of top performers is acceptable. Nevertheless, in times of globalization and the increasing scramble for talent, it can be called into question whether it is favorable to not fully develop the talents of all students. Therefore, we argue that the notion of social justice should again be broadened to its original meaning, taking into account fairness for all students. This study clearly shows that social justice, and consequently educational equity, is more complicated than simply focusing on closing the achievement gap (i.e. not considering the relation with student characteristics).

Regarding social and ethnic equity, this study concludes that social equity decreased over the period 2003–2011, whereas ethnic equity increased during this time span, both regarding math and science achievement. However, results indicate large differences between countries.

This study also has its limitations. First of all, our measures of social status and ethnicity are very limited, due to the available information in TIMSS. Future research should take into account the multidimensionality of both concepts to deepen our understanding of trends in social and ethnic equity in diverse societies. Whereas, for example, the operationalization of ethnicity in this study might be opportune for European societies, it might not come to terms with the notion of ethnicity in other parts of the globe. The same holds for the SES indicator of books at home. Research points out that various indicators of SES represent pupils' SES, leading to different conclusions on social equity when considering various indicators (Sirin 2005). Furthermore, the validity of a SES indicator varies between countries (Yang and Gustafsson 2004), making it easier to find a culturally valid measure of SES for one country compared to others. Although the study of Yang (2003) shows a great stability in home possession items being used to capture SES across countries (even with possessions varying substantially across countries) and shows that the number of books at home is highly related to the cultural capital factor, it also shows that the number of books at home is only lowly related to the general socio-economic factor. Replicating our study with different and more elaborate measures of SES and ethnicity would reveal further insight into the cultural bias of different indicators and deepen and validate insights into equity of educational systems. Future research might also consider Gustafsson's (2007) approach, by relating change in SES or ethnicity to change in achievement, to see whether causal inferences can be drawn on the relationship between these background characteristics and a system's achievement level.

Second, we looked at equity as the non-existence of a relationship between background characteristics and achievement. This operationalization is in line with the mainstream egalitarian vision. But as Roemer (2004, p. 11) indicates, this conceptualization implies that policy makers should aim at eliminating "the influence of not only social connections, family culture and investment, and the genetic transmission of ability, but also the influence of family background on the formation of preferences and aspirations among children". It can be questioned whether the conceptualization used in this study is widely accepted in all countries.

Furthermore, this study showed that there is no consistent relationship between trends in quality and trends in equity across countries. However, in line with Woessmann (2004), this study showed that some countries succeed in combining a positive change in both variables. Whereas cross-country studies show the possibilities of comparing countries in relation to both quality and equity, studying how quality and equity can be combined in one country might reveal more insight into how both goals go hand in hand, mainly in light of the above mentioned critiques on culturally valid measurements of social and ethnic equity across countries. Some studies in one country suggest that a choice needs to be made between quality and equity (e.g. Frempong et al. 2011 in South Africa), however, the longitudinal study of Kyriakides and Creemers (2011) in Cyprus shows that quality and equity in schools goes hand in hand with, or at least do not exclude, each other.

This study was limited to math and science achievement as indicators of educational quality and to social and ethnic equity as indicators of educational equity. As trends in math achievement significantly correlate with trends in science achievement, in primary education the trend in achievement level might be a general trend across cognitive domains. However, other quality and equity indicators need to be investigated to broaden the notion of trends in quality (e.g. non-cognitive educational outcomes like well-being or long-term effects of education) and trends in equity (e.g. equity concerning students with special needs) to shed more light on whether, and to what extent, different forms of equity and quality coincide.

Last but not least, in this study we explicitly opted for controlling only a few variables, as we adhere to the idea that countries can make choices on how to organize their educational system. Nevertheless, it might be assumed that these trends relate to (policy) decisions and reflect the strategies different countries roll out for their educational system. Further qualitative and quantitative research is needed to unravel the prerequisites for educational systems to evolve towards both higher quality and equity.

Acknowledgments We would like to thank Gudrun Vanlaar from our Centre and Sarah Gielen and Wim Van Den Noortgate from the Faculty of Psychology and Educational Sciences Kulak of the University of Leuven (Belgium) for their valuable comments on an earlier version.

Appendix: The Mean of Some Variables Per Country

	HDI	Books		Language at home	
	2000	2003	2011	2003	2011
		M	M	M	M
Armenia	0.65	1.98	1.95	1.94	1.79
Australia	0.91	2.46	2.30	1.90	1.79
Belgium (Flanders)	0.88	2.00	1.94	1.82	1.71
Chinese Taipei	0.59	1.90	1.94	1.72	1.49
England	0.84	2.25	2.04	1.94	1.78
Hong Kong	0.82	1.45	1.80	1.71	1.63

(continued)

(continued)

	HDI	Books		Language at home	
	2000	2003	2011	2003	2011
		M	M	M	M
Hungary	0.79	2.16	2.08	1.99	1.97
Iran	0.65	1.15	1.18	1.52	1.83
Italy	0.83	1.62	1.77	1.89	1.76
Japan	0.88	1.77	1.76	1.98	1.85
Lithuania	0.76	1.74	1.63	1.97	1.83
Netherlands	0.89	2.10	1.91	1.92	1.80
New Zealand	0.89	2.21	2.15	1.87	1.71
Norway	0.92	2.26	2.23	1.92	1.79
Singapore	0.83	1.91	2.05	1.38	1.26
Tunisia	0.64	1.08	1.20	1.39	0.79
United States	0.91	1.94	1.87	1.83	1.83

References

Atkinson, B. A. (2015). *Inequality. What can be done?*. Cambridge, MA: Harvard University Press.

Atweh, B., Graven, M., Secada, W., & Valero, P. (Eds.). (2011). *Mapping equity and quality in mathematics education.*. New York, NY: Springer.

Bourdieu, P. (1986). The forms of capital. In J. Richardson (Ed.), *Handbook of theory and research for the sociology of education* (pp. 241–258). New York, NY: Green Wood Press.

Bower, C. B. (2013). Social policy and the achievement gap: What do we know? Where should we head? *Education and Urban Society, 45*, 3–36.

Breen, R., & Jonsson, J. O. (2005). Inequality of opportunity in comparative perspective: Recent research on educational attainment and social mobility. *Annual Review of Sociology, 31*, 223–243.

Coleman, J. S. (1988). Social capital in the creation of human capital. *The American Journal of Sociology, 94*, 95–120.

Condron, D. J. (2011). Egalitarianism and educational excellence: Compatible goals for affluent societies? *Educational Researcher, 40*, 47–55.

Condron, D. J. (2013). Affluence, inequality, and educational achievement: A structural analysis of 97 jurisdictions across the globe. *Sociological Spectrum, 33*, 73–97.

Eriksen, T. H. (2002). *Ethnicity and nationalism: Anthropological perspectives*. London, UK: Pluto Press.

European Commission. (2016). *Strategic framework for education and training*. Retrieved from http://ec.europa.eu/education/policy/strategic-framework/index_en.htm

Everett, B. G., Rogers, R. G., Hummer, R. A., & Krueger, P. M. (2011). Trends in educational attainment by race/ethnicity, nativity, and sex in the United States, 1989–2005. *Ethnic and Racial Studies, 34*, 1543–1566.

Frempong, G., Reddy, V., & Kanjee, A. (2011). Exploring equity and quality education in South Africa using multilevel models. *Compare: A Journal of Comparative and International Education, 41*, 819–835.

Gulson, K. N., & Webb, T. (2012). Education policy racialisations: Afrocentric schools, Islamic schools, and the new enunciations of equity. *Journal of Education Policy, 27,* 697–709.

Gustafsson, J. E. (2007). Understanding causal influences on educational achievement through analysis of differences over time within countries. In T. Loveless (Ed.), *Lessons learned: What international assessments tell us about math achievement.* Washington, D.C.: Brookings Institution Press.

Hanushek, E. A., & Woessmann, L. (2008). The role of cognitive skills in economic development. *Journal of Economic Literature, 46,* 607–668.

IEA. (2013). *About IEA.* Retrieved from http://www.iea.nl/about_us.html

Johnson, R. S. (2002). *Using data to close the achievement gap: How to measure equity in our schools.* Thousand Oaks, CA: Corwin Press.

Kohlhaas, K., Lin, H. H., & Chu, K. L. (2010). Science equity in third grade. *The Elementary School Journal, 110,* 393–408.

Konstantopoulos, S. (2008). Do small classes reduce the achievement gap between low and high achievers? Evidence from project STAR. *The Elementary School Journal, 108,* 275–291.

Kyriakides, L., & Creemers, B. P. (2011). Can schools achieve both quality and equity? Investigating the two dimensions of educational effectiveness. *Journal of Education for Students Placed at Risk, 16,* 237–254.

Lenkeit, J. (2013). How effective are educational systems? A value-added approach to measure trends in PIRLS. *Journal for Educational Research Online, 4,* 143–173.

Lenkeit, J., & Caro, D. H. (2014). Performance status and change—Measuring education system effectiveness with data from PISA 2000–2009. *Educational Research and Evaluation: An International Journal on Theory and Practice, 20,* 146–174.

Lim, L. (2013). Meritocracy, elitism, and egalitarianism: A preliminary and provisional assessment of Singapore's primary education review. *Asia Pacific Journal of Education, 33,* 1–14.

Liu, H., Bellens, K., Van Den Noortgate, W., Gielen, S., & Van Damme, J. (2014). A country level longitudinal study on the effect of student age, class size and socio-economic status—Based on PIRLS 2001, 2006 & 2011. In: R. Strietholt, W. Bos, J. E. Gustafsson, & M. Rosén (Eds.), *Educational policy evaluation through international comparative assessments.* Münster, Germany: Waxmann.

Luyten, H. (2008). *Empirische evidentie voor effecten van vroegtijdige selectie in het onderwijs* [Empirical evidence for effects of early selection in education]. Enschede, Netherlands: University of Twente.

Machin, S., McNally, S., & Wyness, G. (2013). Educational attainment across the UK nations: Performance, inequality and evidence. *Educational Research, 55,* 139–164.

Mattei, P. (2012). Raising educational standards: National testing of pupils in the United Kingdom, 1988–2009. *Policy Studies, 33,* 231–247.

McCoy, S. K., & Major, B. (2007). Priming meritocracy and the psychological justification of inequality. *Journal of Experimental Social Psychology, 43,* 341–351.

Ministry of Education Singapore. (2009). *Report of the Primary Education Review and Implementation Committee.* Singapore: Ministry of Education.

Mueller, C. W., & Parcel, T. L. (1981). Measures of socioeconomic status: Alternatives and recommendations. *Child Development, 52,* 13–30.

Muthén, L. K., & Muthén, B. O. (2012). *Mplus version 7.0* [computer software].

Nicaise, I., Esping-Andersen, G., Pont, B., & Tunstall, P. (2005). *Equity in education: Thematic review.* Paris, France: OECD Publishing)

OECD. (2005). *School factors related to quality and equity: Results from PISA 2000.* Paris, France: OECD Publishing.

OECD. (2010). *A family affair: Intergenerational social mobility across OECD countries.* Paris, France: OECD Publishing.

OECD. (2012). *Equity and quality in education: Supporting disadvantage students and schools.* Paris, France: OECD Publishing.

Paquette, J. (1998). Equity in educational policy: A priority in transformation or in trouble? *Journal of Education Policy, 13,* 41–61.

Roemer, J. E. (2004). *Equal opportunity and intergenerational mobility: Going beyond intergenerational income transition matrices.* Cambridge, UK: Cambridge University Press.

Rust, K. (1994). *Issues in sampling for international comparative studies in education: The case of the IEA Reading Literacy study. Methodological issues in comparative educational studies..* Washington, DC: US Department of Education, Office for Educational Research and Improvement.

Schleicher, A. (2009). Securing quality and equity in education: Lessons from PISA. *Prospects, 39,* 251–263.

Schütz, G., Ursprung, H. W., & Woessmann, L. (2008). Education policy and equality of opportunity. *Kyklos, 61,* 279–308.

Sirin, S. R. (2005). Socioeconomic status and academic achievement: A meta-analytic review of research. *Review of Educational Research, 75,* 417–453.

Stegmueller, D. (2013). How many countries for multilevel modeling? A comparison of frequentist and bayesian approaches. *American Journal of Political Science, 57,* 748–761.

Unesco. (2013). *Human Development Index (HDI).* Retrieved from http://hdr.undp.org/en/statistics/hdi/

Von Davier, M., Gonzalez, E., & Mislevy, R. (2009). What are plausible values and why are they useful? *IERI Monograph Series Issues and Methodologies in Large-Scale Assessments.* Hamburg: IER Institute, Educational Testing Service.

Woessmann, L. (2004). *How equal are educational opportunities?: Family background and student achievement in Europe and the United States.* Bonn, Germany: IZA.

Yang, Y. (2003). Dimensions of socio-economic status and their relationship to mathematics and science achievement at individual and collective levels. *Scandinavian Journal of Educational Research, 47,* 21–41.

Yang, Y., & Gustafsson, J. E. (2004). Measuring socioeconomic status at individual and collective levels. *Educational Research and Evaluation, 10,* 259–288.

Zajda, J., Majhanovich, S., & Rust, V. (2007). Introduction: Education and social justice. *International Review of Education, 52,* 9–22.

Chapter 8
School Resources and Student Achievement: A Review of Cross-Country Economic Research

Eric A. Hanushek and Ludger Woessmann

Abstract How do school resources affect students' academic achievement? This chapter provides a survey of economists' work on the effect of expenditure and class size on student achievement using different international student achievement tests, with a particular focus on the use of quasi-experimental research methods to address challenges of the identification of causal effects. Overall, the international evidence provides little confidence that quantitative measures of expenditure and class size are a major driver of student achievement, across and within countries. The cross-country pattern suggests that class size is a relevant variable only in settings with low teacher quality. Among other school inputs, descriptive evidence suggests that measures of the quality of inputs and, in particular, teachers are more closely related to student outcomes.

8.1 Introduction

How do school resources affect students' academic achievement? A lot of work on this question has emerged since Jan-Eric Gustafsson (2003) reviewed the literature. In particular, much research has used data from international student achievement

---

This is a slightly extended version of an extract from a much longer article previously published under the title "The Economics of International Differences in Educational Achievement" in the *Handbook of the Economics of Education*, Vol. 3, edited by Eric A. Hanushek, Stephen Machin, and Ludger Woessmann, Amsterdam: North Holland, pp. 89–200, Copyright Elsevier (2011). We are grateful to Elsevier for granting us the right to reproduce the material here.

E.A. Hanushek
Stanford University, NBER, and CESifo, Stanford, USA
e-mail: hanushek@stanford.edu

L. Woessmann (✉)
University of Munich, Ifo Institute, CESifo, and IZA, Munich, Germany
e-mail: woessmann@ifo.de

© Springer International Publishing AG 2017
M. Rosén et al. (eds.), *Cognitive Abilities and Educational Outcomes*,
Methodology of Educational Measurement and Assessment,
DOI 10.1007/978-3-319-43473-5_8

tests to shed new light on the question. Much of this research, in particular from economists working in the field, has focused on challenges of the identification of causal effects by using quasi-experimental research methods. Some of the recent research is in line with the suggestion by Gustafsson (2007) that important analysis could come from changes in the performance of different countries over time. This chapter provides a survey of economists' work on the effect of expenditure and class size on student achievement using different international student achievement tests. Part of this research focusses on the challenge of overcoming possible bias in cross-country estimation, part on the identification of causal effects within countries.

Virtually all nations of the world today realize the research and policy value of student performance data that come from testing the cognitive skills of students. While there is wide variation across nations in testing—differing by subject matter, grade level, purpose, and quality of testing—the idea of assessing what students know as opposed to how long they have been in school has diffused around the world, in part at the instigation of international development and aid agencies. Somewhat less known is that comparative cross-national testing has been going on for a long time. Nations participated in common international assessments of mathematics and science long before they instituted national testing programs. These common international assessments provide unique data for understanding both the importance of various factors determining achievement and the impact of skills on economic and social outcomes.

In the mid-1960s, international consortia started to develop and implement comparisons of educational achievement across nations. Since then, the math, science, and reading performance of students in many countries have been tested on multiple occasions using (at each occasion) a common set of test questions in all participating countries. By 2016, three major international testing programs are surveying student performance on a regular basis: the Programme for International Student Assessment (PISA) testing math, science, and reading performance of 15-year-olds on a three-year cycle since 2000, the Trends in International Mathematics and Science Study (TIMSS) testing math and science performance (mostly) of eighth-graders on a four-year cycle since 1995, and the Progress in International Reading Literacy Study (PIRLS) testing primary-school reading performance on a five-year cycle since 2001.

The research based on the international assessments goes in two different directions: research designed to understand the underlying determinants of cognitive skills and research focused on the consequences of skill differences. Here, we simply focus on surveying the literature on school resources as one group of determinants of international educational achievement, covering both evidence across countries and evidence within different countries. For research on student background and institutional structures of the education system as two other groups of possible determinants, see Sects. 4.2 and 4.4 in Hanushek and Woessmann (2011a). For the second line of research, see Sect. 5 in Hanushek and Woessmann (2011a), as well as Hanushek and Woessmann (2015). Furthermore, Sects. 1–3 in Hanushek and Woessmann (2011a) provide a more detailed discussion of the unique advantages of and concerns with the use of cross-country data, a brief economic motivation to frame the discussions and an overview and critical assessment of the different available international datasets on educational achievement.

The cross-country comparative approach provides a number of unique advantages over national studies: It can exploit institutional variation that does not exist within countries; draw on much larger variation than is usually available within any country; reveal whether any result is country-specific or more general; test whether effects are systematically heterogeneous in different settings; circumvent selection issues that plague within-country identification by using system-level aggregated measures; and uncover general-equilibrium effects that often elude studies in a single country. The advantages come at the price of concerns about the limited number of country observations, the cross-sectional character of most available achievement data, and possible bias from unobserved country factors like culture.

The standards of evidence throughout empirical economics have changed in recent years, sometimes dramatically. The character of change also enters directly into our consideration of cross-country analyses. The analytical designs employed in the cross-country analyses we discuss have developed over time in a way that parallels much of the related micro-econometric work within individual countries. The initial publications of comparative tests across nations by the organizations that conducted the different studies tended to report bivariate associations. Subsequent analyses performed multiple regressions in the form of educational production functions that tried to address the most obvious perils of bias from intervening factors by adding corresponding control variables. While initial studies estimated international educational production functions at the aggregate country level, subsequent studies exploited the full variation of the international micro data.

More recently, several studies have started to employ econometric techniques such as instrumental-variable, regression-discontinuity, differences-in-differences, and different sorts of fixed-effects specifications in order to come closer to identification of causal relationships in the international data on educational achievement. This applies both to the identification of causal effects within countries and to the challenge of overcoming possible bias from unobserved country heterogeneity—e.g., in terms of cultural differences—in cross-country estimation. While these developments are far from complete at this time, we emphasize the issues of identification and interpretation in much of the discussion below.

We limit the coverage of this chapter to studies that make cross-country comparisons. Based on this criterion, we cover only studies that estimate the same specification for different countries or estimate a cross-country specification. Studies that use the international survey data for analysis within a single country will be referenced only insofar as they are directly relevant for the internationally comparative approach.

8.2   International Evidence on Education Production Functions

As is the case in the majority of the literature on educational production, the basic model underlying the literature on determinants of international educational achievement resembles some form of the education production function:

$$T = a_0 + a_1 F + a_2 R + a_3 I + a_4 A + e$$

where T is the outcome of the educational production process as measured, e.g., by test scores of mathematics, science, and reading achievement. The vector F captures facets of student and family background characteristics, R is a vector of measures of school resources, I are institutional features of schools and education systems, and A is individual ability.

When estimating this equation within different countries, studies based on international data face the same methodological challenges as studies restricted to a specific country (see Hanushek 1979, 2002; Todd and Wolpin 2003 for key issues in empirical identification of education production functions). The fundamental challenge is that most inputs in the education production function are likely not to be exogenous in a statistical sense. Leading concerns derive from omitted variables, selection, and reverse causation. A key candidate of an omitted variable is student ability A, most dimensions of which tend to go unmeasured and are likely correlated with other inputs in important ways. An additional concern for research on most of the international tests is their cross-sectional structure which does not allow for panel or value-added estimations, so that temporally prior inputs are usually unobserved. School inputs will often be the outcome of choices of parents, administrators, and schools that are correlated with the error term of the production function. Given this substantial scope for endogeneity bias, least-squares estimates of the equation need to be interpreted with great care, even when they control for a large set of observable input factors. This has led to the development of more elaborate techniques that try to draw on exogenous variation in the variables of interest.

In the following review of the literature, we will refer to the more descriptive studies only briefly and mostly focus on studies trying to address the key identification issues. There is, however, one specific aspect about making cross-country comparisons of estimates obtained from performing the same estimation in different countries: If one is willing to make the assumption that any bias is constant across countries, then a cross-country comparison of estimates is feasible, even if interpretation of the size of each estimate is not.

The main challenges change when it comes to studies estimating cross-country associations. There are both unique advantages and specific concerns with using cross-country data to estimate the determinants of educational achievement. At the most general level, cross-country estimation is able to get around the most pressing concerns of bias from selection but introduces new kinds of omitted variable concerns. Within-country variation is often subject to severe selection problems:

For example, students who choose to attend a well-equipped school may differ along both observable and unobservable dimensions from students taught in poorly equipped schools. While many observable characteristics are often controlled for in econometric analyses, thereby comparing students who are observationally equivalent, within-country estimates may still suffer from selection on unobserved characteristics. In cross-country analyses, one can aggregate the input variable of interest up to the country level, thereby circumventing the selection problem. In effect, the cross-country analysis then measures the impact of, for example, the average expenditure per student in a country on student achievement in the country as a whole. Such cross-country analysis cannot be biased by standard issues of selection at the individual level, as patterns of sorting cancel out at the system level.

The main cost to this—apart from the limited degrees of freedom at the country level—is that unobserved heterogeneity at the country level may introduce new forms of omitted variable bias. For example, cultural factors such as "Asian values" may remain unobserved in the econometric model and correlate both with student outcomes and relevant inputs in the education production function. Education systems—and societies more generally—may also differ in other important dimensions unobserved by the researcher. To address such concerns, the main results of cross-country studies should be checked for robustness to including obvious correlates of the cultural factors as control variables at the country level. Another robustness check is to draw only on variation within major world regions by including regional (continental) fixed effects. More fundamentally, some cross-country studies have started to adopt new techniques directly developed to address such issues of identification in particular contexts, and these studies will be the main focus of the following review.

Early studies that employ the international student achievement tests to estimate similar education production function within different countries include Heyneman and Loxley (1983) and Toma (1996). Early studies using the cross-country variation of international tests to estimate international education production functions on country-level observations include Bishop (1997), Hanushek and Kimko (2000), and Lee and Barro (2001). The first economic study to make use of the vast potential of the international micro data on students' achievement, family background, and school inputs and of the broad array of institutional differences that exists across countries to estimate extensive multivariate cross-country education production functions is Woessmann (2003). While still subject to the prior issues of cross-country identification, employing the rich student-level data on background factors allows to hold constant a large set of observable factors usually unavailable in national datasets.

Table 8.1 presents an example estimation of an international education production function.[1] Using student-level data for 29 OECD countries from the 2003 cycle of the PISA test of 15-year-olds, the model expresses individual student achievement in math as a function of large set of input factors. While this is a basic

---

[1] See Woessmann et al. (2009) for additional background and robustness analyses.

Table 8.1 An example of an international education production function: PISA 2003

	Coef.	Std. err.
STUDENT CHARACTERISTICS		
Age (years)	17.593***	(1.101)
Female	-17.360***	(0.639)
Preprimary education (more than 1 year)	5.606***	(0.703)
School starting age	-3.863***	(0.505)
Grade repetition in primary school	-35.794***	(1.410)
Grade repetition in secondary school	-34.730***	(1.646)
Grade		
7th grade	-47.184***	(4.068)
8th grade	-28.009***	(2.239)
9th grade	-12.486***	(1.337)
11th grade	-6.949***	(2.062)
12th grade	7.030	(4.826)
Immigration background		
First generation student	-9.047***	(1.544)
Non-native student	-9.040***	(1.644)
Language spoken at home		
Other national dialect or language	-23.736***	(2.849)
Foreign language	-8.381***	(1.665)
FAMILY BACKGROUND		
Living with		
Single mother or father	19.349***	(1.842)
Patchwork family	21.272***	(2.032)
Both parents	27.432***	(1.829)
Parents' working status		
Both full-time	-2.479*	(1.325)
One full-time, one half-time	6.744***	(1.063)
At least one full time	13.753***	(1.173)
At least one half time	8.416***	(1.133)
Parents' job		
Blue collar high skilled	0.431	(0.970)
White collar low skilled	2.864***	(0.933)
White collar high skilled	8.638***	(0.988)
Books at home		
11-25 books	5.554***	(0.978)
26-100 books	22.943***	(1.009)
101-200 books	32.779***	(1.117)
201-500 books	49.834***	(1.219)
More than 500 books	51.181***	(1.399)
Index of Economic, Social and Cultural Status (ESCS)	18.114***	(0.524)
GDP per capita (1,000 $)	-1.890*	(1.060)

(continued)

Table 8.1 (continued)

	Coef.	Std. err.
SCHOOL INPUTS		
School's community location		
Town (3,000-100,000)	3.226[*]	*(1.531)*
City (100,000-1,000,000)	10.782[***]	*(1.890)*
Large city with > 1 million people	7.895[***]	*(2.378)*
Educational expenditure per student (1,000 $)	1.174[***]	*(0.405)*
Class size (mathematics)	1.474[***]	*(0.067)*
Shortage of instructional materials		
Not at all	-10.180[***]	*(2.576)*
Strongly	6.720[***]	*(1.300)*
Instruction time (minutes per week)	0.035[***]	*(0.005)*
Teacher education (share at school)		
Fully certified teachers	9.715[***]	*(3.422)*
Tertiary degree in pedagogy	6.573[***]	*(2.010)*
INSTITUTIONS		
Choice		
Private operation	57.585[***]	*(8.355)*
Government funding	81.839[***]	*(22.327)*
Accountability		
External exit exams	25.338[*]	*(10.054)*
Assessments used to decide about students' retention/promotion	12.185[***]	*(1.631)*
Monitoring of teacher lessons by principal	4.557[***]	*(1.343)*
Monitoring of teacher lessons by external inspectors	3.796[***]	*(1.415)*
Assessments used to compare school to district/national performance	2.134[*]	*(1.259)*
Assessments used to group students	-6.065[***]	*(1.301)*
Autonomy and its interaction with accountability		
Autonomy in formulating budget	-9.609[***]	*(2.178)*
External exit exams x Autonomy in formulating budget	9.143[***]	*(3.119)*
Autonomy in establishing starting salaries	-8.632[***]	*(3.251)*
External exit exams x Autonomy in establishing starting salaries	5.868	*(3.980)*
Autonomy in determining course content	0.175	*(1.907)*
External exit exams x Autonomy in determining course content	3.224	*(2.858)*
Autonomy in hiring teachers	20.659[***]	*(2.249)*
External exit exams x Autonomy in hiring teachers	-28.935[***]	*(3.365)*
Students	219,794	
Schools	8,245	
Countries	29	
R^2 (at student level)	0.390	
R^2 (at country level)	0.872	

Notes: Dependent variable: PISA 2003 international mathematics test score. Least-squares regressions weighted by students' sampling probability. The models additionally control for imputation dummies and interaction terms between imputation dummies and the variables. Robust standard errors adjusted for clustering at the school level in parentheses (clustering at country level for all country-level variables, which are private operation, government funding, external exit exams, GDP per capita, and expenditure per student). Significance level (based on clustering-robust standard errors): [***] 1 percent, [**] 5 percent, [*] 10 percent.

Source: Own calculations based on Woessmann et al. (2009), who provide additional background details.

model that does not fully exploit the potential of the international data, the model specification already documents the rich set of background factors available from the student and school background questionnaires. Moreover, the international data display wide variation in many of the potential inputs to achievement, thus allowing for more precise estimation of any effects. At the individual level, the factors include student characteristics such as age, gender, immigration, and preprimary educational attendance and family-background measures such as socio-economic status, parental occupation, family status, and the number of books in the home. At the school level, the model includes resource measures such as class size and shortage of materials, instruction time, teacher education, community location, and institutional factors such as a set of measures of teacher monitoring and student assessment, different dimensions of school autonomy, and their interaction with accountability measures. At the country level, this basic model includes a country's GDP per capita, educational expenditure per student, and the institutional factors of external exit exams, share of privately operated schools, and average government funding of schools.

While the cross-sectional nature of this estimation allows for a descriptive interpretation only, it is worth noting that many measures of students' individual and family background are systematically related to their achievement, as are several measures of the institutional structure of the school system. By contrast, the point estimate on class size, the classical measure of quantitative school inputs, is counterintuitive,[2] and the estimates on the more qualitative school inputs, while positive, are more limited than the background and institutional estimates. The model accounts for 39 % of the achievement variation at the student level and for 87 % at the country level. That is, while unobserved factors such as ability differences are important at the individual level, the model is able to account statistically for most of the between-country variation in academic achievement. These basic result patterns are broadly common to all studies of international education production functions estimated on the different international student achievement tests. Here, we focus on one specific group of determinants, namely school inputs. Sections 4.2 and 4.4 in Hanushek and Woessmann (2011a) discuss the literature on the other two groups of determinants—student and family background, as well as institutional structures of the education system—in greater detail.

---

[2]The coefficient on country-level spending is very small. While it is statistically significant, identification here comes from a very particular margin, as the correlation between spending and per-capita GDP (whose coefficient is negative here) in this model is as high as 0.93. Other studies tend to find a significant positive coefficient on GDP per capita, but not on spending. See Hanushek and Woessmann (2011a) for more extensive discussion.

8.3   Evidence on School Inputs Across Countries

We start with research that uses variation in school inputs across countries.[3] The studies reveal that in general, the cross-country association of student achievement with resources tends to be relatively weak.

When looking across countries, the most straightforward starting point is the simple association between the aggregate financial measure of average expenditure per student and average achievement. Figure 8.1 presents the international association between cumulative spending per student from age 6 to 15 and the average math achievement of 15-year-olds on the 2003 PISA test. Without considering the strong outliers of Mexico and Greece, there is no association between spending levels and average achievement across countries.[4] At the most basic level, countries

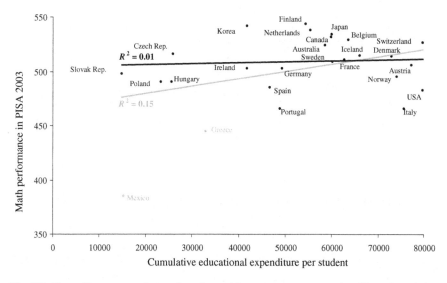

Fig. 8.1 Expenditure per student and student achievement across countries. *Notes* Association between average math achievement in PISA 2003 and cumulative expenditure on educational institutions per student between age 6 and 15, in US dollars, converted by purchasing power parities. *Dark line* regression line for full sample. *Light line* regression line omitting Mexico and Greece. *Source* Woessmann (2007)

---

[3]For a general overview of such studies see Table 2.6 in Hanushek and Woessmann (2011a).

[4]With the two outliers, there is a weak positive association as long as other effects are ignored. Taken literally, the full-sample association suggests that $60,000 per student in additional expenditure (a quadrupling of spending in the low spending countries) is associated with about a half standard deviation improvement in scores. However, once a country's GDP per capita is controlled for, the cross-country association between student achievement and expenditure loses statistical significance and even turns negative, suggesting that the bivariate association is driven by the omitted factor of average socio-economic status.

with high educational spending appear to perform at the same level as countries with low expenditures.

This picture has been evident in many other waves of the different international achievement tests (e.g., Woessmann (2002), Sect. 3.2, for the 1995 TIMSS test). Furthermore, in most cases the lack of a significant positive cross-country association between expenditure per student and educational achievement holds up when numerous other determining factors such as family background and school features (including instruction time) are accounted for in a regression framework. Hanushek and Kimko (2000) and Lee and Barro (2001) perform country-level regressions using different tests and Woessmann (2003) and Fuchs and Woessmann (2007) perform student-level microeconometric regressions using TIMSS 1995 and PISA 2000, respectively.

As discussed above, such cross-sectional analysis has to be interpreted cautiously, even when controlling for a large set of factors. There may be reverse causality, and unobserved country differences—e.g., cultural traits or institutional and political factors—may be correlated with both inputs and outcomes. As a first step to address such worries, one can look at within-country variation over time. By looking at changes in inputs and outcomes, one can rule out unobserved level effects. Thus, Gundlach et al. (2001) calculate changes in expenditure and achievement for individual OECD countries from 1970 t o 1994, and Gundlach and Woessmann (2001) for individual East Asian countries from 1980 to 1994.[5]

The results, depicted in Fig. 8.2, suggest that educational expenditure per student has increased substantially in real terms in all considered OECD countries between the early 1970s and the mid-1990s, and in all considered East Asian countries except the Philippines between the early 1980s and the mid-1990s.[6] Yet, comparing test scores over the same time intervals suggests that no substantial improvement in average student achievement has occurred in any of these countries. Combining the time-series evidence on resources and achievement, it is fair to conclude that substantial increases in real school expenditure per student did not lead to improvements in student outcomes in most of the sampled OECD and East Asian countries. In fact, the experience of many countries is much bleaker than what had been termed the "productivity collapse in schools" in the United States (Hanushek 1997).[7]

---

[5]Achievement data from the international tests at the two respective points in time are linked using U.S. longitudinal achievement data. Increases in educational expenditure are adjusted not only for average inflation, but also for the so-called "Baumol effect" of increasing costs in service sectors with constant productivity. Three different approaches of calculating price deflators for the schooling sector that account for this effect are averaged in the depiction of Fig. 2. For details, see Gundlach et al. (2001), Gundlach and Woessmann (2001), and Woessmann (2002), Sect. 3.3.

[6]Gundlach and Woessmann (2001) show that the resource expansion in the East Asian countries mostly results from government decisions to raise the number of teachers per student.

[7]One potential explanation for this bivariate longitudinal pattern might of course be that students' family background might have deteriorated on average. Students may increasingly be lacking many of the basic capabilities required for a successful education and may thus be increasingly expensive to educate. Such effects may play a significant role in countries with a large inflow of

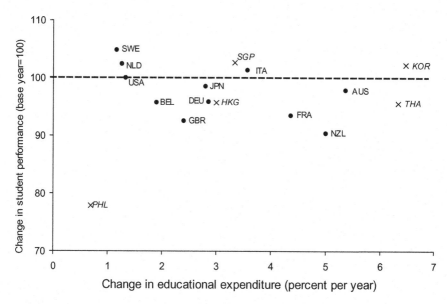

Fig. 8.2 Change in expenditure per student and in student achievement over time. *Notes* Data for OECD countries refer to 1970–1994, data for East Asian countries to 1980–1994. Change in student performance: students' average educational performance in math and science in 1994 relative to base year. Change in educational expenditure: average annual rate of change in real educational expenditure per student in percent. Country abbreviations: Australia (*AUS*), Belgium (*BEL*), France (*FRA*), Germany (*DEU*), Hong Kong (*HKG*), Italy (*ITA*), Japan (*JPN*), Netherlands (*NLD*), Philippines (*PHL*), Singapore (*SGP*), South Korea (*KOR*), Sweden (*SWE*), Thailand (*THA*), United Kingdom (*GBR*), United States (*USA*). *Source* Based on Gundlach et al. (2001) and Gundlach and Woessmann (2001)

More recently, the linking of the PISA tests over time allows for a direct comparison of spending changes to changes in achievement on psychometrically linked tests. As is directly obvious from Fig. 8.3, changes in PISA performance from 2000 to 2012 are not systematically related to concurrent changes in expenditure per student (Hanushek and Woessmann 2015). Countries with large spending increases do not show different achievement trends from countries that spend only little more. The coefficient estimate on expenditure in the simple underlying

---

(Footnote 7 continued)

immigrant students or with rising levels of poverty. But on average, parents in the considered countries have been enjoying higher incomes and better education over time, and the number of children per family has declined. Hence by the later periods, children may actually start schooling with better basic capabilities than before. These issues, however, await thorough econometric analysis.

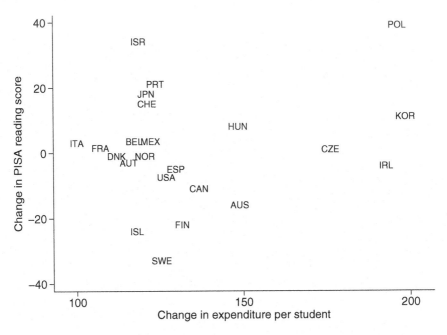

Fig. 8.3 Changes in educational spending and in student achievement across countries. *Notes* Scatter plot of the change in expenditure per student, 2000–2010 (constant prices, 2000 = 100) against change in PISA reading score, 2000–2012. *Source* Hanushek and Woessmann (2015) based on OECD data

first-differenced regression is insignificant, and without the apparent outlier Poland, the point estimate is negative.[8]

Apart from the aggregate expenditure measure, the cross-country variation has also been used to analyze specific resource inputs in cross-sectional analysis. Expenditure per student is an encompassing measure of school inputs which considers not only personnel costs but also material costs. But international comparisons of expenditure may be hampered by the problem of choosing an appropriate exchange rate (Fig. 8.1 uses conversion by purchasing power parities). Because personnel costs make up more than three quarters of total expenditure in nearly all countries, class size lends itself particularly well as a non-monetary input measure for international comparisons which determines a large part of total expenditure. However, using class size instead of expenditure per student yields the same general picture as in Fig. 8.1. Regression analyses that control for family background measures come to similar results. At the country level, Lee and Barro (2001) find a positive effect of smaller student-teacher ratios, but Hanushek and Kimko (2000)

---

[8]Similarly, using data from the first three PISA waves, the working-paper version of Hanushek and Woessmann (2011b) reports insignificant negative coefficient estimates on expenditure per student in first-differenced and fixed-effects models.

find no such relationship.[9] However, country-level analysis may suffer from aggregation bias (Hanushek et al. 1996), as Fertig and Wright (2005) show that the probability of finding statistically significant and correctly signed class-size effects increases with the level of aggregation. Student-level analyses that use data on the actual size of the class of the tested students, rather than ratios of teachers to students at some level, tend to find counterintuitive signs of the coefficient on class size that are often statistically significant (e.g., Woessmann 2003; Fuchs and Woessmann 2007; Table 8.1).

The latter studies also take indicators of the shortage of instructional material, usually reported by school principals, into account. Shortage of material tends to be negatively associated with student outcomes. Measures of instruction time also tend to be significantly related to achievement. By contrast, in multivariate analyses the availability of computers at school is not related to student outcomes, and intensive computer use is negatively related to test scores (Fuchs and Woessmann 2004).

In the student-level studies, measures of teacher education tend to show positive associations with student achievement in cross-country analyses. Drawing on information from teacher background questionnaires in TIMSS, Woessmann (2003) finds positive associations of student achievement with teacher experience and female gender and a negative one with teacher age. In their country-level analysis, Lee and Barro (2001) find a positive effect of teacher salary levels. Similarly, Woessmann (2005b) reports a significant positive coefficient on a country-level measure of teacher salary when added to an international student-level regression. Dolton and Marcenaro-Gutierrez (2011) pool country-level data from international tests in 1995–2006 to show that teacher salaries—both when measured in absolute terms and relative to wages in each country—are positively associated with student achievement, even after controlling for country fixed effects.

In sum, the general pattern of the cross-country analyses suggests that quantitative measures of school inputs such as expenditure and class size cannot account for the cross-country variation in educational achievement. By contrast, several studies tend to find positive associations of student achievement with the quality of instructional material and the quality of the teaching force. While these cross-country associations reveal to what extent different input factors can descriptively account for international differences in student achievement, studies that focus more closely on the identification of causal effects have reverted to using the within-country variation in resources and achievement. This literature is most advanced for the estimation of class-size effects. In the following, we discuss three approaches that have been suggested to estimate causal class-size effects on international data: a combination of school fixed effects with instrumental variables, a regression discontinuity approach that makes use of variation stemming from maximum class-size rules, and a subject fixed effects approach.

---

[9]Using country-level data for data envelopment analysis, Afonso and St. Aubyn (2006) find indications of substantial inefficiencies in the use of teachers per student in most countries.

8.4   Evidence on School Inputs Within Different Countries

The initial within-country studies have used conventional least-squares techniques to focus on developing countries and their comparison to developed countries, a particular advantage of using international data.[10] Relying on data from early international tests, Heyneman and Loxley (1983) suggested that school resources tend to be more closely related to student achievement in developing countries than in developed countries. Hanushek and Luque (2003) did not corroborate this conclusion using the more recent TIMSS data. Michaelowa (2001) uses the regional PASEC data to provide conventional evidence for five countries in Francophone Sub-Saharan Africa.[11]

The problem with such conventional estimates is that resources in general, and class sizes in particular, are not only a cause but also a consequence of student achievement or of unobserved factors related to student achievement. Many features may lead to the joint and simultaneous determination of class size and student achievement, making class size endogenous to student achievement. For example, schools may reduce class sizes for poorly performing students and policymakers may design compensatory funding schemes for schools with large shares of students from poor backgrounds (see West and Woessmann 2006 for international evidence). In both cases, class sizes are allocated in a compensatory manner, biasing the class-size coefficient upwards. In contrast, policymakers may also have high-performing students taught in special small classes to support elite performance. Likewise, parents who particularly care for the education of their children may both make residential choices to ensure that their children are taught in schools with relatively small classes and support their children in many other ways, leading them to be relatively high performers. In these cases, class sizes are allocated in a reinforcing manner, biasing the class-size coefficient downwards. In short, parents, teachers, schools, and administrators all make choices that might give rise to a non-causal association between class size and student achievement even after controlling extensively for family background. Conventional estimates of class-size effects may thus suffer from endogeneity bias, the direction of which is ambiguous a priori.

To identify causal class-size effects, two quasi-experimental strategies have been applied to the international test data (cf. Woessmann 2005b). The first quasi-experimental approach draws on exogenous variation in class size caused by natural fluctuations in the size of subsequent student cohorts of a school (similar to Hoxby 2000). In this case, the quasi-experiment results from the idea that natural fluctuations in student enrollment lead to variations in average class size in two

---

[10]See Table 2.7 in Hanushek and Woessmann (2011a) for an overview of within-country studies on school inputs.

[11]Using PIRLS data, Woessmann (2010) estimates a quasi-value-added model, controlling for retrospective information on pre-school performance, for primary-school students in two Latin American and several comparison countries.

adjacent grades in the same school. Natural birth fluctuations around the cut-off date that splits students into different grade levels occur randomly. Therefore, they lead to variation in class size that is driven neither by students' educational achievement nor by other features that might jointly affect class size and student achievement.

Woessmann and West (2006) develop a variant of this identification strategy that exploits specific features of the TIMSS database. The sampling design of the first TIMSS study, which tested a complete 7th-grade class and a complete 8th-grade class in each school, enables them to use only the variation between two adjacent grades in individual schools. This strategy aims to exclude biases from nonrandom between-school and within-school sorting through a combination of school fixed effects and instrumental variables using grade-average class sizes as instruments. The rationale of this approach is as follows. Any between-school sorting is eliminated in a first step by controlling for school fixed effects, restricting the analysis solely to variation within individual schools. Within schools, the allocation of students to different classes in a grade may also be non-random. Within-school sorting is filtered out in a second step by instrumenting actual class size by the average class size in the relevant grade in each school. Within-school variation in class size is thus used only insofar as it is related to variation in average class size between the 7th and 8th grade of a school. The identifying assumption is that such variation is not affected by student sorting but reflects random fluctuations in birth-cohort size between the two grades in the catchment area of each school. Thus, causal class-size effects are identified by relating differences in the relative achievement of students in 7th and 8th grade within individual schools to that part of the between-grade difference in class size in the school that reflects between-grade differences in average class size.

Figure 8.4 illustrates the basic intuition behind this identification strategy for the example of math achievement in Singapore. The top panel indicates that class-average test scores are *positively* associated with class size, as is the case in most countries—likely reflecting ability sorting of students between and within schools. The middle panel plots the achievement difference between the 7th-grade and 8th-grade class in each school against the same grade difference in class size, which is equivalent to including school fixed effects in a regression framework. Overcoming effects of between-school sorting by removing any difference in overall achievement levels between schools, the size of the positive correlation is reduced substantially, but remains statistically significant. The reduction suggests that poorly performing students tend to be sorted into schools with smaller classes in Singapore. The final step of the identification strategy, illustrated in the bottom panel, additionally eliminates any effects of within-school sorting by using only that part of the between-grade variation in actual class sizes that can be predicted by variation in grade-average class sizes. The picture suggests that class size has no causal effect on student achievement in math in Singapore. Rather, weaker students seem to be consistently placed in smaller classes, both between and within schools.

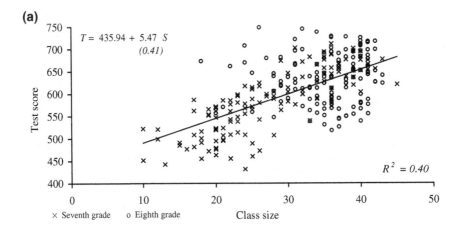

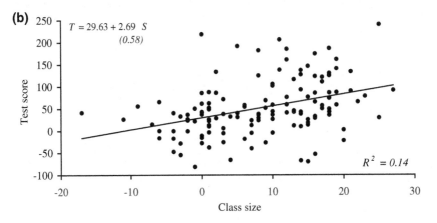

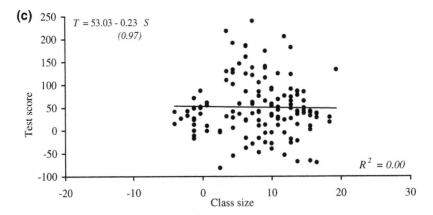

Fig. 8.4 Identifying class-size effects: Singapore as an illustrative example. *Source* Woessmann (2007) **a** All classes, **b** grade difference and **c** grade difference, instrumented

Woessmann and West (2006) implement this identification strategy in microeconometric estimations of education production functions for 11 countries around the world.[12] In line with Fig. 8.4, their results suggest that conventional estimates of class-size effects tend to be severely biased. They find sizable beneficial effects of smaller classes in Greece and Iceland, but reject the possibility of even small effects in four countries and of large beneficial effects in an additional four countries. Additional specification tests support the identifying assumption that students and teachers are not systematically sorted between grades within individual schools. There are no systematic differences at all in the observable characteristics of students or teachers between the two grades in schools in which one of the two adjacent grades has substantially larger average class sizes than the other; there are no systematic differences in the estimated class-size effects between expanding, stable, and contracting schools; and there are no systematic differences in the estimated class-size effects between countries where 7th grade is the first grade of a particular school and countries where it is not so that grade-average class sizes might have been adjusted based on schools' experience with the particular students.

The basic pattern of results is corroborated by a second quasi-experimental identification strategy based on rule-induced discontinuities. Following the study by Angrist and Lavy (1999) for Israel, Woessmann (2005b) exploits the fact that many countries have maximum class-size rules that induce a nonlinear association between the number of students in a grade of a school and average class size. In particular, the association has sharp discontinuities at multiples of the maximum class size that can be exploited to identify variation in class sizes that is exogenous to student achievement. The TIMSS data suggest that 10 West European school systems implement national maximum class-size rules reasonably strictly and with enough sharpness to enable an empirical implementation of this instrumental variable strategy.[13] In all 10 countries, results from identification by rule-induced discontinuities rule out the possibility of large causal class-size effects in lower secondary school. The only statistically significant, but small estimates are, again, in Iceland and, marginally, in Norway.

Woessmann (2005b) shows that these results are robust to several specification tests. Some models control for peer effects, in terms of the mean achievement and family background of each student's classmates, to exclude bias from peer sorting. Controlling for any continuous association between grade enrollment and student achievement by adding enrollment in the specific grade and its squared term as additional controls does not lead to substantive changes in results. When applying the specification to a discontinuity sample of students whose grade enrollment is within a margin of plus or minus 5 or 6 students of the rule-based discontinuities, so that identification does not come from observations far off the discontinuities, the

---

[12]Additional evidence based on the same identification strategy for countries in West Europe, East Europe, and East Asia is presented in Woessmann (2005b), Ammermueller et al. (2005), and Woessmann (2005a), respectively.

[13]The ten West European school systems that employ maximum class-size rules are: Denmark, France, Germany, Greece, Iceland, Ireland, Norway, Spain, Sweden, and Switzerland.

instrument gets weak in about half the countries, while results remain robust in the other half. Excluding especially large schools in each country (of a size three or four times the maximum class size) does not lead to a substantive change in results.[14]

However, as discussed by Woessmann (2005b), some reservations remain with this regression-discontinuity identification strategy (cf. also Urquiola and Verhoogen 2009). In particular, intentional exploitations of the rule by systematic between- and within-school choices might lead to remaining endogeneity in the rule discontinuity approach. Thus, it is possible that parents and schools "play the system": parents particularly keen to ensure low class sizes for their children may make their enrollment decisions—and school principals their acceptance decisions —on the basis of expected class size, and those decisions may be related to student achievement. Still, in the end both quasi-experimental identification strategies come to a very similar pattern of results. Moreover, the source of the potentially remaining biases differs in the two cases, adding confidence that any remaining bias in each strategy is of second-order magnitude.

Both identification strategies reach the conclusion that class size is not a major force in shaping achievement in lower secondary school in any of the countries considered. There is no single country for which any of the specifications showed a statistically significant and large class-size effect. In every case where one of the methods leads to a reasonably precise estimate, a large effect size can be ruled out with considerable statistical confidence. There is only one country, Iceland, where results create confidence that a causal class-size effects exists. However, in both specifications the estimates are relatively small and estimated precisely enough to reject the possibility of a large effect.

The unique value of cross-country research, however, lies in analyses of whether the cross-country differences in estimated class-size effects are systematically related to underlying features of the school systems. Such analyses can improve our understanding of the particular circumstances under which class sizes matter or not. Although causal class-size effects are small at best in all the countries considered, there are still differences across countries. The international evidence shows that the estimated effect size does not vary systematically for children from differing family backgrounds or for countries with different levels of average achievement, economic development, average class size, or educational spending (Woessmann and West 2006; Woessmann 2005b). But the existence of class-size effects is systematically associated with the salary and education level of the teaching force. In both studies, class-size effects were detected only in countries with relatively low teacher salaries and education. The pattern is similar within countries in which the education level of teachers varies. In these countries, the estimated class-size effect tends to be larger in classes that are taught by teachers with lower education. Interpreting average teacher salary and teacher education as proxies for average teacher quality, the results suggest that relatively capable teachers do as well when teaching large classes as when teaching small classes. By contrast, less capable

---

[14]The size of the induced discontinuity in class size is smaller when grade enrollment is larger.

teachers do not seem to be up to the job of teaching large classes, while doing reasonably well in small classes. Consequently, the pattern of international effect heterogeneity suggests that class-size effects occur only when the quality of the teaching force is relatively low.

A third approach to the identification of causal class-size effects tries to avoid bias from non-random sorting of students by using variation within individual students. If the same student is taught two different academic subjects in differently sized classes, the within-student between-subject variation can be used for identification (cf. Dee 2005; Dee and West 2011). The inclusion of student fixed effects, implemented by differencing across subjects, effectively excludes bias from subject-invariant student, family, and school characteristics, observable and unobservable. Unobserved characteristics that vary by subject and are correlated with class size, such as subject-specific fast-track or enrichment classes or teacher characteristics, could, however, still bias this research design. Altinok and Kingdon (2012) implement this identification strategy to estimate class-size effects in up to 45 countries using TIMSS 2003 data, which provide test scores in math and science for each student. Their results provide little support for class-size effects, with only few countries showing significant and sizeable positive effects of smaller classes. Analyzing the cross-country variation in class-size effects, they confirm that class-size effects are larger where teacher qualifications are lower, and also find indication of larger class-size effects in developing countries.

Beyond class-size effects, Ammermueller and Dolton (2006) use the same cross-subject identification strategy to estimate the effect of teacher-student gender interaction in England and the United States using TIMSS and PIRLS data. In most specifications (with the exception of one in England), they find little evidence of a significant effect of the interaction between student and teacher gender on student achievement. Schwerdt and Wuppermann (2011) use the same cross-subject identification with student fixed effects to identify the effects of teaching practices on TIMSS data in the United States. At a more descriptive level, Bratti et al. (2008) use the PISA data to estimate the association of student achievement with cooperative and competitive attitudes towards learning at the individual and school level.

8.5 Conclusions and Outlook

The economic literature on determinants of international differences in educational achievement has applied two main approaches. The first approach exploits the cross-country variation for identification of cross-country associations. The second approach estimates the same association within different countries in order to enhance understanding of whether a factor's importance differs systematically in different settings. Part of the existing work is descriptive in nature, estimating the association of student achievement with certain factors after controlling for the rich set of possible inputs into educational production available in the international background data. But quasi-experimental work has been developed to identify some of the underlying causal mechanisms both in the cross-country and in the within-country approach.

All in all, the international evidence on the role of school inputs in educational production provides little confidence that quantitative measures of expenditure and class size are a major driver of student achievement, across and within countries. Studies using different methods to identify causal class-size effects consistently find no strong effects of class size in most countries. Among school inputs, descriptive evidence suggests that measures of the quality of inputs and, in particular, teachers are more closely related to student outcomes. However, research in this area awaits more work to identify the underlying causal links.[15]

A particular opportunity of the international research is that it can unveil whether certain effects differ systematically across countries. For example, the international pattern suggests that significant class-size effects are only present in systems with relatively low teacher quality. This result raises the cost-effectiveness question of whether student achievement is best served by reducing class size or by increasing the low teacher quality even in the countries where class-size effects are present.

Due to the limited role of differences in expenditures and class size in explaining cross-country achievement differences, it may be tempting to conclude that school systems do not matter so much for student achievement, after all. Nothing could be more wrong than that. Evidence that differences in teacher quality and instruction time do matter suggests that what matters is not so much the amount of inputs that school systems are endowed with, but rather how they use them. Correspondingly, international differences in institutional structures of school systems such as external exams, school autonomy, private competition, and tracking have been found to be able to account for a substantial part of the cross-country variation in student achievement (see Woessmann 2016 for a recent review).

As the economic literature on international evidence on educational achievement has emerged only relatively recently, there is obviously still considerable scope for future advances. A topic unexplored by economists is the international tests in non-traditional subjects, such as foreign languages, civic education, and information technology. More generally, some of the rich background information contained in the international studies could be explored further, and part of it may provide information on relevant non-cognitive skills. For example, Falck and Woessmann (2013) attempt to derive measures of entrepreneurial intentions from the international background data, and Chap. 6 in Woessmann et al. (2009) explores such measures of non-cognitive outcomes as student morale and commitment, non-disruptive behavior, disciplinary climate, and tardiness. Further information on non-cognitive skills may be derived from the international background questionnaires. As a more distant outlook, international testing of non-cognitive skills would be an obvious challenge.

---

[15]More recently, Hanushek et al. (2014) show effects of teacher cognitive skills on international differences in student achievement.

As more and more countries participate in the international tests, the opportunities grow for future research on the determinants of international educational achievement. With the additional variation, the international research will be able to draw on more experience with different inputs and start to analyze additional specific features beyond the broad concepts of input variables analyzed so far. There is also considerable scope for future research to advance identification in quasi-experimental research settings. Furthermore, as more regular tests with reasonable comparability over time become available, a panel structure of international tests emerges that provides longitudinal information within countries. This will allow future research to exploit educational reforms in different countries over time (see Hanushek et al. 2013 for a recent first example). A limiting factor remains the lack of individual-level panel data in the international tests.

In the more distant future, it is tempting to envision what research will be able to do with the sort of achievement data that will be available in 20–30 years from now. The number of participating countries is as high as 52 in TIMSS 2011 and 65 in PISA 2012, and additional countries have signed up to participate in the most recent cycles. With these sets of comparable achievement data for extensive samples of countries being linked to subsequent economic growth, and with the emerging long panels of regular achievement data for large samples of countries, the outlook for future research in the economics of international differences in educational achievement is clearly bright.

References

Afonso, A., & St. Aubyn, M. (2006). Cross-country efficiency of secondary education provision: A semi-parametric analysis with non-discretionary inputs. *Economic Modelling, 23*(3), 476–491.

Altinok, N., & Kingdon, G. (2012). New evidence on class size effects: A pupil fixed effects approach. *Oxford Bulletin of Economics and Statistics, 74*(2), 203–234.

Ammermueller, A., & Dolton, P. (2006). *Pupil-teacher gender interaction effects on scholastic outcomes in England and the USA*. ZEW discussion paper 06-060. Mannheim: Centre for European Economic Research.

Ammermueller, A., Heijke, H., & Woessmann, L. (2005). Schooling quality in Eastern Europe: Educational production during transition. *Economics of Education Review, 24*(5), 579–599.

Angrist, J. D., & Lavy, V. (1999). Using Maimonides' rule to estimate the effect of class size on scholastic achievement. *Quarterly Journal of Economics, 114*(2), 533–575.

Bishop, J. H. (1997). The effect of national standards and curriculum-based examinations on achievement. *American Economic Review, 87*(2), 260–264.

Bratti, M., Checchi, D., & Filippin, A. (2008). *Should you compete or cooperate with your schoolmates?* IZA discussion paper 3599. Bonn, Germany: Institute for the Study of Labor.

Dee, T. S. (2005). A teacher like me: Does race, ethnicity, or gender matter? *American Economic Review, 95*(2), 158–165.

Dee, T. S., & West, M. R. (2011). The non-cognitive returns to class size. *Educational Evaluation and Policy Analysis, 33*(1), 23–46.

Dolton, P., & Marcenaro-Gutierrez, O. D. (2011). If you pay peanuts do you get monkeys? A cross-country analysis of teacher pay and pupil performance. *Economic Policy , 26*(65), 5–55.

Falck, O., & Woessmann, L. (2013). School competition and students' entrepreneurial intentions: International evidence using historical Catholic roots of private schooling. *Small Business Economics, 40*(2), 459–478.

Fertig, M., & Wright, R. E. (2005). School quality, educational attainment and aggregation bias. *Economics Letters, 88*(1), 109–114.

Fuchs, T., & Woessmann, L. (2004). Computers and student learning: Bivariate and multivariate evidence on the availability and use of computers at home and at school. *Brussels Economic Review, 47*(3/4), 359–385.

Fuchs, T., & Woessmann, L. (2007). What accounts for international differences in student performance? A re-examination using PISA data. *Empirical Economics, 32*(2–3), 433–462.

Gundlach, E., & Woessmann, L. (2001). The fading productivity of schooling in East Asia. *Journal of Asian Economics, 12*(3), 401–417.

Gundlach, E., Woessmann, L., & Gmelin, J. (2001). The decline of schooling productivity in OECD countries. *Economic Journal, 111*(471), C135–C147.

Gustafsson, J.-E. (2003). What do we know about effects of school resources on educational results? *Swedish Economic Policy Review, 10*(3), 77–110.

Gustafsson, J.-E. (2007). Understanding causal influences on educational achievement through analysis of differences over time within countries. In T. Loveless (Ed.), *Lessons learned: What international assessments tell us about math achievement* (pp. 37–63). Washington, DC: Brookings Institution Press.

Hanushek, E. A. (1979). Conceptual and empirical issues in the estimation of educational production functions. *Journal of Human Resources, 14*(3), 351–388.

Hanushek, E. A. (1997). The productivity collapse in schools. In W. J. Fowler Jr. (Ed.), *Developments in School Finance, 1996* (pp. 185–195). Washington, DC: National Center for Education Statistics.

Hanushek, E. A. (2002). Publicly provided education. In A. J. Auerbach & M. Feldstein (Eds.), *Handbook of Public Economics* (Vol. 4, pp. 2045–2141). Amsterdam, the Netherlands: North Holland.

Hanushek, E. A., & Kimko, D. D. (2000). Schooling, labor force quality, and the growth of nations. *American Economic Review, 90*(5), 1184–1208.

Hanushek, E. A., Link, S., & Woessmann, L. (2013). Does school autonomy make sense everywhere? Panel estimates from PISA. *Journal of Development Economics, 104*, 212–232.

Hanushek, E. A., & Luque, J. A. (2003). Efficiency and equity in schools around the world. *Economics of Education Review, 22*(5), 481–502.

Hanushek, E. A., Piopiunik, M., & Wiederhold, S. (2014). *The value of smarter teachers: International evidence on teacher cognitive skills and student performance*. NBER working paper no. 20727. Cambridge, MA: National Bureau of Economic Research.

Hanushek, E. A., Rivkin, S. G., & Taylor, L. L. (1996). Aggregation and the estimated effects of school resources. *Review of Economics and Statistics, 78*(4), 611–627.

Hanushek, E. A., & Woessmann, L. (2011a). The economics of international differences in educational achievement. In E. A. Hanushek, S. Machin, & L. Woessmann (Eds.), *Handbook of the Economics of Education* (Vol. 3, 89–200). Amsterdam, the Netherlands: North Holland.

Hanushek, E. A., & Woessmann, L. (2011b). How much do educational outcomes matter in OECD countries? *Economic Policy, 26*(67), 427–491.

Hanushek, E. A., & Woessmann, L. (2015). *The knowledge capital of nations: Education and the economics of growth*. Cambridge, MA: MIT Press.

Heyneman, S. P., & Loxley, W. (1983). The effect of primary school quality on academic achievement across twenty-nine high and low income countries. *American Journal of Sociology, 88*(6), 1162–1194.

Hoxby, C. M. (2000). The effects of class size on student achievement: New evidence from population variation. *Quarterly Journal of Economics, 115*(3), 1239–1285.

Lee, J.-W., & Barro, R. J. (2001). Schooling quality in a cross-section of countries. *Economica, 68* (272), 465–488.

Michaelowa, K. (2001). Primary education quality in francophone Sub-Saharan Africa: Determinants of learning achievement and efficiency considerations. *World Development, 29* (10), 1699–1695.

Schwerdt, G., & Wuppermann, A. C. (2011). Is traditional teaching really all that bad? A within-student between-subject approach. *Economics of Education Review, 30*(2), 365–379.

Todd, P. E., & Wolpin, K.I. (2003). On the specification and estimation of the production function for cognitive achievement. *Economic Journal, 113*(485), F3–F33.

Toma, E. F. (1996). Public funding and private schooling across countries. *Journal of Law and Economics, 39*(1), 121–148.

Urquiola, M., & Verhoogen, E. (2009). Class-size caps, sorting, and the regression-discontinuity design. *American Economic Review, 99*(1), 179–215.

West, M. R., & Woessmann, L. (2006). Which school systems sort weaker students into smaller classes? International evidence. *European Journal of Political Economy, 22*(4), 944–968.

Woessmann, L. (2002). *Schooling and the quality of human capital*. Berlin, Germany: Springer.

Woessmann, L. (2003). Schooling resources, educational institutions, and student performance: The international evidence. *Oxford Bulletin of Economics and Statistics, 65*(2), 117–170.

Woessmann, L. (2005a). Educational production in East Asia: The impact of family background and schooling policies on student performance. *German Economic Review, 6*(3), 331–353.

Woessmann, L. (2005b). Educational production in Europe. *Economic Policy, 20*(43), 446–504.

Woessmann, L. (2007). International evidence on expenditure and class size: A review. In *Brookings papers on education policy 2006/2007* (pp. 245–272). Washington D.C.: Brookings.

Woessmann, L. (2010). Families, schools, and primary-school learning: Evidence for Argentina and Colombia in an international perspective. *Applied Economics, 42,*(21), 2645–2665.

Woessmann, L. (2016). The importance of school systems: Evidence from international differences in student achievement. *Journal of Economic Perspectives, 30*(3), 3–31.

Woessmann, L., Luedemann, E., Schuetz, G., & West, M. R. (2009). *School accountability, autonomy, and choice around the world*. Cheltenham, UK: Edward Elgar.

Woessmann, L., & West, M. R. (2006). Class-size effects in school systems around the world: Evidence from between-grade variation in TIMSS. *European Economic Review, 50*(3), 695–736.

Chapter 9
Exploring the Effects of Following Different Tracks of Study in Upper Secondary Education on Cognitive Test Performance

Lisbeth Åberg-Bengtsson

Abstract The research presented in this chapter explores, using examples from an earlier version of the Swedish Scholastic Aptitude Test [the SweSAT], the possible environmental influence on cognitive test performance with respect to the effects of differences in earlier education. Relatively large differences in results between students having attended different tracks of study in upper secondary school have been noticed in the SweSAT. Obviously, this may be due to initial differences when entering these tracks. However, it may also be assumed that different tracks followed in upper secondary schooling may influence abilities measured by the SweSAT in a different manner. The present study tentatively proposes the effects of track of study both on the observed results in a set of sub-tests and on certain ability factors previously proposed to lie behind performance on the test, after control for marks, at the end of lower secondary education.

The Swedish Scholastic Aptitude Test[1] [the SweSAT] bears great resemblance to entrance tests to higher education used in other countries (e.g. the USA SAT) and is designed to give a measure of aptitude for higher education in a broad sense. It is well known that students from different tracks of study in upper secondary education perform differently on this test, which most likely, and to a great extent, has to do with differences in academic performance which already existed upon entering these tracks. However, it seems plausible that educational and other environmental effects due to attending different tracks in upper secondary schooling may affect students' results on the SweSAT. Investigations of such effects, with

---

[1]For roughly 10 years, the test has been referred to as 'the Swedish Scholastic Assessment Test'. However, at the time of study the established labeling in English was 'the Swedish Scholastic Aptitude Test'.

L. Åberg-Bengtsson (✉)
Department of Educational Research and Development, University of Borås, Borås, Sweden
e-mail: lisbeth.aberg-bengtsson@hb.se

control measures for initial differences, are rare—a fact that leaves open a relatively unexploited and urgent domain. Thus, when dealing with this issue, the present research, adopts a broader perspective than just attempting to contribute to validity issues related to a national entrance test.

9.1 Some Previous Research on the Effects of Schooling on Cognitive Ability Factors

Even though the SweSAT is not a test of intelligence, it still resembles such a test and hence aims to measure multiple abilities with different degrees of generality. Consequently, it seems relevant to take a point of departure in research on intelligence. However, as noticed by Gustafsson (2008), this field "is rich in paradoxes" (p. 31), which relates to the fact that there is ample evidence both for stability and change in intelligence over time. Ceci (1991) pointed to the discrepancy in the literature on the effects of schooling on intelligence test scores, proposing that this may be due to differences in quality of education and that only academically oriented types of programs would have an effect. Also Ackerman and Lohman (2003) posed the question on the extent to which there are differences between different types of programs. Research by scholars who have reported the effects of schooling on intelligence indicates that these effects might amount to approximately 2 IQ units (e.g. Härnqvist 1968a, b).

9.1.1 Effects of Track of Study on Differentiated Ability Factors

Balke-Aurell (1982), in an extension of the Härnqvist investigations, studied two representative samples of the Swedish male population tested at enlistment to military service. On the basis of multiple regression analyses and path models with latent variables, she suggested interaction effects between educational level and general intelligence (g)—the higher the educational level, the stronger the increase in g. In addition, she found effects on specific ability factors from verbal and technical types of education. The effects on special/technical ability were more substantial than those on verbal ability.

Gustafsson (2008) pursued the issue pointed out by Cesi (1991) and Ackerman and Lohman (2003) concerning different influences of different types of programs regarding effects of schooling on mental abilities. Arguing for the need for a better understanding of changes in intelligence, Gustafsson (2008) suggested that the undifferentiated conception of intelligence should be abandoned in favor of multidimensionality. Based on this, he conducted a study in which changes in intelligence over two years of study in a group of 13,906 Swedish males, who followed different tracks in upper secondary education, were focused upon. These individuals were tested at enlistment to military service by an established cognitive test battery recognized to measure fluid ability (*Gf*), crystallized intelligence (*Gc*), and general visualization (*Gv*). A five-factor, latent-variable model fitted to the leaving certificate from compulsory education was used to control for initial differences when entering upper secondary school. Gustafsson's results indicate that there are effects on factors of intelligence but that these effects appear to be restricted to academic programs. Effects corresponding to about 2.5 IQ points per year of schooling were estimated for academic tracks on *g*, also when represented by the *Gf* factor. In addition, at least as strong an improvement was observed in *Gv* for the academic tracks with technical or science orientation, whereas for *Gc* weaker effects were found for most academic and some vocational tracks. Thus, according to Gustafsson, certain schooling experiences seem to cause improvements not only in general cognitive ability but also in more specific abilities.

9.2   The Swedish Scholastic Aptitude Test

The results on the SweSAT can be used as an alternative to marks from upper secondary school when applying for admission to higher education. The test is administered twice a year with a spring version and an autumn version. During the 1990s there were up to 145,000 test takers per year. Thereafter this number decreased to 65,000 in 2007, when it was at its lowest. Since then there has been a new increase—in 2014 nearly 136,000 students took the SweSAT (Ögren 2014). Thus, the test plays an important role for gaining access to university programs and courses for which there is keen competition. A new set of items is constructed for each administration. All questions are multiple-choice format with one correct choice and three or four distractors.

The test has been subjected to a number of changes during its almost four decades of existence. Between 1977 and 1995 the test comprised six sub-tests; until 1992 these were tests of vocabulary; Swedish reading comprehension; diagrams, tables, and maps; 'data sufficiency' (i.e. mathematical related logical reasoning); general information; and study technique. In the spring of 1992, the study technique sub-test was exchanged for English reading comprehension, and in 1996 the general information sub-test was excluded and the number of sub-tests thus decreased from six to five. In 2011 the number of sub-tests was increased to eight, now also involving mathematical problem solving, quantitative comparisons, and sentence completion.

9.2.1   Some Research on the SweSAT

Throughout the years, a relatively large number of investigations and assessments have been conducted on the SweSAT. Only a minor part of this research, namely studies of the dimensionality of the test, will be addressed below. Most of these studies are based on factor analyses of sub-test scores.

Having investigated 10 administrations of the test, Gustafsson et al. (1992) argued for a two-factor structure with an overall factor related to all six sub-tests and a narrower, nested 'knowledge' factor related to the vocabulary (WORD), Swedish reading comprehension (READ), general information (GI), and study technique (STECH) sub-tests. The overall factor, which was hypothesized to measure an 'analytic' dimension of performance, showed the highest correlations with the data sufficiency (DS), that is mathematical related, logical reasoning, and the diagram, tables, and maps (DTM) sub-tests. Åberg-Bengtsson (2005), building on the study by Gustafsson et al. (1992) and her own previous identification of a three-factor model of DTM sub-tests (Åberg-Bengtsson 1999), investigated the internal structure of the entire test. She argued for a 'quantitative factor' related to the DS sub-test and items of the DTM sub-test that demand calculations in addition to merely reading off values when carrying out the tasks. The DS sub-test that was also thoroughly investigated by Åberg-Bengtsson (2005) seems to be essentially unidimensional.

Carlstedt and Gustafsson (2005) studied the construct validity of the SweSAT in relation to the Computerized Enlistment Battery Test (CAT-SEB), an instrument with well-known properties used in enlistment to military service in Sweden. The most important dimensions of the CAT-SEB are g, Gc, and Gv. The main results in Carlstedt and Gustafsson's study showed that the general SweSAT factor represents a mixture of Gf and Gc, of which the latter is the most important contributor to the variance of the test. They also concluded that general intelligence is strongly involved in performance on the DTM and DS test, which supported the earlier interpretation by Gustafsson et al. (1992). In addition, their analyses indicated that the DTM and DS sub-tests should, to a certain extent, be regarded not only as an analytic and 'quantitative' affair, but also as belonging to the Gc domain, which was shown to involve both reading skills and vocabulary.

It may seem reasonable to assume that a spatial or visual ability is heavily involved in the interpretation of diagrammatic tasks of the kind included in the DTM sub-tests, but Carlstedt and Gustafsson (2005) found only a weak relation between Gv and the DS sub-test and even weaker relations to a few of the DTM versions in one of their models, whereas none of their other analyses showed any Gv involvement in the SweSAT. They suggested that it may be single items in the DTM and DS sub-tests that tap Gv and that these effects are not seen in the summed scores. However, Åberg-Bengtsson (1999), in her item-based approach to the DTM sub-test, could not identify a visual dimension.

An observed gender difference in favor of males has been a continuous concern with the SweSAT in general (a phenomenon shared with other similar entrance tests, e.g. the USA SAT I) and with the quantitative sub-tests in particular. In 1991, when the SweSAT was first offered to a larger group of test takers, the difference between the genders amounted to approximately 0.5 standard deviation units (Gustafsson et al. 2000). Over a period of 10 years, the magnitude of the difference decreased to 0.3 (Stage and Ögren 2001), which may be a result of deliberate steps taken by test developers aimed at a more equalized performance between the sexes. However, since the reconstruction of the test in 2011 into a balanced assignment between verbal and quantitative sub-tests and items, the difference between male and female test takers has increased to approximately the same magnitude as 20 years earlier (see, e.g. Ögren 2014).

It has been maintained that the groups are not fully comparable, mainly due to self-selection among male and female test takers. From previous research, it seems reasonable to assume that as much as 0.25 standard deviation units of the observed differences may be caused by males constituting a positively (self-)selected group (e.g. Mäkitalo 1994; Mäkitalo and Reuterberg 1996; Reuterberg 1999; Gustafsson et al. 2000). Thus, these effects may account for the observed gender differences of sub-tests where the differences are relatively moderate, whereas in quantitative sub-tests, such as DTM and DS, they may only partly explain the difference.

Åberg-Bengtsson (1999, 2005) concluded that a part of the gender difference on the SweSAT might be traced to the 'quantitative factor' related to particular DTM items and to the DS sub-test. Reuterberg (1999) as well as Reuterberg and Ohlander (1999) showed that an identified general factor for the English reading comprehension test yielded quite a moderate gender difference in favor of males and that different texts constituting this sub-test might favor either males or females.

9.3 Methodology

The research reported in this chapter is a previously unpublished part of a series of studies on the characteristics of the SweSAT conducted in the 1990s and early 2000s. It is based on models suggested by Åberg-Bengtsson (1999, 2005; see also, Gustafsson and Åberg-Bengtsson 2010). This research builds on the assumption that performance on cognitive tests is neither unidimensional (see, e.g. Carroll 1993; Gustafsson 1984, 1988) nor merely an effect of stable qualities of the individual. Instead such tests may be seen as 'measuring multiple abilities of different degrees of generality' (Gustafsson and Åberg-Bengtsson 2010, p. 101) and be related to context and personal experiences during lifespan. Among the theories adopting multidimensional perspectives on the structure of abilities, a hierarchical structure has been convincingly argued for (e.g. Carroll 1993; Gustafsson 1988, 2008; Horn and Cattell 1966).

Hierarchical factor models (Gustafsson and Balke 1993) may be set up and tested in different ways by so-called oblique higher order (HO) models or orthogonal nested factor (NF) models (Gustafsson and Blake 1993; Gustafsson and Undheim 1996). Figure 9.1 illustrates the two approaches. Hierarchal factor models have in common an overall or general third-order factor influencing all performance and a few broad factors on an intermediate second-order level. The first level is characterized by a number of narrow and specific factors. It has been argued, that in HO modeling, factors are more distant from reality than lower order factors. Counterarguments have been raised that the characteristics of higher order factors

A Higher Order (HO) model   A Nested-factor (NF) Model

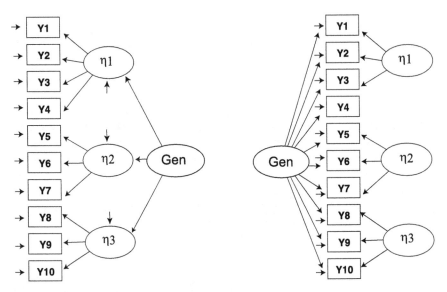

Fig. 9.1 *Left* The HO model with one third-order and three second-order factors. *Right* A NF model with one broad and three narrow dimensions

have to do with a breadth in influence rather than being a question of super-ordination. NF modeling gets to grips with this perceived distance between higher order factors and observed reality, because in such models all factors relate to manifest variables (see, Gustafsson and Åberg-Bengtsson 2010, for a historical perspective and a more detailed discussion of hierarchical modeling approaches).

9.3.1 Selection and Data

Results on the SweSAT from the cohort of individuals born in 1972 who took the test version administered in the spring of 1991 constitute one set of data used in the present chapter. Reasons for choosing this particular administration of the test were that (a) from 1991 and onward the test was offered to a larger group of students than before, and (b) in 1991 both the study technique [STECH] and general information [GI] sub-tests were still included in the test (see the description of the SweSAT above). Reusing a previously identified four-factor model in the current analyses, these two sub-tests were necessary for adequately separating the quantitative and analytic dimensions of the SweSAT (see, Åberg-Bengtsson 2005).

Up to 1994, upper secondary education in Sweden had an organization with five academic tracks (labelled 'lines'), preparing students for higher education and

Table 9.1 Distribution of subjects in the present analysis by track of study and gender

Gender	Track of study					
	Natural sciences	Social sciences	Technological	Liberal arts	Economics	Total
Males	1764	636	2768	61	946	6175
Females	2143	2046	880	634	1670	7373
Total	3907	2682	3648	695	2616	13,548

comprising three years of study, in addition to a large number of vocational tracks attended for two years which did not allow for entry at university level. From the cohort of test takers presented above, those who had attended one of the five academic tracks in upper secondary school were selected for the analyses. The tracks were: the natural sciences line, the technology line, the social sciences line, the liberal arts line, and the economics line.[2]

Marks from the leaving certificate of compulsory education (i.e. lower secondary school) were also used in the analyses. Thus, the group of test takers investigated after list-wise deletion consisted of 13,548 individuals. Table 9.1 gives an overview of subjects in the present analysis by track of study and gender.

9.3.2 Analyses

The analyses were conducted with a structural equation modeling technique, using the STREAMS modeling program (Gustafsson and Stahl 2005) together with the Mplus estimation program (Muthén and Muthén 2006). Below, an analysis of the leaving certificate from lower secondary education containing 17 marks will first be provided. Following this, the SweSAT investigation is presented.

A 'marks model' on the leaving certificate suggested by Andersson (1998) was used to control for initial differences in performance due to selection and self-selection among students when choosing tracks of study. In these computations, an orthogonal NF model with four factors was set up and tested. In this model all observed manifest variables (i.e. the 17 subject marks) were related to a general 'school achievement' (*SchAch*) factor, whereas sub-sets of observed variables were loaded on a number of hypothesized, less general factors. These latter factors were a 'mathematic/science' factor (*MaScie*) related strongly to mathematics and the natural sciences; a 'language' factor (*Langua*), and a relatively broad factor related to a group of practical subjects and the mathematic/science block. Andersson first

---

[2]In later curricula there is a different system for tracks of study, which has somewhat different labeling of the programs. For instance, what is in the present text labeled 'the economics line' comes close to what is now referred to as 'the business management and economics program' (Skolverket 2012).

called this latter factor 'non-verbal' but interpreted it to be a 'spatial/practical' (*SpPract*) factor, which seems a more adequate label.

Two different sets of computations were conducted on the SweSAT data. First, effects of track of study on the observed results of the six sub-tests treated as manifest variables were investigated. In this analysis, track of study and gender[3] were defined as dummy variables. Next, corresponding computations were carried out with the six subtests exchanged for the latent variables in a four-factor model identified by Åberg-Bengtsson (2005). In both sets of computations, a similar series of gradually more complex models were posited and tested.

9.4   Results

Effects of tracks of study on the observed results of the six sub-tests will be addressed first. Thereafter the interest is directed towards effects on the set of factors in the SweSAT as previously identified by Åberg-Bengtsson (2005).

9.4.1   The Sub-test Analysis

In order to investigate the main effects, all six sub-tests were regressed, first on tracks of study, and then on gender. These computations showed that, on the whole, students following the natural sciences line performed considerably better than the other groups of students. However, there was one exception—on the DTM and DS sub-tests, students from the technology line performed equally well as the students from the natural sciences line. The technology students also achieved relatively high results on the GI sub-test. There was a gender difference in favor of males on all sub-tests, especially on the DS and DTM tests. Merging the two models reduced this difference considerably for all sub-tests but it was still significant for the DTM and DS. The pattern for performance on the sub-tests remained roughly the same.

As previously suggested, it is reasonable to assume that the students differed already when entering the different tracks of study in upper secondary school. Thus, the marks model was used as a control instrument. In positioning the controlled models the relations between tracks of study and the marks model factors were set up as casual effects even though it may be argued, from a strictly theoretical way of reasoning, that it would be most correct to set them up as covariances. However, from a structural equation modeling perspective, the positing of such a model would have implied treating these factors as exogenous and endogenous variables at

[3]Gender was included in the analyses even if gender differences were not a main interest in the present study. The reason was to control for gender effects, since, (a) male test takers performed better on the SweSAT than females, as previously stated, and (b) males and females were unevenly distributed by track.

Table 9.2 The six sub-tests regressed on tracks of study and on gender with control for marks from lower secondary school (statistically significant standardized regression weights)

Sub-test	Track of study[a]				Gender[b]
	Natural sciences	Social sciences	Technological	Liberal arts	
DTM	−0.07	−0.04	−0.05	−0.06	−0.10
DS	0.07		0.08	−0.04	
WORD	0.13	0.09		˚0.10	−0.08
READ	0.09	0.06		0.03	
STECH	0.03	0.04	−0.03		
GI	0.15	0.05	0.04		−0.10

[a]Reference group: the economics line
[b]Reference group: male test takers

the same time, which is not appropriate. As the chosen solution was used to control for initial differences only, the above method was judged to be acceptable.

Table 9.2 gives the magnitude of the regression weights when relating the observed results of the six sub-tests to tracks of study and gender with control for marks from the leaving certificate of compulsory (i.e. lower secondary) education. The Root Mean Square Error of Approximation (RMSEA) value of this model was 0.042, which indicates good fit, whereas the $\chi 2$ value was relatively high, $\chi 2$ (240) = 5888. However, this should be seen as a consequence of the inclusion of the marks model, which already had a high $\chi 2$ value.

In this controlled analysis, some statistically significant and quite substantial effects from tracks of study can be noticed. Following the natural sciences line seems to have been most advantageous for achieving good results on the majority of sub-tests, but also attending the social sciences line was quite rewarding, whereas studies on the liberal arts line had a rather good effect on the results of the WORD sub-test. As can be seen from the negative values for all four tracks of study in Table 9.2 with respect to the DTM sub-test, the economics line (serving as the control group) to a higher degree seemed to have prepared the students for handling diagrams, tables, and maps. In this controlled model there are gender differences in favor of males for three sub-tests.

9.4.2 The Latent-Variable Analysis

In the next phase of the study, the observed results of the six sub-tests were replaced with a set of latent variables. These factors emanate from studies on the SweSAT by Gustafsson et al. (1992) and Åberg-Bengtsson (1999, 2005). Before presenting the results of the main analysis a brief account of the four-factor SweSAT model replicated on the present sample will be given.

The SweSAT four-factor model. In this model (Fig. 9.2) the 20 items of the DTM sub-test were included, whereas the sum of scores was used for the other 5 sub-tests (DS, WORD, READ, STECH, and GI). The item approach for the DTM sub-test was necessary for the identification of the quantitative computation (*Quant*) factor (see, Åberg-Bengtsson 1999, 2005). All manifest variables were assumed to load on

Fig. 9.2 The SweSAT model previously argued by Åberg-Bengtsson (2005)

a 'general' SweSAT factor (*Gen*). A 'knowledge' factor (*Knowl*) related to four of the sub-tests (WORD, READ, STECH, and GI) with the aforementioned 'quantitative' factor (*Quant*) nested within this general dimension. In addition, there was another nested factor (*End*) showing some kind of 'end of test' effect for the DTM sub-test. As the '*End*' factor concerns this sub-test only, it will neither be given much further attention, nor accounted for in Table 9.4. However, because it is an important dimension in the DTM sub-test, its inclusion in the analyses was necessary for the estimation processes to run smoothly.

The factor loadings (Table 9.3) in the four-factor SweSAT model in the current study differ only marginally from the ones yielded for the entire population of 19-year-old test takers (Åberg-Bengtsson 2005). The model demonstrated good fit: RMSEA = 0.013, $\chi 2$ (242) = 820.

The latent-variable model. Before setting up and testing the entire model, some main effects were investigated. Regressing the four SweSAT factors on gender gave

Table 9.3 The four-factor SweSAT model (standardized factor loadings)

	Gen	*Knowl'*	*Quant'*	*End'*
DTM 1	0.04			
DTM 2	0.30		0.25	
DTM 3	0.17		0.04	
DTM 4	0.26		0.15	
DTM 5	0.32			
DTM 6	0.25		0.13	
DTM 7	0.16			
DTM 8	0.41			
DTM 9	0.20		0.14	
DTM 10	0.30			
DTM 11	0.19		0.09	
DTM 12	0.31		0.09	
DTM 13	0.23		0.14	
DTM 14	0.27		0.24	
DTM 15	0.34		0.23	
DTM 16	0.32		0.16	0.04[a]
DTM 17	0.34		0.05	0.10[a]
DTM 18	0.37			0.16[a]
DTM 19	0.45		0.05	0.27[a]
DTM 20	0.31			0.39
DS	0.69		0.30	
WORD	0.46	0.64		
READ	0.59	0.42		
STECH	0.63	0.36		
GI	0.55	0.44		

[a]Insignificant value

Table 9.4 The SweSAT factors regressed on tracks of study and on gender with control for marks from lower secondary school (statistically significant standardized factor loadings)

SweSAT factor	Track of study[a]				Gender[b]
	Natural sciences	Social sciences	Technological	Liberal arts	
Gen	−0.06		−0.05	−0.11	
Quant'	0.15		0.17		−0.20
Knowl'	0.23	0.14	0.05	0.16	−0.10

[a]Reference group: the economics line
[b]Reference group: male test takers

statistically significant differences (in favor of males) for the '*Gen*' and '*Quant*' dimensions, whereas no such differences were found for '*Knowl*'. When the SweSAT factors were regressed on tracks of study in a similar way, the students from the natural sciences and technological lines showed better results than the other students on '*Gen*' and much better on '*Quant*' factor. The students of natural sciences succeeded much better in the '*Knowl*' factor than did the students of technology and economics. Also, the students having attended the social sciences and the humanistic lines performed comparatively well in this respect. Analysing loadings with respect to tracks of study and sex at the same time, that is to say, looking at one while controlling for the other, rendered the same pattern. However, the strengths of the loading decreased both for tracks of study and gender, which of course indicates shared variances.

The standardized factor loadings for the final latent-variable model controlled for initial differences as measured by marks from the leaving certificate from compulsory education are presented in Table 9.4. There is a positive effect on the '*Quant*' and '*Knowl*' factors of having attended the natural sciences line, whereas studying social sciences was advantageous for the '*Knowl*' factor only. Studying technology affected mainly the '*Quant*' factor. There seems to be a small, positive effect on the '*Gen*' dimension of following the economics and social sciences lines and particularly so compared to having studied the liberal arts line. Taking into account the marks from lower secondary school as well as effects of tracks of study, there is a gender difference in favor of males in the '*Quant*' and '*Knowl*' factors.

9.5 Conclusions

Despite the fact that the SweSAT is less heterogeneous than, for instance, the CAT-SEB test (Carstedt and Gustafsson 2005) previously referred to and that the control for initial differences is by no means perfect in the present study, the results may still tentatively be interpreted to be in line with arguments that different types of schooling may affect performance on cognitive test differently. Gustafsson (2008) suggested that choice of track of study after compulsory school was important for cognitive improvement and that effects on factors of intelligence were to be restricted to attending academic programs in upper secondary education. The analyses above took a more detailed approach when investigating possible effects on cognitive performance of attending different academic tracks in upper secondary education.

For the sake of completeness, the effects of track of study on the observed results on the sub-tests of the version of SweSAT used in the study were first investigated. As pointed out above, students who had followed the natural science, the social science, and the liberal arts lines obtained better results on the vocabulary sub-test than did the students who had followed the economics and technological lines. This seems logical, as it may be assumed that these latter tracks were more specialized and less generally academic and thus not training as broad a vocabulary as the former.

The same explanation may be suggested for the reading comprehension sub-test, for which the pattern is fairly similar to that of the vocabulary sub-test, even though the tendencies are somewhat weaker. Presumably, textbooks and other tools for learning as well as teaching methods and tasks given to the students on these specialized tracks to some extent differed systematically from the more academic ones. The pattern of the diagram, tables, and maps sub-test is particularly interesting. Here, the economics line students were more successful than students from the other four tracks. One possible explanation is that the use of graphical and tabular representations of quantitative data has been an integral part of the studies in this track to such a degree that it positively affected the outcome of this particular sub-test.

The decomposing of the variance of a test into a factorial structure may give information about the outcome of performance on broader dimensions related to all, or a major part, of the sub-tests. Furthermore, such analyses can also point out interesting features of more narrow and specific factors or factors accounting for a relatively small part of the variance. In the analysis above, all manifest variables load on the overall SweSAT dimension. According to Carlstedt and Gustafsson (2005) this factor is a mixture of Gf and Gc, with the strongest impact for the latter. Whereas the deviations between tracks for the general factor were rather small, more substantial differences were found for both the rather broad '$Knowl$' factor and the more narrow and specific '$Quant$' factor.

It may seem remarkable that the students in the natural science line succeeded substantially better than the other four tracks of study on the '$Know$' factor. Evidently, this factor belongs to the Gc domain and is strongly related both to language abilities and general school achievement (Carlstedt and Gustafsson 2005). Obviously, a lot of things may affect development, knowledge building, and language skills in educational settings. Tentatively, it may be assumed that, for example, attending classes with other students who are highly motivated for studies brings about positive effects for different adequate competencies.

The results concerning the '$Quant$' factor appear to be logical first and foremost with respect to the finding of an effect of having taken natural science or technological studies, which may be assumed to focus on such skills. Obviously, this factor extracts a part of the variance 'invisible' in the observed results for the diagram, tables, and maps sub-test. Thus, it was possible to identify an effect of studies in the natural science and technological lines on a particular dimension of this subtest as well as on the data sufficiency sub-test, even though students from the economics line performed best on the diagram, tables, and maps sub-test as such.

9.5.1 Finally

In the present study, the leaving certificate from compulsory education in the analyses was used to control for initial differences. As has been touched upon above, it may be argued that these marks are not perfect for this purpose and that other selection and self-selection effects may be at stake. However, the marks used are known to be highly correlated with later success in educational situations and may thus be regarded as the best instrument available for control in the current analyses. In addition, the effects that are tentatively pointed out seem reasonable and make sense. Thus, hopefully, the piece of research presented here may contribute to the scientific discussion and, to some extent, broaden our understanding of effects of education on performance on cognitive ability tests.

Acknowledgments The research presented here was carried out within the VALUTA project conducted in 2001–2004 and financially supported by the Bank of Sweden Tercentenary Foundation. The author gratefully acknowledges Professor Jan-Eric Gustafsson for his mentorship for her as a researcher as well as for his guiding and advice during this particular research process.

References

Åberg-Bengtsson, L. (1999). Dimensions of performance in the interpretation of diagrams, tables, and maps: Some gender differences in the Swedish Scholastic Aptitude Test. *Journal of Research in Science Teaching, 36*, 565–582.

Åberg-Bengtsson, L. (2005). Separating the quantitative and analytic dimensions of the Swedish Scholastic Aptitude Test (SweSAT). *Scandinavian Journal of Educational Research, 49*, 359–383.

Ackerman, P. L., & Lohman, D. F. (2003). Education and *g*. In H. Nyborg (Ed.), *The scientific study of general intelligence: Tribute to Arthur R. Jensen* (pp. 275–292). Amsterdam: Elsevier Science.

Andersson, A. (1998). The dimensionality of the leaving certificate in the Swedish compulsory school. *Scandinavian Journal of Educational Research, 42*, 25–40.

Balke-Aurell, G. (1982). *Changes in ability as related to educational and occupational experience* (Göteborg Studies in Educational Sciences, 40). Gothenburg, Sweden: Acta Universitatis Gothoburgensis.

Carlstedt, B., & Gustafsson, J.-E. (2005). Construct validation of the Swedish Scholastic Aptitude Test by means of the Swedish Enlistment Battery. *Scandinavian Journal of Psychology, 46*, 31–42.

Carroll, J. B. (1993). *Human cognitive abilities: A survey of factor-analytic studies*. New York: Cambridge University Press.

Ceci, S. J. (1991). How much does schooling influence general intelligence and its cognitive components? A reassessment of the evidence. *Developmental Psychology, 27*, 703–722.

Gustafsson, J.-E. (1984). A unifying model for the structure of intellectual abilities. *Intelligence, 8*, 179–203.

Gustafsson, J.-E. (1988). Hierarchical models of individual differences and cognitive abilities. In R. J. Sternberg (Ed.), *Advances in the psychology of human intelligence* (Vol. 4, pp. 35–71). Hillsdale, NJ: Erlbaum.

Gustafsson, J.-E. (2008). Schooling and intelligence: Effects of track of study on level and profile of cognitive abilities. In P. Kyllonen, R. Roberts, & L. Stankov (Eds.), *Extending intelligence: Enhancement and new constructs* (pp. 31–49). Hillsdale, NJ: Erlbaum.

Gustafsson, J.-E., & Åberg-Bengtsson, L. (2010). Unidimensionality and interpretability of psychological instruments. In S. E. Embretsen (Ed.), *Measuring psychological constructs: Advances in model-based approaches* (pp. 97–121). Washington, DC: American Psychological Association.

Gustafsson, J.-E., Andersson, A., & Hansen, M. (2000). Prestationer och prestationsskillnader i 1990-talets skola [Differences in school achievement in 1990s]. In *SOU 2000:39, Välfärd och skola: Antologi från Kommittén välfärdsbokslut* (pp. 135–211). Stockholm, Sweden: Social Ministry.

Gustafsson, J.-E., & Balke, G. (1993). General and specific abilities as predictors of school achievement. *Multivariate Behavioral Research, 28*, 407–434.

Gustafsson, J.-E., & Stahl, P. A. (2005). *STREAMS 3.0 User's Guide: Version 1.0.0.* Mölndal, Sweden: MultivariateWare.

Gustafsson, J.-E., & Undheim, J. O. (1996). Individual differences in cognitive functions. In D. C. Berliner & R. C. Calfee (Eds.), *Handbook of educational psychology* (pp. 186–242). New York: Macmillan.

Gustafsson, J.-E., Wedman, I., & Westerlund, A. (1992). The dimensionality of the Swedish Scholastic Aptitude Test. *Scandinavian Journal of Educational Research, 36*, 21–39.

Härnquist, K. (1968a). Relative changes in intelligence from 13–18: I. Background and methodology. *Scandinavian Journal of Psychology, 9*, 50–64.

Härnquist, K. (1968b). Relative changes in intelligence from 13–18: II. Results. *Scandinavian Journal of Psychology, 9*, 50–64.

Horn, J. L., & Cattell, R. B. (1966). Refinement and test of the theory of fluid and crystallize general intelligences. *Journal of Educational Psychology, 57*, 253–270.

Mäkitalo, Å. (1994). *Non-comparability of female and male admission test takers* (Report No. 1994:06). Gothenburg, Sweden: University of Gothenburg, Department of Education and Educational Research.

Mäkitalo, Å., & Reuterberg, S.-E. (1996). *Who takes the Swedish Scholastic Aptitude Test? A study of differential selection to the SweSAT in relation to gender and ability* (Report No. 1996:03). Gothenburg, Sweden: University of Gothenburg, Department of Education and Educational Research.

Muthén, L. K., & Muthén, B. O. (2006). *Mplus: User's Guide*. Los Angeles, CA: Muthén & Muthén.

Ögren, G. (2014). *Högskoleprovet våren och hösten 2014: Provdeltagargruppens sammansättning och resultat* [The Swedish Scholastic Assessment Test spring and autumn 2013: Test takers and their results] (BVM nr 61). Umeå, Sweden: Umeå University. ISSN 1652-7313.

Reuterberg, S.-E. (1999). Textinnehåll och könsskillnader i delprovet engelsk läsförståelse (ELF) [Analysis of content of the English Reading Comprehension (ERC) subtest and associated gender differences] (Rapport nr 1999:6 S, *Fokus på högskoleprovet*, s. 36–42). Stockholm: National Agency for Higher Education.

Reuterberg, S.-E., & Ohlander, S. (1999). *Engelsk läsförståelse i högskoleprovet: En analys av reguljärprov och utprövningsversioner hösten 1998* [English Reading Comprehension in the

SweSAT: An analysis of the pilot test and final version, autumn 1998] (IPD-rapporter, Nr 1999:09). Gothenburg, Sweden: University of Gothenburg, Department of Education.

Skolverket. (2012). *Upper secondary school 2011*. Stockholm, Sweden: Fritzes.

Stage, C., & Ögren, G. (2001). *Högskoleprovets utveckling under åren 1977–2000* [Changes in the SweSAT during 1977–2000] (PM nr 169). Umeå, Sweden: Umeå University, Department of Educational Measurement.

Chapter 10
Empirical Puzzles on Effective Teachers: U.S. Research

Henry M. Levin

Abstract This chapter addresses the knowledge base on selection and evaluation of effective teachers using recent empirical literature from the United States. It finds that the traditional criteria of teacher licensing, educational credentials, and teaching experience show extremely weak relationships to gains (value-added) in student achievement. Combining classroom observations and measures of teacher value-added seem to hold promise in identifying productive teachers among those already employed, but lack applicability in the initial selection of teachers. Differences among teacher training programs in teacher effectiveness are surprisingly small relative to variance within programs. Issues of how to select teachers and how to reward them for their contributions to student and school productivity remain contested without solid evidence to resolve them.

10.1 Introduction

Many countries pursue a continuous quest for ways to improve the training and selection of teachers. But, progress in this direction assumes that we have a strong knowledge-base on what makes teachers effective and how to use this information to improve teacher training and selection. Surely we must have an image of what makes a teacher effective in order to prepare and engage such persons for our classrooms. Traditionally, most countries have required prospective teachers to undertake specific courses and applied experiences in classrooms that qualified them to be teachers. In some cases teacher prospects were also required to take

Chapter for a festschrift in honor of Professor Jan-Eric Gustafsson, University of Goteborg. Previous version presented at a conference on "**Teacher Competence and the Teaching Profession**" Sponsored by the Swedish Royal Academy of Sciences and Wenner-Gren Foundations/KVA, September 10–13, 2014, Stockholm.

H.M. Levin (✉)
Teachers College, Columbia University, New York City, NY, USA
e-mail: hl361@columbia.edu

© Springer International Publishing AG 2017
M. Rosén et al. (eds.), *Cognitive Abilities and Educational Outcomes*,
Methodology of Educational Measurement and Assessment,
DOI 10.1007/978-3-319-43473-5_10

official examinations beyond the university requirements to ascertain the quality of their preparation. It was assumed that these formal qualifications in conjunction with experience provided evidence of their professional competences to teach. Unfortunately, empirical studies of the relation between these requirements and student outcomes have not been able to provide strong validation of these qualifications in terms of teacher effectiveness.

An ambitious study of 25 countries between 2002 and 2004, by the OECD concluded:

> A crucial area in which research has yet to deliver more clear indications concerns the attributes that make a good teacher. This makes it difficult to design a set of standards teachers should meet and to conceive preparation and developmental programmes for teachers, or to devise strategies for dealing with ineffective teachers (OECD 2005: 222).

This intervention reviews the U.S. research on this topic and the dilemma that it raises for designing newer and more effective training programs and for guiding teacher selection. In the next section it reviews briefly the findings on identifying teacher characteristics that predict student learning. This is followed by the shift in research and policy to direct measurement of teacher success and both the uses of these findings and their challenges. The final section raises a range of issues on how to proceed in the training and selection of teachers.

10.2   Evidence on Productive Teachers

Although there is little unanimity on what teacher characteristics are needed for teaching effectiveness, some criteria must be used to establishing standards for training and hiring teachers. Thus, all countries have established qualifications for teaching. These typically consist of some minimum level of education, usually at the post-secondary level, as well as the details of the content of that training which is required for teacher certification and licensing. Beyond this minimum, most countries set out standards for further professional development in the form of additional educational attainment and teaching experience which contribute to teacher effectiveness. Teacher pay is usually set according to the educational attainment and experience of teachers.

Yet, a half century of research that has tried to explore the statistical relationships between teacher certification requirements, teacher education, and teacher experience, on the one hand, and student achievement, on the other, show very weak results. For example, in one of the earliest research studies on this subject, Hanushek (1971) found that student achievement gains were unrelated to the experience or degree level (e.g. Master's Degree) of their teachers. Subsequent summaries of the accumulating statistical literature by Hanushek and Rivkin (2006) as well as summaries of periodic earlier surveys (e.g. Hanushek 1997) provided little support for the assumptions that the conventional measures of teacher qualifications were strongly linked to student achievement. More recent studies have also found little relationship.[1] Examples of the findings on each dimension follow:

Certification Requirements—Because education is the responsibility of the state government in the U.S., there is no national certification requirement for a teaching license. Each of the 50 states sets its own standards. Typically these entail the receipt of a Bachelor's or Master's degree and a range of required courses on educational theory, practice, and subject content as well as supervised practice in classrooms. Some states also require passing scores on examinations of general knowledge, teaching methods, and specific subject knowledge in the teaching field. But, many of the states have permitted a range of alternative paths for meeting the certification or credential requirements to be a teacher (Kane et al. 2008; Boyd et al. 2009). In some states, a scarcity of credentialed teachers has meant that teachers who do not meet the licensing requirements are permitted to teach while under-taking the courses and other requirements for a teaching license. This diversity in the certification status of teachers has provided statistical diversity that permits sophisticated studies of the impact of certification status on student achievement. Most studies suggest that the relationship is weak (Wayne and Young 2003; Kane et al. 2008) meaning that the requirements for a teaching license do not have a profound measured impact on teaching outcomes.

Teacher Education Level—Presumably, the more education that a teacher receives, the more effective the teacher will be. But, clearly this depends on the type of educational experience that is evident. In the U.S. teachers are induced to obtain education beyond the Bachelor's degree by a salary schedule that provides financial incentives for completing additional coursework and degrees. However, only rarely does this link require that the additional coursework be demonstrably tied to sub-stantive educational goals of teacher improvement, and teachers often obtain the additional educational credits by attending conferences or pursuing whatever courses are available within their restricted time schedules. Thus it is not surprising that additional degrees and coursework obtained by teachers show a weak or non-existent relation with student achievement (Wayne and Young 2003; Hanushek 1997; Hanushek and Rivkin 2006). The exception to this is that the effectiveness of mathematics teachers seems to benefit from additional training in mathematics courses (Wayne and Young 2003).

---

[1]It is important to note that many studies only look for a statistically significant relation in which the result was unlikely to be found by chance. But in the context of validating a predictive relation between a criterion and outcome, the magnitude of the relationship is important, not just its rejection of a chance occurrence. I have used the term "little relationship" to characterize situations in which there is no statistically significant relation or the relationship is statistically significant, but trivial (suggesting little impact). For example, one of the largest apparent effects of certification is found in Clotfelter et al. (2007). But the difference in student achievement between teachers who have met the full license requirement and those who lack the requirement is only about 2 per-centiles on a standardized metric of achievement or less than 1 percentile if one makes an adjustment for fadeout of achievement effects based upon studies of that phenomenon. Also see the debate in Goldhaber and Brewer (2000, 2001) and Darling-Hammond et al. (2001).

Teacher Experience—Presumably for teachers, as in all occupations, additional experience increases one's proficiencies and makes one more effective. One of the problems in identifying this statistically is that relatively high teacher turnover in the early years of teaching in the U.S. means that the composition of teachers' characteristics changes by experience levels. If teachers who are less successful leave after teaching for a year or two, some of any apparent positive relation between experience and student achievement will be due to changes in the proficiencies of those who stay as opposed to the causal effect of more teacher experience on student achievement. Teacher experience does seem to be related to student achievement, but mostly in the first years of teaching according to several studies (Rivkin et al. 2005; Staiger and Rockoff 2010; Harris et al. 2014). In contrast, Koedel and Betts (2007) found no impact of either teacher experience or education on student achievement.

Other Qualifications—Although teacher licensing, educational attainment, and experience are the main policy attributes that formally affect teacher training, hiring, and salary, these are not the only qualifications that have been considered in the teacher effectiveness literature. Among those that have also been included in multiple statistical studies is the quality or student selectivity of the undergraduate institutions where teachers received their training, and test results (Wayne and Young 2003). In both cases there are positive relationships for teachers and their students' achievement, although few studies have been done in this area, and the statistical relations are modest.

But there is also skepticism that measuring even a broader set of characteristics of prospective teachers will yield much additional information on specific dimensions that predict their future productivity. Rockoff et al. (2011) undertook a large survey of New York City teachers to gather a wide range of teacher attributes that might be connected with student achievement in mathematics at the elementary and middle school levels. Their teacher data base included multiple measures of the teacher's background such as major field of study, test scores, selectivity of their college, mathematics knowledge, and cognitive ability. In addition, they collected information on personality using the dimensions of the "Big Five": extraversion, agreeableness, conscientiousness, openness, and emotional stability (Digman 1990). They also employed a commercial instrument for prescreening teachers that is supposed to predict performance in the urban classroom. They use all of these data in combination to predict teacher productivity in the classroom as assessed by mathematics gains in student achievement by creating two principal factors, a cognitive and a non-cognitive one. Each has about the same predictive ability, but both are nominal in their apparent predictive impacts. The expanded data set comprises both cognitive and non-cognitive teacher variables. This is far more information on teacher candidates than is available to schools for recruitment and hiring. Yet, this plethora of personal and professional teacher characteristics explains only about 12 % of the variance in student achievement gains in mathematics.

Koedel and Betts (2007) undertook a study of over 1000 teachers and 16,000 students in San Diego to ascertain the impact of measures of teacher quality on the

2nd to 5th grade gains in student reading and mathematics scores. Using information on teacher experience, certification status, field of degree specialization, receipt of master's degree, and other qualifications in specific subjects explained less than 6 % of student gains in mathematics and less than 3 % of teacher effectiveness in reading. Even when they use 50 measures of teacher qualifications (what they call the "kitchen sink" approach), the explained variance in teacher performance that is predicted rises to only about 7 %, and they show that this is overstated statistically. Koedel and Betts (2007: 4) conclude that "The empirical evidence suggests that schools may find it very difficult to identify the best teachers and that even if they do, they may choose not to hire them." Although one comprehensive study in North Carolina finds a more positive statistical relation between teacher characteristics and student achievement, it is an outlier in the literature (Clotfelter et al. 2007) as an overall summary of this literature demonstrates (Harris and Sass 2011). A more recent study has found that early career identification of teacher promise predicts later teacher effectiveness (Atteberry et al. 2015).

10.3 Identifying Effective Teachers

The failure of the many empirical studies to validate a strong relationship between the standard measures of teacher quality and teacher productivity has raised extreme skepticism on issues of how to identify and recruit productive teachers. What is particularly important is that this challenge is not due to teachers showing a narrow range of productivity. When student achievement is measured among classrooms, the differences are dramatic. Hanushek (1971) was the first to explore this phenomenon in a single school district, finding large differences in student achievement across classrooms staffed by different teachers. Individual teachers seem to generate large differences in student results, yet the differences in the teacher characteristics that generate these results are not identified in the empirical literature. Hanushek et al. (2005: 421) show this contrast when they simply specify classrooms staffed by different teachers as explanations for differences in achievement. Using this "teacher-blind" method of identifying classrooms, they are able to explain about eight times as much variance in student achievement in mathematics as when specifying the characteristics of teachers who teach in those classrooms. For reading, the comparison in favor of identifying classrooms of teachers is nine times as great relative to identifying the teachers' characteristics.

In the U.S. these findings have shifted teacher evaluation to a focus on measuring student learning directly in terms of value-added (VA) for each teacher rather than concern about the traditional professional credentials. Of course, this raises interesting questions about initial selection of teachers if one cannot determine their likely productivity until they are hired and one can document their contribution to student achievement, a matter that will be addressed below. VA is a direct measure of student test score gain in a given period of time such as an academic year. Student achievement might be measured at the beginning of the year and the end of a year in specific subjects and adjusted for non-random assignment of students. Presumably, the gain in achievement in raw scores or standardized scores serves to assess the value-added in learning associated with a particular teacher. Within-school differences among teachers in VA of students appear to be large. Hanushek and Rivkin (2010) summarize these differences among a range of studies. Differences among teachers are consistently larger for mathematics than reading. For a standard deviation of teacher effectiveness in mathematics, there is an apparent gain of 0.11–0.36 standard deviations of student achievement in a single year, with a midpoint of about 0.20. For reading the range is 0.08–0.26. In theory, these kind of differences would close achievement gaps by race and income within 3–5 years if the advantages in teacher effectiveness were conferred upon educationally disadvantaged students, but as Haertel (2013) points out, this is a vast overstatement beyond what the evidence supports.

Adoption and diffusion of VA approaches into policy have moved quickly in the U.S., partky because of academic persuasion but largely because the U.S. Department of Education has required states to adopt student achievement as a criterion for teacher evaluation in order to benefit from a program for federal funding. Many states and local school districts have gone farther than mere VA evaluation alone, using the VA results to determine teacher tenure or permanent employment, teacher salaries, bonuses, and teacher dismissals. There are many issues surrounding VA which suggest great caution in its application (Haertel 2013). For example, year-to-year consistency in VA for individual teachers is low, estimated in the range of only 0.2–0.5 in correlations for elementary teachers in one major study (McCaffrey et al. 2009). Accordingly, multiple years of teacher data must be averaged over several years to obtain relatively stable estimates of VA for individual teachers.

Beyond this, students are not randomly assigned to teachers or teachers to students (Rothstein 2010). Although this must be taken into account so that teachers are not punished or rewarded for teaching students of different capabilities, it is difficult to accomplish through existing value-added models. Some teachers are chosen for particular types of students because they are unusually successful with such pupils, for example more academically challenged students. Even if the selected teachers are highly successful with these students, the value added may be less than for teachers of students who are assigned students of higher abilities. Statistical methods may be used to adjust for such student differences, but these are limited to data availability on observable student characteristics, an inadequate basis for statistical controls because of the many unobservables that affect there should be a period after success. Rothstein (2009); Goldhaber et al. (2014); Guarino et al. (2015) apply different statistical models to address this phenomenon and find that differences in estimates of teacher VA can be quite large under different assumptions. These differences emerge especially with different classroom composition of students according to socioeconomic background. The American Statistical Association (2014) has evaluated the statistical modeling and conclusions of the VA literature and has concluded not only that caution in interpretation and policy application is in order, but that "… ranking teachers by their value-added scores can have unintended consequence that reduce teacher quality". The American Educational Research Association (2015) has also issued a statement that urges caution in the use and interpretation of teacher value-added methods and emphasizes the limitations of the knowledge-base for using in high stakes decisions on teacher effectiveness.

Although VA has been proposed and used increasingly for teacher evaluation, it has been used to evaluate only a narrow range of student outcomes, typically reading and mathematics. Many subjects don't lend themselves well to VA measurement such as art and physical education, and subjects that are less standardized in content such as social studies are less suitable for VA comparisons. At the secondary level there may be so few teachers and students in specialized courses, that teacher VA cannot be compared statistically. Different tests for the same subjects also can yield dramatically different results (Papay 2011; Grossman et al. 2014). That is, a teacher VA can be affected simply by which test instrument is used to measure achievement, even if the structure and content of the test is similar.

Another concern of VA is that it provides only a very narrow purview of teacher and school productivity by focusing only on the cognitive component of schooling. Schools are expected not only to improve knowledge and cognitive skills, but also to develop the social and emotional skills and behaviors of students that enable them to interact productively with others and become competent adults (Inkeles 1966). There is strong evidence that educational strategies have a significant influence on the formation of these attitudes and behaviors (Durlak et al. 2011). Empirical literature suggests that the non-cognitive or social and emotional skill domain may be as important or more important in determining workforce productivity (Heckman and Kaust 2012; Levin 2012). Yet, this domain is not measured or considered as a focus of VA assessments except as it affects indirectly the cognitive achievement results.

One attempt to consider the effects that teachers have on cognitive and non-cognitive skills is that of Jackson (2012) who attempts to look at teacher impacts on both student achievement gains and behavioral measures of student behavior. For non-cognitive behaviors that are affected by 9th grade teachers, he collects student data in 10th grade on student absences, dropouts, suspensions, grades, and other dimensions that he views as non-cognitive. He then relates these to their 9th grade teachers in algebra and English, removing the effects of the test results on the non-cognitive outcomes. He finds that teacher effects on test results and non-cognitive measures are weekly correlated, so that cognitive measures can not be assumed to represent the independent effects of individual teachers on non-cognitive outcomes of students. He found that the independent effects by teachers on each type of impact are comparable. But by, limiting evaluation of teacher to cognitive measures of VA omits an important dimension of teacher effectiveness.

Providing strong incentives for teachers to focus on student value-added may encourage narrow effort of teachers towards "teaching to the test". With practice tests provided by test publishers and textbooks that are structure to match the tests, teachers become highly familiar with what will be tested and the testing format. Teachers who seek high VA can concentrate instruction on specific information and repeatedly structure student quizzes and examinations in the test format rather than focusing on broader mastery of subjects or topics that are not reflected on the official tests. It is hardly a surprise to find that careful research has found that teacher induced learning has low persistence with three quarters or more fading out within a year (Jacob et al. (2008). Other research has found that less than one-third of the teacher value-added achievement survives to the next grade (Kinsler 2012). Confirming a similar type of finding, Rothstein (2010) found that the correlation between the initial VA effects and student achievement two years hence was only 0.3–0.5. This suggests that rewards for short-term achievement gains may not be promoting long-term gains.

But, in a pioneering research exercise, Chetty et al. (2013) were able to estimate the relations between value-added of teachers in grades 3–8 for 2.5 million students in a large city and later accomplishments of students such as college attendance and earnings. They found a one standard deviation difference in teacher value-added was associated with an increase in earnings of about one percent at age 28, a modest difference, but one for which benefits exceeded costs. One of the major critiques of this work has been that teachers who had larger gains historically were not incentivized to teach to the test, nor were they measured and evaluated on the test score gains. Thus higher value-added teachers prior to the era of evaluation measurement and high-stakes treatment on results may have been succeeding in other ways that not observable, but are correlated with value-added, and account for the long-term student results. Similar results may not be linked to incentivized and pressurized policies on value-added that lead to teaching to the test

Despite the challenges to the use and interpretation of VA to evaluate teacher effectiveness, its adoption has been meteoric. This rapid adoption in a field that is known for glacial change is particularly surprising in its importance for teacher policy because VA is being recommended and used in many school systems to determine salaries, long-term employment, and termination policies for teachers. Of course, the federal government's promotion of VA and its financial leverage have been key determinants of this rapid adoption. It should be noted that the recent years of economic recession undermined school budgets, making schools particularly vulnerable to the loss of funding by not meeting federal demands for teacher evaluations based upon student achievement.

In contrast to the use of VA, teachers have been evaluated traditionally by their school principals or their assistant principals in larger schools or their department chairpersons in secondary schools. It is useful to know how VA results might differ from principal evaluations in terms of overall teacher rankings and in breadth of coverage. It must be emphasized that principal evaluations in many schools have been a periodic ritual that have been neither systematic nor rigorous. More typically they have required the principal to make a short visit to a classroom on a schedule that was transmitted to the teacher in advance by tradition or agreement. The principal was expected to fill out a standardized form provided by the district which provided a checklist and space for comments or observations on the teacher's lesson plans, lesson execution, and teaching behaviors. In many cases the forms list an obligatory category in which the principal is asked to suggest interventions to improve effectiveness. These have often been treated as vague and gratuitous in nature. The vast majority of teachers were given ratings of good and excellent. In many school systems the teacher evaluation systems have been viewed as a formal and obligatory ritual that avoided deeply critical insights and recommendation to improve teacher effectiveness that might create tensions between principal and teacher. One important assessment is that this superficiality served and still serves an important purpose, to preserve harmony in the school while creating the appearance of an institutional attempt at quality improvement (Bridges 1992).

But, in recent years some school systems have established evaluation procedures that are more accountable for detailed information on teacher performance and greater responsibility for identifying performance challenges and appropriate recommendations to overcome them. Researchers have compared the results of a range of principal evaluations of teachers with VA results. It is important to note that these principal evaluations may be more extensive, detailed, and purposive than the routinized and mandated teacher evaluations required traditional by schools. Jacob and Lefgren (2008) assumed that principals have three key sources of information on teacher performance: formal and informal observations of teachers with students and colleagues; parental feedback on teachers; and student achievement results. Principals were surveyed with a request to provide ratings of teacher performance on pre-specified dimensions of teacher behavior. With statistical controls for demography of the students taught by each teacher, the principal ratings were compared to the value-added results. Among the many findings, the researchers found that the principal ratings tended to coincide for the lowest and highest performing teachers on VA performance, but not those in the middle of the VA distribution. In part this finding was related to the influence of the added dimensions that principals considered in the survey beyond VA. The authors concluded that these additional components have value which suggests combining VA results with principal evaluations for a fuller assessment of teacher performance.

Harris et al. (2014) also compared teacher value-added measures of effectiveness with principal evaluations of teachers. They found that principals value teacher effectiveness in terms of student achievement, but they also value teacher effort and collaboration in rating teacher productivity. More recent work by Harris and Sass (2014) confirms both the findings and the recommendation of combining good processes of principal's evaluation with VA in rating teachers. They find that, in particular, principals value teacher effort and collaboration among other characteristics that may or may not be embedded in VA. What is missing from these assessments is the contribution that student evaluations might add (Marsh and Roche 1997).

10.4 Implications for Teacher Preparation and Recruitment

There are many views on how to improve the preparation of teachers and the recruitment of outstanding teachers. One of the most comprehensive sources on this topic is Darling-Hammond and Bransford (2005) which comprises an effort sponsored by the National Research Council of the U.S. National Academy of Sciences. The contributions are analytical, comprehensive, and provocative and written by noted scholars. But, there are large differences in the prescriptions. In part, this is due to differences in opinions on what constitutes desirable human development and education, a normative question; in part it is due to what instructional strategies are considered effective in reaching these goals, an issue that is amenable to research and evidence. Differences in both perspectives define the directions that are recommended for preparing teachers. When these are overlaid on the different subjects, ages, and special needs of children, the complexity increases manifold. But, the richness of the perspectives magnifies the challenge of how to construct different approaches to education and teacher preparation that might be validated by results.

There has been relatively little empirical research on how specific teacher preparation programs or certification requirements for teachers have different consequences in terms of student results. As noted earlier, teachers with regular licenses and those who lack these credentials by entering teaching through other routes show no differences or only small differences in student achievement (e.g. Clotfelter et al. 2007; Boyd et al. 2006; Goldhaber and Brewer 2000). For example, Harris and Sass (2011) find no evidence that the pre-service training of teachers or their college entrance test scores are linked to their later productivity in student VA.

But, special attention must go to the detailed analysis and comparison of student outcomes for of teacher preparation programs. Boyd et al. (2009) studied 31 different teacher preparation programs in New York City which account for most of the teachers hired in recent years for that city's students. 26 of the programs were traditional university-based programs, and 4 provided other approaches to teacher preparation. They also obtained detailed data on the components that comprised each program. These data were used to link teachers to value-added in student achievement in grades three through eight in English Language Arts and Mathematics. The data set and analyses also provide a rich set of information on student and teacher demographics and other dimensions that may affect student achievement.

The authors found differences among teacher preparation programs in the effectiveness of their teachers with the most productive programs being associated with student gains that reach about 0.04 to 0.05 greater than the average program result. However, these findings are in conflict with the expectations of large differences in effectiveness of teacher training programs. Translated into percentile gains for students, this magnitude of effect size is equivalent to about 2 percentiles. The authors argue that the true effect sizes are larger if adjusted for measurement errors. But, there is also a potential upward bias in their results because of inadequate treatment of potential selection effects. Prospective students select the preparation programs that attract them, and the programs select among the students that apply rather than students being randomly assigned to programs. Although the authors are aware of this challenge and use covariates to control for selection, these are not likely to be adequate to account for the unobservable differences in teachers who chose and/or were chosen into the specific programs that were evaluated. Thus, the results could be partially attributable to the character of the teachers in each program rather than the programs themselves. Finally, it should be noted that if the evidence on fadeout of achievement gains is applicable, the 2 percentiles ultimately melt into 1 percentile advantage or less.

The authors also sought to ascertain which program features were related to teacher effectiveness in the achievement of their students. One particularly salient finding is that for first year teachers, there is a reasonably strong and consistent link between VA and supervised field experiences in classrooms and capstone projects devoted to the study of practice. Although this study is pioneering in its goals and use of data, the authors suggest caution in generalizing the results because of ambiguity in interpretation. Yet, it provides an ambitious and promising format for further research. Harris and Sass (2011) obtain less detailed information on programs and find little evidence that pre-service training other than math courses for math teachers seems to matter in the statistical link between teacher preparation and student achievement.

Goldhaber et al. (2013) evaluated the student achievement outcomes of teachers among teacher preparation programs within the State of Washington and also those from out-of-state. Although differences in educational effectiveness among teachers within each program were substantial, differences in graduates among institutions were almost inconsequential. Unfortunately, this raises the question of how much is known about producing better teachers that can be used to construct new programs or improve existing ones that can substantially improve the teaching force. The modest differences are particularly humbling in contrast to the aspirations to raise student achievement generally and to reduce the substantial achievement gaps by socioeconomic status and race.

In a recent paper, Jacob et al. 2016) are more optimistic in their analysis of a Washington D.C. multi-stage application process which includes written assessments, a personal interview, and sample lessons. Teachers in the top quartile score two-thirds of a standard deviation higher in student achievement gains relative to those in the lowest quartile. But these measures are weakly associated with the probability of being hired, perhaps because teacher-value added is too limited a sole-criterion for measuring teacher effectiveness.

10.4.1 Policy Dilemmas

To improve teacher preparation and selection, we need verification that new policies in those domains will have beneficial effects on the education of the students they will teach.. Depending upon educational goals and how student success is measured, there is only limited information on how changes in teacher preparation and selection will lead to verifiable improvement in educational results. This conclusion is emphasized by Staiger and Rockoff (2010) who conclude that we know so little about the prospect of teacher effectiveness from available information at the time of hiring that it is necessary to monitor teacher progress in terms of student results over a few years before we can draw conclusions on teacher quality and make decisions about retention or dismissal and adjustment of remuneration. That is, our ability to predict teacher effectiveness from all available background information is highly limited as documented above. And the fact that the early years of experience seem to have dynamic effects on teacher performance necessitates avoiding judgments on effectiveness until an adequate time frame is considered. This is particularly important because some teachers may start with larger VA results than others, but benefit less from experience, coaching, and mentoring than those who start from a lower base. This possibility is particularly salient, given the year-to-year variance in VA results among individual teachers.

Since one cannot know a teacher's VA in advance or predict it with any precision from the available teacher characteristics, the use of VA as a primary device for identifying productivity raises obvious challenges for evaluating initial teacher preparation, recruitment, and selection. We must also be mindful that VA is a restricted measure of teacher effectiveness based upon stylized testing in a few subjects and ignoring all of the other dimensions of teacher performance and productive student development. Once employed, a teacher must serve for a number of years before reliable estimates of VA can be used to ascertain effectiveness that merits a long-term contract and other rewards for performance.

There is no ready solution for this dilemma. Deciding whom to recruit and select is unclear and only weakly informed by information on teacher characteristics. Waiting for consistent and stable VA results for several years is also cumbersome and needs to be combined continuously with additional information to encompass other important dimensions of teacher performance. But, most limiting in this process of assessment is the fact that no systematic mechanism is provided to validate changes and differences in teacher preparation with their impacts on teacher performance in schools. If schools hire teachers from a single teacher training institution, they will have no ability to compare their performance with those of other providers. Further, if programs are changing, there is no systematic provision to identify the consequences of those changes, particularly given that the literature shows "small" effects which may be difficult to identify with limited samples of teachers who are hired.

In theory this problem could be resolved through market signaling (Spence 1973). Market signaling is based upon productive organizations hiring their employees under the assumption of uncertainty with respect to their productivity, but utilizing information that has shown promise in the past. The relation between this information and productivity is continuously evaluated for new hires to see how it predicts employee results, and feeds back into subsequent hiring decisions on a continuous basis. To my knowledge, there is no systematic process in any school system that is dedicated to this goal.

A school system composed of multiple schools such as a district or municipality could hire teachers according to whatever criteria it chose. Initial contracts would be renewable for a limited duration, perhaps three years duration. Teacher performance could be evaluated over time and linked statistically to particular teacher characteristics and preparation. This continuous evaluation would uncover patterns of desirability for specific types of teachers and from specific programs which would be used to establish hiring patterns, and the most successful teachers would be provided with long-term or tenured contracts. The use of market signaling would also provide a feedback loop to teacher preparation institutions on the performance of their graduates through market demand. This approach would increase risk-taking in teacher hiring because of the provision to undertake systematic monitoring of teachers from new programs or ones that were changing. It would also allow schools with unique student populations or goals to differentiate their hiring from other schools and for the school system to maintain extensive records on a wide range of teacher characteristics and experiences with teachers from different preparation programs. Using a market signaling model, schools and school systems can influence the market by registering preferences for certain types of teachers and graduates of particular institutions who have been shown to be effective through recruitment and special incentives.

The major challenge is to improve vastly the knowledge-base on what makes a teacher effective. Even with the best of intentions to raise the quality of recruitment into teaching and to improve teacher preparation, we need to validate the consequences of our efforts rather than just assuming that they are effective. Moreover, we need to obtain feedback of results for the benefit of those who are planning new teacher policies and strategies. Bearing in mind that the literature of teacher selection and preparation is far from unanimous, we need to obtain more of a concensus on what is needed to transfer clichés like "attract better teachers" and "improve teacher preparation" into concrete strategies that can be validated for their results. Hopefully, efforts in this direction will take into account far more than just VA, especially given the important of social and emotional learning that has been recognized in recent years.

10.4.2 Some Concerns

In moving forward to validate teacher performance and build a market signaling approach, we must keep in mind certain conclusions:

1. Much has been learned about measuring gains in student achievement in relation to their teachers, using VA. But present value-added approaches are highly incomplete. They are limited to a few specific subjects and knowledge that is tested in constrained testing frameworks that rarely reflect the understanding behind the responses. They are also highly susceptible to test preparation rather than knowledge as suggested by the strong fadeout effects on student performance. They lack attention to teacher effectiveness in addressing social and emotional learning, and they have statistical challenges in stability of results from year-to-year and in addressing the non-random assignment of teachers.
2. Multiple evaluation methods would seem to be more promising in which VA measures are combined with ways of evaluating teacher performance in

non-tested domains. Of particular promise are the use of principal evaluations that are well-structured in terms of dimensions that are evaluated and rigor of evaluations. These might be supplemented with student and parent evaluations. How all of this information might be formulated and combined in assessments also needs to be considered.

3. At present the apparent effects of identifiable characteristics of teachers and teacher preparation programs are small. This suggests that we need to understand both the potential and limits of teacher effectiveness in the larger picture of student performance. Further, we need to understand better the types of non-school factors that need to be improved for student performance and how the non-school factors such as family educational assistance and pre-school enrichment can expand teacher effectiveness.

4. Perhaps the greatest shortcoming of existing research on teachers is the paucity of useful information for developing, identifying, and selecting a highly promising teaching force. The implications of this review of research are that random selection of college graduates for teaching would obtain about as effective a group of teacher prospects as any selection criteria. This seems highly unlikely, but it is hardly challenged by the evidence. We need to provide more systematic understanding for choosing both a pool of potentially effective teachers that can be validated subsequently as well as the market incentives for attracting them. Most notably we must devote considerable effort to validating empirically the consequences of new teacher preparation programs (Grossman and McDonald 2008).

References

American Educational Research Association. (2015). AERA statement on use of Value-Added Models (VAM) for the evaluation of educators and educator preparation programs. *Educational Researcher, 10*(10), 1–5.

American Statistical Association. (2014). *ASA statement on using value-added models for educational assessment.* Retrieved from http://www.amstat.org/policy/pdfs/ASA_VAM_Statement.pdf

Atteberry, A., Loeb, S., & Wyckoff, J. (2015). Do first impressions matter? Predicting early career teacher effectiveness. *AERA Open, 1*(4), DOI: 10.1177/2332858415607834

Boyd, D. J., Grossman, P. L., Lankford, H., Loeb, S., & Wyckoff, J. (2006). How changes in entry requirements alter the teacher workforce and affect student achievement. *Education Finance and Policy, 1*(2), 176–216.

Boyd, D. J., Grossman, P. L., Lankford, H., Loeb, S., & Wyckoff, J. (2009). Teacher preparation and student achievement. *Educational Evaluation and Policy Analysis, 31*(4), 416–440.

Bridges, E. M. (1992). *The incompetent teacher: Managerial responses.* New York, NY: RoutledgeFalmer.

Chetty, R., Friedman, J. N., & Rockoff, J. E. (2013). Measuring the impacts of teachers II: Teacher value-added and student outcomes in adulthood. *American Economic Review, 104*(9), 2633–2679.

Clotfelter, C. T., Ladd, H. F., & Vigdor, J.L. (2007). How & why do teacher credentials matter for student achievement? *Economics of Education Review, 26*(6), 673–682.

Darling-Hammond, L., & Bransford, J. (Eds.) (2005). *Preparing teachers for a changing world: What teachers should learn and be able to do.* San Francisco, CA: Jossey-Bass.

Darling-Hammond, L., Berry, B., & Thoreson, A. (2001). Does teacher certification matter? Evaluating the evidence, *Educational Evaluation and Policy Analysis, 23*(1), 57–77.

Digman, J. (1990). Personality structure of the five factor model. *Annual Review of Psychology, 41*, 417–440.

Durlak, J. A., Weissberg, R. P., Dymnicki, A. B., Taylor, R. D., L, & Schellinger, K. B. (2011). The impact of enhancing students' social and emotional learning: A meta-analysis of school-based universal intervention. *Child Development, 82*(1), 405–432.

Goldhaber, D., & Brewer, D. (2000). Does teacher certification matter? High school teacher certification status and student achievement. *Educational Evaluation and Policy Analysis, 22* (2), 129–145.

Goldhaber, D., & Brewer, D. (2001). Evaluating the evidence of teacher certification: A rejoinder. *Educational Evaluation and Policy Analysis, 23*(1), 79–86.

Goldhaber, D., Liddle, S., & Theobald, R. (2013). The gateway to the profession: Assessing teacher preparation programs based on student achievement. *Economics of Education Review, 34*, 29–44.

Goldhaber, D., Walch, J., & Gabele, B. (2014). Does the model matter? Exploring the relationship between different student achievement-based teacher assessments. *Statistics and Public Policy, 1*(1), 28–39.

Grossman, P., & McDonald, M. (2008). Back to the future: Directions for research in teaching and teacher education. *American Educational Research Journal, 45*(1), 184–205.

Grossman, P., Cohen, J., Ronfeldt, M., & Brown, L. (2014). The test matters: The relationship between classroom observation score and teacher value added on multiple types of assessment. *Educational Researcher, 43*(6), 293–303.

Guarino, C., Reckase, M., & Wooldridge, J. (2015). Can value-added measures of teacher performance be trusted? *Education Finance and Policy, 10*(1), 117–156.

Haertel, E. H. (2013). *Reliability and validity of inferences about teachers based on student test scores* [PDF document]. William H. Angoff Memorial Lecture Series, Educational Testing Service. Retrieved from http://www.nnstoy.org/download/vam-and-student-growth-models/VAM%20Angoff%20lecture%20ETS.pdf

Hanushek, E. A. (1971). Teacher characteristics and gains in student achievement: Estimation using micro data. *American Economic Review, 61*(2), 280–288.

Hanushek, E. A. (1997). Assessing the effects of school resources on student performance: An update. *Educational Evaluation and Policy Analysis, 19*(2), 141–164.

Hanushek E.A., Kain J.F., O'Brien D.M., & Rivkin SG. (2005). The market for teacher quality. NBERWork. Pap. 11154.

Hanushek, E. A., & Rivkin, S. G. (2006). Teacher Quality. In E. A. Hanushek & F. Welch, (Eds.), *Handbook of the economics of education*, Vol 2 (pp 1051–1078). Amsterdam: North Holland.

Hanushek, E. A., & Rivkin, S. G. (2010). Generalization about using value-added measures of teacher quality. *American Economic Review, 100*(2), 267–271.

Harris, D. N., & Sass, T. R. (2011). Teacher training, teacher quality, & student achievement. *Journal of Public Economics, 95*(7–8), 798–812.

Harris, D. N., & Sass, T. R. (2014). Skills, productivity and evaluation of teacher performance. *Economics of Education Review, 40*, 183–204.

Harris, D. N., Ingle, W. K., & Rutledge, S. A. (2014). How teacher evaluation methods matter for accountability: A comparative analysis of teacher effectiveness ratings by principal & teacher value-added measures, *American Educational Research Journal, 51*(1), 73–112.

Heckman, J. J., & Kautz, T. (2012). Hard evidence on soft skills. *Labour Economics, 19*(4), 451–464.

Inkeles, A. (1966). The socialization of competence. *Harvard Educational Review, 36*(3), 265–283.

Jackson, K. (2012). Non-cognitive ability, test scores, and teacher quality: evidence from 9th grade teachers in North Carolina (NBER working paper no 18624). Retrieved from National Bureau of Economic Research website http://www.nber.org/papers/w18624

Jacob, B. A., & Lefgren, L. (2008). Can principals identify effective teachers? Evidence on subjective performance evaluation in education. *Journal of Labor Economics, 26*(1), 101–136.

Jacob, B. A., Lefgren, L., & Sims, D. P. (2008). The persistence of teacher-induced learning. *Journal of Human Resources, 45*(4), 915–943.

Jacob, B., Rockoff, J. E., Taylor, E. S., Lindy, B., & Rosen, R. (2016). Teacher applicant hiring and teacher performance: Evidence from DC public schools (NBER Working Paper Number 22054) Retrieved from National Bureau of Economic Research website http://www.nber.org/papers/w22054

Kane, T. J., Rockoff, J.E., & Staiger, D. O. (2008). "What does certification tell us about teacher effectiveness? Evidence from New York City. *Economics of Education Review, 27*(6), 615–631.

Kinsler, J. (2012). Beyond levels & growth: Estimating teacher value-added and its persistence. *Journal of Human Resources, 47*(3), 722–763.

Koedel, C., & Betts, J. R. (2007). Re-examining the role of teacher quality in the educational production function (Working Paper No 0708). Retrieved from Department of Economics, University of Missouri website http://economics.missouri.edu/working-papers/2007/wp0708_koedel.pdf

Levin, H. M. (2012). More than just test scores. *Prospects, 42*(3), 269–284.

Marsh, H. W., & Roche, L. A. (1997). Making students' evaluation of teaching effectiveness effective: The critical issues of validity, bias, and utility. *American Psychologist, 52*(11), 1187–1197.

McCaffrey, D. F., Sass, T. R., Lockwood, J. R. & Mihaly, K. (2009). "The intertemporal variability of teacher effectiveness estimates. *Education Finance & Policy, 4*(4), 572–606.

McKenzie, P., Santiago, P., Sliwka, P. & Hiroyuki, H. (2005). Teachers matter: Attracting, developing and retaining effective teachers. Paris: OECD.

Papay, J. (2011). Different tests different answers: The stability of teacher value-added estimates across different outcome measures. *American Educational Research Journal, 48*(1), 163–193.

Rivkin, S. G., Hanushek, E. A., & Kain, J. F. (2005). Teachers, schools, and academic achievement. *Econometrica, 73*(2), 417–458.

Rockoff, J. E., Jacob, B. A., Kane, T. J., & Staiger D. O. (2011). Can you recognize an effective teacher when you recruit one? *Educational Finance & Policy, 6*(1), 43–74.

Rothstein, J. (2009). Student sorting and bias in value-added estimation: Selection on observables and unobservables. *Educational Finance & Policy, 4*(4), 537–571.

Rothstein, J. (2010). Teacher quality in educational production: Tracking, decay, and student achievement. *Quarterly Journal of Economics, 125*(1), 175–214.

Spence, M. A. (1973). Job market signaling. *Quarterly Journal of Economics, 87*, 355–374.

Staiger, D. O., & Rockoff, J. E. (2010). Search for effective teachers with imperfect information. *Journal of Economic Perspectives, 24*(3), 97–117.

Wayne, A. J., & Young, P. (2003). Teacher characteristics and student achievement gains: A review. *Review of Educational Research, 73*, 89–122.

Part III
Modelling Measurement Properties

Chapter 11
Measuring Changing Educational Contexts in a Changing World: Evolution of the TIMSS and PIRLS Questionnaires

Ina V.S. Mullis, Michael O. Martin and Martin Hooper

Abstract With each TIMSS and PIRLS assessment, IEA's TIMSS & PIRLS International Study Center at Boston College has improved the quality of the context questionnaire data collected about educational policies and practices. Over the 20 years that TIMSS and PIRLS have measured trends in educational achievement, the questionnaire data have been evolving to measure a stable set of policy-relevant constructs. With trends in valid and reliable context questionnaire scales, changes in students' achievement from one assessment cycle to the next can be examined in relation to changes in the policies and practices of interest to determine whether there are patterns. TIMSS 2015 provided trend results for about a dozen such scales (e.g., *Instruction Affected by Resource Shortages*, *Safe and Orderly School*, and *Early Literacy and Numeracy Activities*) and PIRLS 2016 is expected to provide similar results.

11.1 IEA's TIMSS and PIRLS: 20 Years of Trend Data

IEA (International Association for the Evaluation of Educational Achievement) was founded more than 50 years ago to conduct international comparative assessments of student achievement. The goal was to gain a deeper understanding of how variations in educational achievement related to differences in educational practices. As explained by IEA's first Chair, Professor Torsten Husén from the University of Stockholm, the education systems of the world represented a laboratory to objectively study variations, allowing "comparisons to be made with means more powerful and more sure than artificially set up and costly experimental situations within one country or culture (Husén 1967 pp. 27–28)." Today, IEA's most prominent international assessments are TIMSS (Trends in International Mathematics and Science Study) and PIRLS (Progress in International Reading

I.V.S. Mullis (✉) · M.O. Martin · M. Hooper
TIMSS & PIRLS International Study Center, Boston College, Chestnut Hill, MA, USA
e-mail: ina.mullis@bc.edu; timssandpirls@bc.edu

© Springer International Publishing AG 2017
M. Rosén et al. (eds.), *Cognitive Abilities and Educational Outcomes*,
Methodology of Educational Measurement and Assessment,
DOI 10.1007/978-3-319-43473-5_11

Literacy Study), which have been directed by IEA's TIMSS & PIRLS International Study Center at Boston College since 1993.

Since its first assessments in 1995, TIMSS has collected more than 20 years of trend data about student achievement in mathematics and science, as well as extensive data about the school, classroom, and home contexts for mathematics and science teaching and learning. International assessments of mathematics and science have been conducted at the fourth and eighth grades every four years since 1995, and the TIMSS Advanced assessment of advanced mathematics and physics for students in their final year of secondary school has been conducted three times (1995, 2008, and 2015). PIRLS is an international assessment of reading comprehension at fourth grade that has been conducted every five years since 2001, with the most recent 2016 assessment extended to encompass PIRLS Literacy, a less demanding version of PIRLS, and ePIRLS, an assessment of online reading. About 60 countries and educational entities regularly participate in the TIMSS and PIRLS assessments. The TIMSS and PIRLS international results for the participating countries as well as complete documentation of the methods used to implement the assessments can be found at timssandpirls.bc.edu.

In addition to providing rigorous measures of achievement, the TIMSS and PIRLS assessments ask students, their parents, their teachers, and their school principals to complete questionnaires about their home, school, and classroom contexts for learning. Also, each country completes a curriculum policies questionnaire and prepares a chapter summarizing the structure of its education system, the curriculum, and overall policies related to teacher preparation and instruction, and all this information is published online in the TIMSS and PIRLS Encyclopedias (timssandpirls.bc.edu).

TIMSS and PIRLS update the topic areas to be covered by the achievement assessments and the context questionnaires with each assessment. For example, the *TIMSS 2015 Assessment Frameworks* and the *PIRLS 2016 Assessment Framework, 2nd Edition* each contain a chapter describing the factors or aspects of home, school, and classroom contexts for learning that the questionnaires should cover as well as which student characteristics and attitudes should be included.

11.2 Explaining Trends in Achievement in Relation to a Stable Set of Context Factors

TIMSS and PIRLS provide the assessment results to the public via descriptions of the mathematics, science, and reading achievement in the participating countries, accompanied by detailed reporting of the countries' educational context, policies, and practices. When there is a positive association between achievement and a factor (e.g., number of books in the home, school emphasis on academic success), the results are shown in the International Reports. However, given the cross-sectional survey designs with each student only measured at one point in time, it has been difficult to go beyond descriptive reporting and support causal interpretations of how achievement is influenced by particular school, classroom, and home factors.

The continuing accumulation of TIMSS and PIRLS trend data across successive assessments provides an opportunity to develop explanations of how some factors have been influencing educational achievement over time, partially overcoming the challenges posed by the cross-sectional design. Professor Jan-Eric Gustafsson from the University of Gothenburg began using TIMSS and PIRLS trend data to study causal influences on education within countries a decade ago (Gustafsson 2007). Essentially, by aggregating data to the country level, changes in achievement from one assessment cycle to the next are examined in relation to changes in the context factor of interest to determine whether there is a pattern. In recent years, a number of variations on this basic idea have been used to make causal inferences based on TIMSS and PIRLS results (Liu et al. 2014; Rosén and Gustafsson 2014).

Meanwhile, the TIMSS & PIRLS International Study Center has been working to improve the quality of the data collected about educational policies and practices, so that research using the trend data to provide explanations about educational influences can be more productive. The goal is to eventually use TIMSS and PIRLS trend data to address questions such as: How do trends in educational achievement relate to changes in emphasis on preprimary education? to changes in school safety? to changes in the quality of teaching?

TIMSS and PIRLS have a careful design for developing assessments of trends in student achievement that evolves over time, but unfortunately it has taken more time to develop a stable set of measurable educational context constructs that also can evolve over time. The remainder of this paper describes the process of developing the TIMSS and PIRLS questionnaires over the past 20 years, and the approach currently being used to provide reliable and valid trend measures of context factors and practices that are policy-relevant across countries.

11.3 TIMSS 1995

From initial planning beginning in 1989, TIMSS 1995 burgeoned into the most ambitious international assessment of student achievement conducted until then, with 45 participating countries and an array of data collection instruments consisting of tests and questionnaires given to populations of students in the third/fourth grades, seventh/eighth grades, and the final year of secondary school (Martin 1996). Following the success of the first International Assessment in Mathematics in 1964, IEA conducted a number of important international studies during the 1970s and 1980s, including a second assessment in mathematics (Robitaille and Garden 1989) and two assessments in science (Comber and Keeves 1973; Postlethwaite and Wiley 1992). Then, made possible largely by funding from the United States, TIMSS 1995 encompassed IEA's third assessment of both mathematics and science, and was originally named the Third International Mathematics and Science Study.

At the time, TIMSS 1995 was not planned as a trend study. Based on previous experience with IEA studies, participating countries anticipated that there would be a number of years until the next mathematics and science studies and so they viewed TIMSS 1995 as a golden opportunity to collect as much data as possible. These included veteran countries from previous IEA mathematics and science assessments as well as a burst of new countries participating in their first international assessments. The comprehensive Conceptual Framework that guided questionnaire development in TIMSS 1995 reflected a model developed in IEA's Second International Mathematics Study and still used in TIMSS assessments today, where levels of a country's educational system are represented by three aspects of the curriculum (Robitaille and Garden 1996). The *intended curriculum* represents what students are expected to learn as defined in countries' curriculum policies, the *implemented curriculum* represents what is taught in classrooms, and the *attained curriculum* is what students have learned as measured by TIMSS. The TIMSS 1995 Framework was portrayed as a matrix of system, school, classroom, and student explanatory factors across four dimensions: (1) what students are expected to learn, (2) who delivers instruction, (3) how instruction is organized, and (4) what students have learned.

To address all aspects of the Conceptual Framework, the 1995 questionnaires asked about a wide range of topics and activities. For example at seventh/eighth grade, the School Questionnaire contained a series of lists of topics of interest, such as the degree of influence 15 different school and community groups had on the curriculum taught in their school, the time the principals devoted to 14 different tasks (e.g., giving a demonstration lesson, disciplining students), and who was responsible for another 14 such tasks (e.g., buying supplies, determining teachers' salaries).

With the aim of linking student achievement to instructional activities, the Student Questionnaire, as well as seeking a large amount of demographic information, asked about the frequency of about 20 different classroom activities (e.g., copy notes, look at textbooks, discuss homework) in mathematics lessons and then the frequency of the same 20 activities in science lessons. Also, beyond asking teachers about their demographic characteristics, preparation for teaching, roles and responsibilities, use of homework and assessment, and numerous classroom situations and activities, the Teacher Questionnaire included a substantial number of questions about pedagogy. Separately for mathematics and science, teachers were asked about 22 potential lesson topics, the purpose of the lesson, and to sequence a list of 11 activities (e.g., review, do exercises, watch a film) according to how the lesson should proceed, and more than a dozen additional questions about lesson activities (e.g., writing equations, calling on students, working in pairs). The "Opportunity to Learn" section consisted of approximately 20 pages of sample assessment items and mathematics and science topics, with detailed questions about when the topic was covered in the curriculum, whether each of the items was a good assessment of the topic, and whether students would encounter the topic outside of school. The last section covered teachers' views about acceptable pedagogical approaches to teach particular topics.

11.4 Measuring Trends

After TIMSS 1995, countries became interested in follow-up data and so TIMSS 1999 was conducted as a repeat of 1995 at the eighth grade, but with new items to replace those released after TIMSS 1995. Then, with its third assessment cycle, TIMSS was redesigned to become a trend study. Measuring trends from one assessment to the next requires maintaining a balance between keeping the same instruments from assessment cycle to cycle, and updating the instruments to maximize the relevance of assessment results by addressing the most current learning goals and policy issues. Assessments need to reflect new assessment content (e.g., scientific discoveries), incorporate measures of the most effective policies and practices based on current research, and use the most effective assessment methods based on technological innovations, while carefully respecting the basic principle: If you want to measure change, do not change the measure.

TIMSS and PIRLS are based on assessment frameworks and data collection designs that enable the assessments to evolve gradually over time while maintaining stability from assessment to assessment. The Assessment Frameworks for mathematics, science, and reading, are updated with each assessment cycle to keep abreast with current developments. To address updates in the Frameworks at least one-third of each TIMSS or PIRLS assessment is devoted to new item development, while a substantial percentage of items from the previous assessment (about 60–65 %) are reassessed to provide a foundation for measuring trends. Matrix sampling assessment designs provide for new items to be included with each assessment and previously assessed items to be made available to researchers while maintaining reliable measurement on the underlying achievement scale.

Updating the questionnaires for TIMSS 1999, 2003, and 2007 as well as for PIRLS 2001 and 2006 was approached systematically, but not according to a specific design. The Context Questionnaire Frameworks were updated for each TIMSS and PIRLS assessment to identify which policies and practices should be covered in the questionnaires regarding national/community, home, school, and classroom contexts relevant to teaching and learning, as well as which students' characteristics and attitudes toward learning should be included. Also, each assessment devoted considerable energy to questionnaire development and to increasing the relevance of the data provided about teaching and learning in mathematics, science, and reading. From 1995 to 2007, the questionnaire development process was implemented separately for TIMSS and PIRLS, guided by the TIMSS & PIRLS International Study Center working with the TIMSS Questionnaire Item Replacement Committee (QIRC) for TIMSS and the PIRLS Questionnaire Development Group (QDG) for PIRLS. The final products were based on the collaborative consensus of the National Research Coordinators (NRCs) working on each assessment cycle. The result was a variety of major and minor modifications in the context questionnaires that satisfied the current needs of the participating countries, but made monitoring trends very challenging. The idea of measuring contextual constructs was not central to the process, but several constructs did emerge and these sets of items were often reported through summative indices through 2007.

The changes made from 1995 through 2007 in the TIMSS questions about students' attitudes toward mathematics are described to illustrate progress in identifying and measuring constructs, even though they resulted in little useful trend data. Because the issue of response burden for students, teachers, and principals became central after TIMSS 1995, only some of the 1995 questionnaire items could be carried forward.

Figure 11.1 contains the two individual questions and two sets of items asked in 1995 and again in 1999 that endured in some form through several assessment cycles and became the basis for future context questionnaire scales related to mathematics and to science. The items shown pertain only to attitudes toward mathematics, but the parallel items also were included for science.

Figure 11.2 shows the TIMSS 2003 set of questions about attitudes toward learning mathematics with asterisks (*) indicating the differences between 2003 and 2007. Two items from 1995 and 1999, "Mathematics is boring" and "I like mathematics," were not included in 2003, but rejoined the questionnaires for TIMSS 2007. One item from 2003 was deleted before 2007 based on its complex reading load. The set of items measuring the degree to which eighth grade students value mathematics was administered in TIMSS 2003 and then re-administered in 2007, but having deleted item (d) [denoted with the asterisk (*)] because it overlapped with item (e).

In the TIMSS 2007 International Report, the set of items about learning mathematics was reported as two separate indices, *Index of Students' Positive Affect Toward Mathematics* ("I enjoy learning mathematics," "Mathematics is boring," and "I like mathematics") and *Index of Students' Self-Confidence in Learning*

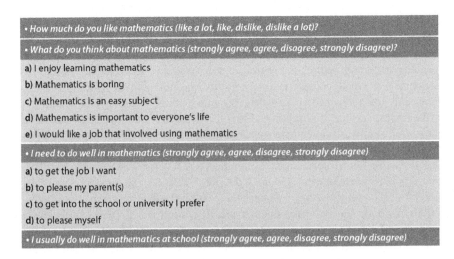

Fig. 11.1 Student attitudes toward mathematics in TIMSS 1995 and TIMSS 1999

> **• How much do you agree (agree a lot, agree a little, disagree a little, disagree a lot) with these statements about learning mathematics?**
>
> **a)** I usually do well in mathematics (from TIMSS 1995 and 1999)
>
> **b)** I would like to take more mathematics in school
>
> **c)** Mathematics is more difficult for me than for many of my classmates
>
> **d)** I enjoy learning mathematics (from TIMSS 1995 and 1999)
>
> **e)** *Sometimes when I do not initially understand a new topic in mathematics, I know that I will never really understand it (not included in TIMSS 2007)
>
> **f)** Mathematics is not one of my strengths
>
> **g)** I learn things quickly in mathematics
>
> * Mathematics is boring (from TIMSS 1995, 1999, added back in 2007)
>
> * I like mathematics (from TIMSS 1995, 1999, added back in 2007)

> **• How much do you agree (agree a lot, agree a little, disagree a little, disagree a lot) with these statements about mathematics?**
>
> **a)** I think learning mathematics will help me in my daily life
>
> **b)** I need mathematics to learn other school subjects
>
> **c)** I need to do well in mathematics to get into the school or university of my choice (from TIMSS 1995)
>
> **d)** *I would like a job that involved using mathematics (from TIMSS 1995)
>
> **e)** I need to do well in mathematics to get the job I want (from TIMSS 1995)

Fig. 11.2 Student attitudes toward mathematics in TIMSS 2003 and TIMSS 2007

Mathematics (Mullis et al. 2008). The second set of items was reported as the *Index of Students Valuing Mathematics*. The indices were additive composites of the students' responses across items, and students were classified into regions according their index scores. The *Index of Students' Positive Affect Toward Mathematics* was used to measure trends between 1995 and 2007, and the other two indices to measure trends between 2003 and 2007. Analyses of the 2007 scale structure of both sets of items documented the three attitudinal dimensions (Martin and Preuschoff 2008).

11.5 PIRLS 2001 and 2006

At its inception, PIRLS questionnaire development benefited from the TIMSS experience, and later TIMSS questionnaires in turn benefited from PIRLS developments. PIRLS was first assessed in 2001, with the second round in 2006, so the TIMSS 2003 questionnaires benefited from PIRLS 2001, and the PIRLS 2006 and TIMSS 2007 questionnaires benefited from TIMSS 2003. Yet, the decision whether to delete an item or retain it, or to retain an item in its original form to measure trends or to revise it to improve measurement, essentially was made item by item for TIMSS by the TIMSS NRCs and for PIRLS by the PIRLS NRCs.

The PIRLS 2001 home questionnaire given to students' parents and caregivers became one of the most important innovations in context questionnaire development. Called the Learning to Read Survey, the home questionnaire provides important information about parental or caregiver emphasis on early learning activities (e.g., read books, play word games) and preprimary education, as well as home resources and parents' education levels and occupations.

Also, the PIRLS 2001 idea of incorporating the Encyclopedia into the questionnaire development process made it possible to reduce School and Teacher Questionnaire burden in TIMSS and PIRLS assessments. Instead of asking all of the principals or teachers about countrywide policies, the NRCs provided such information, and the results were included in cross-country tables supplementing the chapters in the Encyclopedias.

11.6 TIMSS and PIRLS 2011

Confronting how to establish comparability in measuring the topics covered in the context questionnaires became a necessity in 2011, when the trend cycles of TIMSS and PIRLS came together. Countries took advantage of having both TIMSS and PIRLS in 2011 to assess the same fourth grade students in reading, mathematics, and science and be able to relate achievement in these three key curriculum areas to extensive context questionnaire data, including for TIMSS countries the valuable information obtained through the PIRLS home questionnaire. It was readily apparent that comparable context questionnaire data across the three curricular areas was central to the success of this effort.

Working together, the TIMSS & PIRLS International Study Center and the NRCs for TIMSS and PIRLS initiated a plan for developing context questionnaires that paralleled the system used for the achievement data. The TIMSS and PIRLS 2011 Context Questionnaire Frameworks were updated based on a common conceptual model, entitled TIMSS and PIRLS Policy Considerations, which considered student achievement in the context of school environment and classroom instruction, while acknowledging the important roles of curriculum and curriculum coverage, teachers prepared to teach the curriculum, supportive home environments, and student motivation to learn.

The TIMSS and PIRLS 2011 Student, Teacher, School, and country-level Curriculum Questionnaires were developed jointly by the TIMSS and PIRLS questionnaire groups (TIMSS 2011 QIRC and PIRLS 2011 QDG) and during joint meetings of the TIMSS and PIRLS 2011 National Research Coordinators. Context questionnaire development concentrated on measuring constructs related to fostering achievement across countries through context questionnaire scales—sets of items analyzed through item response theory (IRT) methodology that replaced and extended the TIMSS 2007 concept of indices. To develop the scales, many individuals worked to identify constructs that were universal across as many countries as possible and also enduring over time. The process required considerable narrowing of questionnaire topics compared to previous assessments, because each construct needed to be measured by at least five to eight items for satisfactory reliability and validity.[1]

The TIMSS & PIRLS International Study Center guided the process of developing valid and reliable scales to measure those constructs. Consistent with the idea of having fewer constructs with improved measurement of each construct, building a foundation for stable trend measurement was central to the effort. If the newly developed scales were found to be robust, which would require including a sufficient number of items, then further items could be added or deleted with each successive future assessment to keep the constructs up-to-date with recent findings in the literature.

The task included (1) identifying constructs that were important to all three curricular areas for which new scales could be developed to measure trends, (2) identifying other important constructs covered in the questionnaires for which scales could be developed, including reconciling the different formats and wording between the TIMSS and PIRLS versions, and (3) minimizing the burden to an acceptable level. Underpinning the new approach, each questionnaire scale was designed to be reported using IRT scaling methods. The questionnaires were field tested, and the scales evaluated for unidimensionality, reliability, item fit with the Rasch partial-credit model, and relationship with achievement. The questionnaires were modified in light of the field test results and subjected to a final review at a joint meeting of all the TIMSS and PIRLS 2011 NRCs.

The 2011 questionnaire development effort was very successful, yielding nearly 20 context questionnaire scales measuring aspects of student learning and teaching developed in parallel across reading, mathematics, and science. New scales measuring student content engagement as described by McLaughlin et al. (2005) were considered to be an especially important advance compared to previous efforts to collect data about effective teaching. Content engagement refers to the cognitive interaction between the student and instructional content that may be sparked by such strategies as questioning or encouraging students. Examples of other scales included in the home, school, teacher, and student questionnaire include *Early Literacy and Numeracy Activities Before Beginning Primary School*, *School Emphasis on Academic Success*, *Instructional Practices to Engage Students*, and *Student Bullying*.

To continue using the TIMSS attitude scales to illustrate the evolution of context questionnaire development, the TIMSS 2011 International Report (Mullis et al. 2012) contained results for three IRT scales: *Students Like Learning Mathematics* and *Students Confident in Learning Mathematics* (fourth and eighth grades), and

---

[1]As a guideline, Suen's (1990) formula was used to determine the minimum requirements for scale construction: (number of items) * (number of response categories $- 1$) ≥ 20.

• How much do you agree (agree a lot, agree a little, disagree a little, disagree a lot) with these statements about learning mathematics?

a) I enjoy learning mathematics (from TIMSS 1995 and 1999)

b) I wish I did not have to study mathematics

c) Mathematics is boring (from TIMSS 1995 added back in 2007)

d) I learn many interesting things in mathematics

e) I like mathematics (added to scale in 2007)

Fig. 11.3 Student attitudes toward mathematics in TIMSS 2011

Students Value Mathematics (eighth grade only). Similar scales were developed for attitudes to science.

As an example of the evolution of these scales, Fig. 11.3 shows that the *Students Like Learning Mathematics* scale had five items in TIMSS 2011, including three from previous TIMSS assessments (a, c, and e) and two newly introduced in 2011 (b and d).

As described in Martin et al. (2014), these items were scaled using IRT methods (Rasch partial-credit model) and found to make a moderately reliable scale (reliability coefficients in the 0.8–0.9 range for most countries) with a modest relationship to achievement in most countries (average correlation 0.27). Similar to the other context questionnaire IRT scales, the scale metric was chosen such that the average score across all countries was 10 points and the standard deviation 2 points. In addition to the average scale score for each country, the International Report presented the percentage of students in each of three regions of the scale. Students who *Like Learning Mathematics* had a score of at least 11.3, which corresponds to their "agreeing a lot" with three of the five statements and "agreeing a little" with the other two, on average. Students who *Do Not Like Learning Mathematics* had a score no higher than 9.0, which corresponds to their "disagreeing a little" with three of the five statements and "agreeing a little" with the other two, on average. All other students *Somewhat Like Learning Mathematics*.

The TIMSS and PIRLS 2011 approach of using IRT methods to summarize the questionnaire scales, and presenting the results for three regions of the scale (most to least desirable) to aid interpretation represented a big step forward. However, the effort to coordinate the TIMSS and PIRLS 2011 questionnaires while concentrating on scale development required considerable revisions in the previous questionnaires, so it was not possible to measure trends compared to earlier assessments. The plan was to continue using IRT scaling for questionnaire scales and provide trends in TIMSS 2015 and PIRLS 2016. That is, scales that were successful (reliable and useful) in TIMSS and PIRLS 2011 would be available for measuring trends in TIMSS 2015 and PIRLS 2016.

11.7 TIMSS 2015 and PIRLS 2016

In an effort to maintain comparability between TIMSS and PIRLS context questionnaires, development for TIMSS 2015 and PIRLS 2016 began with a joint meeting of the TIMSS 2015 QIRC and the PIRLS 2016 QDG, with each group consisting of NRCs experienced in questionnaire development and policy analysis. Essentially, the purpose of the meeting was to make recommendations for updating the Context Questionnaire Framework, and to triage the scales and items in the 2011 questionnaires based on their value in providing policy relevant information useful for educational improvement. Important for future TIMSS assessments at the fourth grade, it was decided to make the home questionnaire a permanent part of future TIMSS fourth grade assessments.

To update the 2011 scales for TIMSS 2015 and PIRLS 2016, the 2011 data were used to identify scales that needed more construct relevant items to increase reliability and validity, or that had items that did not contribute to measuring the construct and could be deleted. For most scales, only one or two items were deleted, but many scales had new items added to improve measurement of the construct. The goal was to improve each scale while maintaining at least half the items in common between 2011 and 2015/16 to serve as a foundation for trend measurement. Also, some new scales were developed.

After the process of NRC review, field testing, revisions by the TIMSS & PIRLS International Study Center, review and revisions by the QIRC, and final review by the NRCs, the TIMSS 2015 Home, Student, Teacher, and School Questionnaires included about 30 scales at the fourth grade (including those based on the home questionnaire) and 25 scales at the eighth grade.

Figure 11.4 shows the *Students Like Learning Mathematics* scale for TIMSS 2015. To increase reliability and strengthen validity four items (f through i) were added for a total of nine items. Student responses in 2015 to the extended set of nine

---

• How much do you agree (agree a lot, agree a little, disagree a little, disagree a lot) with these statements about learning mathematics?

a) I enjoy learning mathematics (from TIMSS 1995, 1999, and 2011)

b) I wish I did not have to study mathematics (2011)

c) Mathematics is boring (from TIMSS 1995, 1999 and added back in 2007, 2011)

d) I learn many interesting things in mathematics (2011)

e) I like mathematics (added to scale in 2007, 2011)

f) I like any schoolwork that involves numbers (new in 2015)

g) I like to solve mathematics problems (new in 2015)

h) I look forward to mathematics lessons (new in 2015)

i) Mathematics is one of my favorite subjects (new in 2015)

Fig. 11.4 Student attitudes toward mathematics in TIMSS 2015

items were scaled using the IRT partial credit approach, and the resulting scale transformed to the 2011 scale metric. With results from 2011 and 2015 on the same scale, trend comparisons for the *Students Like Learning Mathematics* scale were now possible by comparing average scale scores from the two assessments.

To complement the trend scale score results from the nine-item scale, the cut-points for the three regions were updated to reflect the enhanced scaling and the increase in the number of items. In TIMSS 2015, students who *Like Learning Mathematics* had a score of at least 11.4, which corresponds to their "agreeing a lot" with five of the nine statements and "agreeing a little" with the other four, on average. Students who *Do Not Like Learning Mathematics* had a score no higher than 9.4, which corresponds to their "disagreeing a little" with five of the nine statements and "agreeing a little" with the other four, on average. All other students *Somewhat Like Learning Mathematics*.

11.8   Trends in Context Questionnaire Scales in 2015

The results for the TIMSS 2015 context questionnaire scales will be reported in the TIMSS 2015 International Report (Mullis et al. 2016). These will include a number of the scales from 2011 as well as several newly developed scales at both the fourth and eighth grades, and will show trends when possible. As an example, Table 11.1 presents results for the eighth grade *Students Like Learning Mathematics* scale using preliminary, prepublication data.

Table 11.1 presents the percentage of students in each of the three categories of liking learning mathematics for each country, with countries ordered by the percentage of students who Like Learning Mathematics. The table also shows for each country the average mathematics achievement of students in each category. Because these are preliminary, prepublication results and achievement differences between countries may not be revealed, the achievement data are adjusted so that the overall average achievement score is 500 in each country. Despite this adjustment, the table clearly shows differences in average achievement between the scale categories for each country. On average, mathematics achievement was about 35 points higher for the "Like Learning Mathematics" category than for the "Somewhat Like Learning Mathematics" category, which in turn was about 27 points higher than the "Do Not Like Learning Mathematics" category.

As an indicator of trends, Table 11.1 shows the average score on the *Students Like Learning Mathematics* scale for each country in 2015, as well as the difference between this and the country's average scale score in 2011, together with an indicator of the statistical significance of the difference.

For TIMSS 2015, the TIMSS & PIRLS International Study Center will report trends at both the fourth and eighth grades on scales measuring *Instruction Affected by Mathematics Resource Shortages, Instruction Affected by Science Resource Shortages, Safe and Orderly School, School Discipline Problems, Students Like Learning Mathematics, Students Like Learning Science, Students Confident in*

Table 11.1 TIMSS 2015 eighth grade—students like learning mathematics scale

Note: Preliminary, prepublication data – each country's overall achievement mean set to 500 to remove overall achievement differences among countries.

Reported by Students

Students were scored according to their degree of agreement with nine statements on the *Students Like Learning Mathematics* scale. Students who **Like Learning Mathematics** had a score on the scale of at least 11.4, which corresponds to their "agreeing a lot" with five of the nine statements and "agreeing a little" with the other four, on average. Students who **Do Not Like Learning Mathematics** had a score no higher than 9.4, which corresponds to their "disagreeing a little" with five of the nine statements and "agreeing a little" with the other four, on average. All other students **Somewhat Like Learning Mathematics**.

Country	Like Learning Mathematics		Somewhat Like Learning Mathematics		Do Not Like Learning Mathematics		Average Scale Score	Difference in Average Scale Score from 2011	
	Percent of Students	Average Achievement	Percent of Students	Average Achievement	Percent of Students	Average Achievement			
Botswana (9)	50 (1.1)	520 (2.3)	38 (1.0)	484 (2.6)	12 (0.6)	491 (4.0)	11.4 (0.04)	0.4 (0.06)	◒
Morocco	44 (0.8)	526 (2.6)	40 (0.6)	484 (2.5)	16 (0.6)	475 (2.1)	11.1 (0.03)	-0.1 (0.04)	
Armenia	40 (1.2)	518 (4.0)	41 (1.0)	493 (3.2)	19 (1.0)	476 (4.6)	11.0 (0.05)	0.1 (0.07)	
South Africa (9)	39 (1.2)	509 (5.0)	42 (0.8)	492 (4.8)	19 (1.0)	505 (6.0)	10.9 (0.05)	0.1 (0.06)	
Egypt	39 (1.5)	530 (4.5)	42 (1.0)	481 (3.0)	20 (1.0)	486 (4.1)	10.9 (0.07)	◇ ◇	
Jordan	39 (1.0)	519 (3.7)	38 (0.8)	490 (3.7)	24 (0.8)	491 (3.6)	10.8 (0.05)	0.0 (0.08)	
Kazakhstan	34 (1.3)	509 (6.4)	54 (1.1)	500 (7.0)	12 (0.8)	476 (7.6)	11.0 (0.05)	0.1 (0.07)	
Iran, Islamic Rep. of	32 (1.1)	533 (6.7)	39 (0.9)	493 (4.6)	28 (1.1)	473 (3.8)	10.5 (0.05)	-0.1 (0.07)	
Lebanon	31 (1.3)	527 (5.8)	45 (1.5)	491 (5.8)	23 (1.4)	487 (5.0)	10.6 (0.05)	0.1 (0.08)	
Malaysia	28 (1.0)	535 (4.7)	56 (0.7)	493 (4.1)	16 (0.8)	465 (4.6)	10.7 (0.04)	-0.1 (0.07)	
Turkey	28 (1.0)	537 (6.5)	42 (0.8)	490 (4.4)	30 (1.0)	482 (3.8)	10.3 (0.05)	0.0 (0.07)	
Kuwait	26 (1.1)	518 (5.3)	38 (1.1)	500 (6.5)	36 (1.4)	488 (5.4)	10.1 (0.07)	◇ ◇	
United Arab Emirates	25 (0.7)	536 (3.0)	43 (0.6)	496 (2.2)	32 (0.8)	479 (2.3)	10.2 (0.04)	-0.1 (0.05)	
Singapore	24 (0.7)	537 (3.4)	42 (0.6)	504 (3.9)	33 (0.8)	468 (4.7)	10.2 (0.03)	-0.2 (0.05)	◓
Georgia	23 (1.1)	534 (8.2)	44 (0.9)	502 (6.2)	33 (1.2)	477 (3.9)	10.2 (0.05)	-0.6 (0.08)	◓
Saudi Arabia	21 (1.1)	526 (7.1)	37 (1.1)	502 (5.0)	42 (1.6)	486 (3.4)	9.8 (0.07)	-0.3 (0.10)	◓
Qatar	21 (0.8)	545 (5.0)	41 (0.8)	505 (3.1)	39 (0.9)	475 (2.3)	9.9 (0.04)	-0.1 (0.07)	
Bahrain	20 (0.9)	540 (4.3)	36 (1.0)	503 (3.2)	44 (1.4)	480 (1.8)	9.7 (0.06)	0.0 (0.07)	
Canada	20 (0.8)	547 (3.7)	40 (0.9)	513 (3.3)	39 (1.1)	468 (2.6)	9.8 (0.05)	◇ ◇	
Thailand	20 (0.8)	537 (9.0)	58 (0.9)	493 (4.6)	23 (1.0)	487 (4.8)	10.3 (0.04)	0.0 (0.06)	
Israel	19 (0.9)	513 (6.4)	36 (0.7)	509 (4.4)	44 (1.1)	489 (3.5)	9.6 (0.05)	-0.2 (0.07)	◓
Russian Federation	19 (1.0)	534 (7.9)	48 (0.7)	508 (6.2)	33 (1.1)	469 (5.4)	10.1 (0.04)	-0.3 (0.06)	◓
United States	17 (0.6)	542 (4.4)	36 (0.6)	511 (3.7)	47 (0.8)	478 (2.8)	9.5 (0.04)	0.0 (0.06)	
Malta	17 (0.6)	546 (3.8)	34 (0.7)	509 (2.7)	49 (0.8)	481 (2.0)	9.5 (0.03)	◇ ◇	
Italy	17 (0.9)	556 (4.9)	32 (0.9)	514 (4.3)	51 (1.2)	473 (3.3)	9.4 (0.05)	-0.1 (0.08)	
Chile	16 (0.8)	543 (6.2)	34 (0.9)	508 (3.8)	50 (1.3)	482 (3.0)	9.5 (0.06)	-0.3 (0.07)	◓
Lithuania	15 (0.9)	551 (6.0)	41 (1.2)	505 (3.7)	43 (1.4)	478 (3.6)	9.7 (0.05)	-0.1 (0.07)	
Hong Kong SAR	15 (0.6)	552 (5.2)	39 (0.8)	513 (5.2)	46 (1.1)	474 (5.9)	9.5 (0.04)	-0.1 (0.07)	
New Zealand	14 (0.6)	547 (6.9)	40 (1.0)	510 (4.5)	46 (1.2)	482 (2.5)	9.6 (0.04)	0.1 (0.07)	
England	14 (0.8)	550 (8.2)	39 (1.0)	516 (5.6)	48 (1.4)	477 (4.6)	9.5 (0.06)	0.1 (0.09)	
Sweden	14 (1.3)	560 (6.4)	34 (1.2)	526 (4.1)	52 (1.5)	469 (3.4)	9.3 (0.06)	0.0 (0.07)	
Ireland	14 (0.7)	552 (6.1)	35 (0.9)	517 (3.7)	52 (1.2)	476 (3.2)	9.3 (0.05)	◇ ◇	
Australia	13 (0.7)	552 (5.5)	36 (0.9)	518 (3.7)	50 (1.2)	476 (2.9)	9.4 (0.05)	0.1 (0.08)	
Norway (9)	13 (0.6)	567 (5.6)	35 (1.0)	521 (3.6)	52 (1.3)	471 (2.9)	9.3 (0.05)	◇ ◇	
Chinese Taipei	11 (0.5)	568 (4.2)	33 (0.7)	533 (2.5)	56 (1.0)	468 (2.8)	9.2 (0.04)	0.2 (0.07)	◒
Hungary	11 (0.7)	568 (9.3)	31 (1.1)	518 (5.4)	58 (1.3)	478 (3.4)	9.1 (0.05)	0.0 (0.07)	
Japan	9 (0.5)	558 (5.3)	32 (0.8)	530 (2.9)	59 (1.1)	475 (2.5)	9.2 (0.04)	0.1 (0.06)	
Korea, Rep. of	8 (0.4)	567 (4.7)	34 (0.7)	531 (3.2)	58 (0.8)	473 (2.8)	9.1 (0.04)	0.2 (0.05)	◒
Slovenia	5 (0.4)	561 (10.7)	28 (1.1)	532 (3.6)	67 (1.2)	482 (2.7)	8.7 (0.05)	0.2 (0.07)	◒
Oman	- -	- -	- -	- -	- -	- -	- -	- -	
International Avg.	22 (0.1)	540 (0.9)	39 (0.1)	506 (0.7)	39 (0.2)	479 (0.6)			

Centerpoint of scale set at 10.

( ) Standard errors appear in parentheses. Because of rounding some results may appear inconsistent.

A diamond (◇) indicates the country did not participate in the 2011 assessment.

A dash (-) indicates comparable data not available.

Significantly higher than 2011 ◒

Significantly lower than 2011 ◓

Table 12.1 (continued)

Country	Like Learning Mathematics		Somewhat Like Learning Mathematics		Do Not Like Learning Mathematics		Average Scale Score	Difference in Average Scale Score from 2011
	Percent of Students	Average Achievement	Percent of Students	Average Achievement	Percent of Students	Average Achievement		
Benchmarking Participants								
Dubai, UAE	28 (1.1)	537 (4.6)	41 (0.8)	498 (2.5)	31 (1.0)	471 (2.8)	10.3 (0.05)	0.2 (0.07) ⬦
Ontario, Canada	25 (1.2)	552 (4.1)	40 (1.1)	509 (4.2)	35 (1.4)	458 (3.3)	10.1 (0.06)	0.2 (0.09)
Abu Dhabi, UAE	24 (1.3)	532 (6.8)	43 (1.0)	498 (4.9)	33 (1.4)	481 (4.3)	10.2 (0.06)	-0.1 (0.09)
Norway (8)	17 (0.9)	546 (5.3)	35 (0.8)	515 (3.5)	48 (1.1)	475 (2.4)	9.6 (0.05)	0.1 (0.07)
Buenos Aires, Argentina	17 (1.0)	516 (7.8)	35 (1.0)	508 (5.2)	48 (1.2)	491 (4.4)	9.5 (0.05)	◊ ◊
Florida, US	15 (1.1)	534 (11.4)	34 (1.1)	507 (8.1)	50 (1.7)	487 (5.8)	9.3 (0.07)	0.0 (0.11)
Quebec, Canada	12 (0.7)	541 (5.9)	42 (1.5)	521 (4.5)	46 (1.8)	478 (5.1)	9.5 (0.07)	0.2 (0.08)

Significantly higher than 2011 ⬦
Significantly lower than 2011 ⬇

How much do you agree with these statements about learning mathematics?

| | Agree a lot | Agree a little | Disagree a little | Disagree a lot |

1) I enjoy learning mathematics
2) I wish I did not have to study mathematics*
3) Mathematics is boring*
4) I learn many interesting things in mathematics
5) I like mathematics
6) I like any schoolwork that involves numbers
7) I like to solve mathematics problems
8) I look forward to mathematics lessons
9) Mathematics is one of my favorite subjects

* Reverse coded

Like Learning Mathematics — Somewhat Like Learning Mathematics — Do Not Like Learning Mathematics
11.4   9.4

SOURCE: IEA's Trends in International Mathematics and Science Study - TIMSS 2015

Mathematics, Students Confident in Science, and *Home Resources.* In addition, trends will be reported on *Early Literacy and Numeracy Activities Before Beginning Primary School* at fourth grade and *Students Value Mathematics* at eighth grade. It is anticipated that the analysis of the PIRLS 2016 data will result in a similar situation.

However, the analyses of the 2015 data revealed that a number of the scales at both grades had been updated too much to be appropriate for measuring trends. In particular, developing scales that measure effective teaching remains a challenge. For example, the 2011 scales measuring content engagement needed considerable improvement, and were among the scales updated too much to measure trends. Nevertheless, substantial progress had been made in identifying some constructs that can be measured over time, particularly in the important areas of home and school resources, school safety, and student attitudes toward learning.

In conclusion, the evolution of the TIMSS and PIRLS questionnaires toward providing a stable set of educational context factors has been a slow process. Yet, substantial progress has been made in improving the quality of the data measuring educational policies and practices, and a number of valid and reliable context questionnaire scales will be included in TIMSS 2015 and PIRLS 2016. Such scales create opportunities for research based on relating trends in student achievement to trends in context questionnaire scales in ways that can provide explanations about the factors that influence educational outcomes.

Researchers will be able to use the TIMSS 2015 and PIRLS 2016 data to examine recent trends in mathematics, science, and reading achievement in relation to changes in several context factors measured by robust questionnaire scales, such as school resources and safety as well as students' attitudes toward learning. TIMSS and PIRLS can benefit from this research to improve the existing context questionnaire scales and develop new context questionnaire scales for inclusion in the TIMSS 2019 and PIRLS 2021 assessments.

References

Comber, L. C., & Keeves, J. P. (1973). *Science education in nineteen countries: An empirical study*. Stockholm: Almqvist & Wiksell.

Gustafsson, J.-E. (2007). Understanding causal influences on educational achievement through differences over time within countries. In T. Loveless (Ed.), *Lessons learned* (pp. 37–64). Washington D.C.: The Brookings Institute.

Husén, T. (1967). *International Study of Achievement in Mathematics. A Comparison of Twelve Countries. Volume I*. New York: Wiley.

Liu, H., Bellens, K., Gielen, S., Van Damme, J., & Onghena, P. (2014). A country level longitudinal study on the effect of student age, class size, and socio-economic status – Based on PIRLS 2001, PIRLS 2006, and PIRLS 2011. In R. Strietholt, W. Bos, J.-E. Gustafsson & M. Rosen (Eds.), *Educational policy evaluation through international comparative assessments* (pp. 223–242). Muenster, Germany: Waxman.

Martin, M. O. (1996). Third International Mathematics and Science Study: An overview. In M. O. Martin & D. L. Kelly (Eds.), *Third International Mathematics and Science Study: Technical report. Volume I: Design and development* (pp. 1.1–1.18). Chestnut Hill, MA: TIMSS & PIRLS International Study Center, Boston College.

Martin, M. O., & Preuschoff, C. (2008). Creating the TIMSS 2007 Background Indices. In J. F. Olsen, M. O. Martin, & I. V. S. Mullis (Eds.), *TIMSS 2007 Technical Report* (pp. 281–338). Chestnut Hill, MA: TIMSS & PIRLS International Study Center, Boston College.

Martin, M. O., Mullis, I. V. S., Arora, A., & Preuschoff, C. (2014). Context questionnaire scales in TIMSS and PIRLS 2011. In L. Rutkowski, M. von Davier & D. Rutkowski (Eds.), *Handbook in international large-scale assessment: Background, technical issues, and methods of data analysis*. Boca Raton: CRC press.

McLaughlin, M., Mc.Grath, D.J., Burian-Fitzgerald, M.A., Lanahan, L., Scotchmer, M., Enyeart, C., et al. (2005, April). *Student content engagement as a construct for the measurement of effective classroom instruction and teacher knowledge*. Paper presented at the annual meeting of the American Educational Researchers Association, Montreal, Canada.

Mullis, I. V. S., Martin, M. O., & Foy, P. (2008). *TIMSS 2007 International Mathematics Report: Findings from IEA's Trends in International Mathematics and Science Study at the Fourth and Eighth Grades*. (Chestnut Hill, MA: TIMSS & PIRLS International Study Center, Boston College)

Mullis, I. V. S., Martin, M. O., Foy, P., & Arora, A. (2012). *TIMSS 2011 International Results in Mathematics*. Chestnut Hill, MA: TIMSS & PIRLS International Study Center, Boston College.

Mullis, I. V. S., Martin M. O., Foy, P & Hooper, M. (2016). *TIMSS 2015 International Results in Mathematics*. Chestnut Hill, MA: TIMSS & PIRLS International Study Center, Boston College.

Postlethwaite, T. N., & Wiley, D. E. (1992). *The IEA Study of Science II. Science Achievement in twenty-three countries*. Oxford: Pergamon Press.

Rosén, M., & Gustafsson, J.-E. (2014). Has the increased access to computers at home caused reading achievement to decrease in Sweden? In R. Strietholt, W. Bos, J.-E. Gustafsson & M. Rosen (Eds.), *Educational policy evaluation through international comparative assessments* (pp. 207–222). Muenster, Germany: Waxman.

Robitaille, D. F., & Garden, R. A. (1989). *The IEA study of mathematics II. Contexts and outcomes of school mathematics*. Oxford: Pergamon Press.

Robitaille, D. F., & Garden, R. A. (1996). Design of the study. In D. F. Robitaille & R. A. Garden (Eds.), *Third International Mathematics and Science Study: Research questions & study design* (pp. 44–68). TIMSS Monograph No. 2. Vancouver, Canada: Pacific Educational Press.

Suen, H. K. (1990). *Principles of test theory*. Hilldale, NJ: LEA Publisher.

Chapter 12
General and Specific Factors in Selection Modeling

Bengt Muthén

Abstract This chapter shows how analysis of data on selective subgroups can be used to draw inference to the full, unselected group. This uses Pearson-Lawley selection formulas which apply to not only regression analysis but also structural equation modeling. The chapter shows the connection with maximum-likelihood estimation with missing data assuming MAR versus using listwise deletion. Applications are discussed of selection into the military using factor analysis models for the variables used in the selection.

12.1 Introduction

Modeling with selective subgroups needs adjustments to be able to draw inference to the full group. This is a typical feature in predictive validity studies where a criterion outcome is regressed on or correlated with a predictor variable and the criterion outcome is missing for those not selected. The adjustments draw on Pearson-Lawley selection formulas (Pearson 1903; Lawley 1943–1944; Lord and Novick 1968; Johnson and Kotz 1972) to obtain desired inferences. The Pearson-Lawley formulas assume linear, homoscedastic regression of a set of analysis variables on a set of selection variables. The general Pearson-Lawley selection formulas can be used for deriving means, variances, and covariances for the full population given values of the selected population and vice versa. This chapter shows that Pearson-Lawley selection formulas play a role not only with respect to predictive validity assessment, but also with respect to multiple-group latent variable modeling. The connection between selection and maximum-likelihood estimation under the MAR assumption is illustrated by Monte Carlo simulations and real-data analyses.

B. Muthén (✉)
Graduate School of Education and Information Studies, Social Research Methodology Division, University of California, Los Angeles, USA
e-mail: bmuthen@ucla.edu

© Springer International Publishing AG 2017   223
M. Rosén et al. (eds.), *Cognitive Abilities and Educational Outcomes*,
Methodology of Educational Measurement and Assessment,
DOI 10.1007/978-3-319-43473-5_12

Individuals applying for a certain training program may be selected based on a set of tests and other assessments. For example, students are selected into colleges based on the SAT, GRE, GMAC, or GMAT and job candidates are selected based on personality tests. To understand the quality of such a selection procedure, the tests and assessments are used as predictors of a training program outcome such as grades or job performance. The multiple correlation R value from this regression is viewed as a predictive validity coefficient. The estimation of this coefficient requires data on the program outcome and the predictors, which are available only for those who were selected. The interest is, however, in estimating the coefficient for the population of all applicants, not only those who were selected. Those who were selected are not a random subsample of those who applied, which means that the inference is distorted unless corrections are made. Similarly, screening instruments are used at baseline in psychological studies to determine a subsample that is at risk for certain future behavioral problems and is therefore of interest to follow up for further study. Again, the desired inference is to the population from which the baseline sample is taken, not to the subpopulation that is at risk.

12.2   Predictive Validity in a Simple Example

Consider the following linear regression

$$y_i = \alpha + \beta x_i + \varepsilon_i. \tag{12.1}$$

In a predictive validity context the predictor x is a test score used to select individuals into a training program in which a criterion outcome y is measured at the end of training. Selecting on x, the regression of y on x obtained in the group of selected individuals correctly estimates the regression model for the full, applicant population (see, e.g. Muthén and Joreskog 1983; Dunbar and Linn 1991). In contrast, selecting on y results in biased regression estimates. The two selection cases are illustrated in Fig. 12.1 using the example of Dunbar and Linn (1991) with a regression of y on x using standardized variables with correlation 0.6. The regression model was estimated using (a) a full sample of 5000 subjects, (b) a selected subsample of subjects with x scores above the mean, and (c) a selected subsample of subjects with y scores above the mean.

12.3   Monte Carlo Study of Selection in an SEM

In structural equation modeling, analysis of a selective group typically gives distorted estimates of the parameters for the full group. It is instructive to study the magnitude of such distortions through an example.

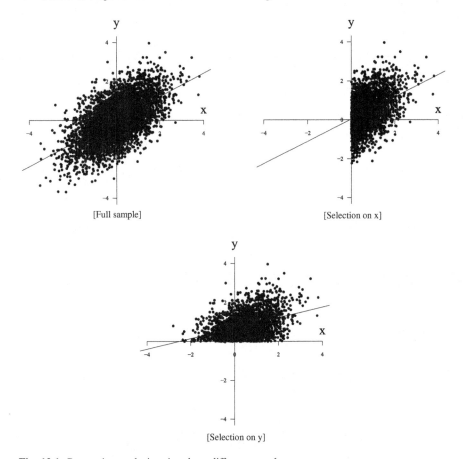

Fig. 12.1 Regression analysis using three different samples

Consider a latent variable version of the selection case of (2). Figure 12.2 corresponds to a hypothetical situation of a selection or screening measurement instrument formed by y_1-y_6, which are indicators of a general factor g and a specific factor s in line with bi-factor modeling. At a later time point a criterion measurement instrument y_7-y_{10} measures a single factor f_2. Consider first the case where the selection variable consists of the unweighted sum of y_1-y_6 so that those with the highest sum form the selected group which are followed up and administered the criterion test. Figure 12.3 shows the data structure, where the unselected group do not have observations on y_7-y_{10}.

The effects of selection on the analysis are illustrated by the following Monte Carlo simulation. A random sample of 2000 subjects is given the y_1-y_6 test and those with the top 50 % summed score are selected and given the y_7-y_{10} test. This procedure is repeated over 500 Monte Carlo replications.

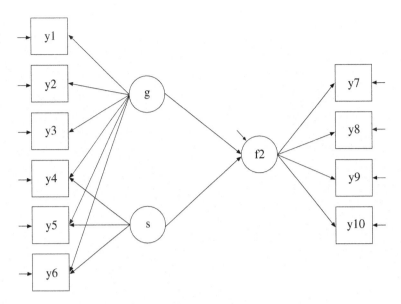

Fig. 12.2 Structural equation model with selection

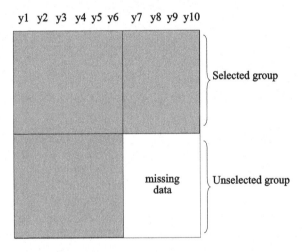

Fig. 12.3 Data structure with selection (non-shaded area represents missing data)

12.4 Using Listwise Deletion

Using listwise deletion, the sample of selected subjects is analyzed with respect to the model for y_1–y_{10} using the ML fitting function. Note that this does not give ML estimates of the parameters in the full sample. With 30 degrees of freedom the mean and variance of the likelihood-ratio χ^2 test are expected to be 30 and 60, but are somewhat overestimated as 32.306 and 72.915 and the 5 % reject proportion obtains a somewhat too high value of 0.108. Still, this implies that the model would often not be rejected.

The results for the parameter estimates are shown in Tables 12.1 and 12.2. The first column shows the population values that were chosen and with which the data were generated. In terms of the selection instrument y_1–y_6, the factor loadings for the general factor g and the specific factor s are clearly misestimated as is seen in the Average column. The 95 % coverage column also shows large deviations from 95 % coverage. Standardized versions of the factor loadings for y_2 and y_5 are shown at the bottom of Table 12.2 as stdlam2 and stdlam5g, stdlam5s. This indicates that the variance explained by the general factor is underestimated and the variance explained by the specific factor is overestimated. This reflects the fact that the selection variable is most closely aligned with g given that selection is based on a sum of all the variables y_1–y_6.

The key parameters of the structural equation relating f2 to g and s show that the influence of g is underestimated and the influence of s is overestimated. It is seen that the variance for g is more strongly underestimated than the variance for s as is expected due to the selection being more closely aligned with g. Table 12.2 shows that this results in a standardized effect of g on f2 that is strongly underestimated as 0.4396 compared to the true value of 0.7. At the same time, the standardized effect of s on f2 is overestimated as 0.6664 instead of 0.506. That is, the relative importance of the two factors is reversed, distorting the true predictive value of the factors in the full population.

For the criterion instrument Table 12.1 shows that the unstandardized factor loadings are well estimated with good coverage. The standardized factor loading for y_8, listed as stdlam8, shows a slight overestimation, which is due to the variance of f2 being underestimated (see the vf2 entry).

The results of the Monte Carlo simulations can be explained via Pearson-Lawley formulas applied to factor analysis. The key results are discussed in Sect. 12.6, whereas Section? presents this in technical terms using matrix formulas.

12.5   Using ML Under MAR

Consider again the model of Fig. 12.2 and the data structure of Fig. 12.3 showing that there is missing data on y_7–y_{10} for subjects who are not selected. In the Monte Carlo study of the previous section, model estimation considered subjects in the selected group who have complete data on y_1–y_{10}. Using the same Monte-Carlo generated data, maximum-likelihood estimation is now applied under the MAR assumption. MAR is fulfilled because the missingness for y_7–y_{10} is determined by the variables y_1–y_6 which are observed with no missingness. Maximum-likelihood estimation uses all available data, that is, not only subjects in the selected group who have complete data on y_1–y_{10}, but also subjects in the unselected group who have data on only y_1–y_6.

Table 12.1 Results obtained by listwise deletion

	Estimates			S.E.	M.S.E.	95 %	% sig
	Population	Average	Std. dev.	Average		Cover	Coeff
g BY							
y1	1.000	1.0000	0.0000	0.0000	0.0000	1.000	0.000
y2	0.800	0.8451	0.0959	0.0944	0.0112	0.958	1.000
y3	0.700	0.5687	0.0752	0.0740	0.0229	0.546	1.000
y4	0.800	0.3624	0.0773	0.0770	0.1975	0.000	1.000
y5	0.700	0.4458	0.0620	0.0638	0.0685	0.040	1.000
y6	0.600	0.2618	0.0638	0.0657	0.1185	0.004	0.978
s BY							
y4	1.000	1.0000	0.0000	0.0000	0.0000	1.000	0.000
y5	0.800	0.8385	0.0889	0.0880	0.0094	0.968	1.000
y6	0.700	0.6785	0.0934	0.0868	0.0092	0.920	1.000
f2 BY							
y7	1.000	1.0000	0.0000	0.0000	0.0000	1.000	0.000
y8	0.800	0.8017	0.0447	0.0454	0.0020	0.940	1.000
y9	0.700	0.7029	0.0428	0.0418	0.0018	0.934	1.000
y10	0.600	0.6007	0.0394	0.0385	0.0016	0.952	1.000
f2 ON							
g	0.700	0.5754	0.0745	0.0748	0.0211	0.592	1.000
s	0.800	0.9566	0.1071	0.1053	0.0360	0.738	1.000
g WITH							
s	0.000	0.0000	0.0000	0.0000	0.0000	1.000	0.000
Intercepts							
y1	0.000	0.7932	0.0314	0.0311	0.6301	0.000	1.000
y2	0.000	0.6202	0.0266	0.0255	0.3854	0.000	1.000
y3	0.000	0.6137	0.0292	0.0302	0.3774	0.000	1.000
y4	0.000	0.8351	0.0334	0.0338	0.6986	0.000	1.000
y5	0.000	0.6745	0.0257	0.0263	0.4555	0.000	1.000
y6	0.000	0.6356	0.0274	0.0292	0.4047	0.000	1.000
y7	0.000	0.6170	0.0367	0.0363	0.3820	0.000	1.000
y8	0.000	0.4921	0.0278	0.0282	0.2430	0.000	1.000
y9	0.000	0.4305	0.0259	0.0265	0.1860	0.000	1.000
y10	0.000	0.3691	0.0275	0.0249	0.1370	0.000	1.000
Variances							
g	1.000	0.3689	0.0546	0.0520	0.4013	0.000	1.000
s	0.400	0.3075	0.0487	0.0481	0.0109	0.492	1.000

(continued)

Table 12.1 (continued)

	Estimates			S.E.	M.S.E.	95 %	% sig
	Population	Average	Std. dev.	Average		Cover	Coeff
Residual variances							
y1	0.600	0.6003	0.0494	0.0479	0.0024	0.946	1.000
y2	0.400	0.3913	0.0340	0.0329	0.0012	0.942	1.000
y3	0.800	0.7925	0.0394	0.0391	0.0016	0.930	1.000
y4	0.800	0.7838	0.0455	0.0463	0.0023	0.942	1.000
y5	0.400	0.4064	0.0272	0.0270	0.0008	0.950	1.000
y6	0.700	0.6883	0.0364	0.0351	0.0015	0.932	1.000
y7	0.700	0.7003	0.0385	0.0410	0.0015	0.968	1.000
y8	0.400	0.3982	0.0240	0.0243	0.0006	0.948	1.000
y9	0.400	0.3974	0.0233	0.0223	0.0005	0.934	1.000
y10	0.400	0.3991	0.0212	0.0209	0.0005	0.952	1.000
f2	0.254	0.2237	0.0350	0.0358	0.0021	0.858	1.000

Table 12.2 Standardized results obtained by listwise deletion

	Estimates			S.E.	M.S.E.	95 %	% sig
	Population	Average	Std. dev.	Average		Cover	Coeff
New/additional parameters							
vy2	1.200	0.6512	0.0292	0.0291	0.3021	0.000	1.000
vy5	1.146	0.6930	0.0312	0.0310	0.2062	0.000	1.000
vf2	1.000	0.6230	0.0556	0.0567	0.1452	0.000	1.000
vy8	1.040	0.6228	0.0495	0.0517	0.1765	0.000	1.000
stdf2ong	0.700	0.4396	0.0422	0.0423	0.0696	0.000	1.000
stdf2ons	0.506	0.6664	0.0413	0.0413	0.0274	0.036	1.000
stdlam2	0.800	0.6302	0.0393	0.0388	0.0304	0.006	1.000
stdlam5g	0.654	0.3227	0.0375	0.0384	0.1112	0.000	1.000
stdlam5s	0.473	0.5534	0.0357	0.0362	0.0077	0.388	1.000
stdlam8	0.784	0.8007	0.0256	0.0256	0.0009	0.896	1.000

The Monte Carlo results for ML are as follows. The likelihood-ratio χ^2 test performs well. With 30 degrees of freedom χ^2 has mean 29.933, variance 61.528, and 5 % reject proportion 0.050, which are all close to the expected values. The parameter estimation works very well as shown in Table 12.3. The ML approach of also using the information on y_1–y_6 for those not selected produces estimates close to the true values for not only the y_1–y_6 part of the model but for the whole model.

As a minor detail, it may be noted that the f2 factor loadings of Table 12.3 have smaller standard errors than those in Table 12.1 using the selected group only. This reflects the smaller sample size when using only the selected group.

Table 12.3 Maximum-likelihood results assuming MAR

	Estimates			S.E.	M.S.E.	95 %	% sig
	Population	Average	Std. dev.	Average		Cover	Coeff
g BY							
y1	1.000	1.0000	0.0000	0.0000	0.0000	1.000	0.000
y2	0.800	0.7983	0.0213	0.0214	0.0005	0.948	1.000
y3	0.700	0.6992	0.0193	0.0199	0.0004	0.952	1.000
y4	0.800	0.7997	0.0262	0.0262	0.0007	0.952	1.000
y5	0.700	0.7011	0.0230	0.0235	0.0005	0.960	1.000
y6	0.600	0.6012	0.0216	0.0217	0.0005	0.948	0.978
s BY							
y4	1.000	1.0000	0.0000	0.0000	0.0000	1.000	0.000
y5	0.800	0.7981	0.0475	0.0466	0.0023	0.938	1.000
y6	0.700	0.6993	0.0441	0.0425	0.0019	0.950	1.000
f2 BY							
y7	1.000	1.0000	0.0000	0.0000	0.0000	1.000	0.000
y8	0.800	0.8004	0.0386	0.0401	0.0015	0.944	1.000
y9	0.700	0.7020	0.0390	0.0375	0.0015	0.926	1.000
y10	0.600	0.5996	0.0356	0.0352	0.0013	0.942	1.000
f2 ON							
g	0.700	0.6981	0.0413	0.0449	0.0017	0.976	1.000
s	0.800	0.8011	0.0612	0.0614	0.0037	0.956	1.000
g WITH							
s	0.000	0.0000	0.0000	0.0000	0.0000	1.000	0.000
Intercepts							
y1	0.000	0.0001	0.0259	0.0265	0.0007	0.964	0.036
y2	0.000	0.0002	0.0234	0.0228	0.0005	0.952	0.048
y3	0.000	0.0013	0.0203	0.0211	0.0004	0.954	0.046
y4	0.000	0.0000	0.0276	0.0268	0.0008	0.942	0.058
y5	0.000	0.0008	0.0242	0.0240	0.0006	0.946	0.054
y6	0.000	0.0010	0.0210	0.0219	0.0004	0.960	0.040
y7	0.000	0.0054	0.0459	0.0467	0.0021	0.958	0.042
y8	0.000	0.0036	0.0392	0.0407	0.0015	0.956	0.044
y9	0.000	0.0019	0.0379	0.0379	0.0014	0.958	0.042
y10	0.000	0.0029	0.0358	0.0353	0.0013	0.940	0.060
Variances							
g	1.000	1.0032	0.0454	0.0457	0.0021	0.954	1.000
s	0.400	0.4013	0.0319	0.0328	0.0010	0.968	1.000

(continued)

Table 12.3 (continued)

	Estimates			S.E.	M.S.E.	95 %	% sig
	Population	Average	Std. dev.	Average		Cover	Coeff
Residual variances							
y1	0.400	0.3990	0.0213	0.0212	0.0005	0.956	1.000
y2	0.400	0.3992	0.0181	0.0170	0.0003	0.922	1.000
y3	0.400	0.4001	0.0155	0.0157	0.0002	0.948	1.000
y4	0.400	0.3984	0.0225	0.0229	0.0005	0.962	1.000
y5	0.400	0.4007	0.0178	0.0179	0.0003	0.954	1.000
y6	0.400	0.3994	0.0167	0.0162	0.0003	0.950	1.000
y7	0.400	0.4006	0.0262	0.0274	0.0007	0.970	1.000
y8	0.400	0.3981	0.0230	0.0229	0.0005	0.954	1.000
y9	0.400	0.3974	0.0224	0.0214	0.0005	0.940	1.000
y10	0.400	0.3993	0.0208	0.0203	0.0004	0.954	1.000
f2	0.254	0.2518	0.0278	0.0283	0.0008	0.944	1.000
New/additional parameters							
vy2	1.040	1.0375	0.0327	0.0328	0.0011	0.964	1.000
vy5	1.146	1.1480	0.0360	0.0363	0.0013	0.952	1.000
vf2	1.000	0.9995	0.0934	0.0977	0.0087	0.958	1.000
vy8	1.040	1.0386	0.0561	0.0587	0.0031	0.962	1.000
stdf2ONg	0.700	0.6995	0.0258	0.0267	0.0007	0.964	1.000
stdf2ONs	0.506	0.5072	0.0336	0.0343	0.0011	0.952	1.000
stdlam2	0.784	0.7839	0.0137	0.0124	0.0002	0.904	1.000
stdlam5 g	0.654	0.6545	0.0156	0.0158	0.0002	0.956	1.000
stdlam5 s	0.473	0.4709	0.0231	0.0245	0.0005	0.970	1.000
stdlam8	0.784	0.7843	0.0189	0.0190	0.0004	0.932	1.000

12.6   Pearson-Lawley Selection Formulas

In the regression example there is one selection variable and it is identical to x. In general, the selection variable need not be the same as x, need not be an observed variable, and need not be a single variable. The Pearson-Lawley formulas assume linear, homoscedastic regression of a set of continuous analysis variables on a set of selection variables. Normal distributions are not assumed. The general Pearson-Lawley selection formulas can be used for deriving means, variances, and covariances for the full population given values of the selected population and vice versa.

Going from the full to a selected population, the means, variances, and covariances of the analysis variables in the selected population are obtained from (1) the means, variances, and covariances of the selection variables in the selected and full population; (2) the covariances of the analysis and selection variables in the full population; and (3) the means, variances, and covariances of the analysis variables in the full population.

Going from a selected to the full population, the means, variances, and covariances of the analysis variables in the full population are obtained from (1) the means, variances, and covariances of the selection variables in the selected and full population; (2) the covariances of the selection and analysis variables in the selected population; and (3) the means, variances, and covariances of the analysis variables in the selected population.

12.7 Pearson-Lawley and Factorial Invariance

As pointed out in Meredith (1964), see also Olsson (1978) and Muthén and Jöreskog (1983), a factor model for a certain population also holds in a selected subpopulation if selection takes place on variables related to the factors and not directly related to the factor indicators. This is in line with regression where selection on x does not change the regression parameters, but selection on y does (Muthén and Jöreskog 1983).

When selection is related to only the factors, the full population factor loadings, factor indicator intercepts, and factor indicator residual variances are not affected by selection but are the same in the selected population. This is a rationale for assuming scalar measurement invariance in multiple-group modeling. The selection effect is absorbed into the factor means and the factor covariance matrix (see, e.g., Muthén and Jöreskog 1983, p. 367; Muthén et al. 1987, p. 440). Consider, for example, the case of a gender covariate influencing the factors. In a two-group analysis based on gender one should therefore expect full measurement invariance. In contrast, consider the gender covariate influencing factor indicators directly, where the direct effects imply that the means of the factor indicators vary across gender not only as a function of the factor mean varying across gender. In this case, selection on gender implies selection on factor indicators and one should not expect full measurement invariance. When selection is directly related to the factor indicators, the factor model does not hold in the selected subpopulation but is distorted as shown in Muthén (1989, p. 83) and illustrated in the Monte Carlo simulation.

For Fig. 12.2 model used in the Monte Carlo study, the factor model for y_1–y_6 is distorted because of selection on the factor indicators. The factor model for y_7–y_{10} is not distorted, however, because the selection is indirect via the factor f2 given that y_1–y_6 do not influence y_7–y_{10} directly. The next section discusses an approach that gives correct maximum-likelihood estimates under this type of selection.

12.8 Predictive Validity of Factors

Structural equation models are useful in predictive validity studies given that factors playing different roles in the test performance can be isolated and used as predictors of criterion outcomes. The use of a bi-factor model such as Fig. 12.2 is studied e.g.

in Gustafsson and Balke (1993), arguing for the value of using both a general and specific factors. While several previous studies indicate that not much increase in predictive power is to be gained from using a differentiated set of ability dimensions, as compared to an undifferentiated composite score (see, e.g. Schmidt and Hunter 1981), Gustafsson and Balke (1993) demonstrate that a bi-factor, orthogonal factor model may bring out a more differentiated pattern of relations between predictors and criteria, and particularly so if a latent variable model is used also for the criterion variables.

Muthén and Hsu (1993) study selection and predictive validity for structural equation models such as those used in Gustafsson and Balke (1993) One of their approaches uses factor scores based on the parameters from the factor model for the predictors estimated from a random sample of the full population. This corresponds to using all subjects of Fig. 12.3. In the case of a random sample, that is, no selection, it is known (Tucker 1971) that with factor score estimated by the regression method, consistent estimates are obtained for the regression of a dependent variable on the estimated factor scores. Although the factor scores have biases, the factor covariance bias and the bias in the covariances of the factors and a dependent variable cancel out in the regression of a dependent variable on the estimated factor scores. In the current case of selection, Muthén and Hsu (1993, pp. 261–262) use Pearson-Lawley selection formulas to show that when a sum of the factor indicators is used as a selection variable, the regression of a dependent variable on the estimated factor scores in the selected group also gives unbiased structural coefficients.

12.9 Selection Based on Factors: Predictive Validity of Admission Tests in the U.S. Military

Given a model such as Fig. 12.2 it is of interest to select subjects based on the factor values instead of a sum of the factor indicators. Muthén and Gustafsson (1994) compare selection based on factors with the conventional selection based on sums of factor indicators used for admission into the U.S. military. Hands-on job performance for nine U.S. army jobs is related to the standard set of ten ASVAB tests as well as twelve experimental tests added to the ASVAB. A bi-factor model is considered for the total number of 22 tests.

A first complication is that it is not known who among the applicant sample was selected and who was not. This means that the data are not structured as in Fig. 12.3 because information on y_1–y_6 for an unselected group is not available. A second complication is that data for the 22 tests are not available for the unselected, applicant group. Only the ten ASVAB tests are available for the applicant group and the twelve experimental tests are only available for the selected, matriculant group. These two complications are resolved by using Pearson-Lawley adjustments in combination with the factor score approach as follows.

As a first step, Pearson-Lawley adjustment is made to the 22×22 sample covariance matrix for the nine jobs in the selected, matriculant group to obtain an estimate of the covariance matrix for the unselected, applicant group. In this adjustment the ten ASVAB tests are used as selection variables given that ASVAB is the standard selection instrument into the military. A 10×10 ASVAB covariance matrix is used for a reference group of 650,278 applicants. A bi-factor factor model is then applied to the 22×22 adjusted covariance matrix and estimated factor scores computed for the selected group in the nine army jobs. The criterion variable of hands-on job performance is then regressed on the estimated factor scores to give unbiased regression estimates in line with Muthén and Hsu (1993). Hsu (1995) shows that standard errors for these regression estimates are well approximated at moderate sample sizes even though the factor score estimation assumes no sampling error in the factor model parameters. Muthén and Gustafsson (1994) show that different profiles of selected subjects are obtained using the factor-based selection versus using the conventional selection. They also argue that the assessment of incremental predictive validity of new tests is better done using a factor model.

12.10   Swedish Military Enlistment Example

A special application of the maximum-likelihood approach under MAR is used for Swedish military enlistment data in Muthén et al. (1994). Enlistment data collection includes: a cognitive test battery; a psychologist's rating of ability to handle strenuous situations; education; medical, and physical tests; and a psychologist's rating of the suitability for being an officer. Performance is measured as two supervisor ratings at the end of the training. Here, the missing data structure features three missing data patterns. Only the individuals scoring in the top 60–70 % of the cognitive test are evaluated for their suitability for being an officer, and performance is only measured for individuals selected as officers. Selection as officer is determined by several other factors than those determining the missing data patterns.

Muthén et al. (1994) use data on the performance of a select group of officers in charge of large units. Because individuals are not followed longitudinally the data come from two sources, a criterion sample of 1208 graduating officers and an enlistment sample. The enlistment sample is created as a random subsample of individuals known to have been selected as officers from the three years that the criterion sample officers were most likely tested. A sample size corresponding to the known selection ratio is chosen so that the maximum-likelihood procedure has the proper ratio of selected and non-selected individuals. A latent variable model is formulated with three latent variable constructs for the four cognitive tests, one construct for the psychologist's ratings, and one construct for the supervisor ratings. In a preliminary analysis, logistic regression is carried out to study predictors of being selected as an officer. In addition to the variables listed above, the location of the enlistment office and the time between the enlistment testing and service are found important and are included in the final latent variable model to avoid selection biases. A useful finding for modifying the selection procedure concerns the time between the enlistment testing and service. While increasing time has a negative effect on selection, it has a positive effect on performance as an officer, presumably due to an age advantage.

12.11 Conclusions

This chapter shows how analysis of data on selective subgroups can be used to draw inference to the full, unselected group. This uses Pearson-Lawley selection formulas which apply to not only regression analysis but also structural equation modeling. The chapter shows the connection with maximum-likelihood estimation with missing data assuming MAR versus using listwise deletion. Applications are discussed of selection into the military using factor analysis models for the variables used in the selection.

References

Dunbar, S. B., & Linn, R. L. (1991). Range restriction adjustments in the prediction of military job performance. In A. K. Wigdor & B. F. Green (Eds.), *Performance assessment for the workplace* (Vol. II. Technical issues, pp. 127–157). Washington, DC: National Academy Press.

Gustafsson, J. E., & Balke, G. (1993). General and specific abilities as predictors of school achievement. *Multivariate Behavioral Research, 28*, 407–434.

Hsu, J. W. Y. (1995). Sampling behaviour in estimating predictive validity in the context of selection and latent variable modelling: A Monte Carlo study. *British Journal of Mathematical and Statistical Psychology, 48*, 75–97.

Johnson, N. L., & Kotz, S. (1972). *Distributions in statistics: Continuous multivariate distributions.*. Chichester: Wiley.

Lawley, D. (1943–1944). A note on Karl Pearson's selection formulae. *Royal Society of Edinburgh: Proceedings, Section A, 62*, 28–30.

Lord, F. M., & Novick, M. R. (1968). *Statistical theories of mental test scores*. Reading, Mass: Addison-Wesley.

Meredith, W. (1964). Notes on factorial invariance. *Psychometrika, 29*, 177–185.

Muthén, B. (1989). Factor structure in groups selected on observed scores. *British Journal of Mathematical and Statistical Psychology, 42*, 81–90.

Muthén, B., & Gustafsson, J. E. (1994). *ASVAB-based job performance prediction and selection: Latent variable modeling versus regression analysis*. Technical report.

Muthén, B. & Hsu, J. W. Y. (1993). Selection and predictive validity with latent variable structures. *British Journal of Mathematical and Statistical Psychology, 46*, 255–271.

Muthén, B., & Hsu, J. W. Y., Carlstedt, B., & Mardberg, B. (1994). *Predictive validity assessment of the Swedish military enlistment testing procedure using missing data and latent variable methods*. Technical report.

Muthén, B., & Jöreskog, K. (1983). Selectivity problems in quasi-experimental studies. *Evaluation Review, 7*, 139–174.

Muthén, B., Kaplan, D., & Hollis, M. (1987). On structural equation modeling with data that are not missing completely at random. *Psychometrika, 52,* 431–462.

Olsson, U. (1978). *Selection bias in confirmatory factor analysis.* Uppsala, Sweden: University of Uppsala (Department of Statistics Research, Report No. 78-4).

Pearson, K. (1903). Mathematical contributions to the theory of evolution. XI: On the influence of natural selection on the variability and correlation of organs. *Philosophical Transactions of the Royal Society, London, Series A, 200,* 1–66.

Schmidt, F. L., & Hunter, J. E. (1981). Employment testing: Old theories and new research findings. *American Psychologist, 36,* 1128–1137.

Tucker, L. R. (1971). Relations of factor score estimates to their use. *Psychometrika, 36,* 427–436.

Chapter 13
Reflections on (Bi) Factor Analysis

Richard J. Shavelson and Edward W. Wiley

Abstract About 20 years ago, Jan-Eric Gustafsson (e.g., Gustafsson and Undheim 1996) used confirmatory factor analysis to examine the hierarchical structure of intelligence, paralleling an earlier extraordinarily thorough exploratory factor analysis reported by Carroll (1993). Gustafsson's model fitting and testing were elegant, he confirmed Carroll's findings, and his work has greatly influenced the field. Wiley et al. (2014) examined the structure of the 2005 revised SAT. We tested alternative models that paralleled proposed score interpretations (e.g., general ability or *g*; quantitative and verbal; quantitative, verbal and writing). Gustafsson's work on bi-factor models led us to an interpretation of the SAT different from the ones we tested but consistent with claims, in part, of those calling for a change in the SAT from a reasoning test to a content-oriented test. We report the results of this follow-up analysis and then summarize research on the influence of general ability on US college admissions tests. We show with bi-factor analysis that both the ACT and the SAT go beyond measuring *g* and capture other aspects of performance predictive of college outcomes (Coyle and Pillow 2008). We conclude by reflecting on the interpretation of factor-analytic findings proposing both cognitive interviews (Ericsson and Simon 1993) and predictive studies to validate proposed factor-analytic interpretations.

Jan-Eric Gustafsson's work on factor analysis has been tremendously influential in psychological, educational and social research. This chapter was written to honor him and his work. As we hope to convince you, even in the writing of this chapter his work led us to improvements of our own work. We are, indeed, indebted to him.

R.J. Shavelson (✉) · E.W. Wiley
SK Partners, Menlo Park, California, USA
e-mail: richs@stanford.edu

R.J. Shavelson
Stanford University, Stanford, USA

© Springer International Publishing AG 2017
M. Rosén et al. (eds.), *Cognitive Abilities and Educational Outcomes*,
Methodology of Educational Measurement and Assessment,
DOI 10.1007/978-3-319-43473-5_13

237

13.1   Introduction

The research reported herein was motivated by the work of Jan-Eric Gustafsson. Gustafsson has made major contributions to statistical methods for finding patterns of relationships or clusters of variables in data. These contributions are conceptual, statistical and practical. Conceptually he was an early pioneer in the development and application of structural equation models with latent variables. Such models demanded that there be a conceptual framework behind any analysis of the covariance structure in a set of variables. Statistically, he pioneered methods for analyzing patterns, most notably for us is his work on bi-factor models—models in which the observed or "… manifest variables relate to more than one factor, and if there is a general factor, it relates to all the manifest variables" (Gustafsson and Åberg-Bengtsson, p. 105). And practically, he created a shell that sat on top of multiple confirmatory factor analytic programs so the user could access these programs without learning the particularly tricky computer languages for running the programs at a time when such shells did not exist.

His development and application of bi-factor or nested models have had an important impact on our understanding of the structure of human abilities (e.g., Gustafsson 1984; Gustafsson and Undheim 1996). More recently this work has contributed to our capacity to deal with multidimensionality in Item Response Theory models (Gustafsson and Åberg-Bengtsson 2010; see also Blömeke et al. 2015).

In what follows, we begin with the application of bi-factor models to college admissions data. We report on the structure of both the Swedish Scholastic Aptitude Test (SweSAT) and the U.S. SAT (SAT) tests, both used in their respective countries for college-admissions decision making. Having extolled the virtues of such factor-analytic approaches to sorting out the contributions of general ability and knowledge, we conclude the paper by raising concerns about the use and interpretation of factor analysis. We make the point that in interpreting the findings, more than goodness of fit of alternative models is needed. More specifically, such analyses need to be augmented by other types of validity, most notably what we call cognitive validity.

13.2   Application of Bi-Factor Models

Here we describe several applications of the bi-factor model to college admissions testing. We begin with Gustafsson's study of the structure of the Swedish Scholastic Aptitude Test (SweSAT) (Gustafsson and Åberg-Bengtsson 2010) and then move to an analysis of the structure of the U.S. SAT, building on our earlier work (Wiley et al. 2014). We conclude this section reporting findings comparing the SAT with another college admissions test, the U.S. ACT (Coyle and Pillow 2008). We examine the extent to which each test demands g and subject knowledge.

13.3 SweSAT College Admissions Test

Gustafsson and Åberg-Bengtsson (2010) used the SweSAT to demonstrate the application of bi-factor analysis to the measurement of psychological constructs. The SweSAT is:

> designed to assess the general ability to successfully pass higher education courses. Reading skills, vocabulary, and skills of reasoning, primarily with quantitative information, are focused on in the test. However, the test lacks a theoretical basis for its construction, and little is known about what the total score computed from the subtests actually measures (p. 111).

Gustafsson eschewed fitting a higher-order factor model to the data preferring, rather, to fit a nested model or bi-factor model. With higher-order factor models, some factors are broad and encompass narrower factors. For example, Verbal Ability might encompass Vocabulary and Reading Comprehension (Fig. 13.1a). Such models follow Thurstone's principle of "'simple structure' in the sense that each factor is associated with a subset of the observed variables and that each observed variable is influenced by only one or a few factors" (Gustafsson and Åberg-Bengtsson 2010, p. 104). In contrast, bi-factor models violate the principle in favor of representing both general and specific factors as first-order factors which are directly linked to observable item responses. So, in the verbal ability example, all items would load on a verbal ability factor and, in addition, vocabulary items would load on a vocabulary factor and reading comprehension items would load on a reading-comprehension factor (Fig. 13.1b).

So, Gustafsson and Åberg-Bengtsson fit a model in which all SweSAT items loaded on a general factor and particular items loaded on one or the other of three nested factors: (1) quantitative reasoning,[1] (2) knowledge, and (3) end-of-test (reflecting items at the end of the speeded test) (see Fig. 13.2). They argued that the bi-factor model links each construct directly to observable performance (test-item responses in this case) rather than indirectly to a one-step removed higher-order construct. The approach seemed immediately sensible and interpretable to us (as did the Gustafsson and Undheim (1996) application of bi-factor analysis to the Wechsler Intelligence Scale for Children).

As to the interpretation of bi-factor analysis of SweSAT scores, Gustafsson and Åberg-Bengtsson (2010, p. 116) noted that:

---

[1]DTM "Items classified as *quantitative* involved more or less complicated arithmetic and calculations in addition to the reading of diagrams, tables, and maps" (Gustafsson and Åberg-Bengtsson 2010, p. 113).

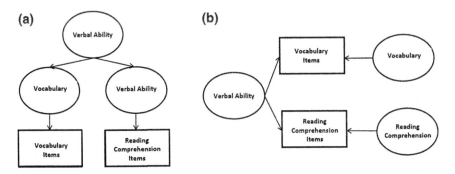

Fig. 13.1 Alternative hierarchical factor models: **a** higher-order factor model and **b** bi-factor or nested factor model

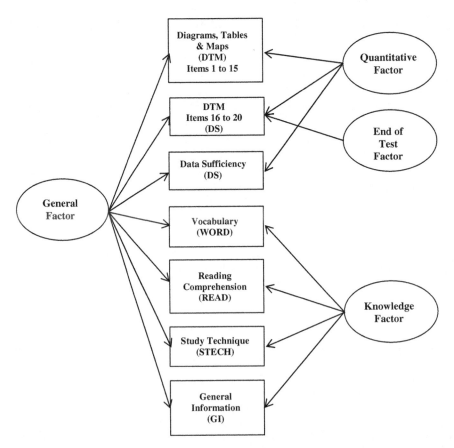

Fig. 13.2 Schematic of a bi-factor model for the SweSAT (adapted from Gustafsson and Åberg-Bengtsson 2010, p. 115)

The main question investigated in the Åberg-Bengtsson (2005) study was whether it is possible to separate the Quant factor from a general factor with the highest relation to the complex problem-solving tests. Such a result would lend support to the hypothesis that this general factor is close to the Gf factor,[2] which is also close to the G factor (Gustafsson 1984). This interpretation is supported by the fact that the two reasoning tests (DS and DTM) are, indeed, the ones most highly saturated by the general factor. The interpretation is also supported by the observation that the second most important factor was Knowl, with relations to the four verbal subtests. This factor, thus, seems to come close to Gc.[3] However, to test these speculations it is necessary to combine the SweSAT with other tests that have known measurement properties [presented next in the paper].

13.4   U.S. SAT College Admissions Test

We were surprised to find that the College Board had not published a factor analytic study of its revised (2005) SAT, historically the U.S.'s "gold standard" in college admissions testing (Wiley et al. 2014). The College Board asked us to conduct such a study.

The 2005 version of the SAT was divided into: mathematics or quantitative reasoning, critical reading, and writing. The College Board considered scores from these three areas to be separable, interpretable sub-scores.

In our published analysis of the SAT structure (based on the October 2010 administration, $N_{Test\ Takers} = 533,824$; $N_{Items} = 170$) we included SAT's three-factor correlated model (mathematics, critical reading and writing) along with several competing models: a general factor model (g); a two-factor correlated model —mathematics and "literacy"; and several others addressing speededness and item difficulty. We found the best fitting and most interpretable structure (replicated in an independent data set; May 2011, $N_{Test\ Takers} = 493,664$; $N_{Items} = 178$) to be the correlated two factor model.

However, in carrying out these analyses we were caught in a bubble of proposed interpretations (critical reading, mathematics and writing) and so did not consider an alternative model, a bi-factor model that includes general ability and nested mathematics and literacy factors (among other competitors). Such a model addresses criticisms that the SAT measures general ability (g) rather than achievement by the nature of its speededness and reasoning-item types not closely related to high school curricula (e.g., Atkinson and Geiser 2009).

---

[2]Gf or fluid intelligence is related to induction, reasoning, problem solving and visual perception (Gustafsson and Åberg-Bengtsson 2010, p. 111).

[3]Gc or crystallized intelligence which is involved in language, reading books and general school learning (Gustafsson and Åberg-Bengtsson 2010, p. 111).

Table 13.1 SAT structure: average factor loadings and factor correlations

Model:	2 Factor		3 Factor	
Factors	Correlated	Bi-factor	Correlated	Bi-factor
General ability (g)	–	0.580	–	0.579
Critical reading (CR)	–	–	0.423	0.219
Mathematics (M)	0.567	0.438	0.496	0.542
Writing (W)	–	–	0.416	0.050
Language (L = CR + W)	0.488	0.138	–	–
Correlations				
L ↔ M	0.710	–		–
CR ↔ M			0.718	
CR ↔ W			0.926	
M ↔ W			0.748	

We reran the October 2010 SAT data to compare both a two- and three-factor model, each with either correlated factors or an uncorrelated bi-factor model with general ability and two or three nested factors. Our findings are presented in Table 13.1.

With the large sample size, all models were statistically significant (consistent with Wiley et al. 2014). For both the two- and three-factor models, the bi-factor approach provided a negligibly better fit than the correlated-factor models but at a cost of model complexity: adding the general factor required more than 160 additional parameters to be estimated. From what we found we believe the additional cost is well worthwhile for the information provided; a luxury with our large samples of persons and items.

If we focus first on the original correlated models (Wiley et al. 2014) it looks as if we have interpretable two- and three-factor models corresponding to the College Board's proposed interpretation of the SAT. Our preference for the two-factor model was one of parsimony supported by the high correlation between the reading and writing factors in the three-factor model (0.926, Table 13.1). Moreover this preference was consistent with trends in language arts in which reading and writing are becoming viewed holistically and in a sense inseparable.

The bi-factor models, however, shed further light on the structure of the SAT and its interpretation. First and foremost, the strongest factor in both the two- and three-bi-factor models is general ability (g, Table 13.1); Atkinson and Geiser (2009) were right. The SAT measures, in part, general ability. Moreover we interpret our findings as providing evidence that the SAT gives greater weight to verbal (or crystallized knowledge, g_c) than quantitative (or g_f aspects of g judging from the three-factor model (average loadings: $g = 0.579$, critical reading = 0.219, mathematics = 0.542, and writing = 0.050). Related, in both the two- and three-bi-factor models there appears to be a strong mathematics factor not accounted for by g.

We conclude from this exercise that the bi-factor model, especially in comparison with the correlated factor models provides important additional interpretable information well worth the additional cost of complexity. Moreover, as we shall see, the findings we reported here are consistent with earlier work examining the interpretation of the SAT and the currently most widely used college-admissions test in the US, the ACT.

13.5   U.S. SAT and ACT College Admissions Tests

A century of research on the SAT (e.g., Lawrence et al. 2003) has consistently shown that the SAT predicts college readiness as indexed by college grade-point-average (GPA) and student retention. When combined with high-school grade-point-average (HSGPA) the SAT provides important college-readiness information, but not the sole information to be used, for college admissions decisions. In 2010 using first- and second-year GPA as criterion measures, the College Board reported that HSGPA correlated 0.56 with both criteria; the SAT correlated 0.56 and 0.55, respectively; and HSGPA and SAT combined correlated 0.64 with both. The same pattern has been observed in successive years (Patterson and Mattern 2013).

Critics (e.g., Atkinson and Geiser 2009, 2015) claim that the SAT is an aptitude measure, that it measures the same thing as general intelligence—"g". There is reason to believe that this is old baggage from the turn of the last century and that the SAT measures both disciplinary achievement and broad reasoning abilities as the College Board claims.

Which claim, then, has empirical support?

Perhaps the most comprehensive study of this question was carried out by Coyle and Pillow (2008). They analyzed two large-scale data sets in which they could test whether the SAT measured only g or whether it measured g and something else about college readiness more closely related to school performance. They had scores for students on the SAT, on measures of g including the Wechsler Adult Intelligence Scale (WAIS, data set 1) and the Armed Forces Vocational Aptitude Battery (ASVAB, data set 2). They also had these students' first- and second-semester college grade-point-averages (GPA). They put all these ingredients into a bi-factor confirmatory factor analysis to address the question of whether SAT only measures g.

The results, replicated with both data sets, are instructive. Below (Fig. 13.2) we present the second data set (with largest sample size). Of particular importance is the finding that the SAT is highly correlated with g (0.78). This provides empirical evidence that the SAT measures g.

Now, look at the bottom of the figure: college GPA at the first-(GPA1) and second-(GPA2) semester of students' freshman year. The goal of an admissions test, including the SAT, is to predict this (and other) college readiness/performance criteria. The sketch in Fig. 13.3 shows that general ability (including information from the SAT) correlates 0.32 with GPA. Not surprisingly and well known, college performance correlates with general ability.

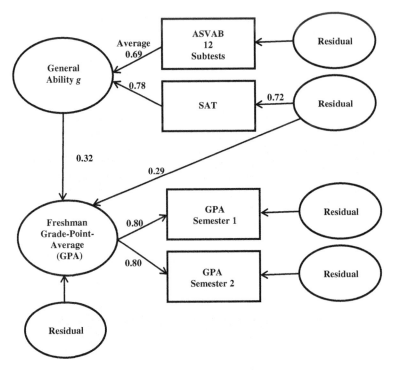

Fig. 13.3 What does the SAT measure: empirical evidence (*Source* Coyle and Pillow 2008, p. 724, adapted from Fig. 13.2a)

However, the story does not end here. Notice the arrow from the SAT's residual term, u_{13}, to GPA. The residual term includes other factors than g and error. The residual correlates about the same as does g with GPA: 0.29. This finding is important. It indicates that the SAT measures not just g but other student characteristics that predict first-year college performance. This result is consistent with the College Board's contention that the SAT taps both reasoning and achievement.

The question arises as to whether the ACT—considered a measure of high-school achievement, one that reflects students' efforts rather than aptitudes—taps g at all, and how well it predicts college GPA. Might it be that the ACT does not correlate nearly as highly as the SAT with g? Might it be that the ACT residual correlates much more highly with GPA than the SAT because it purports to be an achievement test?

Coyle and Pillow (2008) addressed these questions by carrying out the same bi-factor analysis of ACT test scores as they did for the SAT's (Fig. 13.3). Their findings are presented in Fig. 13.4. The ACT correlated as highly with g as did the SAT. Moreover, it does no better predicting college GPA than does the SAT. So while perceptions of the two tests vary, perhaps in some cases for good reason, psychometrically the tests measure very similar things. And the bi-factor model is especially apt in permitting us to draw such conclusions.

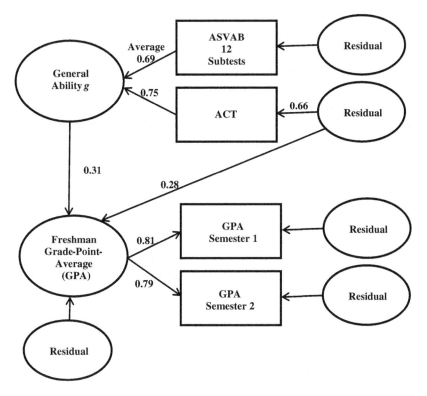

Fig. 13.4 Do the SAT and ACT measure the same or different things? Empirical Evidence (*Source* Coyle and Pillow 2008, p. 724, adapted from Fig. 13.2b)

13.6 Interpretation of Factor Analysis Findings

With some trepidation we conclude these reflections on factor analysis with a caution. The caution is that a factor analyst's work is not complete with the testing of multiple competing models and the selection of the one that fits the data and theory best. Indeed, as the statistician L.J. Savage reminded us: no statistical model is "right." Rather some models are more or less useful for particular purposes in particular contexts.

Indeed, as we specify factor models, we are caught in a contextual or cultural bubble and often miss obvious alternative models that might fit the data equally well. Our initial analysis of the structure of the SAT (Wiley et al. 2014) was so constrained. The further analysis of the structure of the SAT that we carried out for this chapter shed further light on the interpretability of SAT scores. We recognized the importance of the model only upon reflecting on Gustafsson's development and use of nested or bi-factor analytic models.

This said we recognize that factor analysis is built upon covariances (or correlations). Such statistics measure the degree that two variables—any two variables—

rank order objects of measurement similarly. Covariances "don't know" and "don't care about" what is measured. So a mathematics achievement test and a vocabulary test correlate positively and highly but they clearly measure different things. How or why they correlate with each other and other cognitive tests—the "positive manifold"—has been the focus of the study of human abilities for the past 150 years. To say general ability underlies the correlation is simply to restate the case. To formulate the fundamental principles of factor analysis by saying variables correlate with one another because they share common variance is to restate the case. To test alternative models ruling out counterhypotheses is one means of reducing uncertainty about what is being measured. But such model tests are incomplete. And there may be some unidentified model that is more useful.

Without a clearly isolated mechanism underlying observed correlations, then, we can and should do more. Two additional analyses might increase confidence in the validity of proposed factor interpretations. One analysis would be to examine the pattern of correlations among factors predicting convergent and divergent validity to see if they fit theory (Campbell and Fiske 1959). We would expect the factors to fit a pattern of correlations based on theory and empirical research. To the extent the pattern is confirmed, we increase confidence in our interpretation.

A second analysis would examine the extent to which test takers' thought processes are consistent with the proposed factor interpretation (e.g., Ericsson and Simon 1993). If the factor is interpreted, say, as analytic reasoning, we would expect to observe similar cognitive processes in answering the item set or tests that underlie the factor (e.g., Ayala et al. 2002). For example, we (Li et al. 2006) posited four underlying, correlated dimensions to the TIMSS 1999 science-test items: declarative knowledge ("knowing that"), procedural knowledge ("knowing how"), schematic knowledge ("knowing why") and strategic knowledge (metacognitive strategies). We collected students' "think alouds" to items and factor analyzed the item scores. Both the think aloud data and the confirmatory factor analysis provided convergent evidence for the four dimensions.

References

Åberg-Bengtsson, L. (2005). Separating the quantitative and analytic dimensions of the Swedish Scholastic Aptitude Test (SweSAT). *Scandinavian Journal of Educational Research, 49,* 359–383.

Atkinson, R. C., & Geiser, S. (2009). Reflections on a century of college admissions tests. *Educational Researcher, 38,* 665–676.

Atkinson, R. C., & Geiser, S. (2015). The big problem with the new SAT. *The New York Times.* Retrieved March 19, 2016 from http://www.nytimes.com/2015/05/05/opinion/the-big-problem-with-the-new-sat.html?_r=1

Ayala, C. A., Shavelson, R. J., Yin, Y., & Schultz, S. (2002). Reasoning dimensions underlying science achievement: The case of performance assessment. *Educational Assessment, 8,* 101–122.

Blömeke, S., Gustafsson, J.-E., & Shavelson, R. (2015). Beyond dichotomies: Competence viewed as a continuum. *Zeitschrift für Psychologie, Zeitschrift für Psychologie, 223,* 3–13.

Campbell, D. T., & Fiske, D. W. (1959). Validation by the multitrait-multimethod matrix. *Psychological Bulletin, 56,* 81–105.

Carroll, J. B. (1993). *Human cognitive abilities: A survey of factor-analytic studies.*. New York, NY: Cambridge University Press.

Coyle, T. R., & Pillow, D. R. (2008). SAT and ACT predict college GPA after removing *g*. *Intelligence, 36,* 719–729.

Ericsson, K. A., & Simon, H. A. (1993). *Protocol analysis: Verbal reports as data.*. Cambridge, MA: MIT Press.

Gustafsson, J.-E. (1984). A unifying model of the structure of intellectual abilities. *Intelligence, 8,* 179–203.

Gustafsson, J.-E., & Åberg-Bengtsson, L. (2010). Unidimensionality and interpretability of psychological instruments. In S. E. Embertson (Ed.), *Measuring psychological constructs: Advances in model-based approaches* (pp. 97–121). Washington, DC: American Psychological Association.

Gustafsson, J.-E., & Undheim, J. O. (1996). Individual differences in cognitive functions. In D. Berliner & R. Calfee (Eds.), *Handbook of educational psychology* (pp. 186–242). New York: Macmillan.

Lawrence, I. M., Rigol, G. W., Van Essen, T., & Jackson, C. A. (2003). *A historical perspective on the content of the SAT*®. New York: The College Board.

Li, M., Ruiz-Primo, M. A., & Shavelson, R. J. (2006). Towards a science achievement framework: The case of TIMSS 1999. In S. Howie & T. Plomp (Eds.), *Contexts of learning mathematics and science: Lessons learned from TIMSS* (pp. 291–311). London: Routledge.

Patterson, B. F., & Mattern, K. D. (2013). *Validity of the SAT for predicting first year grades: 2011 SAT validity sample* (College Board Research: Statistical Report 2013-3). Retrieved March 19, 2016 from http://research.collegeboard.org/sites/default/files/publications/2013/12/statistical-report-2013-3-validity-SAT-predicting-first-year-grades.pdf

Wiley, E. W., Shavelson, R. J., & Kurpius, A. A. (2014). On the factorial structure of the SAT and implications for next-generation college readiness assessments. *Educational and Psychological Measurement, 74,* 859–874.

Chapter 14
CTT and No-DIF and ? = (Almost) Rasch Model

Matthias von Davier

Abstract Assuring the absence of differential item functioning (DIF) is one of the central goals when constructing a test using either classical test theory (CTT) or item response theory (IRT). One of the most prominent methods of DIF detection is the Mantel Haenzel (1959) procedure that was suggested for this purpose by Holland and Thayer (1986). This test is not only used for DIF detection, a fact sometimes forgotten by educational measurement practitioners, and is often also called the Cochran-Mantel-Haenzel test. The basis of this test is a comparison of odds-ratios of several 2 by 2 tables, which is utilized in educational testing in the context of conditional 2 by 2 tables given the different ordered categories of a variable that represents proficiency or skill levels. In this note, I am expanding existing work that relates the Cochran-Mantel-Haenzel test used in conjunction with a simple sum score variable to the Rasch model. As I have pointed out in previous publications, the simple raw score, being the sum of binary scored responses, has certain desirable features, but is also limited in the sense of how information is used (e.g. von Davier 2010, 2016; von Davier and Rost 2016). In the context of CTT, as well as the use of the Cochran-Mantel-Haenzel procedure in CTT, and its relationship to the assumptions made in the Rasch model, however, the use of the sum score in conditional odds ratios is what brings these important approaches in applied test theory together on a formal mathematical basis.

14.1 Introduction

There have been prior attempts to relate CTT and IRT (Holland and Hoskens 2003; Bechger et al. 2003) as well as attempts to compare extensions of the Rasch model and MH-DIF approaches (Linacre and Wright 1989; Paek and Wilson 2011). However, the current approach, while rooted in the findings of these prior studies tries to approach the issue from a slightly different angle: In this note I focus on

M. von Davier (✉)
Educational Testing Service, Princeton, NJ, USA
e-mail: mvondavier@ets.org

© Springer International Publishing AG 2017

249

M. Rosén et al. (eds.), *Cognitive Abilities and Educational Outcomes*,
Methodology of Educational Measurement and Assessment,
DOI 10.1007/978-3-319-43473-5_14

what is missing, or at least not stated explicitly in the use of (a) the MH-DIF procedure and (b) item-total regressions for test assembly in conjunction with CTT, and how slightly stronger versions of these requirements of 'good items' relate to a model that is virtually identical to IRT or the Rasch model. The basis for this chapter is an examination of tests consisting of binary (correct/incorrect) response variables. However, most results generalize in straightforward ways to tests with polytomous ordinal responses or mixed binary/polytomous tests (e.g. von Davier and Rost 1995; von Davier 2010).

Comparing item analyses to approaches in Biometrics and other fields (Cochran 1954; Armitage 1955), one finds similarities to the assessment of associations between a binary variable and an ordered categorical variable (in test theory this will be very often the sum score). For example, Armitage (1955) states:

> One frequently encounters data consisting of a series of proportions, occurring in groups which fall into some natural order. The question usually asked is then not so much whether the proportions differ significantly, but whether they show a significant trend, upwards or downwards, with the ordering of the groups.

Note that this whole paper is obsolete once it is understood that IRT and some types of nonlinear factor analysis are equivalent (e.g. Takane and DeLeeuw 1987 and more recently Raykov and Marcoulides 2016), and that all of test theory can be covered using a common, unified framework (McDonald 1999). In this note, we hope to add to this discussion by means of a one-by-one comparison of the assumptions made, in particular those of

(a) Absence of DIF versus local independence,
(b) True score + error versus sufficiency of (weighted) total score,
(c) Positive item correlation versus strict monotonicity.

This note also offers a perspective of how these weaker assumptions made in CTT need to be only slightly strengthened to arrive at a model that is virtually identical to the Rasch model or the subgroup of IRT models with sufficient statistics for the person variable (e.g. OPLM & 2PL in the binary case).

Also, several proponents of classical test theory (CTT) on the one hand and the Rasch model (or IRT) on the other hand may need some additional gentle nudging toward the insight that using either approach leads to good test instruments that are compatible with the (seemingly) competing other approach. This insight has its roots in the fact that both approaches, CTT and (unidimensional) Rasch and IRT models are special cases of generalized latent variable models (e.g. Moustaki and Knott 2000; Rabe-Hesketh et al. 2004).

The need to provide a generalized class of models such as the general diagnostic model (von Davier 2005, 2008) grows out of the understanding that several competing hypothesis about the structure of the variables we are aiming to assess can be directly compared and tested against each other if they are specified in a coherent statistical framework. However, there may be cases where several competing hypothesis are indeed providing very similar descriptions of the data while profoundly differing in the underlying assumptions made (von Davier et al. 2012). In other case, several models that appear to be different, or even extensions of another approach may turn out to be mere equivalent versions that can be covered in the generalized modeling framework by means of a reparameterization (von Davier 2013, 2014).

Generalizations of CTT to linear factor models are the predecessors of these generalized (linear and nonlinear) latent variable models. Also, several tests around the world, some of them high-stakes instruments used for highly consequential decisions are still being designed and assembled using the principles of 'vanilla' CTT, together with customary tools to ensure psychometric quality. Among these, procedures for assessing (ensuring the absence of) differential item functioning (DIF) are one of the central foci when constructing a test using either classical test theory (CTT) or item response theory (IRT). Not only Lord and Novick (1968) and others (e.g. Wainer 1988) emphasize the importance of items and their resulting scores as fundamental to the test score. Moreover, ensuring the absence of DIF is considered one of the fundamental goals of test construction in order to provide fair assessments (Dorans 2013). One of the most prominent methods of DIF detection is the Mantel-Haenzel procedure that was suggested for this purpose by Holland and Thayer (1986). This test is not only used for DIF detection, a fact sometimes forgotten by educational measurement practitioners, and often also called the Cochran-Mantel-Haenzel test as methods related to this test have been discussed by Cochran (1954) and Mantel and Haenzel (1959). The basis of this test is a comparison of odds-ratios of several 2 by 2 tables, which is utilized in educational testing in the context of conditional 2 by 2 tables given the different ordered categories of a variable that represents proficiency or skill levels, very often taking the form of observed score groups.

In this note, I am expanding existing work that relates the Cochran-Mantel-Haenzel test used in conjunction with a simple sum score variable to the Rasch model. As I have pointed out in previous work, the simple raw score, being the unweighted sum of scored item responses, has certain desirable features, but is also limited in the sense of how information is used (e.g. von Davier 2010, 2016; von Davier and Rost 2016). In the context of CTT, as well as the use of the Cochran-Mantel-Haenzel procedure in CTT, and its relationship to the assumptions made in the Rasch model, however, the use of the sum score in conditional odds ratios is what brings these important approaches in applied test theory together on a formal mathematical basis. This chapter reviews the assumptions made in the Rasch model and how tests that fulfill these assumptions turn out to be 'good' tests in light of CTT measures of quality, and vice versa, when taking the definition of absence of DIF broadly. While related work pointed out other types of similarities, a direct argument of equivalency under these separately developed sets of preconditions for test quality has not been attempted to my knowledge.

14.2 Notation

Let $X_1, \ldots, X_K$ denote $K > 2$ binary random variables, and let Ω denote the population of respondents on which these random variables can be observed. We will assume for simplicity that the population is finite, and that we can sum over variables observed on samples from Ω. The random variables are representing the scored item responses on a test, and the respondents are represented as members $u \in \Omega$ of a population of potential test takers.

For each respondent, we may define the probability of responding correctly to each of these items X_i. More specifically, let

$$p_{ui} = P(X_i = 1 | u)$$

denote that respondent u produces a correct response on item i. Note that this is not the marginal probability of a correct response, but the probability of a correct response for a given $u \in \Omega$.

Then, for considering a realization of the random variables, let

$$x_{ui} = X_i(u) \in \{0, 1\}$$

denote the binary item response to item i by a respondent u from the population Ω. The code $X_i = 1$ represents correct responses, while $X_i = 0$ represents incorrect responses.

The observed score, the total number of correct responses for a respondent u, aggregated across the K response variables will be denoted as

$$s_X(u) = \sum_{i=1}^{K} x_{ui}.$$

In addition to the item responses, there may be additional random variables that are defined for the population Ω. As an example, background information about each of the potential respondents $u \in \Omega$ can be represented as random variables z_j with $j = 1, \ldots, J$. For a variable that represents gender, for example, z_j, for some j may be defined as

$$z_{ui} = Z_i(u) \in \{male, female\}$$

which may also be coded as $\{0, 1\}$ as it is possible for any binary variable. Note that the additional variables could also represent other types of data, such as answers to items on other tests or questionnaires.

One additional random variable should be considered, one that represents the target of inference. Tests are typically given to make inferences about a skill, or an attribute, often quantitative in nature, which underlies test performance. A 10-item mathematics test is supposed to test more than the performance of students on the

10 items, but rather represent something that speaks more generally about the skill or ability of these students to solve these and similar mathematics problems.

Formally, each respondent u is assumed to possess a level of 'skill', mathematically a continuous random variable Υ, with

$$\tau_u = \Upsilon(u)$$

representing the skill level of respondent u. In different approaches to test theory, there will be different instances of this 'skill level' variable τ. In classical test theory (CTT), the true score, T, can be viewed as a version (a function of) τ specific to a test form, and in item response theory and Rasch models, the 'skill level', τ, will appear in the form of the person parameter, θ, which can also be assumed to be a function of τ.

14.3 Classical Test Theory in a Nutshell

CTT assumes that the observed score $S_X(u)$ can be written as the sum of two components. The foundational equation of the CTT is

$$S_X(u) = T_X(u) + e_X(u)$$

and much has been written about how to interpret these components. The most common setting is that $T_X(u)$ is the expected score on test X for respondent u, assuming either that the test can be repeated indefinitely, or that, based on additional model assumptions, an expected score can be calculated (see the corresponding section below).

Note that this definition of

$$T_X(u) = E(S_X|u)$$

as conditional expectation leads to a number of implications. First, $T_X(u)$ is often referred to as the 'true score', even though it is more accurately described as the conditional expectation of the sum score given respondent $u \in \Omega$.

This conditional expectation is vanishing for all respondents, so for any subset of respondents $U \subseteq \Omega$ we also have $E(e_X|U) = 0$. In particular for subsets of the type

$$U_T = \{u \in \Omega | T_X(u) = T\}$$

As a corollary we obtain that

$$E(e_X|T) = E(e_x|U_T) = \int_{\{u \in \Omega | T_X(u) = T\}} E(e_x|u)p(u)du = 0$$

for any true score T.

Hence, the error variable, e_X, and T_X are, by definition of T_X, uncorrelated in Ω. Therefore, the total variance of the scores $V(S_X)$ can be written as

$$V(S_X) = V(T_X) + E[V(e_X)].$$

Note that this equation decomposes the total variance into the variance of T_X in Ω and the expected variance of the error term e_X. This result follows directly from the definition of T_X and e_X. Measures of reliability and the extent to which a score has validity are, at least in the traditional understanding of these concepts in CTT (Thurstone 1931), based on the correlation of the true score to true scores on other tests that are measures of the same underlying concept, or by means of correlations of the true score and other types of measures that are potentially difficult or expensive to collect, but can be considered the underlying target of inference.

In addition to the foundational assumption of CTT, measures of quality assurance include the selection and assembly of the items as components of the total score. Among these, the most prominent assumptions, or better selection criteria for items, are the absence of differential item functioning (no-DIF) and the presence of (moderate to high) correlations between the item score, X_i, and the total score, S_X.

More specifically, for the absence of DIF, it is assumed that for a number of grouping variables that separates the population into two groups, f and r, the conditional response probabilities by group membership and by total score are the same, that is

$$P(X_i = 1|S_X, f) = P(X_i = 1|S_X, r) = P(X_i = 1|S_X).$$

Expressed as odds ratio for the binary grouping $G: \Omega \rightarrow \{f, r\}$, this equality becomes

$$O_{S_X}(X_i, G) = \frac{P(X_i = 1|S_X, f)}{P(X_i = 0|S_X, f)} \times \frac{P(X_i = 0|S_X, r)}{P(X_i = 1|S_X, r)} = 1.$$

Basically, traditional uses of DIF restrict the study to grouping variables that are of policy relevance such as gender and ethnic minority status. However, there is nothing in the definition that would prevent us from applying the MH-DIF concept broadly, to any binary grouping variables, including those of other items. This use of another item response for splitting the sample is common practice in testing assumptions of the Rasch model (e.g. van den Wollenberg 1982; Verhelst 2001; von Davier 2016).

The Mantel Haenzel (MH) statistic uses a quantity that can be understood as the average odds ratio to test for DIF, more specifically if

$$MH(i, G) = \frac{\sum_{s=1}^{K-1} \frac{N(X_i=1 \wedge f|s)N(X_i=0 \wedge r|s)}{N(s)}}{\sum_{s=1}^{K-1} \frac{N(X_i=0 \wedge f|s)N(X_i=1 \wedge r|s)}{N(s)}} \approx 1$$

we may assume that there is no DIF for item i with respect to grouping variable, G. The expression $N(s)$ represents the frequency of score s. The notation $A \wedge B$ represents the conjunction of events A and B, that is, "A and B" was observed. As an example $N(X_i = 1 \wedge f|s) = N(X_i = 1 \wedge G = f|s)$ denotes the frequency of item i being solved in the focus group given score s. Note that the sum does not include terms for the total scores 0 or K since $P(X_i = 1|S_X = 0) = 0$ and $P(X_i = 0|S_X = K) = 0$ if the item score, X_i, is part of the sum score S_X.

In essence, the MH test statistic is used to check whether the conditional probabilities of success are the same across a variety of subpopulations. Traditionally, DIF analyses includes gender and ethnicity based groupings, but other types of groupings can obviously be used as well.

The positive item-total correlation criterion is based on the rationale that the covariance of the item score, X_i, and the total score, S_X, of which X_i is an additive component, should be in the same direction for all items. The underlying assumption is that the probability of a correct response should increase with increasing true score, which is the expectation of the observed score as defined above.

This covariance can be written as

$$cov(X_i, S_X) = \sum_{x=0}^{1} \sum_{s=0}^{K} P(X_i = x, S_X = s)x \cdot s - E(X_i)E(S_X)$$
$$= [E(S_X|X_i = 1) - E(S_X)]P(X_i)$$

which is nonnegative whenever

$$E(S_X|X_i = 1) \geq E(S_X).$$

Alternatively, the cross product part of the covariance can also be written as

$$\sum_{s=0}^{K} [P(X_i = 1|S_X = s) \cdot s]P(S_X = s) = E[S_X \cdot P(X_i = 1|S_X)]$$

and

$$cov(X_i, S_X) = E[S_X \cdot P(X_i = 1|S_X)] - E(X_i)E(S_X)$$

One straightforward way to ensure positivity is postulating that the conditional probabilities of solving the item given a specific score increase with increasing total score. That is, one may assume

$$P(X_i = 1|S_X = s) \geq P(X_i = 1|S_X = t)$$

for any two scores with $s > t$. This basically ensures that there are more test takers expected to solve the item in groups with higher total scores.

14.4 Rasch Model

With the notations above, the Rasch model assumes the following association between person skill level τ_u and expected performance on a response variable. For all $u \in \Omega$ it is assumed that

$$P(X_i = 1|u) = \frac{\tau_u}{d_i + \tau_u}, \tag{14.1}$$

and, customarily, this definition is used with the transformations $\exp(\theta_u) = \tau_u$ and $\exp(b_i) = d_i$. Hence, the above definition is equivalent to

$$P(X_i = 1|u) = \frac{\exp(\theta_u)}{\exp(b_i) + \exp(\theta_u)} = \frac{\exp(\theta_u - b_i)}{1 + \exp(\theta_u - b_i)} \tag{14.2}$$

which is the form commonly recognized as the dichotomous Rasch model (e.g. Rasch 1966; von Davier 2016). The θ_u is commonly referred to as the person parameter and the b_i is referred to as the item parameter.

Then, for the set of response variables, $X_1, \ldots, X_K$, it is assumed that conditional independence holds. This translates to the assumption that the joint probability of observing responses $x_1, \ldots, x_K$ is given by

$$P(X_1 = x_1, \ldots, X_K = x_K|u) = \prod_{i=1}^{K} \frac{\exp(x_i[\theta_u - b_i])}{1 + \exp(\theta_u - b_i)} \tag{14.3}$$

the product of the item specific responses. the above equation it is easily verified by noting that

$$P(X_i = 0|u) = 1 - P(X_i = 1|u) = \frac{1}{1 + \exp(\theta_u - b_i)}.$$

The expression for the joint probability in Eq. (14.3) can be rearranged so that

$$P(x_1, \ldots, x_K | \theta) = A(x_1, \ldots, x_K) \cdot B[S_X(u), \theta] \cdot C(\theta) \qquad (14.4)$$

with

$$A(x_1, \ldots, x_K) = \prod_{i=1}^{K} [\exp(-x_{ui} b_i)]$$

and

$$B[(S_X(u), \theta)] = \exp[S_X(u)\theta]$$

and

$$C(\theta) = \prod_{i=1}^{K} \left[\frac{1}{1 + \exp(\theta - b_i)} \right]$$

for any skill level $\theta \in \mathbb{R}$. This result can be utilized to calculate the probability of a response pattern given the raw score, S_x. This is done by calculating

$$P(S_X | \theta) = B[S_X(u), \theta] \cdot C(\theta) \left[\sum_{\{(x_1, \ldots, x_k) | \sum x_i = S_x\}} A(x_1, \ldots, x_K) \right]$$

the sum of the probabilities of all response patterns according to Eq. (14.4). For any given response pattern $(x_1^*, \ldots, x_k^*)$ with sum score $\sum x_i^* = S_X$ the conditional probability of observing this particular response vector among those with the same score becomes

$$P(X_1 = x_1^*, \ldots, X_k = x_k^* | S_X) = \frac{\prod_{i=1}^{K} [\exp(-x_i^* b_i)]}{\sum_{\{(x_1, \ldots, x_k) | \sum x_i = S_x\}} \prod_{i=1}^{K} [\exp(-x_i b_i)]}. \qquad (14.5)$$

The above expression is obtained by integrating out the latent skill variable θ, exploiting that the identity holds for every level of θ. The expressions

$$\gamma_K[\mathbf{b} = (b_1, \ldots, b_K), S_X] = \sum_{\{(x_1, \ldots, x_k) | \sum x_i = S_x\}} \prod_{i=1}^{K} [\exp(-x_i b_i)]$$

are commonly referred to as the symmetric functions (e.g. Gustafson 1980; von Davier and Rost 1995; von Davier 2016) for $S_X = 0, \ldots, K$ and S_X is called the 'order' of the function. The result of importance here is that this expression can be utilized to find

$$P(X_j = 1|S_X) = \sum_{\{(x_1,\ldots,x_k)| \sum x_i = S_x, x_j = 1\}} P(X_1 = x_1, \ldots, X_j = 1, \ldots, X_K = x_K|S_X)$$

(14.6)

for any item j and any raw score S_X. Equations (14.5) and (14.6) show that S_X is the minimally sufficient statistic (Fisher 1922) for parameter θ in the Rasch model. It can be further shown that

$$P(X_j = 1|S_X) = \frac{-\left(\frac{\partial \gamma_K[\mathbf{b},S_X]}{\partial b_j}\right)}{\gamma_K[\mathbf{b}, S_X]},$$

that is, that the derivative of the symmetric function with respect to item difficulty b_i can be used in an expression to calculate the conditional score probabilities. The sum in the above Eq. (14.6) runs over all response vectors with the same raw score S_X and with the additional condition that for the item of interest, $x_j = 1$. Most importantly, in the Rasch model the probability of a correct response on item j for raw score group S_X can be calculated without any assumptions about the skill level θ, or its distribution in the population, or about the true score $T_X = E(S_X)$.

14.5 From Rasch Model to CTT

If it can be shown that if the Rasch model holds for a test $\mathbf{X} = (X_1, \ldots, X_K)$, then the classical test theory summary score S_X has 'good' properties, in the sense of that the sum score of this test will provide a satisfactory summary of the data at hand. Hambleton and Jones (1993) pointed out that item response theory (IRT) [and the Rasch model] are strong models, in the sense of that model assumptions made allow derivation of stronger results. As an example, sample independence of parameters and specific objectivity (Rasch 1966) can be derived from these model assumptions, while these cannot be obtained from CTT without making additional assumptions (von Davier 2010, 2016).

14.6 Sufficiency and Total Score

The Rasch model as defined above has some outstanding mathematical features. One of the most salient features is that it turns out that if the Rasch model holds, the total score, $S_X(u)$, is a sufficient statistic for the person parameter, θ_u. In mathematical statistics, a statistic $S = f(X_1, \ldots, X_K)$ is sufficient for a parameter θ if

$$P(X_1, \ldots, X_K | \theta) = P(X_1, \ldots, X_K | S) P(S | \theta)$$

or, equivalently, if

$$\frac{P(X_1, \ldots, X_K | \theta)}{P(S | \theta)} = P(X_1, \ldots, X_K | S).$$

The property of sufficiency can be described as the ability to separate (or eliminate) parameters by conditioning on the sufficient statistics when calculating the unconditional probability of the observed data.

For the Rasch model, the sufficiency of the total score, S_X, allows us to predict the distribution of the response variables, X_i, for all i based on the item parameters, $b_1, \ldots, b_K$. This result means that, if the Rasch model holds, the sum score $S_X(u) = \sum_i X_i$ is all that is needed to summarize the data.

The statistic S_X is the score typically utilized in CTT as the basis for inferences. The fact that this is the sufficient statistics in the Rasch model—a probability model for predicting item responses at the individual level—gives substantial credence to this common choice in CTT. Note that the choice of the unweighted sum score $S_X = \sum x_i$ is, while arguably the simplest form of aggregation, nevertheless a completely arbitrary one (Gigerenzer and Brighton 2009; von Davier 2010). In addition, other IRT models exist that use different assumptions leading to other types of sufficient statistics, not the simple total number correct. As such, there is a clear connection between many, if not the vast majority, of applications of CTT and the Rasch model in that the simple sum score, that is, the total number of correct responses, plays a central role in both approaches.

14.7   Local Independence, True Score, and Error Variance

The assumption of local independence as given in Eq. (14.3) provides a basis for looking at what the expected score for a person u might be. Note that the expected score on a test is what forms the basis of the additive decomposition of observed score, $S_X(u)$, into true score, $T_X(u)$, and error component, $e_X(u)$.

The reasoning is as follows: If the Rasch model holds, we can assume local independence, so that the expected true score can be calculated based on the model equation, summing up the conditional response probabilities across items. That is, we can write

$$E[S_X(u)] = T_X(u) = \sum_{i=1}^{K} P(X_i = 1 | \theta_u) = \sum_{i=1}^{K} p_{ui}$$

for all u. In addition, the error variance of $e_X(u) = S_X(u) - T_X(u)$ can be written as

$$V[e_X(u)] = \sum_{i=1}^{K} p_{ui}(1 - p_{ui})$$

since independence given u holds.

This means that the Rasch model (and more general IRT) will provide direct estimates of the true score and the error variance, if the person parameter, θ_u, is known. This can be used, and is being used, for example in the prediction of expected scores on test forms that have not been taken by a respondent, by means of what is known as 'true score equating'.

14.8   No-DIF

The Rasch model is based on assumptions that apply to all respondents in the population, that is, for all $u \in \Omega$ it provides an expression that relates the probability of success to an item difficulty and a person skill level through

$$p(X_i = x|u) = \frac{\exp(x[\theta_u - b_i])}{1 + \exp(\theta_u - b_i)}.$$

Note that there is no person dependent variable other than θ_u included in the definition of this probability. More specifically, this implies that if the Rasch model holds for all $u \in \Omega$, as given in the expression above, we can conclude that the same probability hold for all levels of θ.

However, there is an even more direct way to show that if the Rasch model holds with items parameters, b_i, for all $i = 1, \ldots k$, we can expect that the MH-test for DIF will turn out such that there is no indication of DIF. More specifically, recall the result that shows how to calculate the conditional probability of a response for a score group. We have obtained

$$P(X_j = 1|S_X) = \sum_{\{(x_1,\ldots,x_k)| \sum x_i = S_x, x_j = 1\}} P(X_1 = x_1, \ldots, X_j = 1, \ldots, X_K = x_K|S_X)$$

(14.7)

for any item j and any raw score S_X if the Rasch model holds. For each grouping variable $G : \Omega \to \{r, f\}$ that separates the population in into members of a focal versus a reference group, we obtain estimates of the relative frequencies

$$\hat{P}(X_j = 1|S_X, f) = \frac{N(X_i = 1 \wedge S_X \wedge f)}{N(S_X \wedge f)}$$

the relative frequency of a success on item j of persons with score S_X in the focus group and

$$\hat{P}(X_j = 1|S_X, r) = \frac{N(X_i = 1 \wedge S_X \wedge r)}{N(S_X \wedge r)}$$

the relative frequency of a success on item j of persons with score S_X in the reference group. It directly follows from the weak law of large numbers that these relative frequencies converge to $P(X_j = 1|S_X)$ if the Rasch model with given parameters holds in Ω. This trivially implies that the odds also converge to the same expected odds

$$\frac{\hat{P}(X_j = 1|S_X, f)}{\hat{P}(X_j = 0|S_X, f)} \rightarrow \frac{P(X_j = 1|S_X)}{P(X_j = 0|S_X)} \leftarrow \frac{\hat{P}(X_j = 1|S_X, r)}{\hat{P}(X_j = 0|S_X, r)}.$$

Finally, this result implies that with growing sample size, all odds ratios in all score groups will converge to the values calculated based on the true parameters and the symmetric functions as given in Eq. (14.7) if the Rasch model holds with item parameters $b_1, \ldots, b_K$ in the population Ω.

Note that there are straightforward extensions that allow for added features to the Rasch model to account for DIF. As an example, for given groups $\{f, r\}$ one could assume that the Rasch model holds, but with different sets of parameters such that

$$P(X_i = 1|\theta, g) = \frac{\exp(\theta - b_{ig})}{1 + \exp(\theta - b_{ig})}$$

in group $g \in \{f, r\}$. This modification allows for group specific item difficulties so that b_{ir} and b_{if} are not necessarily the same (e.g. von Davier and Rost, 1995, 2006, 2016).

However, if the Rasch model holds with the same set of item parameters in all of the whole population, Ω, it follows that there is no DIF for any grouping variable.

14.9 Positive Item Regressions

In CTT, items are typically selected for multiple criteria. Aside from No-DIF and appropriate difficulty level, the main selection criterion is that of assuring positive correlation of the item score variable X_i with the total score S_X. Note that Armitage (1955) and others already aim for a stronger criterion of strict monotonic increasing proportions with increasing score variable (or some other 'natural' ordering of respondents). In the case that the Rasch model can be assumed to hold for a test in some population Ω it is straightforward to show that all item-total correlations are positive.

Recall that the expected item score is given by

$$E(X_i|\theta) = P(X_i = 1|\theta) = \frac{\exp(\theta - b_i)}{1 + \exp(\theta - b_i)}$$

which is strict monotonic increasing in θ. Also, the expected value of the observed score is the true score, which can be calculated as

$$E(S_X|\theta) = T_X(\theta) = \sum_{i=1}^{K} P(X_i = 1|\theta) = \sum_{i=1}^{K} E(X_i|\theta) \tag{14.8}$$

and is also strict monotonic increasing in θ. Finally, the covariance of the item score variable and the total score S_X can be expressed as

$$cov(X_i, S_X) = \int_{\theta} [E(X_i|\theta) - E(X_i)][E(S_X|\theta) - E(S_X)]f(\theta)d\theta$$

which is positive due to the strict monotonicity of $E(X_i|\theta)$ and $E(S_X|\theta)$ and that there exists a θ^* for which $E(S_X|\theta^*) = E(S_X)$ and by means of equation (14.8) and commutativity of finite sums and integration it follows that $E(X_i|\theta^*) = E(X_i)$. Hence, when the Rasch model holds, item-total correlations are positive.

14.10   CTT + Generalized No-DIF + Strict Monotone Item Regression = (Almost) IRT

The previous section has shown that a test designed to follow the Rasch model produces an outcome that has very satisfactory properties when looking at the test from the perspective of CTT. A test constructed by using the Rasch model as a guideline will produce a test in which the simple total score carries all information needed to estimate person skill level, the true score and the error variance can be calculated based on simple item level expected scores, and the test will not have DIF and all item-total correlations are positive.

In this section, the reverse direction is explored. When assembling a test using the basic assumptions of CTT and the customary measures of quality assurance, do we produce an instrument that can be fitted with an IRT model, in particular, the Rasch model?

14.11   CTT Total Score and the Rasch Model

The simple total number of correct responses, also often referred to as the total score

$$S_{\mathbf{X}}(u) = \sum_{i=1}^{K} x_{ui}$$

with binary responses $x_{ui} \in \{0, 1\}$ is compatible with the assumptions made in the Rasch model. It was shown in section that the total score S_X is a sufficient statistic, minimally suffcient statistic, in the Rasch model for the person parameter θ. A more general choice would be

$$W_{\mathbf{X},\mathbf{w}}(u) = \sum_{i=1}^{K} a_i x_{ui}$$

with (typically positive) real-valued weights a_i for $i = 1, \ldots, K$. There is no reason to prefer one over the other just by means of the defnition, indeed, the simple total score is a special case of the weighted score, i.e., $S_X(u) = W_{X,1}(u)$ (von Davier 2010). However, there are legitimate practical reasons to use the unweighted score, in particular if there is little or no information about how to calculate or determine the weights (e.g. Gigerenzer and Brighton 2008; Davis-Stober 2011).

However, there may be good reasons for choosing weights, either based on maximizing the predictive power of a score with respect to some external criterion, or with respect to some unobserved latent variable, or simply in terms of improving the prediction of item scores given the estimate of a person's skill level. It turns out that a number of cases can be identified for which different weighting schemes exhibit a direct correspondence to the sufficient statistic for person ability in an IRT model. Table XYZ gives three prominent examples, the Rasch model (Rasch 1960), the OPLM (Glas and Verhelst 1995) and the 2PL model (Birnbaum 1968).

	Score	Model	$P(X_i = 1|\Theta)$
Simple total score (all weights equal to 1)	$\sum_{i=1}^{K} X_{ui}$	Rasch	$\frac{\exp\cdot(\Theta - b_i)}{1 + \exp\cdot(\Theta - b_i)}$
Pre-specified integer weights ($l_i \in \{0, 1, 2, \ldots\}$)	$\sum_{i=1}^{K} l_i X_{ui}$	OPLM	$\frac{\exp\cdot(l_i\cdot[\Theta - b_i])}{1 + \exp\cdot(l_i\cdot[\Theta - b_i])}$
Single factor model with positive weights ($a_i \in R^+$)	$\sum_{i=1}^{K} a_i X_{ui}$	2PL	$\frac{\exp\cdot(a_i\cdot[\Theta - b_i])}{1 + \exp\cdot(a_i\cdot[\Theta - b_i])}$

The above table provides another indication of how Rasch model and CTT are conceptually and mathematically connected. In both approaches, the simple total score is the central summary of observed response behavior. In the Rasch model this is a consequence of the assumptions made, while in CTT, the simple

(=unweighted) total score is often the central statistic chosen to represent a fallible measure of the true score on a test.

14.12   Absence of DIF—No-DIF 2.0

The no-DIF case when tested will be indicated by a value of the MH-statistic close to 1, see the Sect. 14.3 above. This value represents the odds ratio for the item probabilities in focus and reference group, averaged over total scores. Typically, this average odds-ratio is tested only for a handful of grouping variables such as gender and/or race/ethnicity. However, as pointed out above, the MH-DIF statistic can be calculated for any binary grouping variable.

At this point we need to deviate from the customary checks and propose additional conditions to make the CTT assumptions indeed commensurate with IRT assumptions. Hence, it is being acknowledged that CTT with the usual set of procedures is not based on strong enough assumptions to make the approach equivalent to IRT. However, it should be noted that the assumptions made in addition do not violate customary assumptions or directives for item selection. The absence of MH-DIF is tested by calculating the average over odds ratios, for example, while all that is needed is a slightly stronger assumption that requires the odds ratios in each of the score groups to be 1, that is, instead of the average odds ratio being 1, it is assumed that

$$\frac{P(X_i = 1|S_X, f)}{P(X_i = 0|S_X, f)} \cdot \frac{P(X_i = 0|S_X, r)}{P(X_i = 1|S_X, r)} = 1$$

for all $S_X = 1, \ldots, K - 1$. One may argue that this only provides what was intended when Mantel and Haenzel defined the MH-statistic, namely that across various groupings, the odds ratio is always 1, i.e., that the conditional probabilities in focal and reference group are the same given the conditioning on the total score. This extension, together with the absence of this type of DIF for any other binary grouping variables yields an assumption equivalent to local independence that is common in IRT models. Note that Linacre and Wright (1989) do indeed conjecture that if the same average odds ratio is to be expected in all types of groupings (intervals of total scores or similar) then each of the odds ratios should be in expectation the same. Here we take a slightly different approach and state this as an explicit assumption leading to a stricter criterion for item selection.

More specifically, the response to another item on the test, or an additional item that is not part of the test could also be used to group respondents. Let us assume for items $i \neq j \in \{1, \ldots, K\}$

$$\frac{P(X_i = 1|S_X, X_j = 1)}{P(X_i = 0|S_X, X_j = 1)} = \frac{P(X_i = 1|S_X, X_j = 0)}{P(X_i = 0|S_X, X_j = 0)}$$

so that respondents who solve item j, i.e., $X_j = 1$, are being treated as the focus group and $X_j = 0$ is equivalent to the reference group. Using the definition of conditional probabilities we have

$$P(X_i = 1|S_X, X_j = 1) = \frac{P(X_i = 1 \wedge S_X \wedge X_j = 1)}{P(S_X \wedge X_j = 1)} = \frac{P(X_i = 1 \wedge X_j = 1|S_X)}{P(X_j = 1|S_X,)}$$

so that

$$\frac{P(X_i = 1 \wedge X_j = 1|S_X)}{P(X_i = 0 \wedge X_j = 1|S_X)} \frac{P(X_i = 0 \wedge X_j = 0|S_X)}{P(X_i = 1 \wedge X_j = 0|S_X)} = 1$$

which equivalent to X_i, X_j being independent given S_X. This means that the stronger MH condition applied to one item response variable X_i and another item variable X_j viewed as the grouping variable yields local independence, conditional on the total score. Hence we can write

$$P(X_1 = x_1, \ldots, X_K = x_K|S_x) = \prod_{i=1}^{K} P(X_i = x_i|S_X)$$

as the pairwise local independence extends to the full response pattern probability by the same argument.

14.13 Item-Total Regression 2.0

The previous sections showed how a slightly stronger MH criterion applied to focal and reference groups defined by responses to another item yields local independence given total score. A similar approach will be taken in this section with the goal to extend and strengthen the positive item-total regression criterion. More specifically, recall that the positivity of the covariance of item score and total score can be studied by looking at the cross product of conditional response probability and total score, namely

$$cov(X_i, S_X) = E(P(X_i|S_X) \cdot S_X) - E(X_i)E(S_X)$$

with

$$E(P(X_i|S_X) \cdot S_X) = E(S_X|X_i = 1) \cdot E(X_i).$$

These equivalencies illustrate that higher conditional item response probabilities associated with higher total scores yield a more positive item-total covariance. The criterion of positive item-total covariance can hence be strengthened by assuming conditional item response probabilities to increase strictly with total scores. That is, the strong(er) version of a positive item-total regression requires

$$P(X_i = 1|s) > P(X_i = 1|t)$$

for all total scores $s > t \in \{0, \ldots, K\}$. This condition implies that

$$P(X_i = 1|S_x = 0) < P(X_i = 1|S_x = 1) < P(X_i = 1|S_x = 2)$$
$$< \cdots < P(X_i = 1|S_x = K).$$

Note that the 'spirit' of the positive item-total correlation was not abandoned but strengthened: All items that meet the slightly stronger assumption will also meet the weaker assumption that the item-total correlation is positive.

14.14   An Approximate IRT Model Based on Strengthened CTT Assumptions

The above sections introduced the total score S_X as the basic unit of analyses in CTT and showed that the same quantity is the minimal sufficient statistic for the person ability parameter in the Rasch model. In addition, two slightly strengthened CTT requirements were introduced. One that extends the MH approach of no-DIF requirement to additionally requiring all total score based odds ratios to be equal to 1. Finally, the positive item-total regression requirement was strengthened to the criterion that conditional item success probabilities are required to be strictly increasing with the total score.

These assumptions, and often even the weaker original assumptions with regard to item selection in CTT constructed tests commonly lead to a set of items that, when using the sum score or some other proxy to the true score or underlying ability, align in very systematic ways along the construct we want to measure. An early example can be found in Thurstone (1925) who plotted the relative frequency of success on a number of tasks used in developmental research against the age of respondents in calendar years. Figure 14.1 presents this association. Other examples can be found in Lord (1980) illustrating item-sumscore regressions.

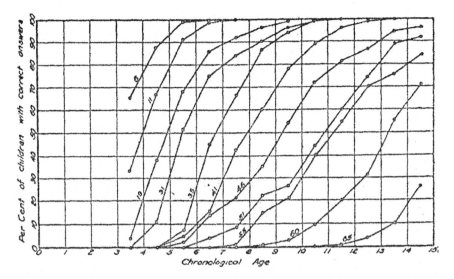

Fig. 14.1 Thurstone's (1925) illustration of item regressions, the relative frequencies of success are depicted as a function of age in calendar years

Given the obvious resemblance of the strictly monotonic item regressions in Fig. 14.1 and the item characteristic curves defined by the Rasch model or more general IRT models, the following approach is proposed: With the assumption that the strengthened versions of the customary CTT item selection requirements are met for $i = 1, \ldots K$ items X_i, define

$$\delta_{i,s} = \log\left[\frac{P(X_i = 1|s)}{P(X_i = 0|s)}\right]$$

for all $s \in \{1, \ldots, K-1\}$ and note that

$$P(X_i = x|s) = \frac{\exp(x \cdot \delta_{i,s})}{1 + \exp(\delta_{i,s})}.$$

Note that Hessen (2005) defined constant log odds ratio (CLOR) models, and also studies the obvious relation of these to the MH procedure. In the in the context of the quantities defined above, CLOR models would be based on $\omega_{ij}(s) = \frac{\delta_{i,s}}{\delta_{j,s}}$ and an assumption is made that these log odds ratios are constant for all ability levels (here: total scores), which specifies that

$$\omega_{ij} = \frac{\delta_{i,s}}{\delta_{j,s}}$$

is a constant for all score groups. It turns out that this is a rather strong assumption, and CLOR models can be shown to be special cases of Rasch models with a (potentially) constrained ability range (Maris 2008). In our context, we will not use the above assumption but build up the argument from the assumed positive item total correlation, or its somewhat strengthened version, the monotonicity of conditional P+ in score groups. While the strengthened assumption is not logically implied by its weaker form (if it was, it would be redundant), it appears that it is often implicitly assumed when studying proportions in levels of a 'natural ordering' of respondents (Armitage 1955).

To continue the line of argumentation, there is the obvious requirement that all probabilities are non-vanishing, so that the δ are well defined. If the strengthened CTT assumption of strict monotonicity of proportions in score groups holds for the data at hand, we have

$$\delta_{i,1} < \delta_{i,2} < \delta_{i,3} < \cdots < \delta_{i,K-1}$$

for all items $i = 1, \ldots, K$. Next we define item-wise and score-wise effects as well as the grand mean of the δ. Let

$$\mu = \frac{1}{K(K-1)} \sum_{i=1}^{K} \sum_{s=1}^{K-1} \delta_{i,s}$$

and let

$$\beta_i = \mu - \frac{1}{K-1} \sum_{s=1}^{K-1} \delta_{i,s}$$

and finally

$$\tau_s = \frac{1}{K} \sum_{i=1}^{K} \delta_{i,s}.$$

by definition we have $\sum_i \beta_i = 0$. Then we can define

$$\hat{\delta}_{i,s} = \tau_s - \beta_i.$$

These $\hat{\delta}$ parameters can be used as approximation to the δ parameters. We can define a probability model by means of

$$\hat{P}(X_i = 1|s) = \frac{\exp(\tau_s - \beta_i)}{1 + \exp(\tau_s - \beta_i)}.$$

The similarity of this model to the Rasch model is evident, and relationships to log-linear Rasch models (e.g. Kelderman 1984, 2006) are obvious. However, there is need to assess how well this approximation works, since strict monotonicity in S and main effects in i are not necessarily assurance enough that the $\hat{\delta} = \tau - \beta$ are close to the δ. Alternatively, one could look at this as an optimization problem and miminize the difference

$$\sum_{i=1}^{K}\sum_{s=1}^{K-1}\left(\delta_{i,s} - [\alpha_i\tau_s - \beta_i]\right)^2.$$

In this case, the derived IRT like model turns out to be

$$\hat{P}(X_i = 1|s) = \frac{\exp(\alpha_i\tau_s - \beta_i)}{1 + \exp(\alpha_i\tau_s - \beta_i)}$$

and similarities to the 2PL IRT model can be observed.

With the implied conditional independence in score groups these yield a model for the full item response vectors. The strict monotonicity of the $\delta_{i,s}$ in s provides support for the use of a simple linear approximation rather than one that utilizes higher order moments of s or τ_s. However, more complex models such as

$$\delta_{i,s} = \sum_{m=0}^{M}\gamma_{i,m}s^m + e$$

can be considered. Given the strict monotonicity and restricted range of item total regressions, however, a linear approximation can be expected to perform well. Note that these models make use of the consequences of assumptions that are slightly stronger than those commonly made in CTT and arrive at models that look a lot like IRT.

14.15   Conclusions

This paper presents an (or yet another) attempt to relate the practices and customary procedures of classical test theory to the assumptions made in the Rasch model and IRT. While Wright and Linacre (1989) and Holland and Hoskens (2003), Bechger et al. (2003), as well as most recently Paek and Wilson (2011) all tackle slightly different angles of this issue, it appears that all parties attempting these types of endeavors agree on some basic similarities. CTT assumes the observed (typically unweighted) sum-score of (often binary) test items as the foundation of all analyses. Note however, that this choice of the aggregate is not 'natural' or 'best' by any means, but that different choices are possible and common in factor analysis as well as in IRT (McDonald 1999; Moustaki and Knott 2000; von Davier 2010). The basis of the sum score S_X as the person measure is extended by showing that the likelihood of solving an item, given this score, is unchanged in different groups under the stricter MH-no-DIF criterion. This yields local independence, a fundamental assumption made in many IRT models. Finally a slightly more rigorous requirement of strict monotone item-total regression yields strictly monotone log-odds, which are finally used to approximate the conditional response probabilities used in MH-DIF and item regressions by IRT type models.

The other direction, deriving 'good' CTT properties based on the Rasch model is much more straightforward. The Rasch model (and other unidimensional IRT models) make sufficiently rigorous assumptions that allow to derive satisfactory adherence to summary statistics used in CTT (unweighted total, or integer weighted, or real valued weighed sum score) as well as the requirement of no-DIF, and finally positive item-total correlations, if the items selected for a test follow these models. DIF can be incorporated in IRT models in a variety of ways, from multiple group IRT models (Bock and Zimowski 1997) with partial invariance (Glas and Verhelst 1995; Yamamoto 1998; Oliveri and von Davier 2014) to models that explicitly examine what split of the sample exhibits direct evidence of item by group interactions (e.g. von Davier and Rost 1995, 2006, 2016).

References

Armitage, P. (1955). Tests for linear trends in proportions and frequencies. *Biometrics (International Biometric Society), 11*(3), 375–386. doi:10.2307/3001775. JSTOR 3001775.

Bechger, T. M., Maris, G., Verstralen, H. H. F. M., & Beguin, A. A. (2003). Using classical test theory in combination with item response theory. *Applied Psychological Measurement, 27*(5), 319–334.

Birnbaum, A. (1968). Some latent trait models and their use in inferring an examinee's ability. In F. M. Lord and M. R. Novick (Eds.), *Statistical theories of mental test scores* (pp. 397–479). Reading, Mass: Addison-Wesley.

Bock, R. D., & Zimowski, M. F. (1997). Multiple group IRT. In W. J. van der Linden & R. K. Hambleton (Eds.), *Handbook of modern item response theory* (pp. 433–448). New York, NY: Springer.

Cochran, W. G. (1954). Some methods for strengthening the common χ^2 tests. *Biometrics, 10*, 417–451.

Davis-Stober, C. P. (2011). A geometric analysis of when fixed weighting schemes will outperform ordinary least squares. *Psychometrika, 76*, 650–669.

Dorans, N. (2013). *Test fairness*. Princeton, NJ (ETS RR-xx-13).

Fisher, R. A. (1922). On the mathematical foundations of theoretical statistics. *Philosophical Transactions of the Royal Society A, 222*, 309368. doi:10.1098/rsta.1922.0009 (JFM 48.1280. 02. JSTOR 91208).

Gigerenzer, G., & Brighton, H. (2009). Homo heuristicus: Why biased minds make better inferences. *Topics in Cognitive Science, 1*(1), 107–143. doi:10.1111/j.1756-8765.2008.01006.x

Glas, C. A. W., & Verhelst, N. D. (1995). Testing the Rasch model. In G. H. Fischer & I. W. Molenaar (Eds.), *Rasch models: Foundations, recent developments, and applications* (pp. 69–95). New York, NY: Springer.

Gustafsson, J.-E. (1980). A solution of the conditional estimation problem for long test in the Rasch model for dichotomous items. *Educational and Psychological Measurement, 40*(2), 377–385 (T270201 R).

Hambleton, R. K., & Jones, R. W. (1993). Comparison of classical test theory and item response theory and their applications to test development. *Educational Measurement: Issues and Practice, 12*(3), 3847.

Hessen, D. J. (2005). Constant latent odds-ratios models and the Mantel-Haenszel null hypothesis. *Psychometrika, 70*(3), 497–516.

Holland, P. W., & Hoskens, M. (2003, March). Classical test theory as a first-order Item response theory: Application to true-score prediction from a possibly nonparallel test. *Psychometrika, 68* (1), 123–149.

Holland, P. W., & Thayer, D. T. (1986). *Differential item performance and the Mantel-Haenszel procedure*. Technical Report No. 86 69. Princeton, NJ: Educational Testing Service.

Kelderman, H. (1984) Loglinear Rasch model tests. *Psychometrika, 49*(2), 223–245.

Kelderman, H. (2006). Loglinear multivariate and mixture Rasch models. In M. von Davier & C. H. Carstensen (Eds.), *Multivariate and mixture distribution Rasch models*. Springer: New York.

Linacre J. M., & Wright B. D. (1989). Mantel-Haenszel DIF and PROX are Equivalent! *Rasch Measurement Transactions, 3*(2), 52–53.

Lord, F. M. (1980). *Applications of item response theory to practical testing problems*. Hillsdale, NJ: Erlbaum.

Lord, F. M., & Novick, M. R. (1968). *Statistical theories of mental test scores*. Reading, MA: Addison-Wesley.

Mantel, N., & Haenszel, W. (1959). Statistical aspects of the analysis of data from retrospective studies of disease. *Journal of the National Cancer Institute 22*(4), 719748. doi:10.1093/jnci/22. 4.719

Maris, G. (2008). A note on "constant latent odds-ratios models and the Mantel-Haenszel null hypothesis". *Psychometrika, 73*(1), 153–157.

McDonald, R. P. (1999). *Test theory: A unified treatment*. Mahwah, NJ: Lawrence Erlbaum Associates, Inc.

Moustaki, I., & Knott, M. (2000). Generalized latent trait models. *Psychometrika, 65*(3), 391–411.

Oliveri, M. E., & von Davier, M. (2014). Toward increasing fairness in score scale calibrations employed in international large-scale assessments. *International Journal of Testing, 14*(1), 1–21. doi:10.1080/15305058.2013.825265

Paek, I., & Wilson, M. (2011). Formulating the Rasch differential item functioning model under the marginal maximum likelihood estimation context and its comparison With MantelHaenszel procedure in short test and small sample conditions. *Educational and Psychological Measurement, 71*(6), 1023–1046.

Rabe-Hesketh, S., Skrondal, A., & Pickles, A. (2004). Generalized multilevel structural equation modelling. *Psychometrika ,69*, 167–190.

Rasch, G. (1960). *Probabilistic models for some intelligence and attainment tests*. Danish Institute for Educational Research: Copenhagen.

Rasch, G. (1966). An individualistic approach to item analysis. In P. F. Lazarsfeld & N. W. Henry (Eds.), *Readings in mathematical social science* (pp. 89–107).

Raykov & Marcoulides. (2016). One the relationship between classical test theory and item response theory: From one to the other and back. *Educational and Psychological Measurement, 76*, 325–338.

Takane, Y., & De Leeuw, J. (1987). On the relationship between item response theory and factor analysis of discretized variables. *Psychometrika, 52*(3), 393-408.

Thurstone, L. L. (1925). A method of scaling psychological and educational tests. *Journal of Educational Psychology, 16*, 433–451.

Thurstone, L. L. (1931). *The reliability and validity of tests: Derivation and interpretation of fundamental formulae concerned with reliability and validity of tests and illustrative problems* (113 p). Ann Arbor, MI, US: Edwards Brothers. doi:10.1037/11418-000.

van den Wollenberg, A. L. (1982). Two new test statistics for the Rasch model. *Psychometrika, 47*, 123–139.

Verhelst, N. (2001). Testing the unidimensionality assumption of the Rasch model. *Methods of Psychological Research Online, 6*(3), 231–271. Retrieved from http://www.dgps.de/fachgruppen/methoden/mpr-online/issue15/art2/verhelst.pdf

von Davier, M. (2005). *A general diagnostic model applied to language testing data*. Research Report RR-05-16. ETS: Princeton, NJ.

von Davier, M. (2008, November). A general diagnostic model applied to language testing data. *British Journal of Mathematical and Statistical Psychology, 61*(2), 287–307.

von Davier, M. (2010). Why sum scores may not tell us all about test takers. In L. Wang (Ed.), Special issue on Quantitative Research Methodology. *Newborn and Infant Nursing Reviews, 10*(1), 27–36.

von Davier, M. (2013). The DINA model as a constrained general diagnostic model—Two variants of a model equivalency. *BJMSP, 67*, 4971. doi:10.1111/bmsp.12003/abstract

von Davier, M. (2014). The log-linear cognitive diagnostic model (LCDM) as a special case of the general diagnostic model (GDM). *ETS Research Report Series*. doi:10.1002/ets2.12043/abstract

von Davier, M. (2016). The Rasch model (Chapter 3). In W. van der Linden (Ed.), *Handbook of item response theory* (Vol. 1, 2nd ed.). Berlin: Springer.

von Davier, M., Naemi, B., & Roberts, R. D. (2012). Factorial versus typological models: A comparison of methods for personality data. *Measurement: Interdisciplinary Research and Perspectives, 10*(4), 185–208.

von Davier, M., & Rost, J. (1995). Polytomous mixed Rasch models. In G. H. Fischer & I. W. Molenaar (Eds.), *Rasch models—Foundations, recent developments and applications* (pp. 371–379). New York: Springer.

von Davier, M., & Rost, J. (2006). Mixture distribution item response models. In C. R. Rao & S. Sinharay (Eds.), *Handbook of statistics* (Vol. 26). Psychometrics. Amsterdam: Elsevier.

von Davier, M., & Rost, J. (2016). Logistic mixture-distribution response models (Chapter 23). In W. van der Linden (Ed.), *Handbook of Item response theory* (Vol. 1, 2nd ed.). Berlin: Springer.

Wainer, H. (1988). *The future of item analysis*. Princeton, NJ: ETS (ETS Research Report No. RR-88-50).

Yamamoto, K. (1998). Scaling and scale linking. In T. S. Murray, I. S. Kirsch, & L. B. Jenkins (Eds.), *Adult literacy in OECD countries: Technical report on the first international adult literacy survey* (pp. 161–178). Washington, DC: National Center for Education Statistics.

Chapter 15
Balance: A Neglected Aspect of Reporting Test Results

Norman D. Verhelst

Abstract An aspect that is often neglected in the reporting of test results is the question of balance: are the results of an individual, small group, or large group, for different meaningful parts of the test, in good balance with each other? This question can be answered in a way which is in a sense orthogonal to the level of performance on the whole test, and which is very flexible as it accepts data collected in an incomplete design and analyzed with an arbitrary unidimensional item response theory (IRT) model. Two such analyses have been published using large groups: the participating countries in the PISA 2000 and 2003 cycles (Verhelst 2012; Yıldırım et al. 2014). The method of analysis considers deviations from the expected profile, i.e. partial scores on a few categories of items, given the results of a unidimensional analysis of the test data of the whole group. For large groups, average deviations are normally distributed, but for small groups like classes or schools, using the central limit theorem might be too optimistic. In this chapter, exact statistical tests are derived. The method will be illustrated using the TIMSS 2011 data for Sweden.

15.1 Introduction

An important characteristic of many large-scale assessments of educational achievement, international or national, is the use of item response theory (IRT), and in particular the use of unidimensional models. In PISA studies (at least in the first five cycles) the Rasch model has been used, while in IEA studies like TIMSS and PIRLS a mixture of the generalized partial credit model (for open ended questions) and the three-parameter logistic model (3PLM, for multiple choice questions) is used. In order to construct league tables—considered by most of the press and government representatives and their political adversaries to be the core business of large-scale surveys—one has to assume that all items (retained after the pilot)

N.D. Verhelst (✉)
Eurometrics, Tiel, The Netherlands
e-mail: norman.verhelst@gmail.com

© Springer International Publishing AG 2017
M. Rosén et al. (eds.), *Cognitive Abilities and Educational Outcomes*,
Methodology of Educational Measurement and Assessment,
DOI 10.1007/978-3-319-43473-5_15

Table 15.1 Frequencies of categories of mathematical items in TIMSS 2011

Content domain		Cognitive domain		Item type	
Category	Frequency	Category	Frequency	Category	Frequency
Algebra	69	Applying	84	CR	97
Data and chance	43	Knowing	79	MC	118
Geometry	42	Reasoning	52		
Number	61				

measure the same latent variable in the same way across all participating students, independently of the language in which the items have been translated and independent of gross cultural and linguistic differences between participating groups.[1]

An undeniable advantage of IRT is the possibility of meaningful comparisons of test performances from non-identical test forms, as in most large-scale assessments incomplete designs are used. As an example, in TIMSS 2011 for Grade 8, 14 different test forms have been used for a total of 215 mathematics items, each test form containing between 26 and 34 items.[2] This flexibility of IRT allows a greater control over different aspects of the items used. In TIMSS 2011 for example the total item pool for mathematics covered four categories of content (algebra, data and chance, geometry, and number), three categories of cognitive operations required by the items (applying, knowing, reasoning) and two item types (constructed response, CR, or multiple choice, MC). In Table 15.1, the marginal frequencies of each of these categories are given.

But the heterogeneity of the tested population together with the multifaceted design of the test items make it difficult to accept that a simple unidimensional IRT model is capable of explaining all of the systematic variance in the test data. This problem may be approached in several ways. One can regret that such a simple model is not sufficient, and look for alternatives; one can try to "prove" that the simple model is not valid and that the league tables (for example) are affected by the non-validity of the model. In TIMSS as well as in PISA, more detailed models are used, but they all are the application of the same model to a sub-set of the items. For example in TIMSS 2011, an analysis is done per category of the cognitive domain, while the three categories are thought of as representing three—intercorrelated—latent variables. Much the same approach is taken in the PISA project. A typical example of challenging the model is given by Kreiner and Christensen (2013) who put in a lot of effort to "prove" that the Rasch model is not "valid" for the "reading" items of the PISA 2006 "reading" data. I think this question of validity versus

---

[1] As we will refer mainly to results of TIMSS and PISA, the participating groups we have in mind are participating countries.

[2] All participants in TIMSS 2011 consider mathematics and science. In this chapter we will report results only for mathematics.

non-validity is a bit trivial, and that the answer Kreiner and Christensen come up with is not constructive at all.

The position taken in this chapter is meant to be constructive: can one learn something from the imperfect fit of the IRT model used which can be useful to the participating groups in a large survey? Concretely, can one say something new and useful when comparing large groups of participants, like countries in TIMSS, or when comparing small groups, like schools or classes?

15.2 Profile Analysis

15.2.1 Basic Idea and Definitions

Let the items of a test (or a test form) be partitioned into a number m (>1) of mutually exclusive categories and assume further that the test score is just the sum of the item scores. One can then compute the score for each item category. Let S represent the test score and let S_j be the score[3] on the set of items that define category j.

The m-tuple $(S_1, \ldots, S_m)$ is called the *observed profile*. Notice that $\sum S_j = S$. For each random variable S_j, the *conditional* expected value $E_s(S_j) \triangleq E(S_j|S = s)$ can be determined, and the m-tuple $(E_s(S_1), \ldots, E_s(S_m))$ is called the *expected profile*. It is immediately clear that $\sum_j E_s(S_j) = s$. The *deviation profile* is defined as the difference between the observed and the expected profile:

$$(D_1, \ldots, D_m) = (S_1, \ldots, S_m) - (E_s(S_1), \ldots, E_s(S_m)), \qquad (15.1)$$

and since the observed and expected profile have the same sum of their components, it follows that $\sum_j D_j = 0$.

Profile analysis exists for a long time (e.g. Greenhouse and Geisser 1959) and refers always to the study of differences between the vectors of the average performances of several groups. Ding (2001) gives an example by plotting the means of men and women on the six sub-scales of the Strong Interest Inventory, not only showing differences in level (women obtaining a larger grand mean than men) but also in pattern (the two lines of the graph are not parallel). If one would follow this tradition, one would concentrate on the *observed profiles*, and all comparisons between groups would inevitably compare levels of performance, just as most of the reports of international surveys concentrate on this aspect of the data. In the area

---

[3]Capital letters are used to designate a random variable and lowercase letters indicate a value of the random variable.

Table 15.2 An example of an observed, an expected, and a deviation profile

	Category A	Category B	Sum
Observed profile	4	2	6
Expected profile	4.406	1.594	6
Deviation profile	−0.406	+0.406	0

of achievement testing, Haberman et al. (2006) have written a critical report on communicating sub-scores (i.e. observed profiles) at the institutional level.

Profile analysis in the present chapter, however, is the study of *deviation profiles,* and it focuses on aspects of the data that are by necessity neglected in psychometrically orthodox approaches to IRT. We illustrate this with a small example with two categories of items (A and B, see Table 15.2).

The interpretation of the values in the deviation profile is clear: it is a comparison (a difference) between what is observed and what is expected under the measurement model used. In the example of Table 15.2, the respondent performs worse than expected on items of category A, and better than expected on items of category B.[4]

From the deviation profile one *cannot* derive:

- the test score;
- the number of items in the test;
- whether there are more or less category A items in the test than category B items; or
- whether category A items are on average easier or more difficult than category B items.

The fact that the deviation profile hides so many things is not a weakness, but represents its strength. It does not tell anything about the level of performance, but only expresses the extent to which the observed profile differs from its expectation (under the measurement model used). Small deviations point to a balanced profile, while large ones show some imbalance.

Deviation profiles can be aggregated, for example,[5] by computing their average in a given group of respondents, even when participants did not answer the same set of items. The meaningfulness of such an aggregation depends on the meaningfulness of the categories. Suppose one wants to build profiles with the categorization "item type" (with categories CR and MC), the fact that not all respondents answer to the same set of items does not matter as long as the categories mean the same thing for all items involved. If one has doubt in this, and one has a hypothesis that

---

[4]The way expected profiles are determined is explained later in the chapter.

[5]Other ways of aggregating are possible. Verhelst (2012) discusses an aggregation based on counting types of profiles.

the MC questions belong to two different categories, then one can always run a profile analysis with the items partitioned into three categories rather than two.

A profile analysis is run under the assumption that the model parameters are known. In a large survey, like TIMSS or PISA, this is not a big problem as far as the item parameters are concerned, since the sample sizes are usually huge and the standard errors of the item parameters are negligible, so the estimates of the parameters can be substituted for the real parameters. However, item knowledge of the item parameters is not always sufficient in order to run a profile analysis. The problem will be discussed later in the chapter.

To run and interpret a profile analysis, two problems have to be solved. One is algebraic—the computation of the conditional expected scores $E_s(S_j)$; the other is statistical—can a statistical criterion be developed to evaluate the seriousness of the deviation between observed and expected profiles. These two problems are discussed in the next two sub-sections.

15.2.2 The Conditionally Expected Scores $E_s(S_j)$

The intuitive meaning of a score (in a test) is the number of "points" a test taker has earned, and often it just means the number of correct answers, corresponding to one point per correct response. In a more technical meaning, the score stands for a sufficient statistic for the latent variable. In the Rasch model, this coincides with the popular meaning of number correct. In the two-parameter logistic model (2PLM) the score in this technical sense is a weighted score, the weights being the discrimination parameters associated with the items. In the three-parameter logistic model (3PLM) a score in this sense does not exist because this model is not a member of the exponential family.

15.2.2.1 The Rasch Model

We start with a brief technical exposé on how the expected scores are computed in the Rasch model. The basic equation of the Rasch model is:

$$P(X_i = 1|\theta) = \frac{\exp(\theta - \beta_i)}{1 + \exp(\theta - \beta_i)} = \frac{\xi \varepsilon_i}{1 + \xi \varepsilon_i} \tag{15.2}$$

where θ represents the latent variable, β_i is the difficulty parameter of item i, and X_i is the response variable for item i, taking the value 1 for a correct and 0 for an incorrect response. The fraction most to the right in Eq. (15.2) expresses the same quantity as the middle fraction, using the one–one transformations:

$$\xi = \exp(\theta) \quad \text{and} \quad \varepsilon_i = \exp(-\beta_i)$$

Rasch (1960) discovered that the conditional distribution of the response patterns given the score is independent of the latent variable θ:

$$P(x_1, \ldots, x_k | S = s) = \frac{\prod \varepsilon_i^{x_i}}{\gamma_s(\varepsilon_1, \ldots, \varepsilon_k)} \tag{15.3}$$

where $\gamma_s(.)$ is a combinatorial function, called the basic symmetric function; s in sub-script is called the order of the function; and the (multivariate) argument of the function (as used in Eq. 15.3) are the ε-parameters of the items. The $\gamma_s(.)$ functions are defined as:

$$\gamma_s(\varepsilon_1, \ldots, \varepsilon_k) = \sum_* \prod_{i=1}^{k} \varepsilon_i^{x_i} \tag{15.4}$$

where it holds that for all i, $x_i \in \{0, 1\}$ and the '*' under the summation sign means that the sum is to be taken over all response patterns for which $\sum x_i = s$. Note that the number of terms in the summation equals $\binom{k}{s}$ and each term is the product of s ε-parameters. Note that $\gamma_0(.) = 1$ for all possible arguments, and, for convenience, we define that $\gamma_s(.) = 0$, whenever $s < 0$ or $s > k$.

The function does not change value if the arguments are permuted, hence the indication "symmetric". To write this in a shorthand notation we define the set E as $E = \{\varepsilon_1, \ldots, \varepsilon_k\}$ whence we can write $\gamma_s(E)$ instead of $\gamma_s(\varepsilon_1, \ldots, \varepsilon_k)$.[6]

Now suppose the items of a test are partitioned into m classes, and according to this partition we form the m sub-sets E_1 to E_m of item parameters, such that for any two sub-sets E_i and E_j, it holds that $E_i \cap E_j = \emptyset$ and $\cup_j E_j = E$. Then, the probability of a response pattern with sub-score vector $(s_1, \ldots, s_m)$ given a total score of $s = \Sigma s_j$ is given by:

$$P(s_1, \ldots, s_m | s) = \frac{\prod_j \gamma_{s_j}(E_j)}{\gamma_s(E)}. \tag{15.5}$$

To find the conditional expected value for a sub-score on category j, it suffices to consider the sub-set E_j and its complement $\bar{E}_j$, and using Eq. (15.5) we find:

$$E_s(S_j) = \frac{\sum_{i=0}^{k_j} i\gamma_i(E_j)\gamma_{s-i}(\bar{E}_j)}{\gamma_s(E)}, \tag{15.6}$$

---

[6]This notation can lead to some ambiguity if two or more parameters have the same value. In such a case we treat them as distinct elements of the set E.

with k_j being the number of items in E_j.

It may be instructive to have a closer look at a special case. Notice that from the definition of the basic symmetric functions (Eq. 15.4), it follows immediately that for any number c:

$$\gamma_s(c\varepsilon_1, \ldots, c\varepsilon_k) = c^s \gamma_s(\varepsilon_1, \ldots, \varepsilon_k).$$

Hence, it follows that Eq. (15.6) does not change value if all ε-parameters are multiplied by the same non-zero constant. Now, consider the case where all items are equally difficult. Without loss of generality we can set, for all i, that $\varepsilon_i = 1$, and it follows that each term in the expansion of $\gamma_s(\varepsilon_1, \ldots, \varepsilon_k)$ equals 1, and the function value itself equals the binomial coefficient $\binom{k}{s}$. The probability mass function P $(s_1, \ldots, s_m|s)$ simplifies to:

$$P(s_1, \ldots, s_m|s) = \frac{\prod_{j=1}^{m} \binom{k_j}{s_j}}{\binom{k}{s}},$$

i.e. the simple multivariate hypergeometric distribution.

15.2.2.2   The 2PLM

When the item parameters are (treated as) known, the 2PLM is an exponential family with respect to the latent variable θ, and the sufficient statistic is the weighted score W defined as:

$$W = \sum_i a_i X_i$$

where a_i is the discrimination parameter of item i. But $a_i \in \mathbb{R}^+$, i.e. it can take any positive value, with the consequence that in general[7] there will be a one–one correspondence between the response pattern and the sufficient statistic W. This implies that for any of the 2^k different response patterns and their associated value of weighted score, there can be only one observed profile $(W_1, \ldots, W_m)$, so that the observed and expected profile are equal and the deviation profile is trivially zero, and of no practical use.

A way out of this problem is to use a restricted version of the 2PLM, where the space of the sufficient statistics is much smaller than the sample space (2^k). For

---

[7]This does not mean that there are no cases possible where several different response patterns lead to the same weighted score, but that they will occur rarely in practice, representing practical insignificance.

example, by restricting the discrimination parameters to positive integers, a flexible model that allows for different discriminations, and at the same time a restricted number of different weighted scores, is created. Suppose there are $k = 12$ items, four having a discrimination equal to 1, four with a value of 2, and four with a value of 3. Then there are $2^{12} = 4096$ different response patterns, but the possible weighted scores are 0, 1, 2, ..., 24 where only 0 and 24 are trivial in the sense that there is a unique pattern that generates them. This model has been studied by Verhelst and Glas (1995) under the name "one-parameter logistic model" (OPLM),[8] where the meaning and the methods of computing of the $\gamma(.)$ functions in this model are also explained in detail.

15.2.2.3   The 3PLM

In this model there is no sufficient statistic for the latent variable, and the expression "computing the conditionally expected sub-scores (given the test score)" has no meaning if one does not explicitly state what one means by "test score". For the purpose of this chapter we will adopt the wide-spread convention of a score as number correct.

Suppose the 3PLM is valid for a test taker v with latent value θ_v, then we can write:

$$P_{vi} \triangleq P(X_{vi} = 1|\theta_v) = c_i + (1 - c_i)\frac{\exp[a_i(\theta_v - \beta_i)]}{1 + \exp[a_i(\theta_v - \beta_i)]}. \qquad (15.7)$$

As in profile analysis the item parameters are supposed to have known values, we can also write:

$$P(X_{vi} = 1|\theta_v) = \frac{\varepsilon_{vi}}{1 + \varepsilon_{vi}}. \qquad (15.8)$$

Equating (15.7) and (15.8), and solving for ε_{vi}, one finds:

$$\varepsilon_{vi} = \frac{P_{vi}}{1 - P_{vi}} = \frac{c_i + \exp[a_i(\theta_v - \beta_i)]}{1 - c_i} \qquad (15.9)$$

This is clearly a function of the item parameters and the latent variable. To indicate the dependency on the latent variable we will use the notation $\varepsilon_i(\theta)$ when the reference to a specific person is not needed. Using the simple structure of (Eq. 15.8) we find that:

---

[8]In this model conditional maximum likelihood estimates of the difficulty parameters are possible. The software is available from the Dutch National Institute of Educational Measurement (CITO). An extended manual is Verhelst et al. (1994). To obtain the software use: http://www.cito.com/ research_and_development/psychometrics/psychometric_software.

$$P(x_1,\ldots,x_k|S = s, \theta) = \frac{\prod [\varepsilon_i(\theta)]^{x_i}}{\gamma_s[\varepsilon_1(\theta),\ldots,\varepsilon_k(\theta)]}, \tag{15.10}$$

and indicating the dependency on θ of any set E of parameters by the notation $E(\theta)$, we find analogously to (Eq. 15.5) that:

$$P(s_1,\ldots,s_m|s, \theta) = \frac{\prod_j \gamma_{s_j}[E_j(\theta)]}{\gamma_s[E(\theta)]}. \tag{15.11}$$

To carry out a profile analysis as originally projected, i.e. using only sub-set averages conditional on the total score (and as we will see later in the chapter, also the whole conditional distribution of the sub-set scores) we would need to compute for all possible observed profiles:

$$P(s_1,\ldots,s_m|s) = \int \frac{\prod_j \gamma_{s_j}[E_j(\theta)]}{\gamma_s[E(\theta)]} g(\theta)\mathrm{d}\theta \tag{15.12}$$

where $g(\theta)$ is the p.d.f. of θ. Most commonly, the distribution of θ is assumed to be the normal one. The evaluation of Eq. (15.11) therefore is time consuming, as an explicit solution of the integral does not exist and numerical approximations—e.g. Gauss–Hermite quadrature—must be used.[9] Therefore, the computations carried out for the sake of this chapter have been based on the use of Eq. (15.11) where the value of θ has been substituted by its weighted maximum likelihood estimate (Warm 1989). The same approach has been followed for items that follow the 2PLM, as Eq. (15.9) applies with $c_i = 0$.

15.2.2.4 The (Generalized) Partial Credit Model

A model suited for polytomous items is the partial credit model (PCM, Masters 1982) and its generalization (GPCM, Muraki 1992). For items allowing a score of 0, 1,..., t_i, the probability of a score j is given by[10]:

$$P(X_i = j|\theta) \propto \exp[a_i(j\theta - \eta_{ij})] \tag{15.13}$$

---

[9]A supplementary problem arises in these approximations, as the quadrature points may take quite large magnitudes, causing often overflow or underflow errors in the computation of the symmetric functions. These errors can be avoided by using specialized software, but this software slows down the computations considerably.

[10]To avoid cumbersome formulae we have chosen a simple parameterization, unlike the one used originally. Notice also the proportional sign in Eq. (15.13). The lacking denominator is just the reciprocal of the proportionality constant and equals the sum of the t_i possible numerators.

where for all items $\eta_{i0} = 0$. In the PCM as originally formulated the discrimination parameter $a_i = 1$, giving rise to a polytomous generalization of the Rasch model. In the GPCM the discrimination parameters can take any positive value; if they can take only positive integer values, one has a polytomous generalization of OPLM. In the PCM and the generalization of OPLM, the ε-parameters are defined as:

$$\varepsilon_{ij} = \exp(-a_i\eta_{ij}), \quad (j = 1, \ldots, t_i),$$

and all conditional probabilities given the total score are independent of θ. The test score itself is $S = \Sigma a_i X_i$. In the general case where the discrimination parameters can take arbitrary positive values, one loses this independency, and one has to work with:

$$\varepsilon_{ij}(\theta) = \exp[a_i(j\theta - \eta_{ij})], \quad (j = 1, \ldots, t_i).$$

As before we work in this case with the simple number correct score, i.e. $S = \Sigma X_i$.

To construct a suitable expression for the combinatorial functions, one uses indicator variables:

$$y_{ij} = \begin{cases} 1 & \text{if } x_i = j, \\ 0 & \text{otherwise,} \end{cases} \quad (j = 1, \ldots, t_i).$$

For a set E of items[11] the combinatorial function is defined as:

$$\gamma_s(E) = \sum_* \prod_i \prod_{j=1}^{t_i} \varepsilon_{ij}^{y_{ij}} \quad \text{or} \quad \gamma_s[E(\theta)] = \sum_* \prod_i \prod_{j=1}^{t_i} [\varepsilon_{ij}(\theta)]^{y_{ij}} \quad (15.14)$$

where the * under the summation sign means all response patterns such that:

$$\sum_i a_i \sum_{j=1}^{t_i} j y_{ij} = \sum_i a_i x_{ij} = s,$$

in the case of the PCM or OPLM and:

$$\sum_i \sum_{j=1}^{t_i} j y_{ij} = \sum_i x_{ij} = s$$

in the case of the GPCM with a simple raw score. Notice that Eq. (15.14) can also be used in case all items are binary, and conversely we can use Eq. (15.15) or Eq. (15.11) in combination with Eq. (15.14) to compute the conditional probability of any response pattern given the test score. So we have developed a general

---

[11]Notice that the ε-parameters of a polytomous item either all belong to the set or all do not.

Table 15.3 Average deviation profile (Sweden) for the content domain

	Algebra	Data and chance	Geometry	Number
Average deviation	−0.492	0.290	−0.318	0.520
Average number of items	9.9	6.1	6.0	8.7
(Minimum, maximum)	(9, 12)	(4, 8)	(4, 9)	(5, 11)

Table 15.4 Average deviation profile (Sweden) for the cognitive domain

	Applying	Knowing	Reasoning
Average deviation	0.277	−0.267	−0.010
Average number of items	12.0	11.3	7.4
(Minimum, maximum)	(6, 17)	(6, 17)	(2, 13)

Table 15.5 Average deviation profile (Sweden) for item type

	CR	MC
Average deviation	0.158	−0.158
Average number of items	13.9	16.9
(Minimum, maximum)	(10, 17)	(12, 20)

approach to compute expected profiles and conditional distributions for any mixture of binary or polytomous items, for use with the 2PLM or the 3PLM. This is what we need in order to carry out profile analyses for the TIMSS 2011 data, as the item collection is precisely such a mixture.

15.2.2.5 An Example: Sweden in the Mathematics Part of TIMSS 2011

For the three categorizations of the mathematics items (see Table 15.1), we have run a profile analysis on 18 large groups of respondents, each group corresponding to the total sample in a participating country. The item parameters are the values obtained in the international calibration.[12] In this example we give the average deviation profiles for the Swedish participants in the Tables 15.3, 15.4 and 15.5. To appreciate the seriousness of the deviations we also include the average, minimum, and maximum (over the 14 test forms) number of items belonging to each category.

It seems that the most dramatic imbalance occurs in the content domain, especially in the categories algebra and number where there is a deviation of about half a score point with respect to the expectation. As the expectation is based on an international calibration where all participating countries contribute, one could say

---

[12]I am indebted to Pierre Foy for his generous help in providing me the necessary results of the calibration.

that Sweden is relatively weak in algebra and geometry (the deviations are negative) and relatively strong in the categories number and data and chance. Of course, one needs stronger arguments than just the information in the foregoing tables to evaluate the seriousness of the deviations. This is discussed in detail in the next section.

15.2.3 Statistics and Profile Analysis

15.2.3.1 The Case of Large Groups

The basic equation in profile analysis is Eq. (15.5) [or Eq. (15.11) when one has to use values of θ] which allows computation of the exact multivariate conditional distribution of the profile $(S_1, \ldots, S_m)$ and hence computation of all possible moments such as the mean vector and variance–covariance matrix. The method followed is complete enumeration, and the main practical problem is double counting or forgetting possible profiles compatible with the test score. Details of the enumeration algorithm for 2, 3, or 4 categories can be found in Verhelst (2012).

Denote the covariance matrix associated with test score s in test form f by Σ_{fs} and the number of respondents having obtained score s in test form f by n_{fs}, then the variance–covariance matrix of the average deviation profile $\Sigma_{\bar{D}}$ is given by:

$$\Sigma_{\bar{D}} = \frac{\sum_f \sum_s n_{fs} \Sigma_{fs}}{n^2} \qquad (15.15)$$

with $n = \sum_f \sum_s n_{fs}$. By the multivariate central limit theorem (CLT) the average deviation is asymptotically normally distributed with mean the zero vector and variance–covariance matrix $\Sigma_{\bar{D}}$ (Eq. 15.15). Since the sum of the components of the (average) deviation vector is zero by definition, the variance–covariance matrix is singular (its column and row sums are zero), but all linear combinations of the components of the deviation vector are also (asymptotically) normally distributed. As in a survey like TIMSS the sample size per country is several thousands, there is no practical objection to use the CLT in testing statistical hypotheses on the average deviation profiles.

In Table 15.6, the variance–covariance matrix for Sweden of the average deviation profile for the content domain is displayed ($n = 5506$), and in Table 15.7 the results of the four univariate tests ($H_{0j}: D_j = 0$) are given. Clearly, all tests give a highly significant result, but given the large sample size, this may be considered "natural". In the example section, we will come back to this result in a broader context.

Table 15.6 Variance–covariance matrix (Sweden) of the average deviation vector for the content domain

Algebra	Data	Geometry	Number
2.276E−04	−6.475E−05	−6.637E−05	−9.649E−05
−6.475E−05	1.802E−04	−4.726E−05	−6.822E−05
−6.637E−05	−4.726E−05	1.777E−04	−6.410E−05
−9.649E−05	−6.822E−05	−6.410E−05	2.288E−04

Table 15.7 Statistical tests for the (Swedish) mean deviation profile

$\bar{d}_j$	$SE(\bar{d}_j)$	$z = \bar{d}_j / SE(\bar{d}_j)$
−0.4922	0.0151	−32.62
0.2901	0.0134	21.61
−0.3183	0.0133	−23.88
0.5204	0.0151	34.40

15.2.3.2 The Case of Small Groups

The use of the CLT may be not appropriate in the case of small groups. Because in all cases considered the score is integer valued, the construction of the exact conditional distribution of the sum $\sum_v S_{vj}$ of the jth component of a profile, given the test score for each the summands, is not hard. It is done by a series of convolutions that are carried out in the same process that generates the distribution for a single test taker.

Suppose that for $n^* < n$ the distribution of the sum of n^* profiles is known. Let t_j^* be the smallest value of the sum of the jth component that has a positive probability, and let T_j^* be the largest such value, and indicate the probability of each value as $p_{n^*}(t)$ for all $t_j^* \leq t \leq T_j^*$. Now consider a profile generated in the enumeration of all profiles compatible with the test score of the $(n^* + 1)$ test taker, and call this the current profile. The score on the jth component of the current profile takes some value, s_j, say, and using Eq. (15.5 or 15.11), we also know the probability p of the current profile. To construct the convolution of the sum so far and the distribution for the new observation, one applies the simple updating rule[13]:

$$p_{n^*+1}(t+s_j) := p_{n^*+1}(t+s_j) + p_{n^*}(t) \times p, \quad \left(t_j^* \leq t \leq T_j^* \right). \tag{15.16}$$

Notice that the update can be used for all components of the current profile at the same time, since the probability p is the probability of the generated profile, not of a

---

[13]The sign ":=" is the assignment symbol (used in many programing languages). Its meaning is to evaluate the expression to the right of it using the current values of the variables. The outcome of this evaluation is the new (updated) value of the variable to the left of the assignment symbol.

single component. To start the algorithm one can define for each component a dummy distribution for all components $t_j^* = T_j^* = 0$ and $p_{0^*}(0) = 1$.

To allow for proper initialization of the updated vector of probabilities, note that:

$$\min(S_j|s) = \max[0, s - \mathrm{maxsc}(\overline{E}_j)]$$
$$\max(S_j|s) = \min[s, \ \mathrm{maxsc}(E_j)]$$

where $\mathrm{maxsc}(E)$ means the maximum score that can be obtained on the set of items whose ε-parameters are elements of E. To have the updating rule (Eq. 15.16) work properly, all probabilities for the updated vector $p_{n^*+1}(t)$ must be initialized at zero for $t \leq T_j^* + \max(S_j|s)$. After the updates for all possible profiles compatible with the current score s, the support for the distribution of the sum of $n^* + 1$ profiles is updated by:

$$t_j^* := t_j^* + \min(S_j|s)$$
$$T_j^* := T_j^* + \max(S_j|s)$$

To find the probability for average deviation profile, notice that the expected profile is completely determined by the model parameters and the test score. So we immediately have:

$$p_n(\overline{D}_j|s_1, \ldots, s_n) = p_n\left[\frac{1}{n}\sum_v [S_j - E(S_j)|s_v]\right] = p_n\left[\sum_v [S_j|s_v]\right].$$

15.3 Examples

In this section two examples will be presented and discussed. Both show a special feature of profile analysis: the number of groups involved in an analysis is in principle unlimited. In the first example we present the deviation profiles for 18 selected countries participating in TIMSS 2011. The second example gives results for a profile analysis with 153 groups, the 153 participating Swedish schools in TIMSS 2011.

15.3.1 An Example with Large Groups

For the first example 18 countries were selected so as to have considerable geographic diversity and a great spread in the ranking of all participating countries. More than 108,000 students were involved, and since TIMSS uses a mixture of the 2PLM, the GPCM, and the 3PLM, a lot of computational work had to be done, since for every participant a weighted likelihood estimate of his/her ability had to be computed and for each of the three categorizations used the combinatorial functions had to be recomputed for each participant,[14,15] to generate the (multivariate) distribution of the sub-scores compatible with the observed test score. In the Figs. 15.1, 15.2 and 15.3, the results of the profile analyses are displayed graphically for the content domain, the cognitive domain, and the item type, respectively. Here are some comments on these figures.

To the right of the names of the countries, their rank number according to their overall performance (in the selected set of 18 countries) is given. The order in which the results are presented is increasing by deviations for algebra (in the content domain), for "applying" in the cognitive domain, and for MC in the item type analysis. The great majority of the deviations are significantly different from zero, but the interesting aspect is the occurrence of different patterns of deviations. The pattern that we saw for Sweden in the content domain, a positive deviation for data and chance and number, and a negative for algebra and geometry, also occurs in Norway, Finland, New Zealand, Australia, and England. For the other countries, the clustering is less clear, although the United States has a pattern in this domain that is rather peculiar: they do better than expected in three categories but substantially worse only in geometry.

In the cognitive domain (Fig. 15.2) it is again the United States that show a unique pattern, being very positive for the knowing category, while most of the other selected countries show a marked negative deviation in this category. A clear exception is Lithuania, with a considerable negative deviation in the reasoning category. It is worthwhile to look at the units on the horizontal axes: they are deviations in score points (items correct) and therefore comparable. In the cognitive domain only two are larger than 0.3 (in absolute value), while in the content domain 23 of the 72 are larger than 0.3.

Figure 15.3 is the easiest to interpret as it reports only on two complementary categories: the two bars for each country have the same length and opposite direction. It may be tempting to attribute positive deviations for MC items to a proneness to guessing, but one should be careful with such an interpretation: the negative deviation for countries like Norway and Sweden does not mean a proneness to non-guessing. It is better to stay near the exact meaning of the profiles: the deviation means a smaller or larger average performance on a category of items than expected under the measurement model used.

To summarize similarities and dissimilarities between countries on all categorizations jointly, one can use the deviations to compute distances between countries

---

[14]There is an exception to this: participants with a zero score or a perfect score trivially generate a deviation profile with all zeros. They are excluded from the analysis, but this applied to <1 % of the participating students.

[15]The total computing time was about 4 s. This may be considered as a ridiculous remark, but it is not. The program is written in FORTRAN and compiled with a highly efficient compiler. The same computations programed in R might easily take more than a 1000-fold of the computing time needed with the FORTRAN program.

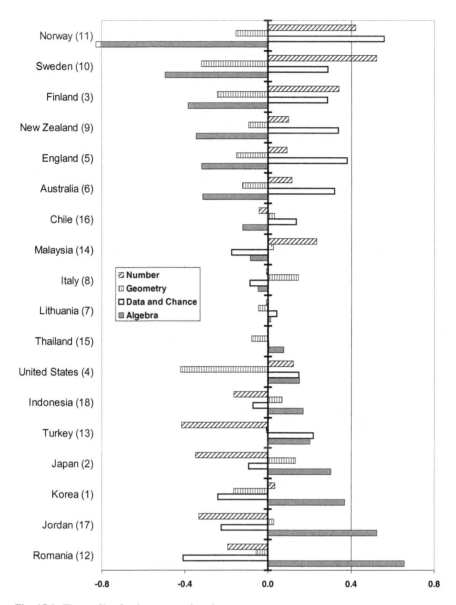

Fig. 15.1 The profiles for the content domain

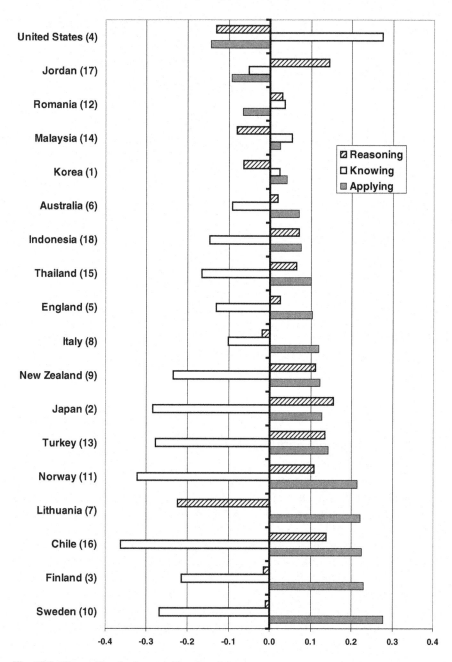

Fig. 15.2 The profiles for the cognitive domain

and then subject the distance matrix to a multidimensional scale analysis. An example of this has been given in Yıldırım et al. (2014).

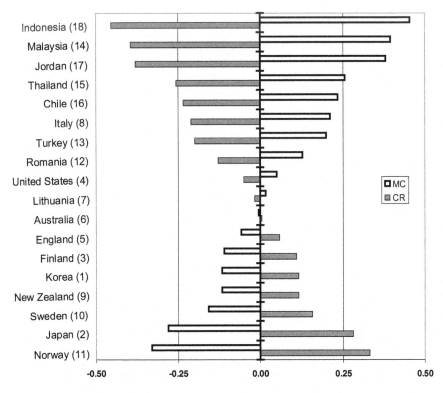

Fig. 15.3 The profiles for item type

15.3.2 An Example with Small Groups

As an example for small groups we present some results on the categories for the four content domains for the 153 Swedish schools participating in TIMSS 2011. The school sample sizes vary from 6 to 58, plus one outlier, of 84 participating students. In Table 15.8 (upper part) the number of schools with a deviation in the lower 5 % and in the upper 5 % of the sampling distribution is given[16] when the parameters from the international calibration are used. Notice that low probabilities correspond to a negative deviation and high probabilities to a positive deviation. In the lower part we give the same frequencies but now from an analysis where the calibration is carried out on the Swedish data only. For this calibration we used the OPLM package (Verhelst et al. 1994) and the item parameters were estimated using conditional maximum likelihood.

---

[16]The primary output of the software is the cumulative probability of the observed average deviation in the exact sampling distribution.

Table 15.8 Number of schools with a significant deviation ($n = 153$)

	Deviation	Algebra	Data	Geometry	Number
International calibration	Negative	126	1	76	0
	Positive	0	106	0	122
Sweden alone	Negative	17	11	14	16
	Positive	18	14	12	18

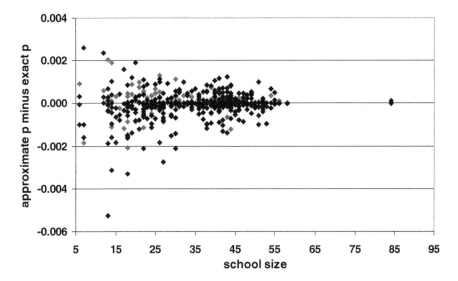

Fig. 15.4 Comparison of exact and approximate cumulative probabilities

The upper part seems only to confirm the results of the profile analysis at country level. Sweden showed a strong relative underperformance in algebra (see Table 15.3; Fig. 15.1) and this is clearly confirmed in the upper part of Table 15.8: 126 schools had a negative significant deviation, and only four schools had a deviation above the median of the exact distribution of average deviations (not shown in the table).

When one does a separate calibration on the data of one country one can detect schools which are relatively strong or weak in some categories. The expected number of schools with a strong positive or negative deviation under the measurement model is 15.3, and one sees that this number is substantially exceeded for all four categories.

Figure 15.4 shows a comparison of the exact and the approximate cumulative probabilities of the observed deviations. The approximate values are the cumulative probabilities based on the assumption of a normal distribution. The vertical axis is the difference between the approximate and the exact cumulative probabilities and the horizontal axis is the school size. Only the results for the content domain are given: the scatter plot contains $153 \times 4 = 612$ points. Two comments on this plot: (1) the difference clearly tends to be smaller the larger the school size (as one would expect from the CLT) and (2) even for very small school sizes the differences are small, all but one being smaller than 0.004 in terms of absolute value. For the other two categorizations we found similar results.

15.4 Discussion

From a statistical point of view profile analysis is a goodness-of-fit analysis of the measurement model used. In fact, it can be considered as a generalization of differential item function (DIF) as it shows that some categories of items function differently in different groups, which may be large groups like countries or small groups, like schools or classes, or even individuals, which represent the smallest possible groups. For a thorough discussion of this in the area of language testing see Verhelst and Banerjee (2016). Every significance found is a signal that the measurement model one uses is not correct. However, this is what we knew beforehand: it would be a bit naïve to believe that a simple model like the Rasch model or the 3PLM can cope with all the cultural and educational differences across the world.

However, profile analysis does permit the identification of greater structure in the deviations from the model, as was clearly shown by the Figs. 15.1, 15.2 and 15.3. A more profound study of these differences might help countries to have a deeper insight into their relative strengths and weaknesses, and this might help them steer their educational systems, for example, by making changes to their national curriculum. Profile analysis on a school or classroom basis may help to detect determinants of deviating profiles and be instrumental in monitoring schools in their educational practice. A lot of work can be done in the area of linking the results of a profile analysis to important background variables.

Is the work done completely? Certainly not, as may be illustrated by the analyses presented in this chapter. For many countries there is an imbalance in their profile, for example, for the content categories, but at the same time there is also an imbalance with respect to the cognitive operations required. So one might ask the—probably naïve—question: is the (relatively) weak performance of Sweden in algebra (Fig. 15.1) due to the fact that they are relatively weak in the cognitive category of "knowing" (Fig. 15.2), i.e. do these two effects strengthen each other, or is Sweden weak in algebra notwithstanding their relative strength in reasoning and applying? Just constructing the bivariate frequency table of categories from two different categorizations (content and cognitive operations) will not be of much help because this table is the same for all participating countries. This question, more generally formulated: "Can one construct a model where the relative effect of categories from different categorizations is made visible in the results of a large survey?" is a challenging one for future research.

References

Ding, C. S. (2001). Profile analysis: Multidimensional scaling approach [Electronic version]. *Practical Assessment, Research and Evaluation, 7* (16).

Greenhouse, S. W., & Geisser, S. (1959). On methods in the analysis of profile data. *Psychometrika, 24,* 95–112.

Haberman, S. J., Sinharay, S., & Puhan, G. (2006). *Subscores for institutions.* ETS Research Series RR-06-13. http://onlinelibrary.wiley.com/doi/10.1002/j.2333-8504.2006.tb02019.x

Kreiner, S., & Christensen, K. B. (2013). Analyses of model fit and robustness. A new look at the PISA scaling model underlying ranking of countries according to reading literacy. *Psychometrika, 79,* 210–231. doi:10.1007/S11336-013-9347-Z

Masters, G. N. (1982). A Rasch model for partial credit scoring. *Psychometrika, 47,* 149–174.

Muraki, M. (1992). A generalized partial credit model: Application of a EM-algorithm. *Applied Pschological Measurement, 16,* 159–176.

Rasch, G. (1960). *Probabilistic models for some intelligence and attainment tests.* Copenhagen: The Danish Institute of Educational Research (expanded edition, 1980). Chicago: The University of Chicago Press.

Verhelst, N. D. (2012). Profile analysis: A closer look at the PISA-2000 reading data. *Scandinavian Journal of Educational Research, 56,* 315–332.

Verhelst, N. D., Banerjee, J., & McLain, P. (2016). Fairness and bias in language assessment. In J. Banerjee & D. Tsagari (Eds.), *Contemporary second language assessment.* (Contemporary Applied Linguistics Vol. 4, pp. 243–260) London: Bloomsbury.

Verhelst, N. D., & Glas, C. A. W. (1995). The one parameter logistic model. In G. H. Fischer & I. W. Molenaar (Eds.), *Rasch models: Foundations, recent developments and applications* (pp. 215–237). New York: Springer Verlag.

Verhelst, N. D., Glas, C. A. W., & Verstralen, H. H. F. M. (1994). *OPLM: Computer program and manual.* Arnhem: Cito.

Warm, T. A. (1989). Weighted likelihood estimation of ability in item response theory. *Psychometrika, 54,* 427–450. doi:10.1007/BF02294627

Yıldırım, H. H., Yıldırım, S., & Verhelst, N. D. (2014). Profile analysis as a generalized differential item functioning analysis method. *Education and Science, 39,* 49–64.

Chapter 16
Views on Classical Statistical Modeling in Competition with the Rasch Methodology

Peter Allerup and André Torre

Abstract During 1979–1980 Jan Eric and Peter Allerup implemented a course at the PhD level under the caption: *Rasch Models in Social and Behavioral Sciences.* It was successfully realized in September/October 1981 near Gothenburg. The late 1970s opened new opportunities regarding the well-known practical problems and limitations of teaching statistical theory supported by empirical analyses on data. In the field of classical factor analyses especially—analyses of high-order contingency tables and analyses carried out by means of Rasch models—such problems were evident. These years provided an efficient means for carrying out such analyses using computers. This chapter will follow some of the tracks used during the course of such research and offers up some reasons why Rasch left classical factor analysis as an analytic statistical method for the benefit of another class of models, originally called *Models for Measurement* by Rasch himself. A couple of visions will be presented on the factor analysis model Rasch developed in 1953, a few years before the release of his book in 1960. These visions will allow the consideration of various aspects of these *Models for Measurement* and their extensions, later re-named as *Rasch models* subsequent to Rasch's death in 1980.

16.1 Introduction

By the end of the 1970s Jan-Eric Gustafsson and I, Peter Allerup, were rather young, and not very experienced researchers in the field of educational research. Our common background was psychometrics formed by Scandinavian people in mathematical statistics and psychology: Herman Wold, Karl Jöreskog, and Dag Sörbom in Sweden and Anders Hald and Georg Rasch in Denmark. Rasch hap-

---

With notes from a research course in Särö 1981.

P. Allerup (✉) · A. Torre
Aarhus University, Aarhus, Denmark
e-mail: nimmo@edu.au.dk

© Springer International Publishing AG 2017
M. Rosén et al. (eds.), *Cognitive Abilities and Educational Outcomes*,
Methodology of Educational Measurement and Assessment,
DOI 10.1007/978-3-319-43473-5_16

pened to be my mentor from 1965 to 1970, when I was employed as a student at the Statistical Institute, Copenhagen University, with professor Rasch as the principal. Certainly, all students employed at the institute were under the heavy influence of Rasch, who repeatedly kept telling us: "Always look at graphs before you compute anything (*man skal tegne, før man kan regne*—in Danish)". We helped him by carefully look for *latent additivity*, which was obviously his favorite empirical structure from the many kinds of data analysis. At the same time he succeeded in communicating his fundamental message about *specific objective comparisons* presented in his book (Rasch 1960) to various colleagues, first of all in Scandinavia, and then subsequently around in the world. In Sweden Leif Lybeck was the person Jan-Eric and I learned to admire, both for Leif's engagement in the views on objective measurements forwarded by Rasch and for his didactic research in mathematics, which matched Rasch's interest in looking for latent additive structures from which, derived as a consequence, theoretical model building could take place.

Jan-Eric was aware of the ideas offered by Rasch via Leif Lybeck, the person who introduced Jan-Eric to the subject. In 1977 Jan-Eric presented a report: *The Rasch Model for Dichotomous Items: Theory, application and a computer program* (Gustafsson 1979). It contained approximately 150 pages and described various theoretical and practical aspects of the so-called simple Rasch Models for two response categories. From the list of contents of his book, you will find headlines like: *Basic concepts; The mathematics of the Rasch Model; Testing goodness of fit; Constructing Rasch scales; Applications; Generalization of the Rasch model;* and a full chapter describing the one parameter logistic model (*PML*) *computer program* for practical data analysis. A section of the book is devoted to a discussion on *unidimensionality*, which is a basic concept in Rasch Models and an attractive property of the classical factor analyses.

During the years 1979–1980 Jan-Eric and I planned to accomplish a course at PhD level under the caption: *Rasch Models in Social and Behavioral Sciences*. It was successfully implemented in September/October 1981 in the small Swedish community of Särö in the neighborhood of Gothenburg, enjoying the pleasant atmosphere created by a conference site being a former, quiet place for retired steam train engine drivers equipped with the special option, that it was possible from their rooms to look to the Swedish King Oscar II's private train station close to the sea.

The late 1970s opened up new opportunities regarding the well-known practical problems and limitations in teaching of statistical theory supported by empirical analyses on data. In the field of classical factor analyses, the analyses of high order contingency tables within analyses carried out by means of Rasch models, such problems were evident. However, while the principles behind factor analyses and the analyses of contingency tables can be studied and discussed mainly considering theoretical insights, the basic concept of objectivity, or the derived concept *item homogeneity,* cannot fully be understood, unless you enter into a kind of "dialog" phase between "theory" and empirical "data analysis". Homogeneity concerns both theory and data. The late 1970s provided an efficient means for such dialogs to take place by the introduction of computer programs and computerized data analyses.

Jan-Eric based his participation at the Särö-course on his PLM program, while I took a starting point for the practical data analyses in a computer program (Andersen 1972) originally developed by Erling B. Andersen and later on refined in a standardized set up (Allerup and Sorber 1977), for the analysis of Rasch's general *M*-dimensional model, i.e. the Rasch model with *M* separate response categories.

The participants at the course were presented with practical data analysis problems, carried out at workshops, viewing the development from classical statistical psychometric analysis to item response theory (IRT) methods, including the models introduced by Georg Rasch. Attempts to generalize the basic Rasch model in terms of two-parameter model (2PML) and a three-parameter model (3PML) were also presented and discussed during the course.

This chapter will follow some of the tracks used during the research course and highlight part of the reason why Rasch left classical factor analysis as an analytic statistical method for the benefit of another class of models, originally called *Models for Measurement*, developed by Rasch himself. The chapter will repeat a couple of visions of the factor analysis model Rasch developed in 1953, a few years before the release of his 1960 book, and will discuss various aspects of these "models for measurement" and their extensions, later re-named *Rasch Models* subsequent to Rasch's death in 1980.

16.2 The Limitations of Classical Factor Analysis According to Rasch

Rasch considered the basic set up in classical factor analysis:

$$x_p = \xi_p + u_p$$

with x_p as a k-dimensional (k items) score vector from individual number p, and u_p a residual random vector with zero mean and variance–covariance matrix:

$$V\{u_p\} = \tau = (\tau_{ij}) \quad \text{for} \quad i,j = 1,\ldots,k.$$

Assuming that the loadings are contained in matrix α, a (k, r)-matrix with rank r and factor vector f_p, of order $(r, 1)$, we then have:

$$\xi_p = \alpha f_p$$

If f_p is a random variable, it is feasible to assume for the variance:

$$V\{f_p\} = \omega = (\omega_{ij}) \quad \text{for} \quad i,j = 1,\ldots,r$$

and for the covariance matrix of factors and residuals:

$$V\{u_p, f_p\} = \pi = (\pi_{ij}) \quad \text{for} \quad i = 1, \ldots, k, \ j = 1, \ldots, r$$

Under these settings the variance matrix for x_p can be taken as:

$$V\{x_p\} = \mu = (\mu_{ij}) = \alpha\omega\alpha' + \alpha\pi' + \pi\alpha' + \tau$$

Note that f_p may be a parameter. In this case the interpretation changes slightly. However, in regular factor analysis further assumptions are usually imposed on the system:

I.	$\pi = 0$	II.	τ is a diagonal matrix	
III.	$\mu_{ii} = 1$ for $i = 1, \ldots, k$	IV.	$\omega_{ii} = 1$ for $i = 1, \ldots, r$	⎰ arbritary
V.	$\omega = 1$ in orthogonal factor models, i.e. I_r [(r, r) identity]			⎱ normalizations
VI.	There is some preference for 0s in the factor pattern matrix α: (a) Spearman: one factor and specifics (b) Holzinger–Burt: zeros in columns (c) Thurstones simple structure: zeros in rows and columns, economizes with loadings $\neq 0$[a]			

[a]*Thurstone* would claim that if rotation to a so-called *simple structure* is objective, in the case of at least three such group factors, then group factor analysis can be done completely objectively using *Burt's* formula, *or Holzinger's bifactor method*

Condition I is not necessary but accepted here and does not change the conclusions provided later. Condition II for independence links to the traditional conditional independence assumptions in latent variables models. Conditions III, IV, and V can be accepted for reasons of mathematical convenience and do not, like condition II, change the final conclusions.

The problem Rasch tried to solve, given the outlined mathematical framework, was to disclose the nature of a set of *common factor loadings* in the case of several sub-populations of a total population. Consequently, if we observe g sub-populations ($h = 1, 2, \ldots, g$) of a total population, each sub-population may be characterized by a variance matrix $\mu^{(h)}$ for the test scores involved. Accepting Condition I leads to the following relation, valid for each sub-population:

$$\mu^{(h)} = \alpha^{(h)} \omega^{(h)} \alpha'^{(h)} + \tau^{(h)}.$$

The aim is to study this relation under the restriction of equal factor loadings for all sub-populations:

$$\alpha^{(1)} = \cdots = \alpha^{(h)} = \alpha.$$

Again it is convenient, however not necessary, to assume all values of $\tau^{(h)}$ to be equal,[1] and the equations for $\mu^{(h)}$ reduce to:

$$\mu^{(h)} = \alpha \omega^{(h)} \alpha' + \tau \quad \text{for} \quad h = 1, \ldots, g$$

The main problem can now be reformulated as a question of the existence of matrices (k, r), $\tau(k, k)$, and $\omega^{(h)}$ (r, r) $(r \le k)$ satisfying the above set of equations.

Making averages $(\cdot)$ for the μ we get:

$$\mu_0^{(h)} = \alpha \omega_0^{(h)} \alpha'$$

where

$$\mu_0^{(h)} = \mu^{(h)} - \mu^{(\cdot)}, \quad \omega_0^{(h)} = \omega^{(h)} - \omega^{(\cdot)}$$

and τ has been eliminated. Solving the equation with respect to $\omega_0^{(h)}$ gives:

$$\omega_0^{(h)} = \left(\alpha' \alpha \right)^{-1} \alpha' \mu_0^{(h)} \alpha \left(\alpha' \alpha \right)^{-1}$$

from which it follows that the (k, k)-matrix i with rank r:

$$i = \alpha \left(\alpha' \alpha \right)^{-1} \alpha'$$

must satisfy the set of equations:

$$\mu_0^{(h)} = i \mu_0^{(h)} i.$$

Matrix i is symmetric and idempotent $i^2 = i$.

The main problem has now been reduced to finding an i-matrix which satisfies this set of relations for $h = 1, \ldots, g$.

Rasch solved this problem by introducing the matrix:

$$\kappa = \sum_{h=1}^{g} \mu_0^{(h)^2},$$

going on to determine its rank r_0 and then splitting it into a product of the form:

$$\kappa = \lambda \lambda'$$

---

[1] If this restriction is not imposed one has to make a few more averages, the results, however will still be elimination of the taus.

where λ is a rectangular matrix of order (k, r_0). Then the solution to $\mu_0^{(h)} = i\mu_0^{(h)} i$ is:

$$i = \lambda \left(\lambda' \lambda \right)^{-1} \lambda'$$

and

$$\alpha_0 = \gamma \lambda$$

The solution α_0 is given with minimal rank and γ can be taken as any arbitrary non-singular (r_0, r_0)-matrix.

It is, consequently clear, that the decomposition of $\mu^{(h)}$ into the common loading-structure:

$$\mu^{(h)} = \alpha \omega^{(h)} \alpha' + \tau \quad \text{for} \quad h = 1, \ldots, g$$

cannot take place with less than r_0 factors.

Rasch presented this result as an indication of the non-specificity of the fundamental factor structure, foreseeing the fact that (later) Rasch models via the concept of specific objectivity—and tests for equal items parameters across sub-populations (called item *homogeneity*)—are in one-to-one correspondence with the basic structure of the model. The idea was already known from an example in traditional statistical analysis: the unambiguous generation of the binomial distribution from a conditional distribution of the one Poisson variate, conditional on the sum of two Poisson variates.

Rasch's concern about specificity must, however, not be confused with the (numerical) statistical test for equal factor loadings across various subpopulations. This problem has been thoroughly discussed by Jöreskog (1971), where similarities and differences in factor structures between different groups were studied. A general model is offered, in which all parameters in the factor analysis models for the different groups may be assigned an arbitrary value or constrained to be equal to some other parameter.

Rasch was here addressing the theoretical requirements for invariance in the structure of factors seen from a point of view of "performing measurements" or "comparisons".

In 1960 he turned a formulation of the basic problem the other way around: What does a theoretical model look like, which satisfies the requirements of consistency or homogeneity? He dealt with this not as a general problem per se, but one brought in specifically when performing comparisons of measurements—whether it be across individuals or across stimuli/items in an educational test.

16.3 The General Rasch Model

Rasch (1967, 1968) generalized his 1960s ideas about measurements or comparisons and constructed a general framework for, what later would be called *general Rasch models for more than two response categories*. Models for "comparisons" or "measurements" were two labels Rasch used to allocate to the models, by stressing the fact that any measurement has a comparison as its starting point.

The general model is based upon a frame of reference constituted by $v = 1, \ldots, N$ individuals responding to $i = 1, \ldots, K$ items, each response $X_{vi} = \mu$ being recorded on a M-dimensional categorical scale, which need not to be ordinal. An example could be $\mu = 1 = $ '*Yes*', $\mu = 1 = $ '*No*' and $\mu = 3 = $ '*Maybe*'. Each item i is characterized by a M-dimensional item parameter $\theta_{i\mu} = \{\theta_{i1}, \ldots, \theta_{iM}\}$ and each individual v likewise characterized by a M-dimensional parameter $\sigma_{v\mu} = \{\sigma_{v1}, \ldots, \sigma_{vM}\}$.

Rasch's key theorem from these years is the following:

On the assumption that the answers of different persons to a set of items are independent stochastic variables for which the probability distributions over M possible categories $\mu = 1, \ldots, \mu = M$ depend on two sets of M-dimensional parameters σ_v and θ_i referring to respectively persons and items, then the validity of the model (below) is a necessary and sufficient condition for complete separability of the two kinds of parameters:

$$P(X_{vi} = \mu) = \frac{e^{\theta_{i\mu} + \sigma_{v\mu}}}{\gamma_{vi}}$$

where $\gamma_{vi} = \sum_{\mu=1}^{M} e^{\theta_{i\mu} + \sigma_{v\mu}}$ is the normalizing constant.

The crucial property of separability is what Rasch meant by objectivity: "During centuries philosophers have disagreed about which concept should be attached to the term objectivity, and on this occasion I am not entering upon a discussion of that matter, I only wish to point out, that the above mentioned separation exemplifies a type of objectivity which I qualify by the predicate specific".[2]

Rasch provided a proof specifically for the necessary and sufficient condition in the special case $M = 2$ response categories (Rasch, not dated, but approx. from 1965 and Rasch et al. 1959), later presented (Allerup 1994) using his original mathematics notation. Notice, that the sufficient statistics for the M-dimensional individual parameters $(\sigma_{v\mu}), \mu = 1, \ldots, M$ are the statistics $(a_{v1}, a_{v2}, \ldots a_{vM})$ where a_{vj} is number of category $\mu = j$ responses across all items, all together adding to K. Andersen (1973), Fischer (1974), Fischer and Molenaar (1995) both established proofs for the

---

[2]My comment: the significance of the outlined data framework of reference is emphasized here, Rasch is actually *restricting and specifying* his concept of objectivity instead of making a general statement about objectivity.

Rasch model as a necessary condition for sufficiency of the individual scores. Fischer and Molenaar (1995) even presented a proof for the general polytomous model based on the concept of "specific objectivity" referred to above.

The research course in Särö was designed as a workshop and was therefore intended to involve data to be analyzed both by this general model and by specializations of the model. Jan-Eric (Gustafsson 1981) and I had planned to involve data from mainly questionnaires from the psychological field and the idea was to let course participants work with empirical data, tests of models, and experience the well-known "Rasch-feeling" of a discourse between the theoretical model construction and empirical structures in the data. In fact, to many participants it came as a surprise that a consequence of a possible misfit of a statistical model could be a revision of "reality", while the model was sustained! Today, this is the part of the well known testing process with Rasch models, in which quite many questions/items can be omitted or eliminated from a questionnaire during the process of test-of-fit of the model.

Perhaps it is because Jan-Eric remember that among the participants were some with excellent cartoonist capabilities that he made a drawing of us as teachers in front of the general Rasch model, wearing a hat, hopefully with maximum likelihood of understanding (the general Rasch model is here presented in the multiplicative structure version).

When Rasch—or his students—operated with the general model, it was always emphasized that *all* analyses should be carried out in a way which accorded with the fundamental separability properties outlined in the theorem above. In practice, it meant performing conditional inference, when items are compared or when individuals are compared. For instance, by looking at the conditional distribution across two items i and j:

$$P\big(X_{vi} = \mu, X_{vj} = \pi | (X_{vi}, X_{vj}) \in \Omega\big)$$

where Ω is a diagonal illustrated in the figure below. For example: if $(\mu, \pi) = (3, 1)$ then $\Omega \in \{(3, 1), (2, 2), (1, 3)\}$.

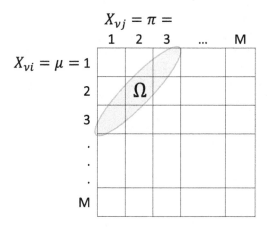

This conditional distribution is independent of the individual parameter σ_v and is dependent on the two item parameters θ_i and θ_j only.

Rasch traced all the new information collected under the general model through rigorous use of such a conditional (distribution) approach in the mathematics behind models. He did so, while using paper and pencil, since only very late in his life, he fully realized the advantage of using a computer. For the practical use of the general model it had the consequence, that estimation and test of model was based on the pairwise comparison technique demonstrated above, a technique that can be unfolded on all (i,j) item combinations and afterwards be reduced to relations for each item. This pairwise technique was adapted by David Andrich and was later on implemented in the computer program RUMM using a one-dimensional specialization of the general model (Andrich 1978).

16.4   Specializations of the General Rasch Model

A clear impression from the Särö meeting, and from many other statistical analyses undertaken later on, that a rigid interpretation and practical use of results drawn by means of the *general M*-dimensional Rasch model is difficult to handle. No restrictions are imposed on the nominal M-dimensional response scale $\mu = 1,\ldots,\mu = M$, and the model structure, therefore allows for a latent M-1 multidimensionality of the individual σ-parameters. In practice, however, the interpretation of parallel subdimensions of the σ-parameters is not straightforward, an attempt which should not be confused with traditional identification problems of subdimensions in, e.g. factor analyses. Søren Risbjerg Thomsen was one of the few people operating with the general model in studies of voting behavior, in which political parties played the role of separate response categories. Here, the electoral behavior was seen as a function of the voters' position on a number of latent dimensions and not as a product of previous voting behavior (Thomsen 1987).

One interesting specialization of the general model, however, arose from part of the workshops in Särö and had Rasch's attention at about that time: The one-dimensional M-category model with fixed numerical scorings of categorical response categories $\mu = 1, \ldots, \mu = M$. Within the *additive* structure of the model: $\theta_{i\mu} + \sigma_{v\mu}$ the set of scorings are denoted as the *scoring function* $\rho_\mu = (\rho_1, \ldots, \rho_M)$ on the hypothesis of one-dimensionality of the M-dimensional item parameters $\theta_{i\mu} = (\theta_{i1}, \ldots, \theta_{iM})$ for $i = 1, \ldots, K$:

$$[\theta_{i\mu}]_{MxK} = [\theta_1, \ldots, \theta_K]'[\rho_1, \ldots, \rho_M]$$

The hypothesis, therefore factorizes the matrix $[\theta_{i\mu}]$ into a one-dimensional item vector $[\theta_1, \ldots, \theta_K]$ and a one-dimensional scoring function $[\rho_1, \ldots, \rho_M]$.

It is easy to derive estimates of $(\theta_1, \ldots, \theta_K)$ and $(\rho_1, \ldots, \rho_M)$ within this additive structure, by minimizing:

$$\min \sum_{i\mu} (\theta_{i\mu} - \theta_i \rho_\mu)^2$$

Allerup and Sorber (1977) found the solution is derived from the fact that under the hypothesis of one-dimensionality the (K, M) matrix $e = (\theta_{i\mu})$ has rank 1, so will $e'e$, and there will be one, large eigenvalue κ. The eigenvectors with $(\theta_1, \ldots, \theta_K)$ and $[\rho_1, \ldots, \rho_M]$ are estimated as the one-dimensional item parameters and one-dimensional scoring function. Evaluation of the hypothesis takes place as a $-2 \log Q$ likelihood ratio test with and without the hypothesis inserted in the likelihood function. The use of a traditional approximate normal theory with minimizing, is due to E.B Andersen's thesis (Andersen 1973). Fischer (1974) derived this one-dimensional specialization of the general Rasch model as a necessary condition for specific objectivity, in line with Rasch's intensive use of pairwise comparisons, which both Fischer and David Andrich during their stays at the Statistical Institute, Copenhagen, learned to accept as the fundamental points of departure for any statistical and philosophical analysis in light of the models.[3]

Andersen (1999) studied the special case with equidistant scoring $(\rho_1, \ldots, \rho_M) = (1, 2, 3, \ldots, M)$ of response categories and discussed the complexity and problems by using various types of scoring functions.

Rasch made the observation, that there are limitations regarding a free choice of values $(\rho_1, \ldots, \rho_M)$ for the scoring function. In fact, it is clear, that the likelihood function for the responses from individual v under the one-dimensional scoring model is:

---

[3]Although Rasch easily mastered multidimensional calculations, he never came around to the use of computers, and therefore, seen from a practical point of view, pairwise comparisons were preferred.

$$P(X_{v1} = x_{v1}, \ldots, X_{vK} = x_{vK}) = \prod_i \frac{e^{x_{vi}(\theta_i + \sigma_v)}}{\gamma_{vi}} = \frac{e^{\sum_i x_{vi}\theta_i + \sum_i x_{vi}\sigma_v}}{\prod_i \gamma_{vi}}$$

where

$$\gamma_{vi} = \sum_\mu e^{\rho_\mu(\theta_i + \sigma_v)}$$

It can be read from here, that the sufficient statistic T_v for the individual parameter σ_v is:

$$T_v = \sum_i x_{vi} = \rho_1 + \rho_2 + \cdots + \rho_K$$

T_v can vary, $0, 1, 2, \ldots, KM$, in the case of equidistant scoring across K items, and, maybe $0, 1, 2, 3, 50, 51, 52, 100, 150$, in case of $K = 3$ items with each item scored on $(\rho_1, \ldots, \rho_M) = (0, 1, 50)$. The point of interest is focused on which numerical values T_v can actually attain. If we calculate the conditional distribution of the K responses from individual v conditional on T_v, this distribution is, of course independent of σ_v because of the sufficiency of T_v:

$$P\left(X_{v1} = x_{v1}, \ldots, X_{vK} = x_{vK} \Big| T_v = \sum_i x_{vi}\right)$$

This distribution can in cases of extreme scoring, e.g. using irrational numbers for $(\rho_1, \ldots, \rho_M)$ like $(\sqrt{3}, e, \sqrt{5}, \sqrt{7}, \pi)$, be singular (probability equals one) in the sense that it is possible to determine which values the X_{vi} actually attain based on the value of T_v.

The problem was addressed by Rasch and discussed during the Särö meeting but no reasonable conclusion was reached.

The importance of the existence of sufficient statistics for statistical model building was part of the Särö meeting and some mathematical statisticians in Scandinavia took the view that part of the Rasch model hierarchy was a product of rather uncomplicated one-to-one correspondences between sufficiency of certain statistics (individual—and item score totals in the data frame of reference) and a model within the exponential class of statistical distribution, thus, ignoring the concept of Rasch's specific objectivity.

It was an obvious step next, therefore, to debate how to "generate" Rasch models and other exponential models by referring to the Swedish mathematician (Martin-Löf 1970, 1974). The way he argued for an exponential distribution followed general reduction principles from "macro states" to "micro states" through the use of *summative* statistics, in accordance with the Austrian physicist Ludwig Boltzmann, who gave an independent argument for the exponential distribution. Rasch and Löf showed a common interest in the number:

$$\begin{bmatrix} a_{oi} \\ a_{v0} \end{bmatrix}$$

for which, in case of the dichotomous Rasch model, $M = 2$ stands for the number of 0-1 matrices with fixed item totals $a_{oi} = (a_{o1}, \ldots, a_{oK})$ and individual scores (totals) $a_{v0} = (a_{v1}, \ldots, a_{vN})$. For Rasch this number was the anchor of specificity when testing the $M = 2$ model, since the conditional distribution [(X_{vi}) being the matrix of all responses]:

$$P((X_{vi})|a_{oi}, a_{v0}) = \begin{bmatrix} a_{oi} \\ a_{v0} \end{bmatrix}^{-1}$$

is independent of both item and individual parameters.[4] For Löf this number played the role of counting the micro states X_{vi} fitting a common macro structure defined by the summative functions a_{oi} and a_{v0}. Löf suggested an approximation formula for calculating this number. Others (see, e.g. Verhelst 2008) have developed elegant approaches for the calculation of approximate values. Rasch's focus was the theoretical specificity, viz. one-to-one correspondence, with the basic model. A useful consequence is, however, the fact that any subgrouping (according to the individuals) of the total response matrix (X_{vi}) leads to:

$$P\left(a_{oi(1)}|a_{oi(1)} + a_{oi(2)} = a_{oi}, a_{v0}\right) = \begin{bmatrix} a_{oi(1)} \\ a_{v0} \end{bmatrix} \bigg/ \begin{bmatrix} a_{oi} \\ a_{v0} \end{bmatrix}$$

which is valid for the sub-group item totals $a_{oi(1)}, a_{oi(2)} i = 1, \ldots, k$ (adding to a_{oi}) for the total (X_{vi}).

This distribution is derived from the basic model in the same way as the hypergeometric distribution is derived as an exact binomial test for equal probabilities of the binomials. For a practical use, approximate values for the three numbers have to be determined, eventually using specialized random sampling techniques (see, e.g. Verhelst 2008). Finally, the "exact principle" of comparing the actual probability $P\left(a_{oi(1)}|a_{oi(1)} + a_{oi(2)} = a_{oi}, a_{v0}\right)$ with the total sum probabilities less that this one, which leads to the conclusion about the hypothesis, that the two sub-groups of the total response matrix (X_{vi}) have consistent item parameters. The division of the total response matrix into two sub-groups thereby offers a possibility of testing, which is not practically assessable form the first, simple uniformly distributed consequence $P((X_{vi})|a_{oi}, a_{v0})$.

Maybe, my memory is wrong, but wasn't it at the Särö meeting we had a computer program constantly running on special 0-1 "switch" matrices?

---

[4]And therefore allows for a test of model which obeys the basic rule of objectivity, viz. independence of the framework parameters.

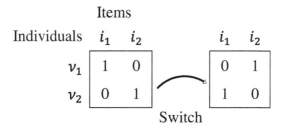

Items

Individuals i_1 i_2 i_1 i_2

Switch

Here four responses to the total response matrix X_{vi} are shown with two individuals v_1 and v_2 responding to two items i_1 and i_2. The demonstrated switch defines a new response matrix X_{vi} but the item totals $a_{oi} = (a_{o1}, \ldots, a_{oK})$ and individual scores (totals) $a_{v0} = (a_{v1}, \ldots, a_{vN})$ remain fixed. Therefore, in principle we have by this a means for generating, successively, X_{vi}-matrices with fixed margins and by this a kind of practical access to counting the number of 0-1 matrices from above.

At the Särö meeting Jan-Eric presented as part of his PML computer program two versions of statistical models, which have both, later on carried the names: *two- and three-parameter Rasch models*. Both types are well known today both in national and international evaluation studies, IEA's TIMSS for instance. Both forms of generalizations are established on the simple $M = 2$ dichotomous Rasch model for two response categories where the frame of reference is a total X_{vi} 0-1 matrix with $\theta = (\theta_1, \ldots, \theta_K)$ and $\sigma = (\sigma_1, \ldots, \sigma_N)$ as one-dimensional items and individual parameters.

The two-parameter model assigns the probability $P(X_{vi} = 1)$ for a correct response:

$$P(X_{vi} = 1) = \frac{e^{\theta_i + \delta_i \sigma_v}}{1 + e^{\theta_i + \delta_i \sigma_v}}$$

The name two-parameter comes from the introduction of the so-called item discrimination parameter δ_i. The significance of δ_i becomes clear when item characteristic curves (ICC), as functions of the individual parameter σ, are compared across items with different θ and δ parameters. The Y-axis measures the probability of a correct response.

The three ICCs demonstrate two parallel item curves (ICC 1 and 3) with the same δ parameter and one item, ICC No. 2 with a δ parameter which is smaller than the two other curves. Users in favor of the two-parameter model accept and appreciate the fact that the red and blue items discriminate better between neighbouring σ-values (i.e. create greater difference in probabilities) because of the steepness of the curves. There is no doubt, however, that differing ICC steepness contradicts the requirements of objectivity behind the ordinary $M = 2$ Rasch model. To see this, one has to remember that it is a consequence of the specificity of the Rasch model, that the following three statements are equivalent (here presented as a brief outline):

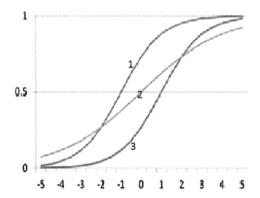

(a) Item totals and individual totals exhaust all information about item difficulty and individual ability (sufficiency).
(b) Individuals can be compared with consistent results, independently of which selection of items is used (objectivity).
(c) The Rasch model can adequately describe the data X_{vi}.

From these statements and a look at the intersecting blue and green ICC curves —especially at the values $\sigma = -4$ (i.e. "weak") and $\sigma = 0$ (i.e. "average") it becomes clear that opposite results are obtained as regards the two individuals probabilities to solve the item correctly. For the individual with $\sigma = -4$ the green item is easier compared to the blue one, while the $\sigma = 0$ individual arrives at the opposite conclusion: the green item is more difficult compare with the blue. Consequently, property (b) is violated, and the outcome of the comparison depends on the choice of items.

During the Särö meeting both practical and theoretical aspects of the use of the two-parameter Rasch model was discussed. It fitted well with the arguments expressed today for applying this model, that too many items must be eliminated during the process of test-of-fit of the simple $M = 2$ Rasch model. The two-parameter model, therefore appear as a kind of practical solution to the fact that the simple $M = 2$ model does not work unless too many items are eliminated.[5] It is but a curiosum, that the two-parameter model also bears the name *Birnbaum alternative*. Seen from an epistemological point of view it is interesting, that Birnbaum while working in the classical psychometric framework, including the normal distribution, nearly as a casual remark (Birnbaum 1968), noticed that the cumulative normal distribution can be well approximated by the logistic function—

---

[5]It is not unusual to eliminate up to 50 % of the items during test-of-fit of the model.

in fact the mathematical expression of the simple Rasch $M = 2$ model. The Rasch model is, thus, seen in this view, just another mathematical expression, which for reasons of mathematical convenience can replace the normal distribution during the psychometric analyses.

It is noteworthy, that the sufficient statistic for the individual parameter σ_v is not actually the raw sum of correct responses across items but instead:

$$T_v = \sum_i x_{vi} = \sum_i \lambda_i \delta_i$$

which is the sum of δ across correctly solved items $\delta_1, \ldots, \delta_K$: $\lambda_i = 0, 1$ depending on non-correct/correct response X_{vi}. In spite of that, in many applications of the two-parameter model, the simple sum of correct responses is still used for secondary statistical analyses.

Finally, we discussed the so called *three-parameter Rasch model* at the Särö meeting, which is another type of generalization of the Rasch model. This generalization was already part of Jan-Erics PML program used at Särö. To the concept of item discrimination embedded in the two-parameter model is now added the idea of guessing φ, the probability that an individual is guessing correctly when responding to a multiple choice item.

The complete three parameter model is a mixture of making a guess and not making a guess. The graph illustrates the situation with ICC curves, in which the responses to two items are not subject to guessing (ICC 1 and 2) while ICC No. 3 never reaches zero to the left because, in this case, this item is subject to a probability of guessing correctly of approximately 20 %.

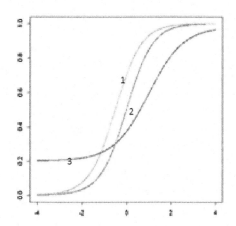

$$P(X_{vi} = 1) = \varphi + (1 - \varphi)\frac{e^{\theta_i + \delta_i \sigma_v}}{1 + e^{\theta_i + \delta_i \sigma_v}}$$

The three-parameter model seems formally to be an imminent solution to a description of "what is going on" in the head of a student sitting at the desk, trying to find the correct answer among multiple choices, who finally gives up and exercises guessing an answer. Critics of the model are often met by the argument that students do guess sometimes, so in order to "meet reality" the basic model must be expanded to comprise reality. The mathematical structure, however, of the displayed three-parameter model can be discussed. Identification and estimation problems have been studied, e.g. by Kyung Han, who makes the points: "*For several decades, the three-parameter logistic model has been the dominant choice for practitioners in the field of educational measurement for modeling examinees' response data from multiple-choice (MC) items. Past studies, however, have pointed out that the φ-parameter should not be interpreted as a guessing parameter*". His study (Han 2012) found logical, empirical evidence showing that neither the *a-*, *b-*, or φ parameters can accurately reflect the discrimination, difficulty, and guessing properties of an item, respectively. In line with Rasch's way of checking, whether a parametric structure is interpretable, another comprehensive study of IRT modeling in the framework of fixed and random effects models (San Martín et al. 2015) concluded specifically for the three-parameter model (3PL): "*Most of the time, the didactic presentation of the 3PL model is carried out in the context of a fixed-effects framework. In this context, the item parameters are interpreted using the item characteristics curves. However, as was discussed in Sect. 2, only identified parameters are accompanied with a statistical meaning. The previous results show that the item parameters of a 3PL model are not identified and, therefore, they are meaningless*".

Could it be, that a more reasonable way of modeling "guessing" take place by introducing an extra response category μ to the existing M response categories? Operationalized by an extension of the M-dimensional item parameter to $\theta_{i\mu} = (\theta_{i1}, \ldots, \theta_{i(M+1)})$? Or creating alternative changes to the simple two- or one-parameter model, rather than the one suggested by the actual introduction of the φ parameter? The displayed three-parameter model is, obviously not a member of the exponential distributions, and, consequently does not enjoy statistical reduction by means of sufficient statistics for neither the items nor the individual parameters. Considered from an extreme interpretation, the three-parameter model in a way defines two, distinct groups of individuals: those who guess consistently at the guessing level φ and those who do not guess but respond according to the Rasch model. Involving a.o. the item parameters $\theta = (\theta_1, \ldots, \theta_K)$. The fact is, that the first guessing group completely satisfies the requirements behind the Rasch model, with identical item parameters and one, fixed individual parameter so that $\theta + \sigma = \log\left(\frac{\varphi}{1-\varphi}\right)$. This creates an obvious item inhomogeneity across the two groups.

16.5   Conclusion

The Särö research course was held at a time near the end of Rasch's life and at the beginning of Jan-Eric's and my academic life. In a way everybody at the meeting was lucky to be familiar with the significance of the concept of objectivity—or specific objectivity—as an essential and long needed approach of analysis, seen from a scientific theoretical point of view. This approach explicitly addressed classical problems of population dependence when making conclusions in the field of educational research.

Certainly, the Rasch models, and the principles behind the models, do not outmatch all old fashioned methods in statistics and do not claim to explain everything. Maybe we should remember some judicious words from earlier?

> To explain all nature is too difficult a task for any one man or even for any one age. 'Tis much better to do a little with certainty and leave the rest for others that come after you (Newton 1703).

The time passed since Särö has also shown that practice may sometimes differ from rigid stands regarding sacred scientific principles. Sometimes we need to compromise:

> The best thing to learn in life is the habit of compromise. Because it's better to bend a little than to break a lot (S. Kirkegaard (not dated)).

References

Allerup, P. (1994). *Rasch measurement, theory of; the international encyclopedia of education* (Vol. 8). Oxford: Pergamon.

Allerup, P., & Sorber, G. (1977). *The Rasch model for questionnaires: With a computer program* (226p). Denmark: Danmarks Paedagogiske Institut.

Andersen, E. (1972). *A computer program for solving a set of conditional maximum likelihood equations arising in the Rasch model for questionnaires.* Princeton, New Jersey: Educational Testing Service.

Andersen, E. (1999). Georg Rasch in memoriam: A discovery journey into a data set. In International Conference International Conference on Large Scale Data Analysis, University of Cologne, Germany.

Andersen, E. B. (1973). *Conditional inference and models for measuring.* København: Mentalhygiejnisk Forlag.

Andrich, D. (1978). A rating formulation for ordered response categories. *Psychometrika, 43*, 357–374.

Birnbaum, A. (1968). Chapter 17.3. In FM Lord & MR Novick(X) (Eds.), *Statistical theories of mental test scores.* Boston: Addison-Wesley.

Fischer, G. (1974). *Ein fürung in die Theorie psychologischer Tests.* Switzerland : Verlag Hans Huber, Bern Stuttgart Wien.

Fischer, G., & Molenaar, I. (1995). *Derivations of the Rasch model, p15, and derivation of the polytomous Rasch models* (p293). Berlin: Springer Verlag.

Gustafsson, E. (1981). *An introduction to Rasch's measurement model.* Paper presented at the research course caption(X). Rasch Models in Social and Behavioral Sciences., Särö, September/October 1981, Eric Clearing House, NJ 08541.

Gustafsson, J. E. (1979). *PML: A computer program for conditional estimation and testing in the Rasch model for dichotomous items.* Reports from. the Institute of Education, University of Goteborg, no. 85.

Han, K. T. (2012). Fixing the c parameter in the three-parameter logistic model. *Practical Assessment, Research & Evaluation,* 17(1).

Jöreskog, K. (1971). Simultaneous factor analysis in several populations. *Psykometrika,* 36(4).

Martin-Löf, P. (1970). *Statistika modeller (statistical models): Anteckningar fran seminarier läsåret 1969–1970 (Notes from seminars in the academic year 1969-1970), with the assistance of Rolf Sundberg.* Sweden: Stockholm University.

Martin-Löf, P. (1974). Exact tests, confidence regions and estimates. In A. W. F. Edwards, G. A. Barnard, D. A. Sprott, O. Barndorff-Nielsen, D. Basu & G. Rasch (Eds.), *Proceedings of Conference on Foundational Questions in Statistical Inference (Aarhus, 1973),* (pp. 121–138). Memoirs, No. 1, Dept. Theoret. Statist., Inst. Math., Univ. Aarhus, Aarhus.

Newton, I. (1703). Principles of philosophy manuscript fragtment (c.1703) add MS 3970.3.

Rasch, G. (1953). On simultaneous Factor analysis in several populations. In *Uppsala Symposium on Psychological Factor analysis.*

Rasch, G. (1960). Probabilistic models for some intelligence and attainment tests. *Munksgaard.*

Rasch, G. (1967). An informal report on a theory of objectivity in comparisons. Psychological measurement theory. In *Proceedings of the NUIFFIC International summer Session in Science at Het Oude Hof Den Haag,* Leiden.

Rasch, G. (1968). A mathematical theory of objectivity and its consequences for model construction. *Paper presented at the European Meeting on Statistics, Econometrics and Managements Science, Amsterdam 2-7 September.*

Rasch, G., Ross, A., Blegvad, M., & Pihl, M. (1959). Erkendelse Vurdering og Valg. *Nordisk Sommeruniversitet.*

San Martín, E., González, J., & Tuerlinckx, F. (2015). On the unidentifiability of the fixed-effects 3PL model. *Psychometrika,* 80(2), 450–467.

Thomsen, R. (1987). Danish elections 1920-79, a logit approach to ecological analysis and inference. Århus: Politica.

Verhelst, N. D. (2008). An efficient MCMC algorithm to sample binary matrices with fixed marginal. *Psychometrika, 73,* 705–728.

Jan-Eric Gustafsson—List of Publications in Chronological Order 1971–2016

This list is an attempt to document all Jan-Eric's major published, scholarly contributions until spring 2016. However, it by no means comprises his complete written production. For example, it does not include unpublished manuscripts and reports, contributions to the public debate in newspapers and magazines, and conference papers and keynotes. As Jan-Eric continues his research, there are obviously more publications of various kind to come.

1971

Gustafsson, J.-E. (1971). *Interaktion mellan individ- och undervisningsvariabler: introduktion och litteraturgenomgång.* Report 34:63, Department of Education, Göteborg University.

1974

Gustafsson, J.-E. (1974a). *Interaktioner mellan individvariabler och listlängd vid glosinlärning.* Report 34:116, Department of Education, Göteborg University.

Gustafsson, J.-E. (1974b). *Verbal versus figural in aptitude-treatment interactions: review of the literature and an empirical study.* Report 35:36, Department of Education, Göteborg University.

Gustafsson, J.-E. (1974c). *Implications of interactions for the experimental research on teaching methods.* Report 35:38, Department of Education, Göteborg University.

1975

Gustafsson, J.-E. (1975a). Interactions and the experimental research on teaching methods. *Scandinavian Journal of Educational Research, 19*(1), 45–57.

© Springer International Publishing AG 2017   313
M. Rosén et al. (eds.), *Cognitive Abilities and Educational Outcomes*,
Methodology of Educational Measurement and Assessment,
DOI 10.1007/978-3-319-43473-5

Gustafsson, J.-E. (1975b). *Om ATI-forskningens nuvarande ståndpunkter samt svar på kritik.* Report 34:133, Department of Education, Göteborg University.

Gustafsson, J.-E., & Wernersson, I. (1975). *Om multivariatanalys med fasta analysenheter och många variabler.* Report 34:132, Department of Education, Göteborg University.

1976

Gustafsson, J.-E. (1976a). *Inconsistencies in aptitude-treatment interactions as a function of procedures in the studies and methods of analysis.* Report 35:46, Department of Education, Göteborg University.

Gustafsson, J.-E. (1976b). *Differential effects of imagery instructions on pupils with different abilities.* Report 35:47, Department of Education, Göteborg University.

Gustafsson, J.-E. (1976c). *Verbal and figural aptitudes in relation to instructional methods. Studies in aptitude-treatment interaction.* Dissertation, Göteborg University.

Gustafsson, J.-E. (1976d). *A note on the importance of studying class effects in aptitude- treatment interaction.* Report 35:52, Department of Education, Göteborg University.

Gustafsson, J.-E. (1976e). *Spatial ability and the suppression of visualization by reading.* Report 35:53, Department of Education, Göteborg University.

1977

Gustafsson, J.-E., & Härnqvist, K. (1977). *Begåvningstyper och undervisningsmetoder* (Ability types and teaching methods. A survey of the MID-project). Stockholm: Skolöverstyrelsen.

Gustafsson, J.-E. (1977a). *The Rasch model for dichotomous items: Theory applications and a computer program.* Report 35:63, Department of Education, Göteborg University.

Gustafsson, J.-E. (1977b). Differential effects of imagery instructions on pupils with different abilities. *Scandinavian Journal of Educational Research, 21,* 1, 157–179.

1978

Gustafsson, J.-E. (1978). A note on class effects in aptitude x treatment interactions. *Journal of Educational Psychology, 70*(2), 142–146.

Gustafsson, J.-E., & Lindström, B. (1978). *Describing and testing aptitude-treatment interaction effects with structural equation models: reanalysis of a study by M J Behn.* Report 35:73, Department of Education, Göteborg University.

Härnqvist, K., & Gustafsson, J.-E. (1978). *International references to Swedish educational research: A citation study.* Report 35:70. Department of Education, Göteborg University.

1979

Fischbein, S., & Gustafsson, J.-E. (1979). *Kunskapsskillnader i skolan: resultat från en tvillingstudie.* Report 39, 1979:14. Department of Education, Göteborg University.

Gustafsson, J.-E. (1979a). *PLM: A computer program for conditional estimation and testing in the Rasch model for dichotomous items.* Report 35:85. Department of Education, Göteborg University.

Gustafsson, J.-E. (1979b). The Rasch model in vertical equating of tests: A critique of Slinde and Linn. *Journal of Educational Measurement, 16*(3), 153–158.

Gustafsson, J.-E. (1979c). *Attitudes towards the school: The teacher and the classmates at the class level and the individual level.* Report 35:75, Department of Education, Göteborg University.

1980

Gustafsson, J.-E. (1980a). A solution of the conditional estimation problem for long tests in the Rasch Model for dichotomous items. *Educational and Psychological Measurements, 40*(2), 377–385.

Gustafsson, J.-E. (1980b). Testing and obtaining fit of data to the Rasch model. *British Journal of Mathematical and Statistical Psychology, 33*(2), 205–233.

Wainer, H., Morgan, A., & Gustafsson, J.-E. (1980). A review of estimation procedures for the Rasch Model with an eye towards longish tests. *Journal of Educational Statistics. 5*(1), 35–64.

1981

Gustafsson, J.-E. (1981). *An introduction to Rasch's measurement model.* Report 1981:02, Department of Education, Göteborg University.

Gustafsson, J.-E., Lindström, B., & Björck-Åkesson, E. (1981). *A general model for the organization of cognitive abilities.* Report 1981:06. Department of Education, Göteborg University.

1982

Gustafsson, J.-E. (1982). *Visualization processes in learning as a function of methods of presentation and individual differences.* Report 1982:09, Department of Education, Göteborg University.

Gustafsson, J.-E., & Svensson, A. (1982). *Family size, social class, intelligence and achievement: A study of interactions.* Report 1982:05. Department of Education, Göteborg University.

1984

Gustafsson, J.-E. (1984). A unifying model for the structure of intellectual abilities. *Intelligence,8*(3), 179–203.

1985

Gustafsson, J.-E. (1985). Measuring and interpreting "g". *Behavioral and Brain Sciences, 8*(2), 231–232.

1986

Härnqvist, K., Gustafsson, J.-E., & Marton, F. (1986). *Pedagogikens gränser och möjligheter: en bok tillägnad Kjell Härnqvist på hans 65-årsdag.* Lund: Studentlitteratur.

1987

Undheim, J. O., & Gustafsson, J.-E. (1987). The hierarchical organization of cognitive Abilities: Restoring general intelligence through the use of linear structural relations (LISREL). *Multivariate Behavioral Research, 22*(2), 149–171.

1988

Gustafsson, J.-E. (1988). Hierarchical models of individual differences in cogni-tive abilities. In R. J. Sternberg (Ed.), *Advances in the psychology of human intelligence* (Vol. 4, pp. 35–71). Hillsdale, New Jersey: Lawrence Erlbaum Associates, Inc.

1989

Gustafsson, J. E. (1989). Broad and narrow abilities in research on learning and instruction. In *Abilities, motivation, and methodology: The Minnesota symposium on learning and individual differences* (pp. 203–237). Erlbaum Hillsdale, NJ.

1992

Demetriou, A., Gustafsson, J.-E., Efklides, A., & Platsdou, M. (1992). Structural systems in developing cognition, science and education. In A. Demetriou., M. Shayer., & A. Efklides. (Eds.), *Neo-Piagetian theories of cognitive development. Implications and applications in education.* London: Routledge.

Gustafsson, J.-E. (1992a). The relevance of factor analysis for the study of group differences. *Multivariate Behavioral Research, 27*(2), 239–247.

Gustafsson, J.-E. (1992b). The Spearman hypothesis is false. *Multivariate Behavioral Research, 27,* 2, 265–267.

Gustafsson, J.-E., & Holmberg, L. (1992). Psychometric properties of vocabulary test items as a function of word characteristics. *Scandinavian Journal of Educational Research, 36*(3), 191–210.

Gustafsson, J.-E., & Undheim, J. O. (1992). Stability and change in broad and narrow factors of intelligence from ages 12 to 15 years. *Journal of Educational Psychology, 84*(2), 141–149.

Gustafsson, J.-E., Wedman, I., & Westerlund, A. (1992). The dimensionality of the Swedish Scholastic Aptitude Test. *Scandinavian Journal of Educational Research, 36*(1), 21–39.

Reuterberg, S.-E., & Gustafsson, J.-E. (1992). Confirmatory factor analysis and reliability: Testing measurement model assumptions. *Educational and Psychological Measurement, 52*(4), 795–811.

1993

Gustafsson, J.-E., & Balke, G. (1993). General and specific abilities as predictors of school achievement. *Multivariate Behavioral Research, 9*(2), 407–434.

Holmberg, L., & Gustafsson, J.-E. (1993). Efficiency of programme handling as a function of verbal and iconic interfaces and individual differences in ability. *Computers in Human Behavior, 9*(2–3), 227–245.

1994

Gustafsson, J.-E. (1994). Hierarchical models of intelligence and educational achievement. In A. Demetriou, & A. Efklides (Eds.), *Intelligence, mind and reasoning—Structure and development. Advances in psychology* (Vol 106, pp. 45–74). Amsterdam: Elsevier.

Härnqvist, K., Gustafsson, J.-E., Muthén, B., & Nelson, G. (1994). Hierarchical models of ability at individual and class levels. *Intelligence, 18*(2), 165–187.

1995

Berggren, U., Carlsson, S. G., & Gustafsson, J.-E. (1995). Factor analysis and reduction of a Fear Survey Schedule among dental phobic patients. *European Journal of Oral Sciences,103*(5), 331–338.

Gustafsson, J.-E., & Undheim, J. O. (1996). Individual differences in cognitive functions. In D. Berliner.& R. Calfee. (Eds.), *Handbook of educational psychology.* New York: Macmillan Library, London: Prentice Hall.

Hakeberg, M., Gustafsson, J.-E., & Berggren, U. (1995). Multivariate analysis of fears in dental phobic patients according to a reduced FSS-II scale. *European Journal of Oral Sciences,103*(5), 339–344.

1997

Gustafsson, J.-E. (1997). Measurement characteristics of the IEA reading literacy scales for 9- and 10-years old at country and individual levels. *Journal of Educational Measurement, 34*(3), 233–251.

Gustafsson, J.-E., & Snow, R. (1997). Ability profiles. In R. Dillon (Ed.), *Handbook on testing.* Washington: Greenwood Press.

1998

Gustafsson, J.-E. (1998). Social background and teaching factors as determinants of reading achievement at classroom and individual levels. *Nordisk Pedagogik, 18* (4), 241–250.

1999

Gustafsson, J.-E. (1999). Measuring and understanding G: Experimental and correlational approaches. In P. Ackerman., P. Kyllonen., & R. Roberts. (Eds.), *Learning and individual differences. process, traits and content determinants.* DC. US. American Psychological Association.

2000

Berntsson, L. T., & Gustafsson, J.-E. (2000). Determinants of psychosomatic complaints in Swedish schoolchildren aged seven to twelve years. *Scandinavian Journal of Public Health, 28*(4), 283–293.

Broady, D., & Gustafsson, J.-E. (2000). *Välfärd och skola*: Antologi från kommittén Välfärdsbokslut. Government document. SOU 2000:39.

Carlstedt, B., Gustafsson, J.-E., & Ullstadius, E. (2000). Item sequencing effects on the measurement of fluid intelligence. *Intelligence, 28*(2), 145–160.

Gustafsson, J.-E., & Reuterberg, S.-E. (2000). Metodproblem vid studier av Högskoleprovets prognosförmåga och deras lösning! *Pedagogisk Forskning i Sverige,* 5,4.

2001

Berntsson, L. T., Köhler, L., & Gustafsson, J.-E. (2001). Psychosomatic complaints in schoolchildren: A Nordic comparison. *Scandinavian Journal of Public Health, 29*(1), 44–54.

Gustafsson, J.-E. (2001a). On the hierarchical structure of ability and personality. In J. Collins & S. Messick (Eds.), *Intelligence and personality: Bridging the gap in theory and measurement.* Mahwah, NJ: Lawrence Erlbaum Associates Publishers.
Gustafsson, J.-E. (2001b). Schooling and intelligence: Effects of track of study on level and profile of cognitive abilities. *International Education Journal, 2*(4), 166–185.

Svensson, A., Gustafsson, J.-E., & Reuterberg, S.-E. (2001). *Högskoleprovets prognosvärde: Samband mellan provresultat och framgång första studieåret vid civilingenjörs-, jurist- och grundskollärarutbildningarna.* Stockholm: Högskoleverket.

2002

Ekblad, S., Gustafsson, J.-E., & Roth, G. (2002). Dimensional analysis of the general health questionnaire by application. *International Medical Journal, 9,* 2.

Gustafsson, J.-E. (2002). Measurement from a hierarchical point of view. In H. Braun, D. Jackson, & D. Wiley (Eds.), *The role of constructs in psychological and educational measurement.* London: Lawrence Erlbaum Associates, Publishers.

Gustafsson, J.-E., & Mårtenson, R. (2002). Review of "structural equation modeling with AMOS basic concepts, applications and programming". *Contemporary Psychology, 47,* 4.

Gustafsson, J.-E., & Myrberg, E., (2002). *Ekonomiska resursers betydelse för pedagogiska resultat: en kunskapsöversikt.* Stockholm: Skolverket.

Ullstadius, E., Gustafsson, J.-E., & Carlstedt, B. (2002). Influence of general and crystallized intelligence on vocabulary test performance. *European Journal of Psychological Assessment. 18*(1), 78–84.

2003

Gustafsson, J.-E. (2003). What do we know about effects of school resources on educational results? *Swedish Economic Policy Review, 10,* 2.

2004

Carlstedt, B., & Gustafsson, J.-E. (2004). Intelligence: theory, research, and testing in the Nordic countries. In R. Steinberg (Ed.), *International handbook of intelligence.* Cambridge: University Press.

Gustafsson, J.-E. (2004). Modeling individual differences in change through latent variable growth and mixture of growth modeling. Basic principles and empirical examples. In A. Demetriou & A. Raftopolous (Eds.), *Emergence and transformations in the mind* (pp. 379–402). NewYork: Cambridge University Press.

Gustafsson, J.-E., & Rosén, M. (2004). Förändringar i läskompetens 1991–2001. En jämförelse över tid och länder. *Forskning i fokus,* Stockholm: Myndigheten för skolutveckling,

Gustafsson, J.-E., & Rosén, M. (2004). Makt och etik i Skolverkets utvärdering av den svenska skolan. Erfarenheter från PIRLS projektet. *Pedagogisk forskning i Sverige. 9*(1), 58–70.

Rosén, M., Myrberg, E., & Gustafsson, J.-E. (2004). *Läskompetens i skolår 3 och 4 – en jämförelse mellan 35 länder*. Stockholm: Myndigheten för skolutveckling.

Tideman, E., & Gustafsson, J.-E. (2004). Age-related differentiation of cognitive abilities in ages 3-7. *Personality and Individual Differences, 36*(8), 1965–1974.

Ullstadius, E., Carlstedt, B., & Gustafsson, J.-E. (2004). Multidimensional item analysis of ability factors in spatial test items. *Personality and Individual Differences.37*(5), 1003–1012.

Yang, Y., & Gustafsson, J.-E. (2004). Measuring socioeconomic status at individual and collective levels. *Educational Research and Evaluation, 10*(3), 259–288.

2005

Carlstedt, B., & Gustafsson, J.-E. (2005). Construct validation of the Swedish scholastic aptitude test by means of the Swedish enlistment battery. *Scandinavian Journal of Psychology, 46*(1), 31–42.

Erickson, G., & Gustafsson, J.-E. (2005). Some European students' and teachers' views on language testing and assessment: A report on a questionnaire survey. *European Association for Language Testing and Assessment.* (EALTA).

Gustafsson, J.-E., & Stahl, P. A. (1995–2005). *STREAMS 3.0. User's Guide for windows*. Mölndal Sweden: MultivariateWare.

Gustafsson, J.-E., & Stahl, P. A. (2005a). *Using EQS with STREAMS 3.0*. Mölndal Sweden: MultivariateWare.

Gustafsson, J.-E., & Stahl, P. A. (2005b). *Using Mplus with STREAMS 3.0*. Mölndal Sweden: MultivariateWare.

Gustafsson, J.-E., & Stahl, P. A. (2005c). *Using LISREL with STREAMS 3.0*. Mölndal Sweden: MultivariateWare.

Gustafsson, J.-E., & Rosén, M. (2005). *Förändringar i läskompetens 1991-2001: en jämförelse över tid och länder*. Report from Department of Education and Didactics, Göteborg University.

Holfve-Sabel, M.-A., & Gustafsson, J.-E. (2005). Attitudes towards school teachers and classmates at classroom and individual levels: an application of two-level confirmatory factor analysis. *Scandinavian Journal of Educational Research, 49*(2), 187–202.

Rosén, M., Myrberg, E., & Gustafsson, J.-E. (2005). *Läskompetens i skolår 3 och 4 i nationell rapport från PIRLS 2001 I Sverige: The IEA Program in International Reading Literacy Study*. Göteborg Studies in Educational Sciences.

Sundgren, M., Dimenäs, E., & Gustafsson, J.-E. (2005). Drivers of organizational creativity: A path model of creative climate in pharmaceutical R&D. *R&D Management, 35*(4), 359–374.

2006

Davidov, E., Yang-Hansen, K., & Gustafsson, J.-E. (2006). Does money matter? A theory-driven growth mixture model to explain travel-mode choice with experimental data. *Methodology: European Journal of Research Methods for the Behavioral and Social Sciences, 2*(3), 124–134.

Gustafsson, J.-E. (2006a). Appendix till Skolverkets rapport "Ett rullande stickprovsbaserat system för kunskapsutvärdering av grundskolans ämnen. Ramverk för ett system för uppföljning av kunskapsutvecklingen i grundskolan. Stockholm: Skolverket.

Gustafsson, J.-E. (2006b). *Barns utbildningssituation. Bidrag till ett kommunalt barnindex*, Stockholm: Rädda Barnen.

Gustafsson, J.-E. (2006c). *Lika rättigheter- likvärdig utbilning: en sammanfattning av studien Barns utbildningssituation – ett bidrag till ett kommunalt barninsex.*

Gustafsson, J.-E., & Rosén, M. (2006). The dimensional structure of reading assessment tasks in the IEA reading literacy study 1991 and the progress in International Reading Literacy Study. *Educational Research and Evaluation, 12* (5), 445–468.

Rosén, M., & Gustafsson, J.-E. (2006). Läskompetens i skolår 3 och 4. In L. Bjar (ed) *Det hänger på språket. Lärande och utveckling i grundskolan.* Lund: Studentlitteratur.

Rosén, M., Gustafsson, J.-E., & Yang-Hansen, K. (2006). Measures of self-reported reading resources, attitudes and activities based on latent variable modeling. *International Journal of Research & Methods in Education,29*(2), 221–237.

2007

Cliffordson, C., & Gustafsson, J.-E. (2007). Effekter av den grundläggande högskoleutbildningens expansion på studerandegruppens sammansättning i B. Askling., R. Foss Lindblad., and G-B Wärvik. (eds.) *Expansion och kontraktion. Utmaningar för högskolesystemet och utbildningsforskare.* Stockholm: The Swedish Research Council.

Gustafsson, J.-E. (2007a). Kommentar till valfrihetens effekter på skolans elevsammansättning. *Friskolor och framtiden- segregation, kostnader och effektivitet*, Stockholm: Institutet för framtidsstudier.

Gustafsson, J.-E. (2007b). Understanding causal influences on educational achievement through analyses of differences over time within countries. In T. Loveless (Ed.), *Lessons learned: What international assessments tell us about math achievement* (pp 37–63). Washington, DC: The Brookings Institution.

Rosén, M., & Gustafsson, J.-E. (2007). The impact of PIRLS 2001 in Sweden. In K. Schwippert (Ed.), *Progress in reading literacy—The impact of PIRLS in 13 countries. Studies in international comparative and multicultural education* (Vol 7, pp. 227–242). IEA: Waxman Publishing Co.

2008

Andersson, L., Allebeck, P., & Gustafsson, J.-E. (2008). Association of IQ scores and school achievement with suicide in a 40-year follow-up of a Swedish cohort. *Acta Psychiatrica Scandinavia, 118*(2), 99–105.

Cliffordson, C., & Gustafsson, J.-E. (2008). Effects of age and schooling on intellectual performance: Estimates obtained from analysis of continuous variation in age and length of schooling. *Intelligence, 18*(1), 143–152.

Cliffordson, C., Giota, J., & Gustafsson, J.-E. (2008). Betyg och betygsättning: Funktioner och effekter. *Resultatdialog 2008*. The Swedish Research Council.

Gustafsson, J.-E. (2008a). Effects of international comparative studies on educational quality on the quality of educational research. *European Educational Research Journal. 7*(1), 1–17.

Gustafsson, J.-E. (2008b). Schooling and intelligence: Effects of track of study on level and profile of cognitive abilities. In P. Kyllonen., R. Roberts., & L. Stankov. (Eds.), *Extending intelligence: Enhancement and new constructs*. New Jersey: Lawrence Erlbaum Associates, Inc. Publishers.

Rosén. M., & Gustafsson, J.-E. (2008). Lesekompetense på 3 og 4 klassetrinn *Der er språket som bestemmer! Lering og språkutvikling i grunnskolen*. Bergen: Fagboksförlaget.

Svedenberg, E., Gustafsson, J.-E., & Svensson, L. (2008). Influences of previous experiences on consumers' reading and use of nutrition information on food packages. A questionnaire study involving structural equation modeling. *Journal of Culinary Science and Technology, 6*(2), 192–205.

Ullstadius, E., Carlstedt, B., & Gustafsson, J.-E. (2008). The multidimensionality of verbal analogy items. *International Journal of Testing, 8*(2), 166–179.

Valentin Kvist, A., & Gustafsson, J.-E. (2008). The relation between fluid intelligence and the general factor as a function of cultural background: A test of Cattell's investment theory. *Intelligence, 36*(5), 422–436.

2009

Gustafsson, J.-E. (2009). Strukturell ekvationsmodellering. In G. Djurfeldt & M. Barmark. (Red), *Statistisk verktygslåda 2*. Lund: Studentlitteratur.

Gustafsson, J.-E., & Myrberg, E. (2009). Resursers betydelse för elevers resultat. In Skolverket: *Vad påverkar resultaten i svensk grundskola? En kunskapsöversikt ombetydelsen av olika faktorer*. (s 160–207). Stockholm: Skolverket.

Gustafsson, J.-E., & Yang-Hansen, K. (2009). Resultatförändringar i svensk grundskola. In Skolverket: *Vad påverkar resultaten i svensk grundskola? En kunskapsöversikt ombetydelsen av olika faktorer*. (s 40–83). Stockholm: Skolverket.

2010

Björklund, A., Fredriksson, P., & Gustafsson, J.-E. (2010). *Den svenska utbildningspolitikens arbetsmarknadseffekter: Vad säger forskningen?* Uppsats: Uppsala: Institutet för Arbetsmarknadspolitiska Utvärderingar.

Gustafsson, J.-E. (2010). Longitudinal designs. In B. P. M Creemers, L. Kyriakides, & P. Sammons (Eds.), *Methodological advances In school effectiveness research*. London and New York: Routledge. Taylor and Francis.

Gustafsson, J.-E., & Åberg-Bengtsson, L. (2010). Unidimensionality and interpretability of psychological instruments. In S. E Embretson (Ed.), *Measuring psychological constructs: Advances in model-based approaches*. Washington, DC: American Psychological Association.

Gustafsson, J.-E., Westling, A., & Alin-Åkerman, B. (2010). *School, learning and mental health: A systematic review*. Stockholm: The Royal Swedish Academy of Sciences.

Zammit, S., Lewis, G., Gustafsson, J.-E., & Dalman, C. (2010). Individuals, schools and neighborhood: A multilevel longitudinal study of variation in incidence of psychotic disorders. *Archives of General Psychiatry, 67*(9), 914–922.

2011

Bergersen, G., & Gustafsson, J.-E. (2011). Programming skill, knowledge and working memory among professional software developers from an investment theory perspective. *Journal of Individual Differences,32*(4), 201–209.

Gunnell, D., Löving, S., Gustafsson, J.-E., & Allebäck, P. (2011). School performance and risk of suicide in early adulthood: Follow-up of two national cohorts of Swedish schoolchildren. *Journal of Affective Disorders,131*, 104–112.

Gustafsson, J.-E., & Yang-Hansen, K. (2011). Förändringar i kommunskillnader i grundskoleresultat mellan 2008 och 2008. *Pedagogisk Forskning i Sverige*, 16, 3, 161–178.

Halleröd, B., & Gustafsson, J.-E. (2011). A longitudinal analysis of the relationship between changes in socio-economic status and changes in health. *Social Science and Medicine*, 72(1), 116–123.

Yang-Hansen, K., Rosén, M., & Gustafsson, J.-E. (2011). Changes in the multi-level effects of socio-economic status on reading achievement in Sweden in 1991 and 2001. *Scandinavian Journal of Educational Research*, 55(2), 197–211.

2012

Gustafsson, J.-E. (2012a). Urval till högskolan i kunskapssamhällets tjänst. I *En högskolevärld i ständig förändring*. Högskoleverket 1995-2012, (s73–80). Stockholm: Högskoleverket.

Gustafsson, J.-E. (2012b). Något om utvecklingen av de internationella studierna av kunskaper och färdigheter. (s 37–46). In T.N. Hopfenbeck., M. Kjernsli., and R. V. Olsen (Red.) *Kvalitet i norsk skole: internationale og regionale undersökelser av leringsutbytte og undervisning*. Oslo: Universitetsförlaget.

2013

Gustafsson, J.-E. (2013a). Causal inference in educational effectiveness research: A comparison of three methods to investigate effects of homework on student achievement. *School of Effectiveness and School Improvement*, 24(3), 275–295.

Gustafsson, J.-E. (2013b). Förändringar i kunskapsbedömningar på individ- och systemnivå i den svenska skolan under 25 år. In I. Wernersson and I. Gerrbo (red.): *Differentieringens janusansikte. En antologi från Institutionen för pedagogik och specialpedagogik vid Göteborgs universitet*, s 45–73. Göteborg: Acta Universitatis Gothenburgensis.

Gustafsson, J.-E., & Erickson, G. (2013). To trust or not to trust?—Teacher marking versus external marking of national tests. *Educational Assessment, Evaluation and Accountability*, 25(1), 69–87.

Gustafsson, J.-E., Yang-Hansen, K., & Rosén, M. (2013). Effects of home background on student achievement in reading, mathematics and science at the fourth grade. In M. O. Martin & I. V. S. Mullis (Eds.), *TIMSS and PIRLS 2011: Relationships among reading, mathematics and science achievement at the fourth grade—Implications for early learning* (pp. 183–289). Boston College, US: Chestnut Hill, MA.

Hansson, Å., & Gustafsson, J.-E. (2013). Measurement invariance of socioeconomic status across migrational background. *Scandinavian Journal of Educational Research*, 57(2), 148–166.

MacCabe, J. H., Wicks, S., Löving, S., David, A. S., Berndtsson, Å., Gustafsson, J.-E., Allebeck, P., & Dalman, C. (2013). Decline in cognitive performance between ages 13 and 18 years and the risk for psychosis in adulthood. A Swedish longitudinal cohort study in males. *JAMA Psychiatry, 70*(3), 261–270.

2014

Erickson, G., & Gustafsson, J.-E. (2014). Bedömningens dubbla funktion – för lärande och likvärdighet. In U. Lundgren., R. Säljö., och C. Liberg. (Red): *Lärande, skola, bildning.* Stockholm: Natur och Kultur.

Gustafsson, J.-E., & Wolff, U. (2014). Läsinlärningens grunder. Individuella differenser, utveckling och träning. *Resultatdialog 2014.* Stockholm: Vetenskapsrådet.

Gustafsson, J.-E., Cliffordson, C., & Erickson, G. (2014). *Likvärdig kunskapsbedömning i och av den svenska skolan – problem och möjligheter.* Stockholm: SNS Förlag.

Gustafsson, J.-E., Lander, R., & Myrberg, E. (2014). Inspections of Swedish schools: A critical reflection on intended effects, causal mechanisms and methods. *Educational Inquiry, 5*(4), 461–479.

Gustafsson, J.-E., Lind, P., & Mellander, E. (2014). *Lära för livet? Om skolans och arbetslivets avtryck i vuxnas färdigheter.* Stockholm: SNS Förlag.

Gustafsson, J.-E., & Rosén, M. (2014). Quality and credibility of international studies. In R. Strietholt, W. Bos, J.-E. Gustafsson, & M. Rosén (Eds.), *Educational policy evaluation through international comparative assessment.* Munster: New York: Vaxmann.

Klapp Lekholm, A., Cliffordson, C., & Gustafsson, J.-E. (2014). The effect of being graded on later achievement: Evidence from 13 year olds in Swedish compulsory school. *Educational Psychology,* 1–19. Published online doi:10.1080/01443410. 2014.933176

Nilsen, T., & Gustafsson, J.-E. (2014). School emphasis on academic success: Exploring changes in science performance in Norway between 2007 and 2011 employing two-level SEM. *Educational Research and Evaluation, 20*(4), 308–327.

Rosén, M., & Gustafsson, J.-E. (2014). Has the increased access to computers at home caused reading achievement to decrease in Sweden? In R. Strietholt., W. Bos., J.-E. Gustafsson., & M. Rosén. (Eds.), *Educational policy evaluation through international comparative assessments.* Munster, New York: Waxmann.

Strietholt, R., Gustafsson, J.-E., & Rosén, M. (2014). Outcomes and causal inference in international comparative assessments. In R. Strietholt, W. Bos, J.-E.

Gustafsson, & M. Rosén. (Eds.), *Educational policy evaluation through international comparative assessments*. Munster, New York: Waxmann.

Thorsen, C., Gustafsson, J.-E., & Cliffordson, C. (2014). The influence of fluid and crystallized intelligence on the development of knowledge and skills. *British Journal of Educational Psychology,84*(4), 556–570.

Yang-Hansen, K., Gustafsson, J.-E., & Rosén, M. (2014). School performance differences and policy variations in Finland, Norway and Sweden. In *Northern Lights on TIMSS and PIRLS 2011* (25–47). Denmark: Nordic Council of Ministers.

2015

Blömeke, S., Gustafsson, J.-E., & Shavelson, R. (2015). Beyond dichotomies. Competence viewed as a continuum. *Zeitschrift fur Psychologie, 223*(1), 3–13.

Ehren, M. C., Gustafsson, J.-E., & Altrichter, H. (2015). Comparing effects and side effects of different school inspection systems across Europe. *Comparative Education, 51*(3), 375–400.

Erickson, G., Åberg-Bengtsson, L., & Gustafsson, J.-E. (2015). Dimensions of test performance in English as a foreign language in different European settings: A two-level confirmatory factor analytical approach. *Educational Research and Evaluation, 21*(3), 1–20.

Gustafsson, J.-E., Ehren, M. C., & Conyngham, G. (2015). From inspection to quality: Ways in which school inspection influences change in school. *Studies in Educational Evaluation, 47*, 47–57.

Gustafsson, J.-E., & Wolff, U. (2015). Measuring fluid intelligence at age four. *Intelligence, 50*, 175–185.

Klem, M., Gustafsson, J.-E., & Hagtved, B. (2015). The dimensionality of language ability in four-year-olds. Construct validation of a language screening tool. *Scandinavian Journal of Educational Research, 59*(2), 195–213.

Klem, M., Melby-Lervåg, M., Hagtved, B., Lyster, S. A. H., Gustafsson, J.-E., & Hulme, C. (2015). Sentence repetition is a measure of children's language skills rather than working memory limitations. *Developmental science, 18*(1), 146–154.

Scherer, R., & Gustafsson, J.-E. (2015a). Student assessment of teaching as a source of information about aspects of teaching quality in multiple subject domains: An application of multilevel bi-factor structural equation modeling. *Frontiers in Psychology, 08*, 1550.

Scherer, R., & Gustafsson, J.-E. (2015b). The relations among openness, perseverance and performance in creative problem solving: A substantive-methodological approach. *Thinking Skills and Creativity, 18*, 4–17.

Sjölund, S., Hemmingsson, T., Gustafsson, J.-E., & Allebäck, P. (2015). IQ and alcohol-related morbidity and mortality among Swedish men and women: The importance of socioeconomic position. *Journal of Epidemiology and Community Health, 69*(9), 858–864.

Wolff, U., & Gustafsson, J.-E. (2015). Structure of phonological ability at age four. *Intelligence, 53,* 108–117.

2016

Gustafsson, J.-E. (2016). Lasting effects of quality of schooling: Evidence from PISA and PIAAC. *Intelligence, (57),* 66–72.

Gustafsson, J.-E., & Nilsen, T. (2016). The impact of school climate and teacher quality on mathematics achievement: A difference-in-differences approach. In T. Nilsen & J.-E. Gustafsson (Eds.), *Teacher quality, instructional quality and student outcome. Relationships across countries.* Berlin: Springer.

Gustafsson, J.-E., Sörlin, S., & Vlachos, J. (2016). *Policyidéer för svensk skola* [Policy ideas for the Swedish school] Stockholm: SNS förlag.

Hansson, Å., & Gustafsson, J. E. (2016). Pedagogisk segregation: Lärarkompetens i den svenska grundskolan ur ett likvärdighetsperspektiv. *Pedagogisk Forskning i Sverige* 21(1-2), 56–78.

Nilsen, T., & Gustafsson, J.-E. (Eds) (2016). *Teacher quality, instructional quality and student outcome. Relationships across countries.* Berlin: Springer.

Rosén, M., & Gustafsson, J.-E. (2016). Is computer availability at home causally related to reading achievement in grade four? A longitudinal difference in differences approach to IEA data from 1991 to 2006. *Large-scale Assessment in Education,4*(1), 1–19.

Yang Hansen, K., & Gustafsson, J.-E. (2016). Causes of educational segregation in Sweden—School choice or residential segregation. *Educational Research and Evaluation, 22:*(1–2), 23–44.

CPSIA information can be obtained at www.ICGtesting.com
Printed in the USA
BVOW06*0823300916

463796BV00003B/4/P